THE
AMERICAN
PRESIDENT

THE AMERICAN PRESIDENT

PHILIP B. KUNHARDT, JR.

PHILIP B. KUNHARDT III

PETER W. KUNHARDT

Foreword by Stephen Skowronek

Introduction by Richard E. Neustadt

RIVERHEAD BOOKS

A MEMBER OF PENGUIN PUTNAM INC.

NEW YORK 1999

Riverhead Books
a member of
Penguin Putnam Inc.
375 Hudson Street
New York, NY 10014

Library of Congress Cataloging-in-Publication Data

Kunhardt, Philip B.

The American President / Philip B.Kunhardt, Jr.,
Philip B. Kunhardt III, and Peter W. Kunhardt.

p.   cm.
Includes index.
ISBN 1-57322-149-X

1. Presidents—United States—History.
2. Presidents—United States—Biography.
3. Presidents—United States—Pictorial works.
I. Kunhardt, Philip B. II. Kunhardt, Peter W.
III. Title
E176.1.K854 1999   99-30869CIP
973'.099—dc21
[B]

Printed in the United States of America

10 9 8 7 6 5 4 3 2 1

This book is printed on acid-free paper. ∞

THE AMERICAN PRESIDENT
The companion volume to the PBS series,
which is made possible through the generous support
of New York Life Insurance Company

CONTENTS

The White House, circa 1889

PREFACE

With its clutter of signs and ordinary lampposts, it looks like streets all across the country, but just down Pennsylvania Avenue in Washington, D.C., is the most important address in the world. In a monumental house conceived and built by George Washington, who almost lived to see it finished, every president since has carried his own burden through its halls, has stood in awe of the gigantic East Room, has thrilled to its great pillars and stately façades, has spent sleepless nights tossing in its beds. The grand house, like the presidency itself, has both remained very much a constant and changed tremendously over the two centuries since John Adams made the mansion his own on November 1, 1800, with the very first night's sleep of a chief executive.

Thirteen years earlier, at the Constitutional Convention in Philadelphia, the idea for the presidency was born. On June 1, 1787, James Wilson of Pennsylvania moved that the executive of the United States consist of a single individual. James Madison, taking notes, recorded the impact of the proposal, which thrust the roomful of buzzing delegates into a sudden and total silence. All knew it was a moment of fateful significance. Wilson believed that a single president could give energy and dispatch to the office, allowing for decisiveness during critical moments in history. But for others the idea seemed fraught with danger, though no one wanted to insult the man sitting in their midst who would almost certainly be named to the job should such an office be created—General George Washington. After "a considerable pause," in Madison's words, Edmund Randolph of Virginia spoke out on behalf of those opposed, calling a solitary executive "the foetus of monarchy," and urging that the office be shared by an executive committee. And so Wilson's proposal was debated on that first Friday in June, and after

days of heated argument and changing opinions, the fateful motion carried. Ever since, the presidency, as one commentator has put it, has been "at the mercy of the accident of personality."

It is the extraordinary procession of these "accidents of personality" that inspired this family team to undertake an exhilarating study of the presidency, which includes not only this book but also a ten-hour PBS documentary series.

In some ways, the presidency is the most exclusive of clubs—by the turn of the twentieth century, just forty-one members, all men, all white, and all Christian. Closer inspection, however, reveals a less static society, one moving inexorably toward greater inclusion. Andrew Jackson was the first to break open the genteel, highly educated ranks represented by the first six presidents. A self-made man hailing from the frontier in western Tennessee, Jackson opened up whole new possibilities in what kind of American could reach the White House. He was followed by a host of figures from equally unlikely backgrounds—a longtime tailor (Andrew Johnson), a fitful tanner (Ulysses S. Grant), a one-time canal boy (James Garfield), and a former rail-splitter (Abraham Lincoln). And though lawyers and career politicians have predominated in the high office, twentieth-century Americans elected a professor (Wilson), a newspaperman (Harding), an engineer (Hoover), and a movie star (Reagan). John F. Kennedy was the first Roman Catholic to reach the White House. Inevitably, the country will elect a woman as president.

As anyone who has toured the White House knows—and 1.2 million Americans do so each year—the mansion's walls prominently display important portraits of past presidents. It was not always so. Though the famous full-length painting of George Washington by Gilbert Stuart has been a feature of the executive mansion since 1800, there was little appetite for any others until the middle of the nineteenth century. It was Andrew Johnson's daughter, Martha, who discovered, while rummaging in the White House attic, a set of six presidential portraits commissioned in the 1850s but then forgotten. Hanging them in the great transverse hall of the state floor of the White House, she opened what was in essence the first presidential portrait gallery in the White House. It was immensely popular and soon was moved into the East Room. Under President Hayes, the gallery was brought up to date by the acquisition of eleven

new paintings, and the collection keeps growing. Each president since has been surrounded by these portraits. They look down upon his comings and goings as a vivid remainder of the relatively few others who have shared his unique station. Their power is symbolic as well as historical. Ronald Reagan, at the opening of his administration in 1980, ordered the portrait of his hero Calvin Coolidge moved onto a prominent wall in the Cabinet Room. George Bush said he did his best thinking during the Gulf War while sitting in the presence of the portrait of Abraham Lincoln. And Richard Nixon, during the depths of the Watergate crisis, used to wander through the White House halls at night talking to the portraits as if to living presences. This book, too, is a presidential portrait gallery, made up not only of oil paintings and of hundreds of rare photographs, but also of words—both ours and of each of the presidents—that open up vistas onto those living presences.

A significant portion of our research time went into searching out the original words of the presidents, not only those existing in widely available published sources, but also those only to be found in manuscript form. And not only the distinguished public utterances, but the little-known, the intensely private, and the humanly revealing, as well as those words that shed light on our own thematic approaches. Chosen out of thousands upon thousands of examples, these words are sprinkled liberally throughout our text, as well as being gathered inside special boxes in each chapter labeled "In His Own Words."

The story of the presidency is, at least in part, a story of human personality under pressure. The administration of George Washington is not fully intelligible without reference to his consuming desire for integrity and to be above politics. John Adams is best illumined by an inspection of his own unique makeup—his learnedness, his irascibility, and most of all his stubborn independence. Again and again a president's personality ends up helping shape his executive performance. Jefferson's expansiveness, Madison's caution, Jackson's ferociousness, Buchanan's timidity, FDR's self-confidence all deeply affected the evolution of the high office. And so questions of character are not only relevant, they are essential. Was a president decisive or indecisive? Rash or thoughtful? Tough-skinned or too sensitive to criticism? Kindly or coldhearted? Did he have a vision for the country he wanted to pursue, or did he become lost in the

A turn-of-the-century view of the White House's north entrance

minutiae of the everyday tasks of the office? Was he proficient in working with others and in enlisting political allies, or was he a loner who withdrew and tried to do everything himself? Was he expansive or petty? Was he honest or dishonest? Did he have a basic trust in the American people or a basic distrust? These questions and others help bring focus to the ways in which presidents have affected the history of the nation.

Our most essential early decision as this project took shape was to treat the presidents thematically, rather than chronologically. Our senior historical consultant, David Herbert Donald, winner of the Pulitzer Prize for biography,

early on put us in touch with Stephen Skowronek, a political scientist at Yale University who specializes in the history of the presidency. His groundbreaking book *The Politics Presidents Make* compares presidents from different eras who shared common dilemmas and who inhabited what he has called similar "political time." Especially qualified to analyze our thematic approach, Skowronek helped us arrange our groupings, following our mandate that each chapter include an early president, two from the middle years, and a modern one who was still alive and could be interviewed today, or at least had lived in the era of moving pictures and recorded sound. With some slight tinkering over the next four years, these categories became the intellectual framework for this book. Skowronek has served as our chief academic consultant, and his Foreword, which explains the importance of looking at the presidents transhistorically, appears on pages *xii* and *xiii*.

Another important alliance that was formed as the project unfolded was with the Harvard scholar Richard E. Neustadt, who has been called by Arthur Schlesinger, Jr., "our most brilliant commentator on the presidency." Neustadt's specialty is analyzing what makes effective presidential leadership; his book *Presidential Power* has been dubbed "an operational Bible for presidents." Our decision to make Dick the sole on-camera commentator for the PBS television series that accompanies this book ended up deeply shaping not only the series but the book as well. He has contributed his own introduction that begins on page *xiv*.

For narrator of the television series, we brought on Hugh Sidey, who has been *Time* magazine's special correspondent on the presidency for four decades. Sidey conducted exclusive interviews for this project with Presidents Carter, Ford, Bush, and Clinton, and these interviews serve as the basis for the chapters on these four presidents. Practically a member of the White House himself, as well as a student of it, Sidey brings a unique perspective to the workings of the Oval Office and the eight presidents he has intimately known (see page *xi)*.

The New York Life Insurance Company, whose board of trustees has included two presidents—Calvin Coolidge and Herbert Hoover—has been the sole sponsor of the television project. Without their enormous support, this venture would not have been undertaken. For five years, as the project has been developed and a nationwide school involvement has materialized around the enterprise, we have worked together as true partners. New York Life is a company ideally suited to present this subject to the nation.

The ten chapters in this book are presented as five pairs of opposites. Those presidents grouped in Chapter 1, "The Heroic Posture," were all national heroes before they ever were candidates. In contrast are the five men in Chapter 2 we have labeled "Compromise Choices"—politicians chosen in many cases for who they were not, rather than for who they were. The "Professional Politicians" grouped in Chapter 3 are contrasted with those political loners of "Independent Cast of Mind" in Chapter 4. Those profiled

in "Family Ties" all seemed born for the high office, while those in "Happenstance" reached the presidency only because of accident and national tragedy. Those grouped in "The American Way" each possessed a burning vision for their country, while those juxtaposed in "The World Stage" made their contributions principally in foreign affairs. And finally, those presidents brought together in Chapter 9—all of whom deliberately stretched the power of the office—are in contrast to the presidents grouped in Chapter 10, who were constrained, for better or worse, by the balanced powers of our overall government.

As we crisscross the boundaries between presidential successes and failures, between greatness and mediocrity, these categories define our focus and shape our text. By taking stock of all the presidents, both those familiar and unfamiliar, and by juxtaposing modern presidents with earlier incumbents, we hope to have given coherence to the sprawling presidential experience. Indeed, the president we treat first within each of these ten chapters represents an archetype that reemerges later in presidents eerily reminiscent of the original. Theodore Roosevelt appears almost like a new Andrew Jackson; William Howard Taft seems in some ways like a resurgence of James Madison; Jimmy Carter closely resembles John Adams and also Rutherford B. Hayes; LBJ echoes Van Buren and also Abraham Lincoln.

It is our hope that our efforts will be of assistance to the American voter. Since our goal has been to see the presidency afresh and to think about its incumbents in new ways, so, too, the process of selection, we believe, can be invigorated by many of these same insights. The search for personal excellence has many pitfalls and blind alleys; for a voter to be able to spot some of them and hold them up to the light of history is citizenship of a high order.

Over the past thirty years, historians have rightly turned away from the old bias of studying history primarily through the stories of its "great white men." And yet the American presidents continue to fascinate. The president is the only elected officer representing the entire nation, and thus has a special obligation to the American people. As has been made clear in the closing years of the twentieth century, the American people still care about the presidency. They believe in it, and rightly insist that it belongs to them.

With Kennedy

Hugh Sidey records the narration for the companion PBS documentary series "The American President." Below, he reflects on more than four decades covering the White House for *Time* magazine, including the presidencies of Truman, Eisenhower and the eight chief executives pictured with him to the right.

With Johnson

A Personal Journey *by Hugh Sidey*

John Kennedy sat forward to listen closely to his space experts. They told him it would cost $40 billion (a huge sum then) and take ten years, and they could not guarantee that the United States would beat the Soviet Union to the moon. Kennedy grimaced, ran his fingers through his hair, then leaned back in his chair in the Cabinet Room. He wanted Americans on the moon—and first. "I want some answers," he told the small group of aides. "Ask the janitor over there if you have to. But I want to know how and when we can get to the moon."

With Nixon

I thought to myself, as I watched and listened to this restless young man of privilege and daring on that April evening in 1961, that with a few words he had launched the nation on a great adventure. And it must have been the same with the visionary Thomas Jefferson, who doubled the size of the United States with the Louisiana Purchase; and the prairie lawyer Abraham Lincoln, who marshaled the most powerful army the world had known to abolish slavery; and Theodore Roosevelt, who sent his engineers to build the Panama Canal. With vision and a free people behind them, these presidents—and the others—profoundly transformed civilization. In our time there is no more effective and powerful political office on the face of the earth.

With Ford

Every one of the forty-one men who have been president has left his mark, some more positive than others. "No president wants to fail," Lyndon Johnson once protested when he was criticized about the Vietnam War. "You do the best you know how." In the midst of that tragic conflict he had won battles for better education and health care. And Richard Nixon, who would be driven from office by the Watergate scandal, had journeyed triumphantly through China, offering American friendship for the first time after twenty-five years of Chinese isolation.

With Carter

The presidency, like democracy, is not an easy journey. "I'm going to give the job to Nixon," JFK once grumped when things were going badly. He knew better. He gloried in "the great chess game," as he called it. That is why so many people now fight for the right to be president. I've ridden along on this historic caravan for more than forty years now. There is no more fascinating and thrilling—and often entertaining—drama that we can witness.

With Reagan

It is my great hope that this book and the public television series it accompanies will allow every reader and viewer to hear the voices and the bugle calls and the church bells, and then feel the excitement of these men calling their nation to the most magnificent efforts in war and peace that humankind has ever known.

With Bush

With Clinton

FOREWORD

by Stephen Skowronek
Yale University

The *American President* invites readers to rethink presidential history and reconsider the men who have held America's top leadership position. The book draws us into the history with an extraordinary collection of photographic and pictorial images, the most comprehensive visual accounting of the principal characters and their environs ever assembled in a single volume. But I would like to draw particular attention to the narrative supported by this artwork. These stunning images are arrayed in the service of an innovative approach to the subject matter. The arrangement and presentation of the material allow us to see familiar figures afresh and to gain new insight into this most enigmatic of institutions.

Familiar as it is, the American presidency has never been easy to understand. The institution has a protean character that defies fixed descriptions and settled explanations. At one moment, it disappoints; at the next, it astonishes. Its history is riddled with eminence and embarrassment, proficiency and paralysis. As each incumbent brings something different to the job, each administration reveals some feature of the position scarcely intimated in the experience of his immediate predecessors.

Writing about an office so mutable and unpredictable is one of the great challenges of political analysis, and no single response has proved entirely satisfactory. But if the presidency does not admit of a definitive history, it does encourage experimentation with different perspectives that might capture one or another of its many aspects. Consider the two most prominently displayed in the literature.

The first approach, "the men and their times," has long been the perspective of choice among biographers and historians. Studies of this sort show us the unique ways in which personality and circumstance interact within the presidential office to determine the fate of particular administrations. Chronological histories of the presidents written from this point of view indicate as well how rare it is for the critical elements to combine in just the right way. The great success stories—George Washington, Abraham Lincoln, Franklin Roosevelt—are few and far between, and they stand out starkly against the long progression of lesser lights.

For those attuned to the frustrations and shortfalls of recent incumbents, these chronological histories are especially instructive. They suggest that our contemporary experience is very much the normal state of affairs in American government. The natural inclination to identify the travails of the sitting president with problems in the governmental system itself is tempered by this perspective on the past, as is the yearning for a leader who will "make the system work." And yet, important as it is to understand the frustration of presidents as part and parcel of the way our system works, this insight will take us only so far. Indeed, for anyone interested in general attributes of the presidential office, a chronological analysis of the struggles of individual characters in particular contexts will prove quite limited. Even those paragons who reached the commanding heights of authority and accomplishment appear fixed in place by this perspective, limited in what they can teach others by the idiosyncrasies of personality and circumstance.

In recent years, an alternative perspective has taken hold that directs our attention more specifically to the institutional development of the presidential office. Studies written from this point of view remind us that though each of our presidents has held the same constitutional position, the governing norms and practical operations of that office have changed over time in rather dramatic ways. Instead of discussing presidential history administration by administration, works on the development of the office typically consider several administrations together in broadly defined eras: the early national period of the founding generation of presidents, the "party period" of the nineteenth-century presidency, and the period of the "modern presidency," ushered in by the New Deal and World War II. Within each of these periods we see a group of presidents who shared similar political resources, technological capacities, and institutional supports, and the coherence of the office can be discerned in reference to common assumptions and expectations about the exercise of power. From this perspective, the key distinctions to be drawn among presidents are not between the "greats" and the lesser lights but between those of one period and the next, as each group is seen to inhabit a very different institution.

This more schematic rendering of presidential history facilitates generalizations about the office, but note that these are generalizations of a particular kind. While similarities among presidents within each period are fairly easy to spot, similarities among presidents in different periods tend to get filtered out. Indeed, when the "modern presidency" is understood as an institution different in kind from all prior forms, and the modern presidents are seen as a coherent group standing apart from the rest, most of presidential history simply loses its relevance. Nearly three-quarters of American presidents predate the modern period, but with the possible exception of the experiences of a handful of historic "greats," the early record would seem to be relegated by this perspective to mere historical interest. The outstanding question is, What can incumbents like Benjamin Harrison or Zachary Taylor possibly tell us about the presidential office as it appears in our own day?

The American President answers this question by establishing a third vantage point from which to view the history of the office. Though the book draws freely on insights made available through more conventional frames of reference, it experiments with a very different temporal arrangement of the material. It does not proceed chronologically though the succession of incumbents, nor does it take up the usual periods of institutional development each in its turn. Instead, the presentation reaches across the standard demarcations of the subject, joining together early and modern presidents around general themes that transcend the particulars of time and place. Each chapter ranges through the whole of presidential history, calling attention to a particular scattering of incumbents that captures something emblematic of the American experience with this office. In this way, the reader gains a sense of those aspects and attitudes of incumbency that constitute the presidency's most enduring qualities.

The thought that breaking up presidential history in this disjointed, out-of-phase fashion might better convey an overarching sense of the whole is but the first of many intriguing notions contained in *The American President*. In its ten thematic sweeps through time, the book is continually juxtaposing presidencies in unexpected ways and shaking up familiar images as it does so. Jimmy Carter's fiercely "independent cast of mind" has always appeared a bit peculiar among the modern presidents, and yet his apparent disdain for professional politicians and his inclination to go it alone politically have deep historical resonance. When Carter's example is joined to those of John Adams, Zachary Taylor, and Rutherford Hayes, the independent stance appears as one of the presidency's most persistent poses. Similarly, the fabled grouping of "greats" is fruitfully broken up here in the service of illuminating less well attended asso-

ciations. George Washington is placed alongside Ulysses S. Grant in a chapter examining the vicissitudes of "the heroic posture." Abraham Lincoln is considered in conjunction with Lyndon Johnson in an exploration of "professional politicians" whose long dedication to their peculiar vocation landed them in America's highest office. Franklin Roosevelt makes his appearance next to Benjamin Harrison to illustrate the influence of "family ties" on presidential history.

To make this organizing principle work, special care had to be taken in crafting the exposition. If, in elaborating these themes, the book had run roughshod over the forty-one different personalities who have held the office, or if it had failed to take into account institutional developments that have transformed that office over time, the end product would be more likely to confuse than enlighten. Several features of the presentation stand out as especially effective in meeting this challenge. The first is that each of the transhistorical themes is rendered through a set of individual presidential vignettes. This means that the office never loses its human face and that critical institutional developments within it are always kept in view. More striking still is the extent to which the presentation allows the presidents to speak for themselves, expressing the major themes in their own words. Breathing life into the framework of the book, this technique serves to make the history accessible even to those who might not have a detailed prior knowledge of it.

Finally, there is the pictorial and photographic support that instantly contextualizes each story and provides a visual accounting of the passage of time. This skillful integration of structure, narrative, and imagery provides a powerful synthesis and makes an important contribution to our understanding of the American presidency. But of course *The American President* is by no means an exhaustive account of the subject. Perhaps the most attractive feature of this book is that in opening up presidential history to an alternative way of thinking, it prompts readers to experiment with its method for themselves. Reshuffling the pieces on our own, we may discover other, as yet hidden connections among the old stories. I can think of no better way to keep this venerable history vital.

INTRODUCTION

by Richard E. Neustadt
Harvard University

As Edward Corwin wrote some sixty years ago, the presidency of the United States has been an office "of uncertain content." So it was in 1787, when the Constitution was drafted, and so it remains today.

This uncertainty is due in part to the spare yet general language of the drafting of the Constitution, which has been subject to reinterpretation in successive generations. For the first forty years, to take just one example, the presidential veto over legislation was thought to apply only to bills affecting presidential powers. Another source of uncertainty as to the office of our chief executive is the uncomfortable fact that most of the presidential powers are shared—Constitutionally and practically—with other institutions independent of a president's command. In that respect, the presidency is weaker than it first appears or than its numerous, importunate constituencies expect. And a third source of uncertainty is the office's relatively stronger role in foreign affairs than domestic affairs—a strength, however, that depends on events abroad, which a president, again, for the most part cannot control.

Because the content of the presidency is uncertain, the person of the president takes on added importance. The manner in which the individual brings his (someday her) mind and energies to bear on the events that frame his time is crucial to the way the office is conceived and executed in that time. The incumbent's own experience, enthusiasms, ideas, interests, prejudices, working style, and temperament will markedly affect what happens in the office and what comes out of it.

The times, of course, can limit or strengthen a president and often do, but he, in turn, makes use of them—or doesn't.

That is why what follows in this book and in the television series it accompanies is oriented to the human histories of the forty-one individuals who so far have occupied the office. Were the institution cut-and-dried, required to perform in the same fashion all the time, those histories would be both less important than they are and less revealing of the presidency in our political system. But the institution is what Corwin said it was.

The uncertainty that dogs the office, heightening the effect of individuals in it, derives most basically from the deliberate competition between president and Congress envisaged in the terms of the Constitution. For example, the "executive power"—which is never defined—is vested in the president, whose duty also is to "take care that the laws be faithfully executed." But it is Congress that creates executive departments, decides their jurisdictions, spells out their programmatic duties, adds the funds to perform those duties, and by hallowed practice investigates the performance. So it becomes clear that Congress has "executive" powers too.

Or consider this: The president is commander-in-chief of the armed forces, and since Thomas Jefferson's time has sometimes sent them into battle overseas on his own motion. But only Congress has the constitutional right to declare war, and Congress, every two years, sets the size and composition of those forces. Also, the president sends and receives ambassadors, a duty construed from the start to put him in charge of foreign relations. But those he sends must be confirmed by action of the Senate. Should they negotiate a treaty and he sign it, the Senate has to consent before it takes effect. Should he wish to send money abroad, Congress must first appropriate it; should he send troops, Congress must agree to pay, as it also must with weapons and munitions. Regarding troops, he has to state his reasons; according to the law (though never yet in practice), Congress can remove them after sixty days, rejecting his rationale. Only if he drops atomic bombs does Congress have no comeback—save impeachment. But every president since Truman has learned, in awe, from his experience that nuclear weapons are for show, not use.

Or consider this: While Congress is the legislature in our system, the president, in Dwight Eisenhower's phrase, is also "part of the legislative process," not only wielding his veto (which the House of Representatives and Senate both, by a two-thirds vote, can override), but also having the duty to recommend "such measures as he judge necessary and expedient."

These are what we conventionally call "checks and balances" in our government. There are others as well, including the sovereign rights of states within their constitutional limits, which the courts can amend, from time to time, by interpretation, but not abolish altogether. In a comparable category are the rights of citizens, and by extension those of the private sector in our economy, not least the press. And very specifically, in another example of checks and balances, senators and members of the House are forbidden to hold executive appointments simultaneously; there cannot be

A young Richard Neustadt working as an adviser to Harry Truman.

congressional cabinets at the president's end of Pennsylvania Avenue.

Most of these checks and balances derive directly, though not avowedly, from British experience, our founding fathers having all been former British subjects. For example, the check that forbids members of Congress from simultaneously holding executive appointments keeps American presidents from doing what King George III was famous for, his so-called "corruption" of Parliament—building majorities with rewards in the form of appointments to administrative posts.

Moreover, president and Congress are competitive because both represent the American people, and so both can claim to represent the source of sovereignty in popular government. But they do so in different ways, for different terms, as they are nominated and elected by different constituencies. Only the president (and, of course, his running mate) is nominated in primary elections or state conventions all across the country and then chosen by popular vote in general elections held state by state on the same day. Just a third of the senators are chosen at the same time, and then for terms of six years rather than the presidential four. Representatives are chosen from geographic districts within states—usually smaller than states—not only when a president runs but also every second year. They are nominated in party primaries or conventions, as is he, but within their state or district, not throughout the country, and then elected by the voters in the same jurisdiction, a far smaller body than the president's fifty-state electorate.

As aggregates, both the Senate and the House represent the whole country. But so does the president, one person. The House can always claim to be most up-to-date in its representation, but every four years the president makes the superior claim of a nationwide vote. Individually no House member (or senator, for that matter) can match that.

Senators and members of Congress have limited influence, at best, in primaries for presidential nominations, or in the national conventions that confirm the results, now shades of their former selves. Presidents are usually at least as limited in influence upon the state or district bodies that nominate representatives and senators, even those nominally of their own party. For in fact the local and state parties are not the same as the quadrennial national party at presidential elections. Money for campaigns can be a binding tie (and has been, on occasion, almost from the start). But by and large, local party affairs remain local, and state affairs state, in the conduct of nominations. In modern times, primary elections for the presidential nomination do lessen the influence of statewide party organizations, once supreme at national conventions, but that influence was usually less congressional than gubernatorial, so Congress scarcely loses by the change.

In short, the constitutional separation of president from Congress is reinforced by the separateness of their respective nominating processes and their electoral constituencies. That is why the separation flourishes, and has flourished, for the most part, since George Washington took his oath of office in 1789. And since the separation rests securely on those different political bases, checks and balances assure perpetual competition, because the president and Congress, each speaking "for" the country, share so widely in each other's functions.

That competition can be muted by concern for dangers from abroad, as was the case when President Washington began, and in the two world wars, and from time to time during the Cold War. Or it can be muted by concern for truly national crises, as in the secession crisis of 1861 or the collapse of the U.S. banking system in 1933. And it always can be tempered by comity among those engaged in governing—but of that our party politics offers no guarantee.

Given these circumstances, individuals are bound to matter in and to the presidency. Underlining this book, therefore, is the thought that a review of the first forty-one may help us as we choose the next president.

Each individual president exists and works in a specific social, economic, technological, and environmental framework, dominated by certain prevailing ideas and trends. All these condition politics and thus what given presidents find they can do, or feel they must attempt. Each also exists in a specific frame of time, defined by modes of communication. For James Monroe, six weeks was not too long to wait for diplomatic correspondence from across the Atlantic. By Lincoln's time the interval had shrunk, with the advent of steamships, to twelve days. After 1867, the laying of the transatlantic cable made communication almost instantaneous—but instant pictures did not come for more than another century.

From 1789 until the eve of World War II, there virtually was no "institutional environment" for the presidency. The president had a private secretary or two (Lincoln in the Civil War had just two!), paid out of his own pocket until the twentieth century, and otherwise depended for all things he wanted done on the federal departments, with their heads in his cabinet, or the military chiefs and their services, or friendly souls in Congress and out, not least in his hometown.

The entire executive establishment consisted only of some 600 civilians when George Washington took charge. By the 1840s the number had risen to some 40,000, and by 1900 to some 100,000. Only in Franklin Roosevelt's time did it rise to a million, just before World War II. After the war it never fell below 2 million until Bill Clinton's time, when it was reduced by perhaps an eighth.

The White House was slow to change. As late as the war, FDR had only eleven civilian assistants, along with a budget-office staff of career civil servants. JFK's assistants amounted to twenty-two, a doubling in sixteen years, mostly because of Truman and Eisenhower innovations. Then, very shortly, President Nixon increased the number by a factor of five, to well over 100. The Clinton staff is larger still. Most of the load that was delegated to departments, or the military, or congressional leaders, or friends (and relatives) by presidents from Washington through Herbert Hoover and the early Franklin Roosevelt is now done, supervised, critiqued, or redone by presidential staff, many at the White House, and more at associated agencies "across the street" in two executive office buildings. Today, 2,000 or so people work for the presidency in the Executive Office of the President; 500 or so work for the president in the White House (clerical help included); 100 or so serve as top staffers; and ten to twenty aides have daily personal access to the president.

This enormous growth of staff has actually been less responsive to administrative needs than to those of politics and technology. It reflects fast-rising public expectations of the presidency, which now is supposed to win wars, resist terror, keep public order, end recessions, guard against depressions, keep prices down and jobs up, save the environment, preserve social security, fight crime and drugs, maintain personal honor, serve as an example to the young, and with it all show "fiscal responsibility." Such expectations are now fed by electronic media, as well as the print press, which have been engaged in massive bursts of instant communication from all quarters simultaneously. What is communicated has to have a basis in events, but with the world at the disposal of the media, thanks to satellites, events from somewhere, about something, are a dime a dozen.

This naturally complicates the substance of policy and its communication to Congress, to agencies, and to the public. Recent presidents have wished to have their own aides—not a department head's, not someone else's—to work and advise on all aspects of all policies. Furthermore, the burgeoning press corps, always pressing, consists not just of "working stiffs," as in pre-television times, but also of reporters, whom television has transformed into celebrities. They, like all such, want their service fast and hot. In President Truman's time, his press secretary had two professional-level assistants. The number nowadays is over forty.

The institutional presidency is not an unmixed blessing for a president. Staffs are too large to be intimate, which means they are too remote to serve reliably as interpreters of what "the boss" really wants. They are subject to becoming "more royalist than the king." They also may attract to themselves more business than is useful for him. Worse still, they may confuse their own interests with his. And since transition funds are now available to bridge the gap between election and inaugural, all too many staff assistants may be young campaigners on their first federal assignment, as ignorant of Washington as the president-elect might be himself, and unprepared to help him master what he needs to know.

Despite staffs and the problems that go with them, recent presidents appear to experience the office in much the way their predecessors did. For the heart of the job is unchanged. It is the making and communicating of decisions, most of which do not originate with the president himself: their long histories are best known to others; their

Richard E. Neustadt at work on *The American President.*

deadlines are set by fixed dates or events substantially beyond his control; and they reach him late, at the end of the process, with advisers split on what to do. All presidents, even recent ones, have faced such choices with the help of a few trusted persons, perhaps three or four, rarely more, who constitute an ultimate inner circle. They may be aides, or cabinet members, or close friends, or family members, like Milton Eisenhower and Hillary Rodham Clinton. What is crucial is that they are each of the president's own selection—someone he turns to repeatedly and who trusts him in turn. Those few may be the only people that a modern president thinks of as his real "staff," the many others nominally in that category notwithstanding. In this regard, his subjective situation has a lot in common with that of every predecessor back to General Washington.

This book proceeds on that premise. It proceeds on the further premise that while history does not literally repeat itself, the situations of some presidents objectively resemble those of many others in certain characteristic ways.

In the final chapter of this book the authors turn to cardinal features of our constitutional design, its checks and balances. These separated institutions that share powers engage as they must in endless competition; they tend toward stalemate in the short run, and are slow to respond to slender majorities, though they are capable of registering national consensus with rapidity. But consensus is not easily reached, save for events so grim and clear-cut that time may not allow for proper remedies. And competition can easily get out of hand, leading toward legislative stasis and administrative chaos. For a country as extensive and diverse as ours, there must be something good about this separated system, since it has endured now for 211 years and plainly has a future. But its potential for failure in the eyes of most proponents of all policies much of the time, and its extraordinary messiness, not to say expense, both in delaying and

in implementing what it does get done, engender critical and sometimes despairing pleas for reform of one kind or another from deeply concerned thinkers—and have done so ever since the eighteenth century.

A discussion of checks and balances seems a fitting way for this book to close. For complicated reasons bound up in history—not quite what Madison expected but more or less consistent with his basic views—the system he created manages to shake off every decade's effort to erase its fundamentals for the sake of theory. Nevertheless, it does continue to change incrementally at the margins, responding to the pulls and tugs of social, economic, and technological development. The responses can lag, some are perverse, and all have unintended consequences. Injustice often follows. To rational minds the process is a mess. No one can fail to fume at some of its results. Yet in this country, so far, we have had only one civil war. Of all our presidential thinkers, Madison, I dare say, would have been almost satisfied by that. Most of the time, I am prepared to join him.

But that is a perspective from inside the States. When I go overseas, as periodically I do, I cannot help but notice how our separated system reinforces tendencies toward continental self-absorption, disappointing what our friends abroad expect from the world's oldest democracy and only superpower. They forget that even our most generous phase of genuine concern for our allies—and for endeavors with them—got kick-started by the threat of Joseph Stalin. German submarines precipitated our engagement in World War I, Japanese bombers did the same for World War II, and Stalin played a crucial part in setting off the retrospective Golden Era of the Marshall Plan. Left to our own devices we incline toward isolation.

The complicated workings of our separated system, with president and Congress independent yet intertwined, are a contributory cause of this isolation. Actions are so fraught with emotion, and yet so far from final—almost every issue can be and usually is reopened for discussion—that the energy and interests of our leaders are consumed, with little left for the outside world save when it forcibly intrudes. From an eighteenth-century perspective, Madison, I think, would not have minded. From a twenty-first-century perspective—oh, how our allies do mind! Sympathy tempers my share in his satisfaction.

PART ONE

THE CANDIDATE

Washington, D.C., in the 1860s

George Washington

William Henry Harrison

THE HEROIC POSTURE

CHAPTER ONE

America has turned to war heroes for more than a third of its
presidents. But war and politics don't necessarily mix.

Ulysses S. Grant

Dwight D. Eisenhower

From the beginning, the presidency has beckoned to national heroes. Renowned for their service in time of war, they seem to many to stand above politics, holding out the possibility of a special kind of leadership. Twelve generals have held the highest office, as well as a half dozen others of lesser rank whose wartime heroism helped get them elected. The most revered of all was our first chief executive, the great hero of the Revolution, General George Washington. He was America's only classical hero, cut in the mold of the ancient Romans. And he was entrusted with the presidency not so much for his generalship as for his restraint and civility and love for his country. The presidential powers granted him under the new Constitution were awesome; yet as commander-in-chief, his authority was to take place under the umbrella of Congress, which retained the power to declare war as well as to raise and regulate the armed forces. From the beginning it was to be a civilian government. And George Washington, understanding this completely, went on to set a model of restraint.

James Monroe: major in the Continental Army

Rutherford B. Hayes: Civil War general

James Garfield: Civil War general

Benjamin Harrison: Civil War general

William McKinley: major in the Civil War

Like the four generals in this chapter, the two men above were also military leaders of heroic stature. At the top is Andrew Jackson, hero of New Orleans and the seventh president. Below him is Zachary Taylor, hero of the Mexican War and the twelfth president.

The generation after Washington produced two more soldier-presidents. The first was General Andrew Jackson, the hugely popular hero of the War of 1812, so admired he continued to receive write-in votes for president for decades after his retirement and death. But by 1840, with the election of the next soldier-president, the idea of heroism itself had changed. With the rise of party politics in America, military men were no longer looked to so much for their qualities of leadership as they were recognized by their parties as potent political commodities. The sixty-eight-year-old former Indian fighter and one-time governor of Indiana Territory, William Henry Harrison, became the first presidential candidate deliberately molded to appeal to public opinion. And in an outburst of hoopla befitting the age, the old general was propelled into office almost in spite of himself.

Harrison's presidency was part of a national trend. Between 1824 and 1856, every presidential election but one included a military hero. William Harrison was soon followed by professional soldier Zachary Taylor, the rough-hewn hero of the War with Mexico, who was himself the object of savvy political handlers. And when the New England war veteran Franklin Pierce ran for president, it was against his former superior officer in Mexico, General Winfield Scott. Party professionals turned to military heroes because of their customary lack of political enemies and because they appealed to a general public increasingly distrustful of lifelong politicians. Appearing to be the antithesis of men like Martin Van Buren, whose chief allegiance lay to himself and to his own political party, generals seemed to belong to the entire country. And unlike sophisticated partisans like Henry Clay and Daniel Webster, they had earned national respect on the fields of battle. Although their opponents criticized them as mere military chieftains, soldier candidates remained popular with the public at large.

But it was one thing to win presidential elections and another to master the presidency itself. And with the sudden natural deaths of both Harrison and Taylor, a crucial question was still unanswered: could military men, other than a rare giant like Washington, be expected to rise to the immense challenges of the presidency? The question was answered, at least in part, in the aftermath of the Civil War, when the country turned to one of the greatest military leaders it has ever produced, Ulysses S. Grant. Elected in large part by Northern veterans, Grant turned out to be one of the least successful presidents in American history, far too inexperienced and unfocused to serve in the distinguished tradition of George Washington.

Grant's failures, however, did not stop other soldier-politicians from running for president, and Republican war heroes occupied the White House for much of the remainder of the nineteenth century. In these decades the votes of veterans remained decisive and presidential campaigning took on a noticeable military air. The single Democratic victor during this entire

Theodore Roosevelt: lieutenant colonel in the Spanish-American War

Harry Truman: major in World War I

John F. Kennedy: Navy lieutenant in World War II

George Bush: Navy lieutenant in World War II

era was Grover Cleveland, whose complete absence of a war record came back to haunt him. When he made the decision midway through his term to return captured Confederate flags to the South, and then went on to veto hundreds of what he considered improper Civil War pension bills, he quickly lost much of his popularity. The next election went to Republican Benjamin Harrison, the sixth in a line of Civil War generals in the presidency.

By the turn of the century, Civil War generals were no longer available; they either had all died off or were getting too old to run. Not wishing to break with their successful formula, Republicans reached out for a major, William McKinley, who had enlisted in the Union Army as a teenager. And then, after Theodore Roosevelt, who had served briefly in the armed forces during the Spanish American War, the twentieth century turned for its presidents to a long line of civilians. The age of the generals appeared to be over. But then came the hero of World War II, Dwight David Eisenhower.

Of all the presidents with military backgrounds, General Eisenhower seemed most similar to George Washington. Like Washington, Ike appeared to be above politics; early on no one even knew whether he was a Democrat or a Republican. And although he was far more politically motivated than anyone realized, throughout his presidency he remained a committed centrist, working hard trying to hold the entire country together. In the years since Eisenhower, seven of the past eight presidents served in the military. Bill Clinton is the one exception. And two of them—John F. Kennedy and George Bush—were distinguished for their wartime heroism.

All in all, America has turned to war heroes for more than a third of its presidents. Coming from outside the normal political system, they appear to transcend the grubby exchange of politics, representing honor and duty rather than barter and compromise. And military men who have reached the White House have usually acted with military restraint. Possessing a first-hand knowledge of the horrors of war, they may have been less willing than civilians to commit men and women to battle.

Still, Americans retain a measure of skepticism about soldier-presidents, partly because military valor is a poor predictor of presidential leadership. In times of crisis and impending war, the country usually elects civilians and not generals. The greatest wartime presidents—Abraham Lincoln and Franklin D. Roosevelt—had virtually no military experience at all.

But America itself was born in war, and her first, and many say greatest, president was himself a general. And so, at regular intervals the country returns to its origins, raising up yet again to high office the military hero.

GEORGE WASHINGTON

1789–1797

America's First Hero

Any memoirs of my life . . . unconnected with the general history of the War, would rather hurt my feelings than tickle my pride," George Washington once wrote. Washington's life is inextricably linked to the Revolution, but over time it has been largely forgotten that his true heroism sprang less from his accomplishments as a military man than from qualities deep inside him: his character and his vision.

"My politics are plain and simple," he wrote. "I think every nation has a right to establish . . . [a] government under which it conceives it shall live most happy." And another time he added, "I think I see a *path*, as clear and as direct as a ray of light."

A farmer's son from tidewater Virginia, from early on George Washington was drawn to the military. He was tall, enormously strong, and a superb horseman, who proved himself virtually invulnerable during the French and Indian War. "I have a constitution hardy enough to . . . undergo the most severe trials," he boasted. "[And] by the all-powerful dispensations of Providence, I have been protected . . .; for I had four bullets through my coat, and two horses shot under me, yet escaped unhurt, altho' death was levelling my companions on every side of me!"

In the years that followed, a Virginia plantation called Mount Vernon became home to this Indian fighter turned farmer. Overseeing thousands of acres and hundreds of slaves, he turned himself into one of the country's wealthiest citizens, marrying a rich and socially prominent widow, Martha Custis. Rather than intellectual or imaginative, George Washington was pragmatic and thorough. Easily embarrassed by his lack of learning, he was not a good conversationalist and he had a legendary temper. He loved to hunt and he loved music. And when he was a political representative in the House of Burgesses, his opinions about public affairs grew steadily stronger. "For my own part, I shall not undertake to say where the line between Great Britain and the colonies should be drawn," he once wrote. "But one ought to be drawn. . . . The crisis is arrived when we must assert our rights."

Revolution broke out in April 1775, and at the age of forty-three Washington reluctantly agreed to serve as commander-in-chief of a Continental Army. But he never considered himself a professional soldier, just a citizen defending his country.

"It has been determined in Congress that the whole army . . . shall be put under my care," Washington wrote Martha on June 18. "I have used every endeavor in my power to avoid it . . . but . . . a kind of destiny . . . has thrown me upon this service. . . . It was utterly out of my power to refuse."

This was the object of his heart's desire—Mount Vernon, overlooking the Potomac. Yet he always seemed to be leaving his gracious mansion to serve the people. Inheriting land from his father, he bought tracts himself, acquiring even more from his marriage to the twenty-seven-year-old wealthy widow Martha Custis. Assisted by land grants, Washington finally owned 80,000 acres, including his own village of several hundred slaves.

THE COUNTRY'S ADULATION

Washington arrived in New York City to be sworn in as the country's first president after an eight-day journey from Mount Vernon. No greater hero ever traveled to his destiny in like manner. The 235-mile route his carriage took had been one long ribbon of jubilation. Cannons boomed in every town and hamlet, dust from thousands of ecstatic horsemen enveloped him, maidens in white, fireworks, bonfires, speeches, and lavish banquets greeted him the entire way. Women and children spread flowers before him and sang. Finally arriving in New York, he was rowed across the Hudson River on a barge. The city seemed to be on the verge of exploding as cannons fired and church bells clanged. It was actually frightening for Washington to see the intensity of adulation the people had for him.

For eight years he led his fellow countrymen, convincing them to fight on, even when the cause seemed lost. It wasn't his generalship that made him stand out, however. It was the way he attended to and stuck by his men. His soldiers knew that he respected them and cared about them, and that he would share their severe hardships. "My brave fellows, you have done all I asked you to do," he once exhorted, "and more than could be reasonably expected, but your country is at stake: your wives, your houses, and all that you hold dear. You have worn yourselves out with fatigue and hardships, but we know not how to spare you."

At war's end, Washington faced a final crisis, one that was building inside his own army. His men, who had forgone pay for as long as six years, had learned that a nearly bankrupt Congress was considering never paying them. "If retiring from the field they are to grow old in poverty," Washington wrote indignantly, "then I shall have learned what ingratitude is." In 1782, with official peace talks still in progress, Washington himself was approached to join an armed rebellion against Congress and allow himself to be set up as king. But the officer who made this proposal simply did not understand George Washington's character.

"You could not have found a person to whom your schemes are more disagreeable," he wrote back. "Banish these thoughts from your mind." When he later heard rumors that his disgruntled officers were moving ahead with a planned military coup d'état, he asked them to meet with him at Newburgh, New York, where they assembled on March 15, 1783.

"Gentlemen," he spoke, addressing the crowded room. "As I was among the first who embarked in the cause of our common Country; as I never left your side one moment, but when called from you on public duty; as I have been the constant companion and witness of your Distresses . . . it can *scarcely be supposed* . . . that I am indifferent to [your] interests. But . . . this dreadful alternative, of either deserting our Country in the extremest hour of her distress, or turning our Arms against it, . . . has something so shocking in it that humanity revolts from the idea. . . . I spurn it, as every Man who regards liberty . . . undoubtedly must."

A silence passed over the assembled group. Then Washington drew out a letter from a congressman, addressing the soldiers' grievances. But the aging commander could not read the text, and was forced to resort to a pair of eyeglasses.

"Gentlemen, you will permit me to put on my spectacles," he said, "for I have not only grown gray but almost blind in the service of my country."

This simple gesture brought tears to the eyes of his men. By his selfless example, Washington had shamed the conspirators out of their plot.

Other new countries have had generals come to the helm, to rule as military dictators. Nothing like that happened following the American Revolution, largely because of George Washington.

In 1783, three and a half months after a final peace treaty was signed, Washington resigned his commission and returned to Mount Vernon, he hoped for good. "I am to become a private citizen on the banks of the Potomac," he wrote gleefully. "Free from the busy scenes of public life, I am retiring within myself."

The very fact that he refused to hold on to his military authority or to seek political or financial reward for his years of service astonished the country. And when word of it reached King George III of England he exclaimed, "If true, then he is the greatest man in the world."

"It is said that every man has his portion of ambition," Washington once wrote. "I may have mine I suppose as well as the rest; but . . . my only ambition is to do my duty."

Four years after his resignation from the Army, Washington reluctantly agreed to come out of retirement and preside at a Congressional Convention in Philadelphia. Here he helped shape a new, national Constitution, which called for a single chief executive to be known as "president." All knew that there was only one man who could fill the position, and in the following year, an unopposed George Washington was unanimously elected by a total of sixty-nine electors.

"My leaving home to take upon myself the execution of this office was the greatest personal sacrifice I have ever . . . been called upon to make," Washington later wrote. "I [felt] very much like a man who is condemned to death does when the time of his execution draws near."

On April 30, 1789, the fifty-seven-year-old war hero, dressed in a dark brown suit and wearing a steel-hilted dress sword, stood on the balcony of Federal Hall in New York City. There, before a great crowd below, he answered the oath the Constitution had mandated, adding his own prayer at the end, "so help me God."

"I walk on untrodden ground," Washington wrote soon afterward. "There is scarcely any part of my conduct which may not hereafter be drawn into precedent."

Appearing in formal dress at weekly public receptions, President Washington would bow and speak to each guest but never become so familiar as

NOT A KING, BUT A PRESIDENT

On the balcony of New York's Federal Hall before an immense crowd below, George Washington swore he would faithfully execute the office of president. Everything was new. The words had never been uttered before. The Constitution being sworn allegiance to was only months old. Here, taking office, was its first leader—not a king to reign over the new nation's people but a president to carry out their will. It was the most daring experiment in government upon which humankind had yet embarked. If the Constitution worked, it would revolutionize history. "This Constitution is really in its formation a government of the people . . . in which all power is derived from and, at stated periods, reverts to them," Washington had stated. "It is purely a government of laws, made and executed by the fair substitutes of the people alone." Later he would add that the American form of government was "a new phenomenon in the political and moral world, and an astonishing victory gained by enlightened reason over brute force."

George and Martha Washington

Washington loved a woman he could not have—tall, witty, teasing Sally Cary Fairfax, wife of one of his close friends. He married instead a tiny widow, Martha Dandridge Custis, so short she barely reached his chest. Martha came with plenty of money, a prerequisite for George, who dreamed of owning an enormous farming enterprise. She was the opposite of his scolding mother—quiet, nonjudgmental, and utterly devoted. And in place of romance, Washington came to value friendship. "Love is a mighty pretty thing," he wrote years later to a step-granddaughter, "but, like all other delicious things, it is cloying. . . . Be assured . . . that all our enjoyments fall short of our expectations, and to none does it apply with more force than to the gratification of the passions." Homely, placid, completely apolitical, Martha ran an efficient household and was a dutiful wife, referring to Washington as her "old man," and addressed by him as his "dear Patsy." She hated being left alone at Mount Vernon, and during the war she sometimes visited her husband in camp, especially at winter quarters, where she not only gave comfort to the general but ministered to the sick as well. Expecting a well-deserved retirement together after the war, Martha was devastated when Washington was elected president, and refused to accompany him to his inauguration. But as First Lady she quickly made herself indispensable, opening her Philadelphia parlor every Friday afternoon to a different assortment of men and women, and hosting a dinner party once a week for as many as could fit around the presidential dinner table.

to shake hands. He called his advisers his "first characters," and invented the presidential cabinet. And on a wild tract of land along the Potomac River, he chose the location for a new capital city that would one day bear his name. He himself laid the cornerstone for the Capitol building and picked out the site for what would become the White House.

To make it absolutely clear that the president was not a king, Washington backed away from wielding too much power, refusing to interfere with Congress. And when war broke out between France and Britain, he ardently opposed taking sides in the conflict, issuing a proclamation of neutrality.

"My policy has been to be upon friendly terms with, but independent of, all the nations of the earth," he noted.

Only once did Washington actually put his uniform back on and lead an army into the field—against fellow Americans in western Pennsylvania. Settlers there were refusing to pay tax on whiskey, and had tarred and feathered federal officers. Washington easily put down the rebellion, but even then he quickly tempered his actions, issuing a blanket amnesty to all the rebels.

His peaceful approach to politics ultimately hurt him, though, and throughout his second term he was vilified for his refusal to take sides in the European conflict.

"I [was] . . . accused of being the enemy of one Nation, and subject to the influence of another," he wrote Thomas Jefferson; "and . . . in such exaggerated and indecent terms as could scarcely be applied to . . . a common pickpocket."

March 3, 1797, was George Washington's final day in office. Setting the precedent for a two-term limit and the civil transfer of power, he confessed, "I shall resign the chair of government without a single regret."

By the time he left office, the country had formed its own national character, in large part by borrowing George Washington's. And when he died just three years later at age sixty-seven, an emotional tribute on the floor of Congress summed him up this way: "First in war, first in peace, first in the hearts of his countrymen." In his farewell address to the nation he himself had said what most mattered to him, warning his country about foreign entanglements and about the danger of partisanship within the republic. "I shall carry to my grave the hope that your Union and brotherly affection may be perpetual; that the Constitution may be sacredly maintained; and that free government . . . the ever favorite object of my heart . . . will be the happy reward of our mutual cares, labors and dangers."

Martha had her parties, too. They were held on Friday nights and were always terminated by nine o'clock, the President and Lady Washington's bedtime.

THE FIRST PRESIDENT'S "FIRST CHARACTERS"

President Washington confers with his two most trusted advisers, Thomas Jefferson (seated at left) and Alexander Hamilton (standing).

For his cabinet and the 350 or so positions the first president had to fill, Washington was determined not to take family, friends, wealth, or social standing into account but instead to select men whom he termed "the first Characters," those who held the greatest reputations in the fields and locales of the jobs he was filling. "My political conduct and nominations must be exceedingly circumspect," he commented, always aware of the precedents he was setting. "No slip into partiality will pass unnoticed. . . . By having Mr. Jefferson as the head of the Department of State, Mr. Jay of the Judiciary, Hamilton of the Treasury, and Knox of that of War, I feel myself supported . . . extremely well." Although the men closest to him were brilliant, strong, and opinionated, Washington would not be bullied by them or take sides, even though Hamilton and Jefferson were in utter disagreement. Jefferson thought Hamilton was a monarchist; Hamilton was convinced Jefferson would turn the government over to the mobs. "I believe the view of both of you are pure, and well meant," the President once lectured his warring cabinet ministers. "Why then, when some of the best Citizens in the United States, Men . . . who have no sinister views to promote, are to be found, some on one side, and some on the other . . . should either of you be so tenacious of your opinions as to make no allowances for those of the other? . . . I have a great . . . esteem . . . for you both, and ardently wish that some line could be marked out by which both of you could walk."

George Washington, with Pierre L'Enfant in 1791, surveys the land for the new capitol city and helps choose the site for the executive mansion.

Washington never lived in the White House—or what was then referred to as the President's Mansion—but his vision and persistence created it, as well as the city that would rise around it and bear his name. In 1789 when the new capital city was first being discussed, an old friend of the President's applied for the job as the proposed city's planner and architect. Designer-artist Pierre Charles L'Enfant had left France in 1777 to fight in the American Revolution; he had even painted Washington's portrait at Valley Forge for Lafayette. Impressed with the man and his talents, Washington gave him the capital job. The city L'Enfant proceeded to design was spacious and grand, but the edifice he had in mind for the President's Palace was so immense and splendid and kingly, it offended Secretary of State Thomas Jefferson and oth-ers in the fledgling U.S. government. Subsequently the temperamental, uncompromising L'Enfant was dismissed, leaving foundations already dug for a rectangular building almost 700 feet long and more than 200 feet in depth. Over the farms and marshlands and woods that still harbored deer and bear, L'Enfant had driven wooden stakes to delineate the monumental city he envisioned. Washington was willing to yield on the palace but not on L'Enfant's city. To move ahead again on the future executive mansion, a design competition was announced. Nine proposals were made, including the work of James Hoban, whom Washington had met in Charleston and had called for an audience with in Philadelphia. Having been able to make his sketches on the actual site, Hoban won hands down, especially since the President was the head judge. The construction of the largest building in the U.S. took almost a decade, and Washington never saw it completed. He died at age sixty-seven, just seventeen days before the new century was rung in and nine months before his successor, John Adams, moved into the President's Mansion. Washington left much behind, especially a legacy of courage and character that would define American ideals for centuries. As a final gift to his country, his last will and testament freed his slaves, setting a remarkable example to generations that would follow.

More than sixty years after Washington's death, a hand-colored stereo photograph shows what his Mount Vernon tomb looked like (above). The painting at the right by John Vanderlyn, like most paintings of Washington, failed to capture the man.

1774: For my own part, I shall not undertake to say where the line between Great Britain and the colonies should be drawn; but I am clearly of [the] opinion, that one ought to be drawn, and our rights clearly ascertained. I could wish, I own, that the dispute had been left to posterity to determine, but the crisis is arrived when we must assert our rights.

1789: At the beginning of the late War with Great Britain . . . it was known . . . that the resources of Britain were, in a manner, inexhaustible, that her fleets covered the Ocean, and that her troops had harvested laurels in every quarter of the globe. Not then organised as a Nation, or known as a people upon the earth—we had no preparation. Money, the nerve of War, was wanting. The Sword was to be forged on the Anvil of necessity: the treasury to be created from nothing. If we had a secret resource of a nature unknown to our enemy, it was in the unconquerable resolution of our Citizens, the conscious rectitude of our cause, and a confident trust that we should not be forsaken by Heaven.

1783: From the observation I have made in the course of this War . . . I am decided in my opinion, that if the powers of Congress are not enlarged, and made competent to all general purposes, that the Blood which has been spilt, the expense that has been incurred, and the distresses which have been felt, will avail us nothing; and that the band, already too weak, which holds us together, will soon be broken; when anarchy and confusion must prevail.

1787: I almost despair of seeing a favourable issue to the proceedings of our Convention, and do therefore repent having had any agency in the business. The Men who oppose a strong and energetic government are, in my opinion, narrow minded politicians, or are under the influence of local views.

1788: The proposed Constitution . . . is provided with more checks and barriers against the introduction of Tyranny . . . than any Government hitherto instituted among mortals.

1788: I . . . always hoped that this land might become a safe and agreeable Asylum to the virtuous and persecuted part of mankind, to whatever nation they might belong.

1796: Against the insidious wiles of foreign influence . . . the jealousy of a free people ought to be constantly awake; since history and experience prove that foreign influence is one of the most baneful foes of Republican Government.

George Washington was the only president never to live in the White House, but he was deeply involved in it from its inception. Its very location was a personal victory—for it was to be situated not far from his home, Mount Vernon. It was Washington who brought in the Irish-born architect James Hoban (whose original 1792 design for the house appears here). Washington drove the first stakes that sited the mansion, and personally requested such features as the East Room and the oval drawing room. And though the building was not completed until after his death, Washington lived long enough to inspect it in nearly finished form.

A century after Washington's death there never was a doubt in anybody's mind who was father of our country or who our greatest president. Here a group of young enthusiasts, some of whom were the grandchildren of slaves, admire the general's toga, an embellishment by the sculptor Greenough who sought a Grecian look.

A Manufactured Hero

William Henry Harrison enjoyed playing the role of humble, backwoods hero. "The high office . . . was never, for a moment the object of my ambition," he wrote before his election in 1840. "I would have preferred to remain with my family in . . . *our log cabin* . . . rather than become engaged in political or other disputes." But despite his pretense to log-cabin origins, he was actually heir to one of the oldest and most distinguished families in America. He was a classically educated Virginian whose father had been a signer of the Declaration of Independence.

As a young man, with a commission signed by George Washington, Harrison had been sent to help patrol the Western frontier, establishing himself as an Indian fighter. "My sword is almost my only patrimony," he wrote his brother in 1794, "but while I wear that sword and the livery of my country, I will not disgrace them."

In 1798 Harrison entered politics, and by age twenty-seven he had become governor of the newly created Territory of Indiana, a post he held for the next twelve years. During this time he built a luxurious Governor's Mansion, which became known as Grouseland. Here William Harrison's principal duty was to oversee relations with Native Americans across a vast tract of wilderness.

"I was appointed sole commissioner for making . . . treaties . . . with the North Western tribes of Indians," he wrote. "[Because of] the violence and injustice with which they have been treated by some of our Citizens, . . . the American name has become almost universally odious to [them]. . . . To remove these impressions has been my constant aim."

Ignoring Governor Harrison's good intentions, President Thomas Jefferson sent word from the White House that he wanted him to use any means possible to obtain Indian lands.

"A short time evinced the wisdom of the plan prescribed by the President," Harrison wrote. "By my own personal exertions in securing the friendship of the chiefs . . . by admitting them at all times to my house & table, my propositions for the purchase of their lands were successfull beyond my most sanguine hopes. . . . In the course of seven years the Indian title was extinguished to the amount of fifty millions of acres."

On August 12, 1810, the Shawnee leader Tecumseh descended upon the Governor's Mansion and warned that his people would not sit still if their lands were threatened again. Harrison recorded the incident as follows: "Tecumseh . . . avowed . . . that it was [his] object . . . to form a combination of all the Indian Tribes in this quarter to put a stop to the encroachments

For his presidential campaign twenty-eight years after the Battle of Tippecanoe, Harrison was depicted as ignoring his subordinates' attempt to keep him from danger and heroically riding into the Indian advance on a white charger.

In the early years of the nineteenth century two powerful Indian chieftains began putting together a confederation of tribes stretching from Florida to Canada to oppose white advances. They were Tecumseh, a well-respected Shawnee chief, and his brother, Lalawethika, known as The Prophet. As military conflict became imminent, the Prophet made his headquarters on the Tippecanoe River in Harrison's territory. "I have determined to commence offensive operations against them immediately," the Governor decided, "and to make a sweeping blow at them beginning with the Prophet at Tippecanoe." Instead of Harrison's "sweeping blow," the Indians surprised the U.S. soldiers. A battle ensued, with heavy U.S. losses.

This is an early photograph of an oil portrait of William Henry Harrison, painted by the New England artist Albert Gallatin Hoit. Armed with a letter of recommendation from family friend Daniel Webster, Hoit had convinced candidate Harrison to sit for the painting in Cincinnati on May 25, 1840. Later he made numerous copies of his portrait and allowed them to be photographed by daguerreotypists. Harrison himself sat for a daguerreotype shortly after his inauguration, making him the earliest president to be recorded by the two-year-old invention. That photograph, by the Philadelphia practitioner Justus Moore, has long since disappeared.

Though the Battle of Tippecanoe (above) was criticized at the time as a victory with many too many U.S. casualties, it helped lead to Harrison's goal—the termination of the Indian confederation.

Above is the image of Harrison that the Whigs were trying to convey in 1840—a humble, log-cabin-dwelling farmer on the banks of the Ohio River, here greeting a wounded Tippecanoe comrade-in-arms.

of the white people. . . . That the Americans had driven them from the sea coast, and would shortly, if not stopped, push them into the Lakes, that they were determined to make a stand where they were."

When Harrison learned that more than 500 warriors had joined Tecumseh along the banks of the Tippecanoe River in Northwestern Indiana, he personally led troops there and prepared for battle. But before dawn, the Indians attacked first.

"Indians were in the Camp before many of my men could get out of their tents," Harrison reported the next day in a dispatch to the Secretary of War. "Confusion for a short time prevailed, but aided by the great activities of the officers I was soon enabled to form the men in order. . . . About daylight the enemy were finally put to flight after having penetrated to, and killed men in the very center of our Camp. Our killed and wounded amounted to 179."

Harrison's political enemies called it a "horrible butchery" and charged him with military incompetence. But over the years, his victory at Tippecanoe became increasingly romanticized as one of the great episodes of American heroism.

"The heroes who fell at Tippecanoe," he wrote, "experienced the common lot of war. . . . Such a victory over such an enemy could not be achieved without great loss."

Twenty-eight years after the battle, Tippecanoe became the rallying cry for Harrison's bid for the presidency. In an era when political party leaders controlled presidential elections, Harrison was a candidate of the Whig Party, which advocated a weak president and a strong Congress. Selected because he was seen as electable, he was cleverly packaged by Whig handlers not just as a war hero but as a reluctant candidate from the back woods. When John Tyler of Virginia was named Harrison's vice presidential running mate, their rousing campaign slogan became "Tippecanoe and Tyler Too."

Harrison's campaign became the best-organized and most exciting ever seen up to that time. Music and whiskey and coonskin caps swamped every hamlet; barbecue smoke, banners, and balloon rides filled the air. In Cleveland a group of Whigs created a huge tin ball which they proceeded to push all the way to the state capital of Columbus. "Keep the ball rolling" became the Harrison motto, implying that the ball would "roll over" the Democrats in November.

Drawing out an astonishing 82 percent of all eligible voters, Harrison ended up with 53 percent of the vote and overwhelmed his opponent in the electoral college. "You have undoubtedly seen it . . . stated that I am a very decrepit old man," he stated in glee. "You now perceive, however, that these stories are false. . . . I am not the old man on crutches nor the imbecile they say I am."

But in fact, Harrison was exhausted and frail when he prepared to leave for Washington in early 1841. And when he said goodbye to his fellow townspeople, he seemed to know instinctively that he would not be coming back. "This may be the last time I have the pleasure of speaking to you on earth," he said. "I bid you farewell; if forever, fare thee well."

On Inauguration Day, it was windy and cold, and Harrison refused to wear a coat or hat. His address was the longest inaugural in U.S. history, lasting nearly two hours. By the time the new president returned to the White House, he was chilled and utterly exhausted, and called for an alcohol rub. Over the next four weeks, plagued by thousands of office seekers, Harrison found his health declining. "The job seekers pack the White House every day," he wrote in despair. "They pursue me so closely that I can not even attend to the necessary functions of nature."

What kind of president William Henry Harrison would have made will never be known. Exactly one month into his presidency he died of pneumonia. He was the country's first president to die in office, and his death helped establish a new precedent for the orderly transfer of power to the vice president. Harrison's final words were spoken to a doctor, but may have been for Vice President John Tyler. "Sir, I wish you to understand the true principles of the government. I wish them carried out. I ask nothing more."

In 1839, in a letter to an author who had requested information, William Henty Harrison became autobiographical for one of the few times in his life.

I was born at the seat of my father called Berkley . . . 25 miles below Richmond VA on the 9th of Feby 1773. . . . Having received a classical education I commenced the study of medicine. . . . Not liking the medical profession . . . [I] explain[ed] that dislike to Gov. Lee of Virginia who . . . recommended me to go into the army. I immediately acquiesced. . . . In 24 hours from the first conception of the idea of changing my profession I was . . . in the 11th U.S. Regt. of Infantry. . . . I was ordered to . . . Cincinnati. . . . The village of Cincinnati [was] then composed of 25 or 30 log cabins. . . . I certainly saw more drunken men in those 48 hours succeeding my arrival at Cincinnati than I had in all my previous life. The prospect was certainly not very encouraging to a youth . . . who had been tenderly brought up.

In a separate writing, Harrison completed the story. The rule which I made shortly after I entered the Army . . . was not drink on any occasions whatever unless I was thirsty. It was this determination which saved me from the terrible fate of four fifths of my brother officers, that number at least having died from the effects of intoxication.

Though Harrison is most famous for the battle of Tippecanoe, his most successful victory came later at the battle of the Thames (above). Here, on October 13, 1813, in present-day Ontario, he soundly defeated the combined British and Indian forces. Among the slain was his old enemy the great Shawnee leader Tecumseh.

On heroism: The successful warrior is no longer entitled to . . . fame. . . . To be esteemed eminently great it is necessary to be eminently good. The qualities of the general and the hero must be devoted to the advantage of mankind.

After an exhausting two-week journey by boat, stage coach, and train, Harrison arrived in Washington from Cincinnati (above) having addressed crowd after crowd along the way and shaken tens of thousands of hands. His inauguration (below) was held on a blustery fourth of March. His address was the longest ever and the crowd was the largest since George Washington had been inaugurated in New York half a century before.

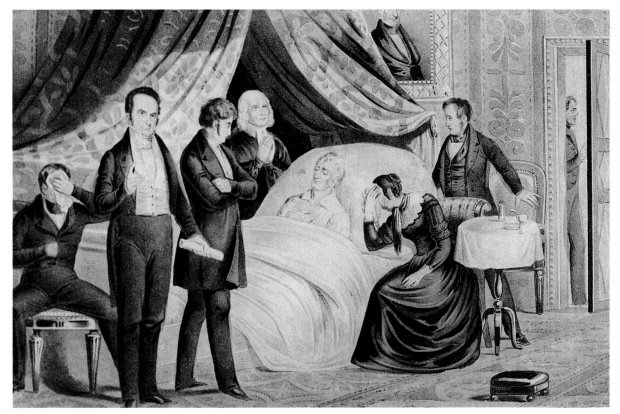

Harrison spent the final eight days of his single month in office in bed, fighting his declining health. Early on April 4, the President died. This contemporary engraving of the death scene shows Secretary of the Treasury Thomas Ewing seated at far left with Daniel Webster, the secretary of state, standing beside him. The mourning woman is Harrison's niece.

THE FIRST WHITE HOUSE FUNERAL

What distinguished Harrison's short tenure was not his life in the White House, but his death and the precedents it established. The most telling was the matter of vice presidential succession, never before tested, which would eventually become resolved as the "Tyler precedent." But there were also matters of official ceremony. Since there had never been a White House funeral before, it was not at first known who should be in charge of arrangements. Secretary of State Daniel Webster decided upon Alexander Hunter, marshal of the District of Columbia. Hunter directed that the White House be draped in black. When Washington ran out of black material, more was dyed. The White House windows were hung with black crape, and the columns were joined by wide, black, drooping ribbons of material. In the great rooms mirrors and chandeliers were covered over. Harrison's coffin with its glass window was first on display to the public in the entrance hall. The funeral in the East Room was by invitation only. The casket

IN MEMORY OF

PRESIDENT WM. H. HARRISON,

WHO DEPARTED THIS LIFE, APRIL 4, 1841, AGED 68,

Deeply lamented by 16 Millions of people.

lay on a table in the middle of the room. Around it circles of dignitaries and family formed, with President Tyler and the cabinet in the inner circle. Every church in Washington seemed to be represented by its clergy. The huge room was packed, with the dress uniforms of the foreign ministers making them stand out like peacocks. After the funeral the coffin was carried outside and hoisted onto a black funeral car that had been constructed out of a wagon. The Marine band played dirges. Soldiers fired salutes. The funeral car was pulled by black-draped horses, each led by a black groom in white uniform. The procession of horses and pallbearers and marshals and dignitaries moved away from the White House portico and headed for the Congressional Cemetery, where Harrison's body would remain until a funeral train made the journey home to Ohio in the spring. This became the model of funerals for presidents to come. The details would change, but the basic ingredients and their dramatic effect would remain the same.

ULYSSES S. GRANT

1869–1877

In Over His Head

Ulysses S. Grant once wrote, "It was my fortune, or misfortune, to be called to the office of Chief Executive without any previous political training." And another time he added, "I did not want the Presidency, and I have never quite forgiven myself for resigning the command of the army to accept it. . . . War and politics are so different."

His story contains an important warning: that the capacities for presidential leadership do not always reside in military heroism. For Grant's presidency as a whole was a miserable failure, an echo of his early years before the war, when he failed at nearly everything he ever attempted.

"I was born . . . at . . . Ohio," wrote Grant about the start of those years. "My father carried on the manufacture of leather. . . . I detested the trade." Later he admitted, "I didn't want to go to West Point. . . . My father had to use his authority to make me go."

After graduation from the Military Academy, Grant went on to fight in the Mexican War, then spent three years alone on the West Coast on duty, apart from his wife and family. It was when he returned home that his life turned into one long struggle to survive.

"I was a poor man, with a family," Grant later remembered. "I worked very hard . . . for our support. . . . If nothing else could be done, I would load a cord of wood on a wagon and take it to the city for sale." Ultimately he did what he had hoped he would never have to do: work in the family leather business.

Neighbors in Galena, Illinois, remembered a man who drank too much and suffered long bouts of depression. Friends spoke of his expressionless face and his vacant eyes. The extraordinary and troubling fact about Grant was that the only thing that ever aroused him was war.

"I remember my own feelings about the war when it commenced," Grant later said in an interview. "I could not endure the thought of the Union separating. . . . It was this feeling that impelled me to volunteer."

Because of public knowledge about his drinking, Grant was slow to gain a commission in the rapidly expanding Union Army, even though West Point graduates were in demand. But once in place, he led his men with such confidence that he was soon promoted to general.

"A successful general needs health and youth and energy," Grant commented. "I had a physique that could stand anything. Whether I slept on the ground or in a tent, whether I slept one hour or ten . . . made no difference. I could lie down and sleep in the rain without caring."

Grant during his presidency (left) and during the Civil War: June of 1864 at Cold Harbor (right)

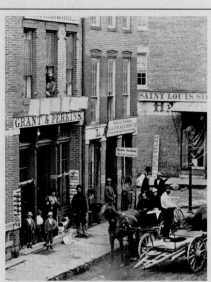

The Grant leather store in Galena, Illinois.

On his early life: I detested the [leather] trade, preferring almost any other labor; but I was fond of agriculture, and in all employment in which horses were used. . . . When about eleven years old, I was strong enough to hold a plough. From that age I did all the work done with horses. . . . At the age of seventeen . . . I went to West Point.

On his middle initial: In answer to your letter of a few days ago asking what "S" stands for in my name I can only state *nothing*. It was a mistake made . . . when application was first made . . . to West Point. . . . After I received my Diploma and Commission, with the "S" inserted, [I] adopted it and have so signed my name ever since.

To his future wife: My Dear Julia. . . . I have never mentioned any thing about love in any of the letters I have ever written you. . . . What an out I make at expressing anything like love or sentiment. . . . You can have but little idea of the influence you have over me Julia. . . . If I feel tempted to do any thing that I think is not right I am sure to think, "Well now if Julia saw me would I do so" and thus . . . I am more or less governed by what I think is your will.

1849: officer in the Mexican War

1859: civilian before the Civil War

1861: brigadier general

Standing just five feet seven inches, weighing 150 pounds and smoking as many as twenty cigars a day, Grant looked less like an imposing general than like the hundreds of thousands of ordinary soldiers who came to trust him as one of them. A taciturn man of long silences and immobile features, he had a stomach for violence. "[At] Shiloh . . . I saw an open field . . . so covered with dead," he wrote, "it would have been possible to walk across the clearing, in any direction, stepping on dead bodies, without a foot touching the ground."

Once, during the Vicksburg campaign, credible charges of drunkenness were leveled against him. An aide to the secretary of war, sent to investigate, reported that Grant was too valuable a general for such stories to be paid attention to. President Lincoln agreed.

"I am sober as a deacon no matter what is said to the contrary," Grant assured his wife Julia in a letter.

By 1864, he was promoted to the rank of lieutenant general. No one since George Washington had ever held this permanent rank. Grant now had the full responsibility for conducting the war.

"President Lincoln . . . said that he did not care to know what I wanted to do. . . . He wished me to beat Lee; how I did it was my own matter," remembered Grant. "Here then [was] the basis of all plans. . . . First to use the greatest number of troops practicable against the Armed force of the enemy. . . . Second; to hammer continuously at the . . . enemy, and his resources, until by mere attrition, if in no other way, there should be nothing left to him."

With terrible bloodshed, Grant's strategy worked. And on April 9, 1865, Confederate general Robert E. Lee surrendered at Appomattox Courthouse. "When news of the surrender first reached our lines," wrote Grant, "our men commenced firing a salute of a hundred guns in honor of the victory. I at once sent word, however, to have it stopped. The Confederates were now our prisoners, and we did not want to exult over their downfall."

Grant returned at war's end to his hometown of Galena, to a hero's welcome. And by 1868 the Republican Party had convinced him to run for president. "I certainly never had either ambition or taste for political life," Grant commented. "[But] nothing so popularizes a candidate for high position as military victories." Later he added, "I owed my honors and opportunities to the Republican party, and if my name could aid it I was bound to accept."

An adoring public overlooked the fact that everything Grant had ever tried outside of war had ended in failure. Instead, they assumed that Grant's proven capacity for leadership in wartime would translate into an ability to handle the job of the presidency, and he was overwhelmingly elected.

1862: major general

1863: major general

1864: major general

1865: lieutenant general

On the Mexican War: Texas was originally a state belonging to Mexico. . . . I am always ashamed of my country when I think of that invasion. . . . I know the struggle with my conscience during the Mexican War. . . . I do not think there was ever a more wicked war. . . . I thought so at the time, when I was a youngster, only I had not moral courage enough to resign.

On the start of the Civil War: It made my blood run cold to hear friends of mine . . . deliberately discuss the dissolution of the Union as though it were a tariff bill. I could not endure it. . . . I wanted to leave the country if disunion was accomplished.

On his rising rank: I never thought of commands or battles. I only wanted to fight for the Union. That feeling carried me through the war. I never felt any special pleasure in my promotions. I was naturally glad when they came. But I never thought of it.

On the Battle of Vicksburg: The enemy used in their defence explosive musketballs. . . . Their use is barbarous, because they produce increased suffering without any corresponding advantage to those using them. . . . If the Vicksburg campaign meant anything . . . it was that there are no fixed laws of war.

On Lee's surrender: When I left camp that morning I had not expected so soon the result that was then taking place, and consequently was in rough garb. I was without a sword . . . and wore a soldier's blouse for a coat, with the shoulder straps of my rank to indicate to the army who I was. When I went into the house, I found General Lee. . . . What [his] feelings were I do not know. As he was a man of much dignity, with an impassible face, it was impossible to say whether he felt inwardly glad that the end had finally come, or felt sad over the result, and was too manly to show it. . . . General Lee was dressed in a full uniform which was entirely new, and was wearing a sword of considerable value. . . . In my rough travelling suit . . . I must have contrasted very strangely to a man so handsomely dressed . . . and of faultless form.

On May 21, 1864, stopping to rest in the Wilderness on the way to Richmond, Lt. General Grant leans over the shoulder of an officer and studies a map (above). After the war, Grant was greeted home by the cheering citizens of Galena, Illinois (right). He had lived there only a year before the war, working in a branch of the family leather business, so hardly anyone in the town knew him then. Everybody had come to know who he was by this time, though. For, early in the war, his victories along the western rivers had given him national prominence. The sudden notoriety hadn't changed the careless way he operated. He dressed in a plain soldier's uniform, paid no attention to protocol, operated out in the field with his troops, wrote his own orders, seemed immune to danger, and made his men feel they could not lose. Now, with his great victories in the east, he was hailed as nothing less than savior of the Union. No wonder Galena wanted to celebrate his return.

Less than four years later, Grant finds himself on the portico of the Capitol, drawing his inaugural speech from his breast pocket and reading his first words as president of the United States.

Once in the White House, Grant's principal concern was for the plight of black Americans, especially in the South. Having fought alongside black soldiers in the Civil War and having helped slaves gain their freedom as American citizens, he was determined not to see them lose it again.

"My civil career commenced . . . at a most critical time," wrote Grant. "In some localities in the Southern States . . . bands of men, masked and armed, had made their appearance. . . . Properly known as 'Kuklux Klans,' [their] objects . . . were by force and terror to . . . deprive colored citizens of the right to . . . a free ballot; to suppress schools in which colored children were taught, and to reduce the colored people to a condition closely akin to that of slavery."

At times, as when he aggressively prosecuted the Klan, or as when he supported a Constitutional amendment giving black men the vote, Grant seemed determined to further racial justice in the country. But too often he vacillated, or lost his concentration, allowing white supremacists to reassert their dominance in the South. And he let one of his finest qualities, loyalty, which had made him absolutely indispensable to Abraham Lincoln, lead him astray in relations with members of his own administration.

Grant regularly ventured over to the lobby of the nearby Willard's Hotel to smoke his cigars, and people learned to come by to try to influence him. He naively allowed himself to be used by so many unscrupulous individuals that he began to be ridiculed in the press.

"I [was] . . . the subject of abuse and slander scarcely ever equaled in political history," Grant later said. "Charges were openly made of corruption on the part of the President or those employed by him."

It was soon clear that Ulysses Grant possessed little of the firmness he had shown in the Army. And though he was personally honest, his administration was scandal-ridden. He was as deaf to misdoings as he was to music—he could barely recognize "Hail to the Chief."

"Mistakes have been made . . . and I admit," wrote Grant in his 1876 annual message to Congress. "[But] failures have been errors of judgment, not of intent."

Grant was never able to put an end to the graft and corruption that undermined his presidency. By the end of eight years, every single one of his executive offices had come under Congressional investigation.

"I never wanted to get out of a place," Grant later said, "as much as I did to get out of the Presidency."

But after he left office, Grant's bad luck continued. Four years later he made an unsuccessful third bid for the presidency. And that failure was followed by still another. Always trusting others more than he should, he became the victim of a stupendous Wall Street fraud that left him utterly bankrupt. Desperate to provide for his wife and children, sixty-two-year-old Grant took the advice of his friend Mark Twain and began writing his memoirs as a source of income. He had barely begun work when a final crisis threatened. During the summer of 1884, while he was eating a piece of fruit, he grabbed his throat and exclaimed, "I think something has stung me from that peach." Grant's cigar habit had caught up with him. He had developed cancer of the throat. By the following summer, working hard to complete his memoirs at a cottage in the Adirondacks, Grant knew the end was near. "There cannot be a hope of going far beyond this time," he confessed. "It is nearly impossible for me to swallow. . . . It pains me even to talk."

Writing in extreme pain, he produced a brilliant autobiography, of lasting literary value. And he forced himself to stay alive until he completed it. Perhaps not surprisingly, Grant chose to write almost nothing at all about the loneliness and misery of his early life; and he commented only briefly on events of his presidency. Instead, he wrote about the only time in his life he had truly succeeded—in war.

"Now, scarcely twenty years after the war, we seem to have forgotten the lessons it taught," he wrote. "But this war was a fearful lesson, and should teach us the necessity of avoiding wars in the future. . . . A conflict between races may come up in the future, as did that between freedom and slavery before. . . . [But] I feel that we are on the eve of a new era, when there is to be great harmony between Federal and Confederate. I cannot stay to be a living witness to the correctness of this prophecy; but I feel it within me that it is to be so."

IN HIS OWN WORDS

On public speaking: You all know how unaccustomed I am to public speaking, how undesirable a talent I think it is to possess, how little good it generally does, and how desirous I am to see more of our public men follow the good example . . . I have set them.

On following his own judgment: The only time I ever deliberately resolved to do an expedient thing for party reasons, against my own judgement, was on the occasion of the . . . inflation bill. I never was so pressed in my life to do anything as to sign that bill, never. . . . I wrote the message with great care, and put in every argument I could call up to show that the bill was harmless. . . . Well, when I finished my wonderful message, which was to do so much good to the party and country, I read it over, and said to myself: 'What is the good of all this? You do not believe it. You know it is not true.' Throwing it aside I resolved to do what I believed to be right—veto the bill! I could not stand my own arguments.

On selfishness in government: All the romance of feeling that men in high places are above personal considerations and act only from motives of pure patriotism, and for the general good of the public, has been destroyed.

On the South after the war: The South has been in many ways a disappointment to me. . . . I hoped that Northern capital would pour into the South, that Northern influence and Northern energy would soon repair all that war had wasted. But that never came. Northern capitalists saw that they could not go South without leaving self-respect at home, and they remained home. . . . I hoped much from the poor white class. The war, I thought, would free them from a bondage in some respects even lower than slavery; it would revive their ambition; they would learn what we in the North know so well, that labor is a dignity, not a degradation. . . . But they have been as much under the thumb of the slave-holder as before the war.

On civil rights for blacks: Social equality is not a subject to be legislated upon, nor shall I ask that anything be done to advance the social status of the colored man, except to give him a fair chance to develop [the] good in him, give him access to the schools, and when he travels let him feel assured that his conduct will regulate the treatment and fare he will receive.

During May 23 and 24, 1865, thousands upon thousands of blue-uniformed soldiers formed up at the Capitol, which still showed the black mourning crape that honored Lincoln, who had died in April. To celebrate the Union victory, the war department had called for a grand review and Washington got one, the most illustrious parade the city had ever seen. It ran all the way down Pennsylvania Avenue and past the reviewing stands where General Grant, still wearing a black mourning ribbon for Lincoln on his arm (above), watched with pride.

During his presidency the left side of Grant's face (above) made him seem much younger than the grizzled right suggested (below). Although he really didn't like being chief executive, Grant was philosophical about it. "The responsibilities of the position I feel, but accept them, without fear," he said. "The office has come to me unsought; I commence its duties untrammeled. I bring to it a conscious desire and determination to fill it to the best of my ability to the satisfaction of the people."

Moving into the White House with the Grants was their immense family portrait by William Cogswell, which was hung in the Red Room.

It was the Gilded Age, and the Grants tried to make the White House reflect the trend toward ornamentation by elaborately redecorating the East Room. They also expanded the greenhouse, introduced a billiards room, built a gracious new stable, and landscaped much of the property. The General left clouds of cigar smoke wherever he went, would only eat well-done beef or pork, never poultry or lamb, took long carriage rides in the afternoons, put up with in-laws who literally moved in, re-created Civil War battles with his famous general friends, who visited often, worked at his desk about four hours a day, stayed close to the press, and on the whole tried to enjoy himself. His biggest personal moment came on May 21, 1874, with the wedding of his vivacious, eighteen-year-old daughter Nellie. The summer before she had been shipped off to Europe in hopes of reining in her enthusiasm for fun, but instead she was wined and dined by royalty and returned head over heels in love with an Englishman, Algernon Sartoris. Years later people looked back on the White House wedding as one of the most brilliant ever held in America. No expense was spared. The decorations, the flowers, the food, the presents on display, the eight bridesmaids, the Marine band, the bridal gown of white satin with an overskirt of lace were all glowingly written about by a herd of reporters enormously grateful to have been let in on Washington's social event of the decade.

Mrs. Grant, who was widely admired, became a national figure as first lady.

The Grants' only daughter, Nellie, was given a magnificent wedding in the East Room.

The President shaved his mustache and chin for this profile made especially for his wife.

For his eight years in office President Grant was always surrounded by his memories of war.

[handwritten note]

July 3. p.m.

When Grant could no longer talk, he communicated with his doctor in scribbled notes like this one, made twenty days before his death.

Grant's last days were spent in a cottage lent to him on Mount McGregor near Saratoga Springs, New York. Working hard to finish his memoirs in a race against death from throat cancer, Grant dashed off a series of poignant notes to his personal physician, John H. Douglas.

June 23, 1885: Dr. . . . I can feel plainly that my system is preparing for dissolution in three ways; one by hemorrhages, one by strangulation and the third by exhaustion. . . . I [have] been adding to my book and to my coffin. I presume every strain of the mind or body is one more nail in the coffin. . . . I will not push to make more notes for the present.

June 27: My mouth hurts me and cocaine ceases to give the relief it did. . . . I presume I will be obliged to have my mouth washed out when I am to take some dinner.

June 28: Can't you bring in more air? It is hot. . . . Is there not danger of . . . mucus coming up and flowing into the windpipe some day?

July 4: Dr. I ask you not to show this to any one . . . until the end. Particularly, I want it kept from my family. . . . Under these circumstances life is not worth living. . . . If it is within God's providence that I should go now I am ready to obey His call without a murmur.

July 5: About an hour ago I coughed up a piece of stringy matter about the size of a small lizard. . . . How much may a man reduce in weight who ought to reach 180 pounds . . . up to 195? I am now down to about 130.

July 10: In two weeks . . . the second vol. [will be] ready to go to the printer. I will then feel that my work is done.

mid July: [T]he disease . . . must be fatal in the end. . . . The fact is I think I am a verb instead of a personal pronoun. A verb is anything that signifies to be, to do or to suffer. I signify all three.

This is the living room of the cottage where Grant spent his final days. On the porch outside and in this room he paid little heed to visitors, a steady stream of whom came to pay their respects or silently show their awe for him by standing outside for hours at a time. Sometimes, Grant would look up from his paper (top) and wave. In his favorite wicker chair on the porch, bundled in blankets and warmed by a wool hat (right), the dying general makes some final changes in his monumental manuscript. Ulysses S. Grant died at Mount McGregor at 8:00 A.M. on July 23, 1885.

DWIGHT D. EISENHOWER

1953–1961

The Heroic Image

A vigorous Dwight Eisenhower signals victory at the Republican National Convention in 1952. "I accept your summons," he said. "I will lead this crusade." Below, a relaxed Ike flashes a victory signal.

No general in history ever faced as complex or momentous a military assignment. Eisenhower was the Allied Commander of all European Forces, overseeing an invasion of Europe across Hitler's defenses. On the night of June 4, 1944, it was Eisenhower who gave the official order that launched D-Day.

"Soldiers, sailors and airmen of the Allied Expeditionary Force," he addressed his troops. "You are about to embark upon the greatest crusade toward which we have striven these many months. . . . You will bring about the destruction of the German war machine. . . . Your task will not be an easy one. Your enemy is well trained, well equipped and battle-hardened. He will fight savagely. . . . We will accept nothing less than full victory. Good luck and let us all beseech the blessing of Almighty God upon this great and noble undertaking."

It was the largest amphibious assault in history, involving 250,000 soldiers, sailors, and airmen. And Hitler's Atlantic Wall was breached. Eisenhower himself reported the victory: "The Allied force, which invaded Europe on June 6, has utterly defeated the Germans by land, sea and air."

When Eisenhower returned home after the war, the public response to him was overwhelming. He was a hero who seemed to fit his times exactly—a humble, honest, clean-cut kind of man the country could feel good about.

"I am not the hero," Eisenhower said in his home town of Abilene, Kansas. "I am the symbol of the heroic men you people, and all the United States, have sent to war."

By far the most popular man in America, Eisenhower exuded friendliness, interest, and goodwill. But he was also a person of considerable inner reserve and a need to control, a more complicated man than he seemed to be on the surface. Possessing an intense desire to be well liked, and working hard to keep people happy, he had been forced to come to terms with a prodigious temper. "I learned long ago," he once admitted, "that the one thing that is damaging to anybody that aspires to a position of leadership of any kind—he must learn to control his temper."

Nicknamed "Little Ike" as a boy, Eisenhower had revealed his strong temper at an early age. Especially ferocious when he felt he had been treated unfairly, his anger was sometimes turned mercilessly on himself. "There was an old apple tree," he remembered late in life, "and I was there crying as hard as I could and beating this . . . tree with my fists and they were all bleeding and messy." With Ike sent to his room by an angry father, it was his mother who nursed his hands and spoke with him about learning how not to hurt

Fresh from victory in World War II, Ike was chief of staff in 1946 when this picture was taken in Hawaii. The first time he had been mentioned seriously for the presidency was back in 1943. In 1948 he was approached by both parties. "Starting in 1911 when I went to West Point, until 1951, which was forty years later, I had never by any inkling of my own given an indication of my political beliefs. It was not proper, and I wouldn't do it." Finally, as supreme commander of the North Atlantic Treaty Organization, Ike was pressured by Senator Henry Cabot Lodge into admitting he was a confirmed Republican and he went on to head the 1952 Republican ticket.

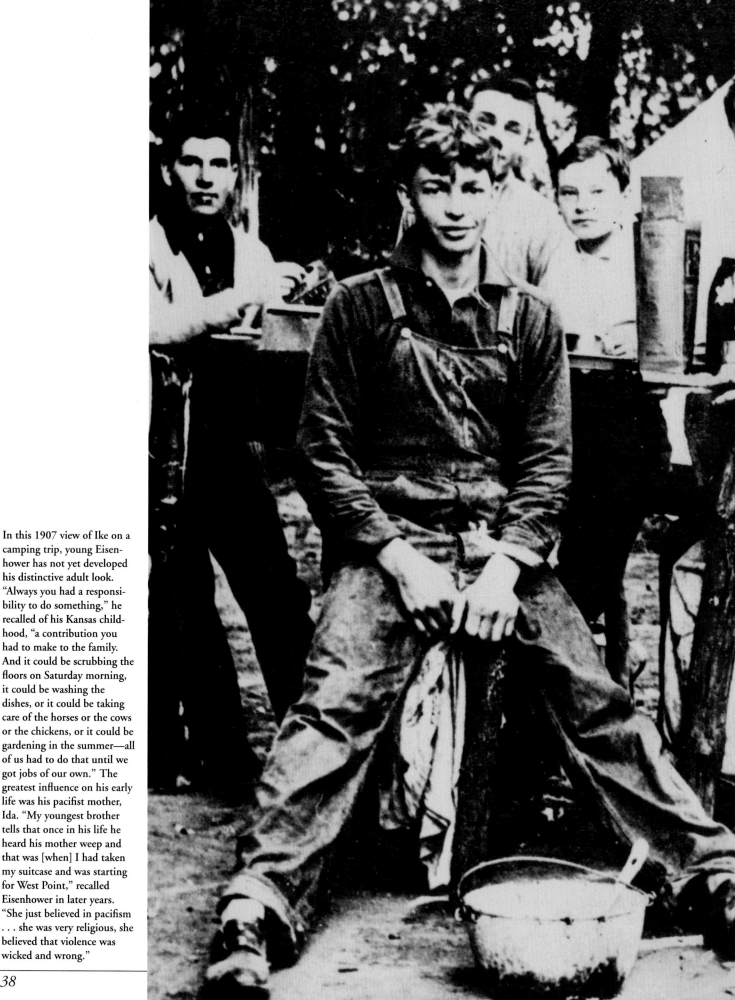

In this 1907 view of Ike on a camping trip, young Eisenhower has not yet developed his distinctive adult look. "Always you had a responsibility to do something," he recalled of his Kansas childhood, "a contribution you had to make to the family. And it could be scrubbing the floors on Saturday morning, it could be washing the dishes, or it could be taking care of the horses or the cows or the chickens, or it could be gardening in the summer—all of us had to do that until we got jobs of our own." The greatest influence on his early life was his pacifist mother, Ida. "My youngest brother tells that once in his life he heard his mother weep and that was [when] I had taken my suitcase and was starting for West Point," recalled Eisenhower in later years. "She just believed in pacifism . . . she was very religious, she believed that violence was wicked and wrong."

himself. "I think this was one of the most important moments of my life," Eisenhower remembered, "because since then I've gotten angry many times but I have tried to keep from showing it."

As a career military man Eisenhower learned what Ulysses S. Grant had learned—that war and politics don't mix. And after World War II, at the height of his popularity, he refused to let his name be entered for the 1948 presidential campaign. "No man since Washington," he said, "has been elected unless he definitely desired it." But four years later his supporters finally convinced him to run.

"The first campaign . . . was quite an adventure," Ike said later. "It was something completely strange in the life of a soldier."

Eisenhower proved to be a skilled politician. He threw himself into the presidential race as if it were an Allied invasion. Careful not to speak out on any issue that might tarnish his heroic image, he focused mainly on Truman's war in Korea. And when he vowed to personally end it, saying, "I shall go to Korea," he easily won the election.

"When I came to the Presidency," Ike commented, "the country was rather in an unhappy state. I tried to create an atmosphere of greater serenity and mutual confidence. . . . You go through three and a half years of active warfare [when] something can happen every minute. It's a thing you have to learn to live with. And I had to, in a different way, learn the same lesson in the White House."

In the 1950s Ike gave the country a real sense of trust. It didn't matter that the first president to have press conferences filmed for television could be inarticulate, often mixing up his words. It was all part of his unique charm.

"I'm going to try to be just as truthful as I can be," he said at one press conference. "And I believe this: I think even people who would classify themselves probably as my political enemies do believe I'm honest. They may call me stupid, but I think they think I'm honest."

In the White House Eisenhower refused to speak out publicly on difficult issues. Fearful that by taking a controversial stand he could jeopardize his huge popularity, he avoided committing himself to matters of racial justice and wouldn't comment on the anti-Communist witch hunts of Senator Joseph McCarthy. At cabinet meetings he rarely spoke. While others gave reports, the President listened and doodled. His presidential style was the antithesis of that of his outspoken predecessor, Harry Truman. Instead, Ike instituted layer upon layer of executive bureaucracy, all part of a military-style reorganization of the White House. But while Eisenhower may have appeared out of touch and isolated within a complex hierarchy, in reality he stayed involved in every important decision. His years in the White House would later become known as his "hidden-hand" presidency.

"One of the things about the presidency," he revealed in an interview, "is the way you have to be prepared to jump just like a mountain sheep from one jag to another jag and you're always on the alert. You have to be."

True to his campaign promise, Eisenhower ended the fighting in Korea, and over time developed a reputation as a man of peace. He refused to go to war in Indochina or to join in a European attack on Egypt over the Suez Canal. He believed that personal diplomacy was the best way to ease foreign crises. Traveling the world aboard the brand new Air Force One, he "waged peace," as he described it. "If you are keeping the peace," he said, "if you are in other words keeping a war from breaking out, that is waging peace."

Ike and Mamie Geneva Doud pose for a wedding portrait in 1916. "I'll tell you about meeting her," he once reminisced about how he first got to know the pretty little eighteen-year-old outside an officers' club in Texas. "It was about a month after I joined my regiment and I was supposed to go on guard duty. . . . One lady I knew . . . called me over . . . and said. . . 'I just want you to meet these people.' And it turns out. . . she said to them . . . 'This is the man who is the woman hater of the post.'. . . This intrigued this little girl and when I said 'sorry folks I've got to go inspect the guard' and [I] turned to the girl and I said 'would you like to walk with me, see what inspecting the guard is?' . . . Yes, she thought she would. . . . From there on I used rather bulldozing methods — I just drove all the rest of them away."

In a December 1943 photograph, Ike takes a place behind FDR in Sicily. A similar meeting had occurred earlier in Tunis when Ike was hoping he would be appointed Supreme Allied Commander in charge of the enormous D-Day invasion of Europe called Overlord. "The President arrived in mid-afternoon," Ike later wrote, "and was scarcely seated in the automobile when he cleared up the matter with one short sentence. He said, 'Well, Ike, you are going to command Overlord.'"

Increasingly sensitive to the danger of nuclear war, Ike proposed that the United States and the Soviet Union open their respective airspace and share their nuclear stockpiles. And he invited Soviet Premier Nikita Khrushchev to Washington and convinced him to join him at a summit meeting in Paris to discuss a ban of all nuclear testing. It was a first major step toward defusing the high level of nuclear tensions in the world.

But Eisenhower's caution as president was at least in part self-serving. Still wishing above all to maintain his popularity, in the controversial area of defense he tried to please everyone. While he stood up to the Pentagon and cut military spending, at the same time he preached a philosophy of peace through strength. And even as he portrayed himself as above all a peacemaker, he authorized covert CIA activities against foreign governments that led to the toppling of regimes in Guatemala and Iran.

He also secretly approved a series of U-2 spy plane missions to photograph Russian missile sites. It wasn't until he was accused of allowing the United States to fall behind the Soviets in missile production that the public saw for itself the angry side of Eisenhower's complex personality.

"If anybody believes that I have deliberately misled the American people," Ike said sternly at a press conference, "I'd like to tell him, to his face, what I think of him. This is a charge that I think is despicable. And I get tired of saying that defense is to be made an excuse for wasting dollars. I don't believe we should pay one cent for defense more than we have to. But I do say this, our defense is not only strong—it is awesome!"

In fact, although Eisenhower publicly criticized America's nuclear buildup, it was largely just talk. He passively stood by as the country's nuclear arsenal grew from 1,000 warheads to 18,000. And he insisted on carrying out activities that could potentially undermine his peace efforts with the Soviets. Just one week before the Paris Peace Summit of 1960 his instincts got the best of him—he couldn't resist approving one last U-2 reconnaissance flight into Russian airspace.

"I was sure that sooner or later we were going to have this whole thing discovered," he later admitted. "But the information we were getting was so valuable that I continued."

During that last mission, the U-2 plane was shot down by the Soviets. At first Eisenhower denied knowledge of the mission, then finally admitted that it was he who had authorized it. At the Paris Peace Summit, an angry Nikita Khrushchev ridiculed Ike's reputation for honesty, then stormed out. Eisenhower was devastated. His final opportunity to leave a lasting legacy of disarmament had failed.

"Looking back on eight years you will say, 'Well, now what did we get done?'" Eisenhower later ruminated. "You have to recognize the political conditions under which they were done. . . . Too many people don't really understand how our government works. Remember this, unless something is good and both sides accept it, it's not lasting."

Ike presided over an era of peace and prosperity, but by the end of his presidency, even he recognized that he had allowed nuclear proliferation to spin dangerously out of control.

"Disarmament is a continuing imperative," he said in his farewell address. "I confess that I lay down my official responsibilities in this field with a definite sense of disappointment. As one who has witnessed the horror and lingering sadness of war—as one who knows that another war could utterly destroy this civilization, I wish I could say tonight that lasting peace

40

is in sight. . . . Now, on Friday noon, I am to become a private citizen. . . . I am proud to do so. I look forward to it. Thank you and good night."

In many ways he was the embodiment of the American dream—the small-town boy who rose to heroism and to the highest office. But Ike finally couldn't live up to George Washington's example. Unlike the first president, who was equally concerned with his personal reputation but in the end was willing to risk it all on behalf of his principles, Eisenhower wasn't. For while he genuinely wanted a more peaceful world, Ike was unwilling to put his reputation on the line on behalf of disarmament. The master at controlling his public persona had become a prisoner of his own heroic image.

By June 1945, the war in Europe had ended and Ike was home. The canyons of New York City were alive with jubilation as Americans thanked their consummate hero. Just a month later the first atom bomb would be tested at Alamogordo, New Mexico, and Hiroshima, Nagasaki, and Japanese surrender would follow in August.

In his farewell address, Eisenhower warned the American people about the dangers of excessive militarism. It was a warning squarely in the tradition of America's first soldier-president, George Washington.

My fellow Americans: . . .
This evening I come to you with a message of leave-taking and farewell, and to share a few final thoughts with you, my countrymen. . . . We now stand ten years past the midpoint of a century that has witnessed four major wars among great nations. Three of these involved our own country. Despite these holocausts America is today the strongest, the most influential and most productive nation in the world. . . . We face a hostile ideology—global in scope, atheistic in character, ruthless in purpose, and insidious in method. . . . Until the latest of our world conflicts, the United States had no armaments industry. American makers of plowshares could, with time and as required, make swords as well. But now we can no longer risk emergency improvisation of national defense; we have been compelled to create a permanent armaments industry of vast proportions. Added to this, three and a half million men and women are directly engaged in the defense establishment. . . . This conjunction of an immense military establishment and a large arms industry is new in the American experience. . . . In the councils of government, we must guard against the acquisition of unwarranted influence, whether sought or unsought, by the military industrial complex. We should take nothing for granted. Only an alert and knowledgeable citizenry can compel the proper meshing of the huge industrial and military machinery of defense with our peaceful methods and goals, so that security and liberty may prosper together. . . . As we peer into society's future, we—you and I, and our government—must avoid the impulse to live only for today, plundering, for our own ease and convenience, the precious resources of tomorrow. We cannot mortgage the material assets of our grandchildren without risking the loss also of their political and spiritual heritage. We want democracy to survive for all generations to come, not to become the insolvent phantom of tomorrow.

One fine day, in the middle of Ike's reign, the gates to the White House are thrown open and citizens large and small make a decorous entrance.

On a goodwill tour in 1955 President Eisenhower listens intently to India's Prime Minister Jawaharlal Nehru, who was helping the United States in its negotiations with China and North Korea. Ike liked to say that instead of waging war he was waging peace.

After his 1955 heart attack, Ike shows the nation he's still alive and kicking.

Because of the extensive rebuilding of the White House during Harry Truman's Administration, few changes occurred during the eight years that followed. In some ways this was a symbol of Eisenhower's whole presidency, in which the bold leadership of FDR and Truman was replaced by a new era of standpatism. Eisenhower took no interest in the most pressing moral challenge of his era—race relations. And during his two terms there was no progress in the areas of desegregation, urban renewal, the environment, or education. In the place of governmental activism, Ike encouraged private-sector prosperity, meeting often with corporate leaders and financiers over games of golf. One of his few improvements to the White House grounds was to establish a putting green on the South Lawn. Having never had a house of their own, the Eisenhowers bought one, a farm, in Gettysburg, Pennsylvania, and Mamie spent much of her time planning its remodeling, decorating, and furnishings. Emboldened by her successes in Gettysburg, in 1960 Mamie furnished the diplomatic reception room of the White House with historic American antiques, an idea that would flower under the Kennedy Administration, just on the horizon.

Toward the end of his second term, a haggard President Eisenhower addressed the nation concerning the U-2 crisis and the failed Paris summit.

At right, a few of the many moods of the thirty-fourth President.

The spic and span of the General's military years is reflected in Ike's White House, as liberal amounts of spit and polish get applied.

Franklin Pierce

James A. Garfield

COMPROMISE CHOICES

CHAPTER TWO

As political parties gained power, party bosses searched for candidates
they could control, or at least rally behind.

Warren G. Harding   Gerald R. Ford

Unlike the early years of the nation, when great men like General Washington rose to the presidency by their own stature, the years after 1840 witnessed political parties often bypassing their leading men in favor of compromise choices. At national conventions, these candidates came out of the shadows, selected less for who they were than for what they could do for their party. In contrast to the recognizably great but often controversial figures of the day, compromise choices were safe, if all too often mediocre.

The leading figure of the Democratic Party in 1844 was former president Martin Van Buren, who once again sought the high office. But his opposition to the immediate annexation of Texas had alienated voters in the South and elsewhere. Sensing Van Buren's political weakness, five other Democrats at the Baltimore convention increased their efforts to steal the nomination from him. Since a two-thirds majority was required to win, it was soon clear that the widespread field would splinter the vote and that

James K. Polk was the first dark horse candidate to be elected president. A man of little charisma but lots of grit, Polk (above in an 1844 engraving) was available when it became clear that former President Martin Van Buren was unwilling to support the majority position of his party on the annexation of Texas. Abraham Lincoln (below, with running mate Hannibal Hamlin) is often described as a dark horse, though in his case he was a serious contender for the 1860 Republican nomination from the outset. "I suppose I am not the first choice of a very great many," he had written. "Our policy, then, is to give no offense to others—leave them in a mood to come to us if they shall be compelled to give up their first love."

Van Buren could not gain the nomination. On the night of May 28, with the convention deadlocked and the party in danger of splitting along North-South lines, political operatives stayed up through the night promoting an unlikely nominee, the twice-defeated candidate for his state's governorship, James K. Polk of Tennessee. Though Polk had earlier been prominent in Congress he had by now sunk into some obscurity, appearing to be on a professional losing streak. But he was a personal friend of Andrew Jackson and was considered acceptable by both Northern and Southern delegates. Possessing a reputation as a stalwart who believed above all else in loyalty to his party, he was perceived as the perfect compromise choice to break the deadlock. The following day, on the ninth ballot, Polk was unanimously nominated, becoming the first dark horse candidate in U.S. history. The Democrats had learned how to break a deadlocked convention, and how to keep their national party from splitting apart. But for the first time in American history a presidential contender was a man who was not a leading national figure.

When the Democratic Party once again turned to an outsider, in 1852, it was to the truly obscure figure of Franklin Pierce, who had been out of political office for more than a decade. Described by one author as "the darkest of dark horses," Pierce replayed the Polk story as farce. His name did not even surface at the party convention until the thirty-fifth ballot; he was not finally nominated until the forty-ninth. And his dismal performance in the presidency raised serious concerns about the entire practice of turning to dark horses. It was clearly not good enough just to have an acceptable compromise; it behooved parties to put forward viable leaders as well. And yet many of the most qualified men continued to be passed over.

By the late 1880s, after a succession of dark horses that included Rutherford B. Hayes and James A. Garfield, British political observer James

The compromise candidate was a direct offspring of the nominating process that reigned in America during its middle period—the heyday of political parties. When conventions became deadlocked after many ballots, leaving a party in danger of splintering, dark horse candidates helped delegates compromise and break the logjam.

Bryce wrote of the dreary procession of American presidents and blamed it on the need of political machines for safe candidates. "Speaking generally, the note of the dark horse is . . . colourlessness. . . . A native mediocrity . . . is proved by the fact that the dark horses who have reached the White House, if they have seldom turned out bad presidents, have even more seldom turned out distinguished ones. . . . From the time when the heroes of the Revolution died out, no President except Abraham Lincoln . . . displayed rare or striking qualities. . . . The President has been . . . since 1829, a party man, seldom much above the average in character or abilities."

The last true dark horse to be propelled into the White House was one of the least successful presidents ever to hold the office. Chosen with the aid of the proverbial smoke-filled room, Warren G. Harding was the unqualified creation of political handlers. A pleasant and fun-loving man, and himself not politically corrupt, he possessed no moral compass or presidential vision, and his administration became one of the most scandal-ridden in U.S. history.

But even in Harding's time the nominating process was changing and party bosses were losing their power over conventions. Under the influence of the Progressive movement, several states began instituting presidential primaries, whereby the general public became the selector of national convention delegates, previously the appointees of party leaders. It was a major step toward the democratization of presidential election. But as late as 1968, only 38 percent of convention delegates were chosen by the public in primaries. Then, in the wake of the 1968 Democratic convention, at which party members threw the nomination to Hubert Humphrey, a man who had failed to enter even a single primary, a new wave of reform swept over the political scene, which led to the institution of presidential primaries in a majority of states. Presidential candidates were now responsible not so much to party leaders as to the American people, to whom they appealed increasingly through the medium of television. Political conventions ceased to be what they had been for over a hundred years: vital deliberative bodies where platforms were hammered out and key compromises made and candidates truly chosen. They became instead largely media events and times of party celebration. With the decline of conventions, and indeed of political parties themselves, dark horses per se were no longer possible.

Still, there continue to be compromise choices in the modern era. Gerald Ford was the compromise choice of Richard Nixon, who under the Twenty-fifth Amendment was obliged to name a replacement for resigning vice president Spiro Agnew and could not risk naming anyone incapable of obtaining speedy confirmation in Congress. And in a sense Jimmy Carter, a relative unknown who seemed to come out of nowhere to win the nomination, was a modern example of a dark horse.

Compromise choices have served their purpose in our political history, allowing majorities to rally around acceptable and safe figures. In a real sense they represent the democratic process at work. But they have also produced a legacy of mediocrity. James Bryce's famous critique remains as relevant today as when it was first uttered over a century ago in the heyday of professional politics. Safety is not what leadership is all about, and there is no substitute for personal excellence in a presidential candidate.

The nineteenth president, Rutherford B. Hayes (above), was a dark horse candidate who went on to win the national elections, but only by a hair; the final electoral vote in 1876 was 185 to 184. Today, with powerful party bosses no longer a factor and with nominations determined at the primaries, the term "dark horse" is used to denote an unexpected late bloomer, like Jimmy Carter (below) who was not prominent in his party but came on with a sudden, unexpected rush as the election approached.

As a congressman, then as a senator, the magnetic, young New Englander with the stiff, military neck, small features, and opaque gray eyes was one of the most popular politicians in Washington.

FRANKLIN PIERCE

1853–1857

The Dark Horse President

Franklin Pierce spent most of his life in Hillsboro, New Hampshire, the son of a Revolutionary war hero and a kindly though hard-drinking mother. After attending Bowdoin College in the new state of Maine, where he began a lifelong friendship with the future writer Nathaniel Hawthorne, Pierce practiced law, then turned to politics. At age twenty-seven he was elected one of New Hampshire's five congressmen. A heavy social drinker always ready for a rowdy night on the town, he soon became one of the most popular men in Washington. "I have been leading, I need not say, a very agreeable life," he wrote home.

In 1834, after two years as a Washington bachelor, he married Jane Means Appleton, the shy, tubercular daughter of a famous Congregationalist minister, who seemed almost the opposite of her boisterous husband. Jane hated Washington, hated politics, and hated most of all her husband's heavy drinking. When Pierce refused to change his ways, his wife Jane returned alone to New Hampshire, where their first child was born. What followed was the first in a string of almost crippling personal disasters: the baby boy, named Franklin, Jr., died in infancy. Both Pierces were devastated. Later, a second son, Frank, would also die, leading a distraught Franklin Pierce to take refuge in religion. "We should have lived for God," he wrote in his diary, "and have left the dear ones to the care of Him who is alone able to take care of them and us."

Fighting liquor, sadness, ill health, and religious doubt, in 1840 Pierce finally renounced alcohol. "It is a body-destroying, heart-breaking, dangerous habit," he wrote. "I will no longer take a drop of any kind of stimulant."

A year and a half later he quit the Senate and returned to New Hampshire to try to rebuild his family life. Still fearful of the social drinking that went along with politics, he turned down the nomination for governor of his state and then the position of attorney general in President Polk's cabinet. "When I resigned my seat in the Senate in 1842," he explained, "I did it with the fixed purpose never again to be voluntarily separated from my family except at the call of my country in time of war."

That call came in 1846, when the United States went to war with Mexico over Texas. It was not long before Brigadier General Pierce found himself leading 2,500 men south of the border. But the glory Pierce yearned for eluded him. "My horse . . . fell under me upon a ledge of rocks," he recorded, "by which I sustained a severe sprain in my left knee. I became exceedingly faint."

Hit in the groin by the pommel of his saddle, Pierce strapped himself

During his early years in Washington, Franklin Pierce was always ready for a bibulous night on the town. When finally persuaded by his wife to give up politics and return to his law practice in New Hampshire, he left behind hardly any Congressional record at all except some bills on Revolutionary War pensions. Among a Senate of giants, he had always been a follower, a protege of his elders and in need of their adulation. While president, Pierce made copies of his official portrait and presented them to his cabinet. One of those copies is reproduced above.

Pierce didn't really understand himself, especially his frailties and failings. He never, for instance, should have pushed himself into the Mexican War; he was not made of the stuff to fight and lead troops. Posing in uniform (above), he merely looked the part. His actions in the field were strewn with mishaps and injury, with falling mounts, knee sprains, saddle blisters, diarrhea attacks, and fainting spells. The presiding general, Winfield Scott, thought Pierce unfit for the saddle. Even so, a few years later he was being talked of as presidential material—a true dark horse in the election of 1852, when the profile below was taken. The Democratic convention had balloted forty-eight times, eliminating all the famous candidates, before handing the nomination to the unknown Pierce on the forty-ninth.

onto his horse to stay in action. Even so he was unfairly called a coward and told by General Winfield Scott to leave the field.

Though New Hampshire welcomed him home a war hero, Pierce was haunted by what he knew was a disappointing record. "I hate war in all its aspects," he wrote in his diary. "I deem it unworthy of the age in which I live."

In the presidential campaign of 1852, Pierce's name was originally nowhere in the running. He had been retired from politics for more than a decade and was virtually unknown to the majority of delegates at the Democratic convention. Battling for the nomination were the leading men of the party—Lewis Cass, James Buchanan, William Marcy, Sam Houston, and Stephen A. Douglas. But as the convention unfolded in the city of Baltimore, it was soon clear that none of these men could win even a simple majority, much less the required two-thirds vote. What was needed was a compromise choice around whom the party could coalesce, just as it had done eight years earlier around James K. Polk. Finally, on the thirty-fifth ballot, Franklin Pierce was first suggested. Pierce was so obscure in national politics that he had no enemies, and his open support of Southern interests made him acceptable to the South. On the forty-ninth ballot he won the nomination.

Pierce's opponent in the national election was none other than his commanding officer from the Mexican War, "Old Fuss and Feathers," General Winfield Scott. In the presidential campaign, Scott mocked Pierce's war record and insisted he was not fit to serve as president. He even released a book purporting to describe Pierce's military heroism—it was tiny in size and contained only blank pages. But in November, with the support of all the slave states, Pierce won the election. The *New York Tribune* lamented, "We have fallen on great times for little men."

Just two months before his inauguration, the President-elect was traveling by train with his wife and their young son Bennie, when tragedy struck again. Their train derailed and was badly wrecked. Pierce and his wife were merely shaken up, but eleven-year-old Bennie was crushed to death in front of their eyes. Mrs. Pierce never got over the shock. She refused to accompany her husband to Washington, and Pierce had to face the presidency still reeling from his personal tragedy. "I presume you have heard of the terrible catastrophe upon the railroad, which took from me my only child," he wrote a friend. "How I shall be able to summon my manhood and gather up my energies for the duties before me it is hard for me to see."

By far his most serious duty concerned the nation's struggle over the future of slavery. North and South were splitting apart over which new territories would allow slavery and which wouldn't. Choosing as his secretary of war Mississippi's Jefferson Davis, Pierce unequivocally sided with the pro-slavery South. "Involuntary servitude is recognized by the Constitution," he wrote, "and stands like any other admitted right. I fervently hope that the question of slavery is at rest."

To appease the South, Pierce enforced the Fugitive Slave Act, which was extremely unpopular in the North. Then he imprudently backed the Kansas-Nebraska Act, which permitted new western territories, even those long assumed to be slave-free, to decide for themselves if slavery should spread there. It was the chief domestic action of Pierce's administration, and it alienated him throughout the North.

The Kansas-Nebraska Act led to the most bitter fighting ever experienced in Congress, epitomized by the physical assault on Massachusetts' Charles Sumner by South Carolina's Preston Brooks: "Violent attack from the North finds its inevitable consequence in the growth of angry defiance in the South," Pierce proclaimed.

In May 1856, war over slavery broke out in Kansas. Unable to unite the Democratic party or offer positive leadership to his tormented country, Pierce was passed over for a second term when his party turned instead to James Buchanan. In his final message to Congress, rather than bowing out gracefully, the President lashed out against Northern abolitionists.

In March 1857 Franklin Pierce returned to New Hampshire having helped bring the nation to the brink of civil war. As a national rupture drew ever closer, he revealed his true views in a letter to his old friend Jefferson Davis, now the leader of Southern secession. "If I were in the Southerners' places, after so many years of aggression, I should probably be doing what they are doing," he wrote. "If our fathers were mistaken when they formed the Constitution, then the sooner we are apart the better."

When his letter was intercepted and published in the newspapers, it destroyed Pierce's remaining credibility in the North. Reviled as a traitor, despised even in his own state, an embittered Franklin Pierce became increasingly reclusive. When his beloved wife died in 1863, he lost his last remaining reason to live. For twenty years he had not touched a drop of alcohol. Now once again he gave in to his appetite for liquor. "After the White House what is there to do but drink?" he said. And that's exactly what the dark horse from New Hampshire did—he drank himself right into the grave.

Alone in Washington and mourning the recent, violent death of his only living son, Pierce (shown above and below) was almost paralyzed with fear on the snowy March morning of his inauguration. Yet he gave a commendable address, using no written text or even notes. His Southern sympathies were soon articulated. "I believe that involuntary servitude," he said, "as it exists in different states of this Confederacy, is recognized by the Constitution. I believe that it stands like any other admitted right, and that the states where it exists are entitled to efficient remedies to enforce the Constitutional provisions." In his inaugural oath Pierce became the only president to refuse to say "I solemnly swear," substituting the words, "I solemnly affirm." His old college friend and biographer, Nathaniel Hawthorne, had a high regard for the new President. "I have come seriously to the conclusion that he has in him many of the chief elements of a great ruler," he wrote a friend. "He is deep, deep, deep. . . . Nothing can ruin him."

IN HIS OWN WORDS

On the death of his first child, Franklin, Jr.: I received this morning a letter from my dear kind mother-in-law from which I learn that I am no longer, what I rejoice to be, a father. The little boy died on the fifth. He who has lived thirty years in this world of ours—seen its vanity . . . and felt its miseries—ought not to suffer at or look over the demise of an infant, but alas what has our experience or what has philosophy to do with the feelings of a father.

On turning down President Polk's offer of the attorney generalship: Although the early years of my manhood were devoted to public life, it was never really suited to my taste. I longed, as I am sure you must often have done, for the quiet and independence that belong only to the private citizen; and now, at forty, I feel that desire stronger than ever.

On keeping government out of social work: I readily and, I trust, feelingly acknowledge the duty incumbent on us all as men and citizens . . . to provide for those who, in the mysterious order of Providence, are subject to want and to disease of the body and mind; but I cannot find any authority in the Constitution for making the Federal Government the great almoner of public charity throughout the United States.

On slavery: I fervently hope that the question [of slavery] is at rest, and that no sectional or ambitious or fanatical excitement may again threaten the durability of our institutions or obscure the light of our prosperity.

During the secession crisis of 1860: I wish I could indulge higher hope for the future of our country, but the aspect of any vision is fearfully dark and I cannot make it otherwise.

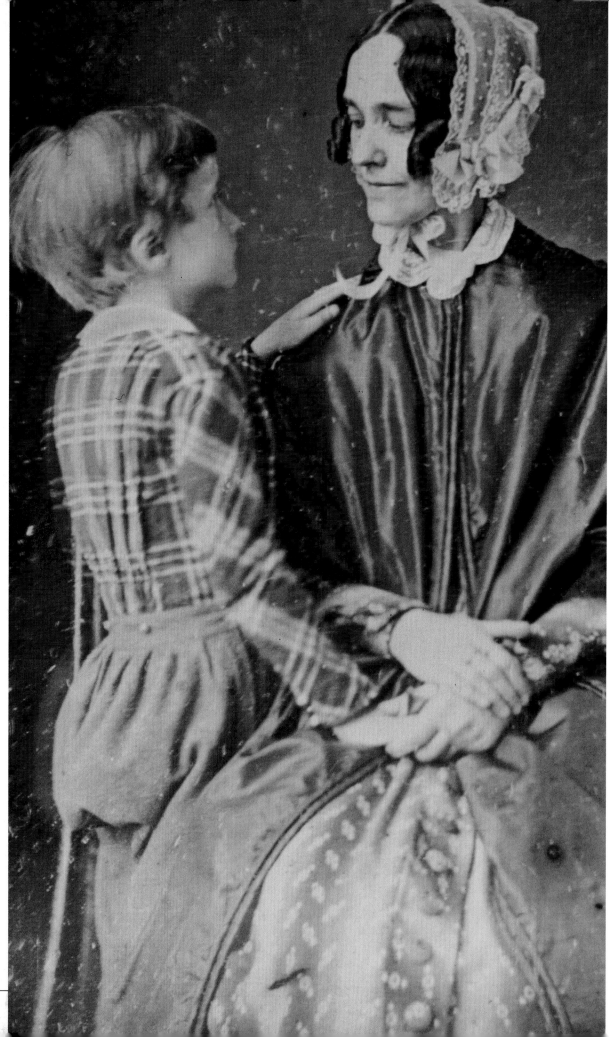

In 1835 Pierce married Jane Means Appleton, the delicate, sickly daughter of a Congregationalist minister who had once been president of Bowdoin College, from which the young New Hampshire charmer had graduated. Life was not kind to the couple. Having lost her first son as an infant and her second at four years, here Jane Pierce looks adoringly at her third son, Bennie. Practically giving up on her husband when he ignored her wishes and went off to fight in the Mexican War, Jane's passion for Bennie now consumed her. When he heard of his father's nomination, Bennie told her, "I hope we won't be elected for I should not like to be at Washington and I know you would not either." His father was elected, but before the inauguration eleven-year-old Bennie was killed in a railroad accident before his parents' eyes. The stricken, Calvinistic Jane, sure her husband's presidency had been purchased by the sacrifice of Bennie, stayed home in bitter mourning while Franklin went to Washington and numbly tried to preside over the country.

Franklin Pierce was a good man who didn't understand his own shortcomings. To his credit, he loved his wife and reshaped himself so that he could put up with her aristocratic, nervous ways and show her real affection. He was one of the most popular men in New Hampshire, polite and thoughtful, easy and good at the political game, charming and fine and handsome. And he was genuinely religious. And yet he was a timid man with a shallow, rigid, old-fashioned mind which could not cope with a changing America. In addition, Pierce was hounded by guilt, temptation, and just plain bad luck.

A scholarly, energetic, introspective, thin-skinned, driven man, James Garfield was the last of the politically potent log-cabin presidents. It was in his deprived childhood that the secret fires of inferiority-fueled ambition began burning, urging him from then on to come out on top in whatever he took on.

JAMES A. GARFIELD

1881

Awaiting Destiny

James Abram Garfield was his own kind of politician. He was the only preacher ever to become president; all his life he believed that a higher power was leading him onward and that a great destiny lay in store for him. "The law of my life [has been] never to ask for an office," he once wrote. "Had I done so I should feel that I was marring the plans of God."

But he also struggled with painful self-doubt, much of which went back to his dirt-poor origins, and to the loss of his father when he was only a child. "Let no man praise me because I was poor and without a helper," he wrote in midlife. "Hardly a day passes . . . [that] does not make me feel my inferiority."

It was destiny, and the Gospel, he said, that saved his life and turned him from work on a canal boat to the pursuit of education and preaching. After listening to an evangelist at the age of nineteen, he was baptized in the Church of the Disciples of Christ. "By the providence of God I am what I am, and not a sailor," he confided to his diary.

He began preaching the Gospel almost every Sunday and eventually was ordained as a minister in his church. But there was always a reckless and ambitious side to Garfield, and an inner sense that he was destined for bigger things. "I know without egotism that there is some . . . slumbering thunder in my soul," he proclaimed, "and it shall come out!"

After attending Williams College, in Massachusetts, Garfield began a life of teaching, rising from professor of classics at Western Eclectic Institute to president of the small Ohio college. But still he was restless. "My heart will never be satisfied to spend my life in teaching," he wrote a friend. "I think there are other fields in which a man can do more."

He turned first to the law and then to politics, running for a vacant state office and winning. Soon he was being spoken of as the "preacher/politician," known for his eloquence, his passion, and his opposition to slavery. Then, in 1861, came the Civil War.

He joined the Union Army as a lieutenant colonel, and perceived the war as a holy crusade. "I am for striking, striking and striking again, till we break them," he said as he led 4,000 men to victory in the mountains of Kentucky. "God . . . is the commander in chief of our armies," he wrote, "and God will take care of the grand consequences."

He rose to the rank of major general. Then, with the war still in progress, Garfield was elected to Congress. It was a seat he would hold for the next seventeen years; never once would he lose a single election.

He treated politics as if it were a form of teaching—or preaching. With

Left fatherless at the age of two, young Garfield (above) was brought up by his strong-willed, religious mother, who was never, during his whole life, far from his thoughts. Once he revisited his birthplace: "I walked over the lonely farm that was once my home, my earliest home. Strange and mingled indeed were my feelings when I stood upon the spot where I was born. . . . [In] the log fire . . . I traced a thousand fantastic figures of giants on fiery steeds and hosts embattled for war. . . . I again seemed tumbling on the floor with brothers and sisters. . . . I was ten again." Once, as a student, he pondered his feelings for his mother, as he studied a daguerrian portrait of her: "I gaze on her form written in silver with a pen of fire. She speaks not, but is calm as in her days of quiet when I nestled in her lap, and in my childish curiosity asked her 'where is heaven?' and 'who made the stars?' She told me that God made them and heaven was his home, and we must all die before we went there. When I found that she must die sometime I cried, and tried to make her promise me that she would not die." To his diary he later confessed her abiding influence: "At almost every turning point in my life she has been the moulding agent."

The jowly twenty-two-year-old on the right above is James Garfield, the teacher of this Greek class at Hiram College in 1853. Already he had taken a shine to one of his pupils, Lucretia Rudolph, "Crete" for short, who is beside him. It was a long, difficult romance. Whenever the subject of marriage came up, Garfield would grow agitated and depressed and, as an antidote, turn to other women. "I went to visit Lucretia," Garfield wrote during the courtship. "We love each other and have declared it. . . . But . . . I am not certain that I feel just as I ought towards her. There is no delirium of passion." Later, upon receiving a letter from another girlfriend, Garfield wrote, "Oh my God to what end didst thou create such an infinite power of loving." Married to Crete in 1858, Garfield shows off his beard to his bride's young sister (below).

an expertise in finance, he became popular and well respected, and was soon being referred to as the "spokesman" of his party. But though he was increasingly mentioned as a presidential possibility, the year 1880 was never intended to be Garfield's year.

At the Republican convention, held inside a specially built wooden auditorium in Chicago, three men vied for the nomination. After a hiatus of four years Ulysses S. Grant was seeking an unprecedented third term, opposed by James Blaine, of Maine. Far behind those two was John Sherman of Ohio. Garfield, who served as a delegate-at-large, was to put forward the name of fellow Ohioan Sherman.

But during his nominating speech, it was Garfield himself who drew the attention of the crowds. From this point on he, not Sherman, was considered Ohio's dark horse. "Delegates from all quarters . . . are openly expressing the wish that I was the Ohio candidate," he wrote home to his wife Crete. "So much of this is said as to put me in constant danger of being suspected of ambitious designs."

On the thirty-fourth ballot of a deadlocked convention, the Wisconsin delegation announced it was shifting sixteen votes to General Garfield. The announcement brought silence, then vigorous cheering. On the next ballot a stampede commenced. Soon, ten thousand voices were chanting his name as the whole convention endorsed James Garfield.

That summer, from his house in Mentor, Ohio, Garfield became the first candidate to conduct a front porch campaign. A telegraph office was set up on his property so that he could keep up with unfolding news and transmit his speeches and remarks to the newspapers. Thousands showed up to lend their support, including a delegation of black Republicans, for whom Garfield was a hero. Running against him was General Winfield Hancock, himself a last-minute dark horse nominee, and in November, Garfield won by a slim margin and was elected the twentieth president of the United States.

He was one of the best prepared men ever to have reached the presidency, with a thorough grasp of every aspect of government. But he was soon calling the office "a bleak mountain," in large part because of frustrations due to office seekers. "My God! What is there in this place that a man should ever want to get into it?" he wrote. "These people would take my very brain, flesh and blood if they could." Within weeks he was writing, "My day is frittered away by the personal seeking of people when it ought to be given to the great problems which concern the whole country."

His lack of self-confidence and need to please in some ways made him unsuited for the office. As president there was no way he could please everyone, and no way to withdraw into scholarly pursuits. "I love to deal with doctrines and events," he admitted. "The contests of men about men I greatly dislike."

Garfield's key challenge as president centered on a system of patronage called "senatorial courtesy," by which senators held de facto veto power over federal appointments within their home states. Garfield had long disliked the tradition. "It is one of the most corrupt and vicious practices of our times," he observed. "It virtually robs the President of his power of appointment and puts a dangerous power in the hands of the Senate."

At the center of the controversy stood a powerful Republican boss, Senator Roscoe Conkling, now demanding to control a key appointment in New York. Garfield was eager to keep Conkling happy, but he also was determined to make his own nomination. When Conkling refused to support the president's choice, an angry Garfield decided not to back down. "Of course I deprecate war," he wrote, "but if it is brought to my door the bringer will find me at home."

It became a duel to the finish between the dark-horse-become-president and one of the major forces of his own political party. In an age of presidential weakness, which had set in after Lincoln, few thought Garfield had the backbone to face Conkling down. But in a series of masterful decisions and confrontations, the President outmaneuvered the master politician. And when the Senate saw the public's mounting approval for Garfield, they voted to ratify his nomination. It marked the end of the dominance of senatorial courtesy, and the beginning of a new era of mounting presidential power and prestige. "[It is a] question of whether the President is a registering clerk of the Senate or the Executive of the United States," Garfield wrote to a friend.

Less than four months into office, Garfield was gunned down in a Washington railroad station. Dropping to the floor, he gasped, "My God, what is this?" The shooter was a religious fanatic named Charles Guiteau who saw himself as the hand of destiny.

All efforts were focused on saving Garfield's life. Alexander Graham Bell was brought in to search for the elusive bullet. At the White House an air-conditioning system was built; one hundred pounds of ice each hour kept the critically ill President cool throughout the sweltering summer. Appalled and spellbound, many Americans awaited daily medical bulletins that updated the President's condition.

Garfield lingered on week after week. It was the longest period of presidential disability in the nation's history, until Woodrow Wilson suffered a stroke four decades later. "Don't be disturbed by conflicting reports about my condition," he wrote to his mother at one point in the summer. "It is true I am still weak, and on my back; but I am gaining every day, and need only time and patience to bring me through." Finally, in September, two months after the shooting, he was moved to the New Jersey shore. Three hundred men laid down a half a mile of track so that a special train could wheel him right to the front door of his seaside cottage. Propped up before an open window, the weakening President gazed out on the waves.

He was such a mixture of a man: preacher, scholar, soldier, politician, an introspective self-doubter who could be passionately committed to causes. He was a drifter in life, a dark horse who had, as if miraculously, become president. "Few men in our history have ever obtained the Presidency by planning to obtain it," he once wrote. "In most cases it is got as the result . . . of accident." And to a friend he had once written, "my life has been made up of a series of accidents, mostly of a favorable nature."

On September 19, 1881, with his beloved wife close by at his side, James Abram Garfield died. Though he had been president only two hundred days, the loss was felt as a national tragedy unparalleled since the death of Lincoln. Americans had come to revere this president, whose rise from poverty to the highest office seemed to embody America at its best. Garfield had attained something that had eluded Franklin Pierce: leadership, on his own terms.

The Civil War's youngest Union major general, Garfield was elected to Congress with the war still raging. He was a candidate for the presidency in 1880, and his steady, showy, articulate integrity made him attractive to American voters. Outwardly he didn't really want to be president much. And yet, underneath he wanted it almost too much, and didn't even know it, for Garfield could not control his lurking ambition, even when it disagreed with what his intellect told him. At key moments in his life, no matter how much he denied it, he turned hypocritical and grasping, momentarily discarding all the decent things he stood for. Still, his background almost ensured success. He was a Greek and Latin scholar, a college president, a teacher and preacher and Civil War major general, an orator, a long-term congressman, a newly elected senator and, of course, a family man. James Garfield could have reached for the stars had not a crazed assassin gunned him down four months after his inauguration.

Inauguration Day in Washington (above) was cold and snowy. "[We] reached . . . the senate at 11:30," Garfield wrote in his diary. "Thence to the east portico of the rotunda . . . [where] I read my inaugural—slowly and fairly well—though I grew somewhat hoarse towards the close." In the weeks afterward, Garfield was anything but joyous. His precious time, he felt, was being swallowed up by irreverent people and irrelevant problems. Where, now, he wondered, were the intervals during which he used to take note of a beautiful sunset or a heaven of stars? In fact, Crete and he sometimes did find time to watch sunsets, from the south porch of the White House.

Garfield was a serious family man. Here are his five children, Mary, Harry, James, Irving, and Abram.

Lucretia Rudolph Garfield

From the start Garfield's bright, young classics student Lucretia had a lot to put up with. Her erratic and unreliable sweetheart summed up the problem: "I think that passion is the most difficult one in my nature and at times it seems perfectly untamable. . . . May God hide from me the day when I am sold to licentiousness and lust." As they moved toward marriage, with Garfield torn between her and another woman, Crete made it known that she was perfectly willing to give him up unless he came clean with her. "How many times have I felt," she wrote him, "that if you would only love me just enough to come and tell me all, I could endure to know the worst; but to see you shrink away from me as though you could not endure my presence, and hide from me the truth, was almost more than I could bear. . . . I would say to you this hour, go and marry Rebecca. . . . [She] is a good and noble girl, in many aspects far my superior but she loves you no better than Crete. If however you love her better, if she can satisfy the wants of your nature better . . . Crete can give you up." Even after they committed themselves to marrying, his unpredictable behavior and her doubts continued. "My heart almost breaks," she wrote three months before the ceremony, "with the cruel thought that our marriage is [to be] based upon the cold stern word duty." It would be years before the two understood each other completely and their passions finally matched. "If I could . . . write out the story of Crete's life and mine," Garfield confided to his diary after thirteen years of marriage, "the long and anxious questions that preceded . . . the adjustment of our lives to each other, and the beautiful results we . . . are now enjoying, it would be a more wonderful record than any I know in the realm of romance."

Garfield and his daughter Molly (Mary) pose during his Congressional years, when he was widely known as the best speaker in the Republican Party. A philosopher in government, Garfield was a brilliant writer of prose, and made heavier use of the Library of Congress than any of his colleagues. He loved his privacy, his intellectual pursuits, and his family life.

Garfield was the second American president to be assassinated; now in the hearts of his countrymen he joined Abraham Lincoln (above). The assassin had stalked Garfield for weeks before gunning him down in a Washington railroad station less than four months after his inauguration. The wounded President was brought back to the White House, where Alexander Graham Bell searched for the elusive bullet with electrical devices. After trying to keep him cool with a makeshift air-conditioning system, his doctors removed Garfield from the sweltering capital and took him to his summer retreat on the New Jersey shore by special train. Three hundred men worked through the night laying a half mile of track from the railroad line to the front door of the cottage, and from an easy chair Garfield could watch the ocean and feel the sea breeze. But not even this could save him for long from what he called "the Silent City," and two and a half months after the shooting the country was mourning him in death (below).

The elaborate decorations that bedecked the White House in 1881 reflect the intense national mourning following James Garfield's assassination and death.

WARREN G. HARDING

1921–1923

"I Should Never Have Been Here"

Warren G. Harding was an obliging, generous-spirited, amiable man who could not bear to offend anyone. The son of a self-taught veterinarian and doctor who was always in debt, he had grown up insecure. As a young man he tried teaching and railroad work and selling insurance before settling on the printer's trade. He acquired the *Marion Star,* a bankrupt Ohio newspaper, and over the years he built it into one of the most successful journals in the state. "Success is not founded so much on capital," he once said, "as it is on industry, stick-to-itiveness and ability to do things."

His wife, Florence Kling de Wolfe, became his business partner and would always be Harding's biggest supporter. Their marriage, however, was not a happy one. Harding nicknamed her "The Duchess" for her formidable ways, and took repeated stays away from her in a Michigan sanitarium. He also began to travel whenever he could, using free railroad passes acquired through his newspaper. He would meet people all over the state, and was soon filling his life with politics. His silver voice and penchant for alliteration helped make him into an accomplished speaker, and his genuine warmth made even hostile audiences feel that he understood them and was speaking directly to each person. "If I say so myself, I do think I turn out a good speech," he once bragged.

Harding served as state senator and then as lietenant governor of Ohio. He had striking good looks and a faculty for pleasing people, qualities that helped him win a seat in the U.S. Senate, where he served six years, though with little distinction.

The Republican convention of 1920 took place during one of the worst heat waves ever to hit Illinois. Inside the barnlike Chicago Coliseum the two favorite candidates each peaked early, but neither would withdraw, leaving a stalemate. With the temperature on the floor hitting 106 degrees, and with the delegates restless, the way was opened for a dark horse compromise.

"The only thing I really worry about is that I might be nominated," Harding had written six months earlier. "That's an awful thing to contemplate." But he had also written, "I have decided to make the plunge and play the big game."

In a suite on the thirteenth floor of Chicago's Blackstone Hotel, the famous "smoke-filled room," would-be kingmakers came and went through the night of June 11, trying to decide whom they would back in the morn-

Six-year-old Warren Harding, shown here with his sisters, was called Winnie by his family. He loved animals and avoided fistfights.

Even though at school he had excelled only at spelling, at sixteen the handsome young man became a teacher.

Harding's Airedale, Laddie Boy, who brought the President his morning paper and retrieved his golf balls, was a favorite of the press and even got interviewed.

One of the causes of Harding's bouts with depression was his less-than-happy marriage to a local Marion woman, Florence Kling de Wolfe (above). Five years older than he, Florence was a divorcée with a son when she set her sights on the young Harding. Though he felt more fear than love for her, he was constitutionally unable to say no, and at twenty-five Harding married her. The Duchess, as he somewhat jokingly called her, watched over his every move and made herself indispensable to Harding. She became his business partner and managed, among other things, the home delivery of the *Star,* at that time a novelty. Harding's wayward eye and her auto-cratic demeanor eventually sent him into the arms of another woman. But throughout it all, Florence remained his biggest defender. "She makes life hell for me," the publisher (below) might growl, but still he clung to her. And during the heady days of the presidential campaign of 1920 she wrote, "No matter what comes into my life, I shall always regard this summer as one of the greatest epochs of my life."

ing. According to one report, Harding was asked in the wee hours of the night was there any secret in his life that might embarrass the party. He might have mentioned why five times he had checked himself into a Michigan sanatarium, or his weak heart, or his meager education, or his ten-year affair with the wife of an Ohio friend, which was still going on and would eventually lead to blackmail. Instead Harding reportedly thought awhile and then answered no, there was no impediment that might disqualify him.

What the smoke-filled room flirted with, the convention itself proceeded to effect. By the tenth ballot on the following day, Warren G. Harding had received 200 more than the necessary votes and the convention declared his nomination unanimous. "The fates . . . have drawn me into the presidential race," he remarked.

Once nominated, Harding set out to win. Like Garfield, he campaigned from the porch of his Ohio home, emphasizing his dislike of Woodrow Wilson and the danger, as he saw it, of the League of Nations. "The President . . . has been irresponsible much of the time," he proclaimed. "He has . . . unmistakable flights of mental disturbance."

Unlike the internationally oriented idealist Woodrow Wilson, Harding was dedicated to "America First," and he promised the country a return to the good old prewar days of "normalcy," as he called it, led by someone who wasn't trying to be a giant. "I am not an outstanding and dominant individual," he said. "I am really more anxious about the tranquillity of our country." And in a soon-to-be famous address he said, "America's present need is not heroics, but healing; not nostrums, but normalcy; not revolution, but restoration."

Instead of marching forward into a new world, Harding was asking America to regress into an old one. And his soothing, blurred message based on rural nostalgia led him and his running-mate Calvin Coolidge to overwhelming victory over the Democratic team of James M. Cox and Franklin D. Roosevelt. Commenting on Harding's victory, Woodrow Wilson scoffed, "How can he lead when he does not know where he is going?"

Once elected, Harding was suddenly struck by the reality of what had happened. "I am just beginning to realize what a job I have taken over," he wrote. "God help me, for I need it." Acutely aware of his own shortcomings, Harding was determined to have a group of the best minds about him. Some of his cabinet choices were excellent, such as Charles Evans Hughes as secretary of state and Herbert Hoover as secretary of commerce. He stood up for these choices against considerable criticism—his strongest, best act as president. But he also wanted to reward Republican friends, and in a few his trust was utterly misplaced. This was especially the case with his campaign manager, Harry Daugherty, whom he made attorney general, and with Albert B. Fall, whom he named secretary of the interior. And with a particularly ill-qualified man whom he put in charge of the Veterans' Bureau—Col. Charles Forbes.

For a while Harding's presidency cruised along smoothly. He normalized relationships with former enemy states, lowered taxes to stimulate economic recovery and improved government budgeting. And recognizing the impact that automobiles would have, he supported a massive highway construction program. His close friends were primarily the wealthy, like Henry Ford and Thomas Edison. Again and again Harding sided with big business, refusing to support a minimum wage for workers, and always siding with company owners during union strikes. "The coal and railway strikes

. . . had no excuse," he said on one occasion. "American business is not a monster. It is the guardian of our happiness."

In the White House Harding was a hardworking president. But increasingly he found the job overwhelming. Intellectually undisciplined, he changed his mind often and stumbled in his efforts to please everyone. "I listen to one side and they seem right," he said, "and—God!—I talk to the other side and they seem just as right! I can't make a damn thing out of this problem."

With but a single secretary and a staff of just two dozen, Harding found himself increasingly taxed. Once, faced with a large stack of official papers, he admitted to an aide he was in over his head: "I am not fit for this office and should never have been here."

By his third year in office, Harding was exhausted and in poor health. His blood pressure was too high, he was overweight, and he suffered shortness of breath. And then came word of a brewing scandal in the Veterans' Bureau, involving Harding's personal friend and appointee Charles Forbes. Though he privately chastized Forbes, Harding failed to denounce him publicly or expose his crimes. Instead he allowed him to resign and flee the country, as he himself retreated into a cocoon of silence, and attempted to sweep the scandal under the rug. A month later Forbes's associate Charles Cramer killed himself. And ten weeks after that a close associate of Attorney General Harry Daugherty also committed suicide. Harding was finally realizing how deeply tainted his administration was. "My God, this is a hell of a job," he said on one occasion. "I have no trouble with my enemies. But my damn friends . . . my goddamn friends. . . . They're the ones that keep me walking the floor nights!"

In the summer of 1923, to escape Washington, Harding commenced a cross-country tour to culminate in Alaska, the first presidential visit there ever. He described the trip as his "voyage of understanding," and for a while in Alaska, Harding seemed to relax. But the scandals in Washington were weighing heavily on his mind. One day, according to Herbert Hoover, Harding asked his trusted secretary of commerce for advice. "If you knew of a great scandal in our administration, would you for the good of the country and the party expose it publicly or would you bury it?" he asked. "Publish it," Hoover replied, "and at least get credit for integrity on your side." But Harding didn't dare take Hoover's advice. Filled with dread, and sticking to a murderous speaking schedule, he began to talk about "dire consequences." Once when his ship suffered a minor accident at sea, Harding was heard to remark, "I hope the boat sinks."

Returning down the West Coast, the President was struck by a violent stomach disorder, which was diagnosed as ptomaine poisoning from tainted crabs. In San Francisco, he was put to bed in the presidential suite of the Palace Hotel. A few days later, while Florence was reading to him, he suddenly broke out in a sweat, turned pale, and stiffened. "I don't know what happened to me," he said to his wife, "a very strange, sinking feeling that I have never experienced before." Although the color returned to his face, and Florence continued to read, it was only minutes before President Harding was dead.

He was one of the most popular presidents in the history of the country, until after his death, when the scandals began to surface. The worst became known as Teapot Dome, an illegal oil-leasing scheme within the Interior Department. Although the president himself was not directly impli-

A born booster, Harding played every instrument in the local band, joined every civic club he could, and spoke in public whenever the opportunity arose. His mellifluent voice, his streams of alliteration, and his actor's movements entranced audiences.

At the notification ceremony after the 1920 Republican Convention, Warren G. Harding accepts his party's nomination. He likened his victory to his favorite game—poker. "I feel like a man who goes in with a pair of eights," he said, "and comes out with aces full."

Like McKinley twenty-four years earlier, Harding campaigned from his porch in Ohio, the state that had provided six of the last nine elected presidents. Here an overflow crowd has gathered at the front porch to hear promises of a return to the good old days—"not agitation, but adjustment; not surgery, but serenity; not submergence in internationality, but sustainment in triumphant nationality."

cated, it was his best friends in government who had committed the worst crimes. His former secretary of the interior, Albert Fall, became the first cabinet officer ever convicted and sent to prison.

Harding's chief presidential failure was his unwillingness to root out the corruption, or to offer his country any true moral leadership. Inhabiting an increasingly complex presidency with enormous responsibilities, Harding found himself unable to rise to the challenge. And the man who always so needed to be adored, the dark horse who could never say no, ended up one of the most vilified presidents in American history.

Always beset by rumors—that he had "Negro blood," that his health was bad, that he was having another affair—Harding took refuge in poker behind closed doors and in serving alcohol to friends in his private quarters during Prohibition. His beloved golf was played out in public.

Posing for a bust gave Harding time to contemplate his simple philosophy: "I like to preach the gospel of understanding in America, the utter abolition of class . . . the maintenance of American institutions . . . and above all continued freedom for the United States, without dictation or direction from anybody else in the world."

Unlike his predecessor, Woodrow Wilson, Harding flung open the White House to an adoring public. "I cannot hope to be one of the great presidents," he once commented. "But perhaps I may be remembered as one of the best loved."

In the early 1920s the times were mellow and the President could take a daily constitutional on his horse, exploring the city of Washington without fear.

On his final trip West—dubbed his "voyage of understanding"—the President and Florence greet admirers from the rear of their campaign train.

Harding's body was brought across the continent to Washington, where it lay in state in the East Room. The grief-stricken First Lady had refused to have an autopsy performed, leading to cruel speculation that she had poisoned him.

With the casket in place, the funeral parade forms outside the White House. Even though his tenure in office had been innocuous, Harding was dearly loved and the country was moved by his sudden death. It was not until later that the Teapot Dome scandal and others emerged, proving Harding's administration to have been deeply tainted by corruption. And then Nan Britton's *The President's Daughter* was published, claiming Harding to be the father of her child. Though Harding is believed to have been falsely accused by Britton, the accusations severely tarnished his reputation.

Healing the Nation

Gerald Rudolph Ford, Jr., in many ways was the perfect choice to restore America's broken confidence after Richard Nixon. Straightforward, honest, a man of recognized decency, he traced his personal qualities back to his Midwestern childhood. Raised in Grand Rapids, Michigan, by his mother and stepfather, he didn't learn that he was adopted until he was almost fifteen. "My stepfather was a magnificent person," Ford remembered, "and my mother equally wonderful. So I couldn't have written a better prescription for a superb family upbringing."

He grew up to become an outstanding football player, serving as captain of his high school team, then playing all through his years at the University of Michigan. At Yale University, where he attended law school, he worked on the side as a football coach. When he returned home at the end of World War II, in which he served overseas as a navy combat officer, it was with a new feeling for public service. "I came back a converted internationalist," he recalled, "and of course our congressman at that time was an avowed, dedicated isolationist. And I thought he ought to be replaced. Nobody thought I could win. I ended up winning two to one."

"I had just taken the oath of office along with all the other freshmen and this man walked up to me and he said, 'I'm Dick Nixon from California. I welcome you here in the House Chamber.' That was January of '49."

For twenty-five years Ford served in the House of Representatives, specializing in military matters and the budgeting process. In 1964 he was appointed Minority Leader, with his highest ambition to become speaker of the House. In 1968 he watched fellow Republican Richard Nixon become elected president alongside Spiro Agnew. Four years later, in the midst of Nixon's reelection campaign, Ford learned about Watergate.

"I was dumbfounded by the stupidity of the Watergate break-in," Ford later said, "and on the Monday following that break-in, or perhaps it was Saturday night, I had a meeting with John Mitchell, who was then in charge of Nixon's campaign. 'Well,' I said to John, 'did the President, did the White House, did you know anything about this stupid break-in?' And John looked me right in the eye and said, 'Absolutely not.' So on that assurance I took the firm stand that it was not a White House–conceived or –executed operation."

Even as the Watergate controversy was heating up, Nixon's vice president was in his own trouble. In the summer of 1973, it was disclosed that

Little Gerald would not learn he was adopted until he was a teenager.

At the University of Michigan, Ford played first-string center in his senior year, after which he got offers from the pros. "In those days you didn't have a scholarship but our coach got me a job over at the University Hospital, where I waited on tables. About every three months I'd give blood, for which I was paid twenty-five dollars."

In September 1974 at Camp David, President Ford is deep in thought. The following day he will pardon Richard Nixon.

Friendly since the time they first met in 1949, Congressman Ford and Senator Nixon pose together two years later. Unlike Nixon, who was headed for the vice presidency, Ford never hungered for the White House. "When I first ran for the Congress I had an ambition to be a good legislator, and when I got to Washington as a member of the House my ambition was to be a very good legislator. And shortly after getting there . . . I could see what a wonderful experience it would be to be Speaker of the House."

In 1948, in the midst of campaigning for a seat in Congress, Ford married Betty Bloomer, a recent divorcée who had modeled, had danced at Martha Graham's studio in New York, and was now a fashion coordinator for a Grand Rapids department store. The matron of honor at their wedding confided to the bride, "Betty, I want to warn you. Jerry's mistress will not be a woman. It will be his work."

Spiro Agnew had received bribes from building contractors while he served as governor of Maryland. To escape prosecution he was attempting to make a plea bargain. "About two days, maybe one day before the story broke," Ford recalled, "Nixon invited me to come down to the executive office in the old executive office building. I had no reason to know why I was being called.

"I was minority leader. He asked me to come down there, and for an hour and a half, we sat there and talked very informally—reminisced about our long friendship. It was a strange conversation. I finally got a call to come to the floor of the House immediately, for a vote. So I left. I got on the floor and two or three of my colleagues on the Republican side grabbed me and said, 'Agnew's resigning.' That was the first real knowledge I had that he had taken that action."

Ford suddenly knew that Nixon was considering him as a replacement for Spiro Agnew. Nixon's preference would have been John Connally of Texas, but support for a Connally appointment did not exist in Congress, and Nixon knew it. He would be forced to do what party leaders had so often done at traditional national conventions: look for somebody who could command a majority, somebody safe. The search for a compromise led directly to Gerald Ford.

"Well, that night I was home with Betty," Ford remembered, "and about eight-thirty after dinner I got a call from Mel Laird and Mel said, 'I'm down at the White House. Would you accept the nomination for vice president if it was offered?' And I said I guess I would. I knew if I was offered it I would accept it but I never thought that being vice president would lead to being president."

Just after Ford became vice president, Archibald Cox, the Watergate special prosecutor, was fired, and the White House scandal became even more heated. In the midst of Congressional talk of impeaching Richard Nixon, Ford suddenly found himself also in the line of fire. "It was very, very uncomfortable," he recalled. "I disagreed privately with some of the actions that were taken by the Nixon White House. I never had good relations with Haldeman and Ehrlichman and Chuck Colson. My personality, my background didn't fit with them. So I felt that President Nixon was getting some bad advice. And it was a very narrow path for nine months. If I was critical of Nixon, the press and the public would have said, well, he was trying to undercut Nixon so he will get the job. On the other hand, if I stayed too loyal it might appear that I was supporting somebody who was involved in this very unwise action. So I had to go down this narrow path of not supporting him too much or not criticizing him too frequently. It was not a pleasant experience."

On Thursday August 1, 1974, Ford received a phone call from Alexander Haig telling him there was a "smoking gun"—evidence that Nixon was involved in the Watergate cover-up. "Al Haig [asked] to come over and see me," Ford remembered, "to tell me that there would be a new tape released on a Monday, and he said the evidence in there was devastating and there would probably be either an impeachment or a resignation. And he said, 'I'm just warning you that you've got to be prepared, that things might change dramatically and you could become president.' And I said, 'Betty, I don't think we're ever going to live in the vice president's house.'"

On August 9, following Richard Nixon's resignation, Gerald Ford escorted him out of the White House. "That was very sad because of our long personal friendship with Dick and Pat," Ford said. "That's a sad situation when you see a couple that had been good friends who [were] leaving under those very tragic circumstances."

And then Ford turned and went back inside the White House, which was his White House now. "Our children were there, and I had of course almost immediately the responsibility of going into the East Room, where I had to be sworn in and where I had to make an acceptance speech. And I couldn't prepare my speech until twenty-four hours or less beforehand, because up until the last minute we weren't sure what President Nixon was going to do. And I had a wonderful speechwriter, Bob Hartman, and he handed me the copy and I read it. He had a knack of saying what I would say. It came to one sentence. I said, 'Bob, we ought to strike this.' And it was the sentence, 'Our long national nightmare is over.' And Bob Hartman said to me, 'If you strike that, I'm quitting!' So I left it in and it turned out to be the most memorable line in my remarks—and it was a wonderful line."

The first thing President Ford had to do, as he saw it, was to relieve the country, to show that here was a decent, respectable new person in the White House, who wasn't at all like Richard Nixon, and that the country could relax again. And Ford did it brilliantly for thirty days. Then, pursuing the same objective, he pardoned Nixon in advance of any litigation in order, in his mind, to get rid of the whole situation. The idea of a trial that would run over a period of months, keeping all the issues of Watergate alive, seemed to him no way to reassure the country and turn things around. But Ford hadn't anticipated the very serious effect that his pardon would have on his own prestige in office. From then on, a considerable part of the electorate thought that he was part of the Nixon conspiracy, that this was a payoff of some kind, a quid pro quo deal. Ford never regained the solid national support that he had in his first thirty days. "I have to say that most of my staff disagreed with me over the pardon," Ford later remembered. "But I was absolutely convinced that it was the right thing to do."

As president, Ford worked hard to heal the nation. Unlike Nixon, who had virtually ignored his cabinet, Ford reestablished normal ties. He offered amnesty to young people who had fled the draft during the Vietnam War. And responding to the worst recession since the Great Depression, he called the first White House summit on the economy, and went on to make his mark in the area of federal budget cutting. But with an increasingly hostile Democratic Congress, Ford's initiatives were often stopped dead in their tracks. And with the economy failing to turn around, his public support all but disappeared.

"My greatest disappointment was that I couldn't turn the switch and all of a sudden overnight go from an economic recession to an economic prosperity," Ford remembered. "That was the greatest disappointment domestically."

Ford's greatest success as president was in demonstrating for two and a half years—which is all the time he had—that the presidency could be decently administered by responsible people. "I hope historians will write that the Ford administration healed the land," said Gerry Ford, "that I restored public confidence in the White House and in the government."

A quarter century after their first meeting, Ford wistfully watches his old friend Nixon depart the White House by helicopter the morning following his resignation. With the fall of Vice President Spiro Agnew in 1973, Ford had been appointed vice president in his stead, and now, in just a few minutes, he would be sworn in as president. Betty Ford stands beside her husband, close to David Eisenhower and his wife, Nixon's daughter, Julie.

Nine days into his presidency, the Fords still had not moved into the White House. Instead the new president commuted from his home in Alexandria, Virginia. Here, with Betty at the door, he leaves for work in a baseball cap, carrying the day's newspapers.

IN HIS OWN WORDS

On his parents: I had a wonderful mother and I was equally blessed to have a superb stepfather. My mother divorced my real father when I was less than a year old. My real father was abusing her physically and mentally and she took me by train from Omaha where I was born, to Grand Rapids, where her parents were. I never knew that I was an adopted son until I was about fifteen.

On his heroes in the presidency: I think Ike did a fine job as president. As a matter of fact, a president has the prerogative of having three portraits in the Cabinet Room of former presidents. I picked Abraham Lincoln, Dwight D. Eisenhower and Harry Truman.

On LBJ: Lyndon Johnson was a very, very skilled member of Congress. He was tough personally—he was very tough on me. Had some unkind statements, but basically he was a good, decent tough guy.

On his qualification for office: I had good exposure to presidents, to presidential problems, and so the combination of minority leader and vice president made me highly qualified to assume the presidency when Nixon resigned.

On Richard Nixon: Nixon was a long-time friend who made a very stupid mistake. So I have to look at the overall, which I think was a good record, and concede that everyone is human and you can make mistakes that are very unfortunate and regrettable.

On the future of the presidency: A person who has the right character and the right motive can handle the job. We don't need to change the duties and responsibilities. We have to make sure the person the American people elect has the qualifications that are essential for the circumstances that are presented to him as our chief executive.

On America: I think it's a great country that something like that could happen to somebody with my background. I get very irritated with people who make a profession of bashing America. I detest the cynics, the skeptics. In my lifetime, our country's got a pretty good track record.

After the decision was made to withdraw from Vietnam, President Ford shuts the world out for a moment (above). Years later he talked of the American evacuation. "The North Vietnamese overran South Vietnam and were right on the outskirts of Saigon, and that's where the crunch came. At that point, because Congress lost its guts and wouldn't put the money up to help our allies, we were faced with a critical situation—how we could evacuate all the Americans from Saigon and as many of our South Vietnamese friends as possible. The net result was we did a good job."

In 1976 Ford swims for the camera while trying out the new White House pool.

On election night in the Oval Office a tired President Ford gets leaned on by his daughter, Susan, before conceding to Jimmy Carter. "I lost the presidential election," Ford said, "[but] we did the best we could and darn near won—against tough odds." Though the pardon of Nixon had blurred his accomplishments, it didn't erase them. By the end of Ford's administration, Americans once again felt trust in the presidency.

With his characteristic good humor and optimism, the President chats on the phone from his private study in the residence of the White House. On having held the land's highest office, Ford says, "I look back and wonder how it ever happened to me."

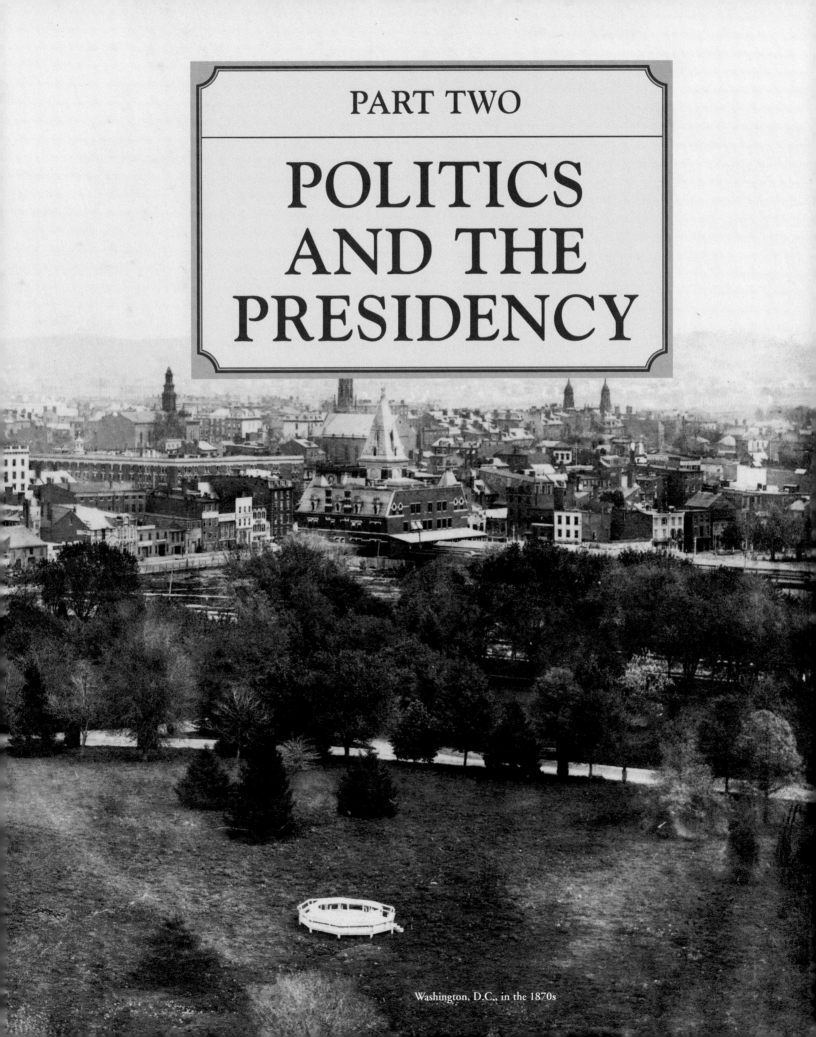

PART TWO

POLITICS AND THE PRESIDENCY

Washington, D.C., in the 1870s

Martin Van Buren

James Buchanan

THE PROFESSIONAL POLITICIAN

CHAPTER THREE

Political skill and a passion for politics are essential to the presidency.
But in times of crisis much more is needed.

Abraham Lincoln

Lyndon B. Johnson

In the nation's early years, participation in political affairs was considered a duty and an honor, but not a way of life. Public-spirited men like George Washington and Thomas Jefferson donated large periods of their lives to national service, but always considered themselves first and foremost private citizens and eagerly anticipated their return to private life. Though members of Congress might be openly partisan, seeing it as their job to represent regional interests, the ideal president was to strive to be free of partisanship, for he alone represented the American people as a whole. Despite real differences between Federalists and Democrat-Republicans, all six of the first presidents believed in a presidency above party. "We are all republicans; we are all federalists," said Thomas Jefferson in his first inaugural address. And when his friend James Monroe received all but one of the 232 electoral votes cast in 1820, demonstrating the effective collapse of a two-party system, the period became known as the "era of good feelings."

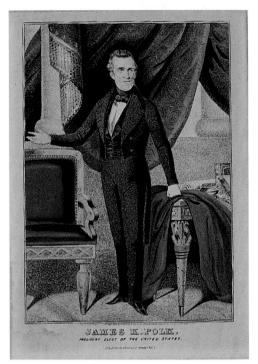

JAMES K. POLK,
PRESIDENT ELECT OF THE UNITED STATES.

James K. Polk, the studious speaker of the House and then governor of Tennessee, became president in 1845 by hitching his star to expansionism. A consummate politician, Polk added a vast area to the United States, including Texas, New Mexico, and California.

As Collector of the Port of New York in charge of a thousand Customhouse employees, Chester A. Arthur marshaled his men in behalf of New York's Republican machine until he was ousted by the reforms of President Hayes in 1878. Arthur was nominated for vice president by the Republicans in 1880, and his march to the top was the only time a machine henchman made it to the White House.

All this changed in the late 1820s and '30s, as politics began emerging as a professional vocation. A new breed of president now arose, on one hand clever, cunning, and driven by ambition, on the other highly skilled in bargaining and in forming coalitions. The man who exemplified the new breed was the New York politician Martin Van Buren. Detesting the blurring of political distinctions and identities that were inherent in Monroe's "era of good feelings," Van Buren called for a resurgence of partisan politics. Political parties, he argued, served a powerful public good, offering opportunity for Americans to vent real political differences. "[They can] rouse the public to exertion," he wrote, "excite a salutary vigilance over our public functionaries, and prevent that apathy which has proved the ruin of Republics." By holding together diverse geographic sections of the country, national parties could serve as antidotes to sectionalism. And as democratic organizations, Van Buren argued, they enabled more people to take an active part in government. Putting lessons he had learned at the state level to good use, Van Buren became the mastermind of Andrew Jackson's rise to the presidency and then went on to help create the national Democratic party. Following Van Buren's guidance, Jackson instituted the tradition of political patronage, by which presidents increased in strength through their ability to reward political allies. Ever since, the presidency has been a thoroughly political office.

Political expertise does not necessarily lead to success in the presidency. Van Buren himself, one of the shrewdest politicos of them all, was unable to cope with the country's economic collapse in the 1830s. And James Buchanan, an extraordinarily gifted career politician, was personally incapable of rising to the awesome challenge of secession. In general, however, in the years since Andrew Jackson, it has been the most openly political presidents who have made the most effective leaders. Not content to allow Congress to be the leading force in government, these presidents have applied all their political skills to the job of leadership, variously cooperating with, pressuring, or bypassing altogether the legislative branch. Abraham Lincoln, who is remembered best for his statesmanship and for his honesty, was perhaps the toughest and most wily politician of the nineteenth century. In an extraordinary example of a president's taking charge, he refrained from convening Congress into special session in 1861 in order to gain free reign to conduct the crucial opening months of the Civil War. Astutely mastering the power of patronage, he lined up crucial support for his own renomination. Federal office holders he had benefited were expected to contribute liberally to his campaign chest. And during key congressional votes Lincoln did what no president had ever done—he personally contacted members of Congress and persuaded them in his direction.

The master politician of the twentieth century was Franklin D. Roosevelt. Like Lincoln, Roosevelt demonstrated the great potential of the professional politician—the creative energy and power generated by fine-honed political skills. Elected president four times, FDR so strengthened the high office that he actually ended up weakening the historic ties between the presidency and the national party system. But his successful example insured that others would follow in his footsteps. And with the notable exception of Dwight D. Eisenhower, and to a lesser extent of Jimmy Carter and Ronald Reagan, ours has been an era in which professional politicians have held the presidency.

Of all of the presidents of the modern era, Lyndon B. Johnson was the quintessential legislative insider; no figure in U.S. history possessed more skill in legislative politics. And LBJ used all his enormous powers of persuasion to bear on the tasks of his presidency. His achievements in civil rights and his programs for a "Great Society" led to a landslide electoral victory in 1964. But then the Vietnam War began to spin out of control, and LBJ suffered a tragic reversal.

In many ways Lyndon Johnson represented the culmination of the purely professional politician. Presidents since, in the age of television, have been forced to place ever greater emphasis upon achieving public support and increasingly less on political bargaining and negotiation. But the Constitution forced politics upon the presidency by providing the chief executive too few exclusive powers and thus requiring persuasion to make up for the lack. Persuasion is the essence of presidential politics, an art form that requires a love of the game and a deep insight into people. The presidents who have made the greatest impact on history have done so as skillful partisan leaders. William Howard Taft failed at the presidency largely because he despised its requirements; he summed it up once in a private letter when he wrote, "politics . . . make me sick."

The most effective presidents didn't feel that way—they enjoyed the art of politics and wholeheartedly embraced it. John F. Kennedy may have summed it up best when he said, "No President . . . can escape politics. If he insists he is President of all the people, and should therefore offend none of them . . . he has dealt a death blow to the democratic process itself."

But Americans have always been ambivalent about government, and suspicious of people who make politics their life's work. When times are good and there is economic expansion, a professional politician may seem a very desirable thing—a person who can bob and weave his way through our complicated system of government. But when times are bad, when economic crisis threatens or war breaks out or governmental scandal erupts or civil unrest sweeps the nation, then the country demands a higher level of national leadership. It is then that Americans look to a president who is not just a politician, but who is above all a statesman.

It looked as if Franklin Roosevelt was merely following in his cousin's footsteps as he mounted the political ladder, but once in office he proved to be an astute and fearless player of the political game.

A pragmatic politician, like his hero John F. Kennedy, Bill Clinton has long been an expert at adapting to changing circumstances. He has also been a brilliant campaigner, and his 1996 reelection was by sizeable margins. In 1998 the politician would stumble, becoming the first president to be impeached since Andrew Johnson. But even at the depth of his personal troubles, he maintained a strong political standing with a majority of Americans.

MARTIN VAN BUREN

1837–1841

"The Little Magician"

All his life Martin Van Buren rankled under his public reputation. "If I had possessed a [tenth] of the skill in subtle management," he once wrote, "and of the spirit of intrigue . . . upon the strength of which . . . my opponents . . . gave me the title of 'magician,' I could have turned aside the opposition without much difficulty."

He was the first president born an American citizen, and he belonged to a generation with a new way of seeing things. A Dutch tavernkeeper's son from Kinderhook, New York, he rose rapidly in New York state politics, and between 1817 and 1821 he put together a political machine beyond anything that had ever existed before in the United States. He understood the importance of the press, of local committees, and of mass meetings, and he advocated strict party loyalty and organization. Unlike most politicians, who needed to be ever in the limelight, he preferred working quietly behind the scenes. "I make it a point never to write . . . the folk of Washington," he once noted, "unless I feel confidence that my doing so will lead to success. . . . I prefer to move step by step." As one contemporary put it, "he rowed to his object[s] with muffled oars."

Friendly and sociable, always impeccably dressed, the savvy, red-haired Dutchman also had a certain coldness. When his wife of eleven years died of tuberculosis in 1819, all he said was that he felt an "anxiety." And he could be ruthless in his political dealings, switching positions on key issues to further his career. "The imputation of non-commitalism . . . became . . . the parrot-note of my adversaries," he scoffed. "[They] regarded me as . . . never so much in my element or so happy as when employed in concocting and advancing political intrigues."

In 1821 he was elected to the U.S. Senate and got his chance to try out his political skills in Washington. In contrast to older leaders, who disapproved of partisan politics, Van Buren saw political parties as a positive good—a way to allow the public to vent political differences. Building ties to key congressmen and newspaper editors, he worked at rebuilding the old connections between New York and Virginia. "In the rough and tumble presidential canvass of 1824," he wrote, "I made my debut in the art and business of President-making."

In 1827, with a new presidential election approaching, Van Buren placed his powerful political machinery behind the candidacy of Andrew Jackson. And when Jackson was elected president the following year, Van

Most of Van Buren's many nicknames had a slightly pejorative tone. Not only was he "the little magician," he was "the red fox of Kinderhook" and "the flying Dutchman" and "Little Van." Here, shown already losing his red hair, is a young Martin Van Buren with the symbols of his legal profession—scroll, pen, and book.

Dressed immaculately as usual, Martin Van Buren poses for a daguerreotype portrait.

MARTIN VAN BUREN'S WHITE HOUSE

After eight years of putting up with a president from Tennessee, Washington society seemed ready for a dose of Eastern Yankee fashion. Martin Van Buren lacked a proper education and was insecure intellectually, but he was nothing short of sparkling on social occasions. A longtime widower with four grown sons, who soon moved in with him at the executive mansion, he at first was at a loss for someone to run the festivities. The former first lady Dolley Madison solved that. She introduced Martin's oldest son, Abraham, who was serving as presidential secretary, to her South Carolina cousin, Angelica Singleton. Before long they married, and Angelica was then given the title of official White House hostess. Her receptions were lavish, punctuated by a "living picture" she had seen young Queen Victoria perform in England. On a raised platform Angelica presented herself statue-like in a flowing white gown, a somewhat outlandish tableau that could not have done the president's already fragile reputation much good. Nor did the fact that copper bathtubs and a heating system were installed during the Van Buren years. In a three-day speech on the House floor, Congressman Charles Ogle charged the President with profligate spending of government money on presidential luxuries and painted the Little Magician as a dandy who used finger bowls to dip his "pretty tapering soft, white lily fingers, after dining on fricandaus de veau and omelet soufflé." It was a thundering Whig effort to miniaturize Van Buren and make him seem kingly and foppish beside the manly, log-cabin qualities of his opponent in the next election, William Henry Harrison. In truth, Van Buren lived simply and spent only about half as much on refurbishing the drafty palace as had his predecessor, Andrew Jackson.

Buren was named his secretary of state. It was a triumph for Van Buren's new approach to politics.

In late March 1828, Van Buren arrived in the nation's capital to meet the new president and begin their official relationship. "It was dark when I reached Washington," Van Buren later recalled. "A solitary lamp in the vestibule and a single candle in the president's office gave no promise of the cordiality with which I was, not withstanding, greeted by General Jackson on my visit to the White House. . . . This was our first meeting as political friends . . . and he received [me] with most affectionate eagerness. . . . From that night [on,] relations . . . were inviolably maintained between that noble old man and myself."

Van Buren became Andrew Jackson's chief political ally and alter ego —calming opposition, wooing the press, putting a good spin on Jackson's use of the spoils system. Watching him at work, one observer wrote, "He glides along as smoothly as oil and silently as a cat, managing so adroitly that nobody perceives it." Pudgy and balding next to the tall war hero of a president, he was the perfect balancing force to Jackson's impetuosity—calm and collected and always aware of political dangers. "You will say that I am on my old track—caution," he once wrote to the president. "But my dear sir, I have always thought, that considering our respective temperaments there was no way in which I could better render you that service which I owe you."

They began taking daily rides together, becoming so close that others grew jealous and began to criticize. "He sticks as close to the President as a blistering plaster," said one. "When Jackson dances, it is Van Buren who plays the fiddle," said another. Cartoonists portrayed him as ever lurking on the sidelines—as a sorcerer, a sly fox, a backward monkey, a satyr. And when he sided with Jackson against the rest of the cabinet over the snubbing of Peggy Eaton, the wife of the secretary of war, a major administrative crisis erupted.

To the cabinet members and their wives Peggy seemed a morally tainted woman; it was rumored that she had shared hotel rooms with her husband before they were married. But to Jackson and Van Buren she was a woman to be defended and the president turned it into a major test of wills. With rancor spreading throughout the administration, in the spring of 1831 Van Buren came up with a plan. He would step down from his post to allow the president to clean house. "[By] resigning [I hoped] to throw off the hounds," he wrote, "by whom personal character is hunted down."

Following Van Buren's advice, Jackson requested the resignations of all of his cabinet members, leading to the first cabinet purge in the history of the presidency. Then, in 1832, after a brief stint as minister to England, Van Buren was brought back as Andrew Jackson's new vice president. It was a nomination so controversial Jackson called for a national convention to ratify it, the first-ever national convention of the Democratic Party.

Once again Van Buren became Jackson's right-hand man, serving to smooth choppy waters left in Old Hickory's boiling wake. But on the central issue of Jackson's second term—his war on the U.S. Bank—even Van Buren could not modify the general's ferocious attack. "The bank . . . is trying to kill me," the old general told him. "But I will kill it!"

In 1836, with Andrew Jackson's endorsement, Van Buren was elected

Cool and analytical, and by his own account "a good listener," Van Buren always refused to make enemies needlessly and knew how to await his opportunities. He maintained his political sagacity into old age.

IN HIS OWN WORDS

Martin Van Buren in 1840.

What follows are excerpts from Van Buren's autobiography:

On his parents: My mother's maiden name was [Hoes] . . . and she was regarded by all who knew her as liberally endowed with the qualities and virtues that adorn the female character. My father was an unassuming amiable man who was never known to have an enemy. Utterly devoid of the spirit of accumulation, his property, originally moderate, was gradually reduced until he could but ill afford . . . the education of his children.

On parties: political parties are inseparable from free governments and are highly useful to the country. . . . Doubtless excesses frequently attend them and produce many evils, but not so many as are prevented by the maintenance of their organization and vigilance. The disposition to abuse power, so deeply planted in the human heart, can by no other means be more effectually checked; and it has always therefore struck me as more honorable and manly . . . to recognize their necessity, to give them the credit they deserve.

On his supposed immoderation: As far back . . . as Mr. Monroe's administration, a quantity of very extravagant French furniture was purchased for the Presidential mansion . . . and among the rest, a parcel of spoons, which were alleged to be of pure gold. These, with other portions of that furniture, were still at the White House in my time. I was charged with having purchased them, and the alleged extravagance made matter of accusation against me in the canvass.

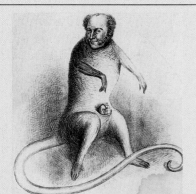

Van Buren's critics likened him to a variety of animals, including a fox, a monkey, and in this case an opossum. In his pouch are three choices to serve as his vice president, including, in the center, James K. Polk.

He was the perfect complement to Andrew Jackson, whom he served for eight years as chief adviser. Many saw him as the wily fox of the Democratic party. Jackson disagreed, calling him "one of the most frank men I ever knew, with talents combined with common sense." But then there was Thurlow Weed, the devoted Whig enemy of both Jackson and Van Buren, who referred to the Little Magician's "non-commitalism" —his habit of sitting on the fence on almost all controversial issues. Calling him "a phenomenon in political duplicity," Weed branded Van Buren as the antithesis of a man of the people, always out for himself. Another political enemy, John Quincy Adams, thought he possessed "an obsequiousness," a "sycophancy," and a "profound dissimulation." Adams concluded acidly, "The most disgusting part of his character" was his "fawning servility." Van Buren hated his reputation as a self-serving politico and worked hard to change his place in American history. In old age he wrote an autobiography, as well as a treatise on American politics, the first ever of its kind. Political parties, he argued, were a positive force for good in society. As democratic organizations they enabled the people to take a greater part in government. Again and again in his autobiography, he attempted to show himself as the political heir of both Jefferson and Jackson. But in fact he was something quite new on the American scene—the first modern, professional politician, and the father of American party politics.

the country's eighth president. In his inaugural address he promised a continuation of the good times of the Jackson presidency. But less than two weeks into his administration a major financial crisis erupted. As panic spread across the country, local banks began refusing to pay off their depositors. "The situation of the . . . banks . . . is a matter [for] the gravest consideration," Van Buren wrote. "You cannot form an adequate idea of the dreadful state of the money market."

Critics charged that it was Andrew Jackson's destruction of the U. S. Bank that had led to the crash, and that a new national bank was now needed to reverse it. But determined not to depart from his predecessor's key commitment, Van Buren presented a counterproposal—the establishment of an independent Treasury. In a striking act of presidential leadership, he united his critics around a new course of action.

Van Buren's idea for an independent Treasury would be the central accomplishment of his presidency, preparing the way for what would become the backbone of the U.S. financial system for the next seventy years. In the short-run, however, Van Buren prolonged the recession and deepened it into a significant depression.

In foreign affairs, Van Buren was largely successful, intervening in a border dispute between Maine and Canada that might easily have led to a war with England. Refusing to side with the inflamed Maine militia, Van Buren chose instead to exercise cautious diplomacy.

But if Van Buren's political instincts served him well in foreign affairs, they failed him when it came to humanitarian issues. His Indian removal policy, which he inherited from Andrew Jackson, resulted in the deaths of thousands of Cherokees. And when African slaves took control of the *Amistad,* a Spanish vessel that had sailed into American waters, Van Buren showed his customary coolness and ordered the slaves to be shipped to Spanish Cuba. A more compassionate Federal Court ordered that the slaves be freed and returned to their homeland.

As the election of 1840 approached, the economy took another sudden plunge downward. This time there was nothing Van Buren could do to restore public confidence. In his last months in office, he watched as a new political party, the Whigs, adopted the Democrats' methods to elect their own candidate. A pro–Van Buren newspaper wrote, "We have taught them how to conquer us."

He had pioneered the art of the professional politician, and for thirty-five years exercised it with unparalleled success. Now he quietly returned to Kinderhook, New York, where, true to form, he calmly and rationally accepted his own defeat. "I have at last got home," he wrote soon afterward. "My health has never been better, nor my spirits either. The result causes me no personal regrets." He would go on to make another bid for the presidency, as a third-party, free-soil candidate, losing to Zachary Taylor. Later, in old age he would write a groundbreaking book on politics. "There [was] . . . scarcely one day during which I [was] . . . wholly exempted from the disturbing effects of partisan agitation," he once reflected. But, he went on to say, if political parties contend "with fairness and moderation, the very discord which is thus produced may . . . be conducive to the public good."

A daguerreotype of the ex-President from the 1850s

A broken wet-plate glass negative offers up
this sober portrait of the fifteenth President.

JAMES BUCHANAN

1857–1861

"Avoiding Conflict"

From his mansion, known as Wheatland, near Lancaster, Pennsylvania, James Buchanan reigned as one of the most successful politicians of his age. His elegant home came to symbolize a man for whom appearances were all-important. Ever since his college days, when he was expelled for drunkenness and insolence, he determined that his public reputation would from then on be impeccable.

From the same generation as Martin Van Buren, Buchanan was learned and ambitious and possessed an extraordinary memory. He had been elected five times to the House of Representatives, had astutely read the times during the rise of Andrew Jackson, and had shifted political parties to become a Democrat. "I distinctly recollect [how a] Senator . . . urged me to change my party name," Buchanan later recalled. "In that event he said he would venture to predict that, should I live, I would become President of the United States."

In 1832 he was named Andrew Jackson's minister to Russia. Though to Buchanan his overseas ministry was tantamount to banishment, it turned out to be a political godsend, keeping him out of the country during a heated period in which his career in Congress might easily have been cut short. He served in the Senate during Van Buren's administration, and in 1844 he made his own bid for the presidency. When he lost the nomination to fellow Democrat James K. Polk, he reluctantly accepted the position of secretary of state. But he detested working for a man he considered his inferior.

"My life is that of a galley slave," he wrote. "I have to do the important drudging of the administration without the power of obtaining offices for my friends. . . . I have no power. I feel it deeply."

Critics noted his careful self-promotion and how he regularly shifted his position on controversial issues. He opposed tariffs one minute, free trade the next. He was for unregulated banking, and then against it. President Polk wrote, "All his acts and opinions seem to be with a view to his own advancement." But he was also a strong believer in maintaining ties between North and South. "Disunion," he once said, "is a word which ought not to be breathed amongst us even in a whisper."

By the 1850s, having survived four decades in politics, Buchanan was hailed as the only man who could hold the country together. And in 1857, under the shadow of a new capitol building still under construction, he was inaugurated the country's fifteenth president. "I have no other object of earthly ambition," he wrote privately, "than to leave my country in a peaceful and prosperous condition."

In younger days Buchanan was captured by a daguerreotype, which was later copied and heavily retouched. A brilliant professional politician, whose career spanned four decades, he would end up, in one contemporary's words, "a bewildered functionary."

Here, on East King Street in Lancaster, Pennsylvania, is the future President's law office, occupying the second floor of the building in the center.

His practically senile secretary of state, Lewis Cass, stands to Buchanan's right in this 1859 photograph of a president with members of his cabinet.

For all his success in building compromise and shaping consensus, Buchanan had no personal political machinery. He hated rallies, trips, and making speeches. He did not project well, and had no charisma in a crowd. He operated, instead, through letters, which he wrote in great number to the people who held the political power in the different counties of Pennsylvania. He loved small gatherings, was a great conversationalist, and often consumed several bottles of Madeira during an evening of talk, though never showing any effects. He was at ease with common folk, aristocrats, politicians—just about everybody as long as the group was small. In the four years he was president, Buchanan treated his cabinet like family; that small group of ministers was just about the right size for him. The highlight of the President's day was a two- or three-hour cabinet meeting, and a week seldom went by when he didn't issue dinner invitations to these substitutes for the family he never had. It was said of him, falsely, that his cabinet controlled him, actually made the decisions. Because the old-fashioned, Southern-inclined men he had chosen thought the same way he did, when everybody agreed on everything, it gave the appearance of a strong cabinet and a weak president. Actually Buchanan didn't like to make presidential decisions on his own. He liked the backing of the old boys he had selected and he liked presenting a united front. Buchanan hovered over his ministers like a mother hen. He was sure he could do

In contrast to Van Buren, Buchanan was tall, his large head topped by graying blond hair. He was a meticulous dresser; some even called him a dandy. And since one eye was nearsighted, he often tilted his head, which some thought an intimate gesture while others were certain it was a sign of deceit. He was a man of contradictions: a learned expositor of the Constitution, he was dignified and shrewd, but he was also stiff and self-seeking and almost utterly humorless. One friend said, "I do not think he ever uttered a genuine witticism in his life."

The only president never to marry, in the absence of a first lady he turned to Harriet Lane, an orphaned niece whom he had earlier adopted. "I feel that it is not good for a man to be alone," he wrote, "and should not be astonished to find myself married to some old maid who does not expect from me any romantic affection."

But in reality Buchanan had no intention to marry, ever since an engagement years earlier had ended in tragedy. Back in 1819, when his wealthy fiancée, Ann Coleman, heard rumors that he was interested in her only for her money, she had angrily broken off the engagement, and then suddenly and mysteriously died. Whether it was suicide was never determined, but Ann's father was convinced that Buchanan was responsible and had called him a murderer. In his grief, Buchanan had written him a plea. "You have lost a child, a dear, dear child. I have lost the only earthly object of my affection. . . . I have now one request to make; . . . deny me not. Afford me the melancholy pleasure of seeing her body before interment." The twenty-eight-year-old's letter was returned unopened. He was banned from the funeral and ostracized by his townspeople. For the rest of his life, Buchanan was overly cautious and fatalistic in almost everything he attempted.

But the last thing America needed in 1857 was timidity or fatalism. What it needed was a president who could boldly face the nation's problems and bridge the widening chasm between North and South. What it had instead was a Northern president deeply inclined toward Southern interests, including slavery. "My election so far as I was personally concerned, was a very small matter," Buchanan wrote. "But . . . the right of the people of a territory to decide the question of slavery for themselves, was a subject of vast importance. . . . The Constitution . . . expressly recognizes the right to hold slaves as property."

Even before his inauguration Buchanan had made a damaging mistake. When the case of the captured slave Dred Scott came to trial at the Supreme Court, Buchanan had secretly and improperly contacted Justice Robert Grier of Pennsylvania and convinced him to vote the pro-slavery line. It was the work of a cunning politician, but it would backfire. In the court's ruling against Scott, Chief Justice Roger B. Taney pronounced that blacks were not citizens of the United States and were "so far inferior, that they had no rights which the white man was bound to respect." Though Buchanan got what he wanted in the Dred Scott decision, his action virtually ensured that there would be civil war.

The Dred Scott decision was followed by a crisis in Kansas, where Buchanan's backing of a pro-slavery state government helped set off bloody fighting. Then, on October 17, 1859, abolitionist John Brown seized the federal arsenal at Harpers Ferry, Virginia, and called for a massive slave uprising. Although the revolt was put down by federal troops, John Brown—through his capture, trial and execution—ignited the land. "On the day of Brown's execution," Buchanan noted, "bells were tolled in many places [in the North] as if he were a martyr. . . . [This] inflamed the Southern mind with intense hostility against the North, and enabled the disunion agitators to prepare it for the final catastrophe." With political pressure mounting against him, all Buchanan wanted was to get out of office peacefully and leave the nation's problems to somebody else. But though he refused to run for another term in 1860, he also refused to support the leading candidate of his party, Stephen A. Douglas, thereby splitting the Democrats and guaranteeing a Lincoln victory in the fall. It was then that the disastrous final months of Buchanan's administration began.

"From . . . December 1860 . . . until March 4, 1861 . . . was by far the most important period of [my] administration," he wrote. "No public man was ever placed in a more trying and responsible position."

Following his lifelong pattern of avoiding conflict, Buchanan came out on both sides of the issue. Secession was unlawful, he said, but then he backed off. "The question fairly stated is: Has the Constitution delegated the power to coerce a State into submission which is attempting to withdraw from the [Union]? . . . After much serious reflection, I have arrived at the conclusion that no such power has been delegated."

As civil war marched steadily closer, it was charged that the president was deliberately harboring traitors within his government. His secretary of war, John B. Floyd, of Virginia, was accused of ordering shipments of arms from Northern arsenals to be sent south. "It is true that . . . Floyd made the attempt," Buchanan blasted back. "But I arrested the order . . . before a single gun was sent. . . . The charges against me . . . were abhorrent."

On December 20, 1860, South Carolina seceded from the Union. Buchanan threw up his hands and said there was nothing more he could do. From this point on, Congress ignored his leadership. His political power and influence were finished.

In the end he was vilified, considered a traitor by both North and South. His portrait, hanging in the Capitol rotunda, was taken down to prevent it from being defaced. "When I parted from the Executive Mansion," Buchanan later recalled, "I said to President Lincoln: 'if you are as happy, my dear sir, on entering this house as I am in leaving it and returning home, [then] you are the happiest man in this country!'"

On March 4, 1861, James Buchanan went home to his Pennsylvania plantation. "I . . . often warned my countrymen of the dangers which surrounded us," he wrote. "I shall carry to my grave the consciousness that I at least meant well for my country." History would label him as cowardly, weak, senile, and vacillating. In truth, he was a lonely, limited man who mistook politics for statesmanship.

their jobs better than they could. Fussy and critical, he was always sticking his nose into their business, yet he was a father figure to them as well, very much admired. Behind his back they called him The Squire. Buchanan's own family included his twenty-two nieces and nephews and his thirteen grandnieces and grandnephews, many of whom he helped support and some of whom lived in his Southern-style mansion outside of Lancaster. Of these the most beloved was Harriet Lane, whose guardianship he had assumed after she had been orphaned at seven. Buchanan saw to it that Harriet was watched over and cared for as she grew up in Lancaster. Good-natured and filled with an exuberant spirit, she grew into an exciting young lady who could wheedle anything out of her old uncle, even an extended trip to London when he was the U.S. ambassador to Great Britain. There, as the hit of Queen Victoria's court, she learned the ways of the world. During Buchanan's bachelor presidency, which followed, Harriet was more than willing to turn her life over to him and act as first lady, planning his entertainments and presiding over his table. In return, she was always the center of attention, with her bright laugh, low-cut dresses, and hoop skirts. Although she didn't marry until later, she was for those four years a leading belle of Washington, and a new song was even written in her honor, "Listen to the Mocking Bird," to which she liked to waltz, even though her uncle found dancing in the White House improper.

One of the most capable hostesses in White House history, Harriet Lane was also well informed on political issues.

James Buchanan on slavery:

I believe it to be a great political and a great moral evil. I thank God, my lot has been cast in a state where it does not exist. But . . . I know it is an evil at present without a remedy . . . one of those moral evils from which it is impossible for us to escape without the introduction of evils infinitely greater.

The Constitution . . . expressly recognizes the right to hold slaves as property in states where slavery exists. This, then, is not a question of general morality, affecting the consciences of men, but it is a question of constitutional law. . . . The southern states have rights guaranteed to them, and these rights I determined to maintain, come weal, come woe.

The abolitionists . . . scattered throughout the slave holding states pamphlets, newspapers and pictorial representations . . . calculated . . . to excite the wild and brutal passions of the slaves to cut the throats of their masters.

These are the injurious effects produced by the Abolitionists upon the slave himself. Whilst, on the one hand, they render his condition miserable by presenting to his mind vague notions of freedom never to be realized, on the other, they make it doubly miserable by compelling the master to be severe, in order to prevent any attempts at insurrection.

There are many, I fear very many, in the Northern States who place their consciences above the Constitution of the country, and who would, as jurors, rescue a fugitive slave from servitude against the clearest testimony, thinking, at the time, they were doing God's service.

How easy would it be for the American people to settle the slavery question forever. . . . All that is necessary to accomplish the object, and all for which the slave States have ever contended, is to be let alone.

As many contemporaries noticed, Buchanan's head often inclined to one side, a posture made more conspicuous by a nervous twitch or jerking he could not control. His delicate, fair skin looked well scrubbed, as if he'd just come out of a bath. A high, white stock which encased his neck and jowls became his hallmark.

Buchanan had been sworn into office in the shadow of the partially completed new dome of the Capitol. On his last day in office, the scaffolding still showed where the mighty crown would eventually rise.

ABRAHAM LINCOLN

1861–1865

Politics with a Purpose

If James Buchanan represented the professional politician unable to cope with great events, his successor came to stand for the exact opposite. Yet for twenty-six years Abraham Lincoln was as concerned as Buchanan was with his own political advancement. "No man knows, when that presidential grub gets to gnawing at him," he once admitted, "just how deep it will get until he has tried it."

Brought up in rural Indiana, Lincoln was required by his father to perform what he called "the roughest work a young man could be made to do." With a strong distaste for manual labor, he launched out on his own and began attracting attention in Illinois. He was friendly, he was honest, and he was a beguiling storyteller. And he soon began to take an interest in local politics. "Every man is said to have his own peculiar ambition," he wrote in his first political address. "I have no other so great as that of being truly esteemed by my fellow men, by rendering myself worthy of their esteem."

The 1830s and '40s saw Lincoln's rapid ascent in Illinois politics. Three times elected to the state legislature, he became a lawyer, a Whig operative, and a recognized expert at forming coalitions. Like Van Buren, he learned how to keep secrets, how to trade favors, how to use the press to his advantage. And he cultivated his relationship with the party hierarchy.

"I am for the regular nominee in all cases," he once said. "The man who is of neither party is not, and cannot be, of any consequence."

Those who knew him best came to speak of his ruthlessness. One colleague said, "He handled men remotely," like "pieces on a chessboard." But he also became known for his humor and his frankness.

In February 1860, Lincoln made an adroit maneuver while on a speaking trip to New York City. Just before delivering his address at the Cooper Union, he visited Mathew Brady's photographic gallery and had his picture taken. Brady made a print of the three-quarter-length figure, did some artful retouching, especially softening Lincoln's face, then made a copy negative, which was used to produce thousands of cartes de visite, one of which is shown above. The picture also found its way into influential publications such as *Harper's Weekly,* which ran the spread at left of "the prominent candidates" just before the Republican convention. Later, Lincoln liked to attribute his victory to a combination of the speech and the photograph.

This photograph of Lincoln was taken in Springfield, Illinois, soon after the 1860 Republican convention. Though he would be billed to the public as "Honest Abe" and "the rail splitter," he was in fact a cagey, prosperous lawyer who had long been on retainer with the Illinois Central Railroad.

Lincoln liked to look windswept. Here, in this 1857 picture by Alexander Hesler, the photographer tried to tame his hair but the politician ran his fingers through it to keep it rumpled. "This coarse, rough hair of mine was in a particularly bad tousle at the time," he smiled, "and the picture presented me in all its fright."

Lincoln rarely spoke of his early years, but when he did, he chose his words carefully.

My grandfather's [name] was Abraham,—same of my own. . . . [He] was killed by the Indians. . . . Owing to my father being left an orphan at the age of six years, in poverty and in a new country, he became a wholly uneducated man.

My father . . . removed from Kentucky to . . . Indiana, in my eighth year. We reached our new home about the time the state came into the Union. It was a wild region, with many bears and other wild animals still in the woods. There I grew up.

There were some schools, so called; but no qualification was ever required of the teacher. . . . There was absolutely nothing to excite ambition for education. . . . Still somehow, I could read.

Away back in my childhood . . . I got hold of a small book . . . , "Weem's Life of Washington." I remember all the accounts there given of the battlefields and struggles for the liberties of the country. . . . I recollect thinking then, boy even though I was, that there must have been something more than common that those men struggled for.

As a junior congressman in largely Democratic Washington, Lincoln found he had little influence. And when he publicly opposed President Polk's war against Mexico, he became unpopular back home. After a single term of office, he returned to Illinois deeply discouraged.

"From 1849 to 1854," he later related, "[I] practiced law more assiduously than ever before. . . . I was losing interest in politics, when the repeal of the Missouri Compromise aroused me again."

The event became the turning point in Lincoln's life. The Missouri Compromise of 1820 had drawn a line to keep slavery exclusively in the South. Its repeal meant slavery could now spread into Kansas and Nebraska and throughout the West. "It amounts to this," Lincoln responded, "if any one man chooses to enslave another, no third man shall be allowed to object." Lincoln's speeches began to take on an increasing urgency. "This covert zeal for the spread of slavery I cannot but hate," he said in October 1854. "I hate it because of the monstrous injustice of slavery itself."

The cause reignited Lincoln's political career. In 1856, he committed himself to the newly formed Republican party. And in a race for the Senate two years later, he entered a series of debates with Illinois Democrat Stephen A. Douglas. Though Lincoln subtly tailored his message to the politics of his audience, he steadfastly stuck to his basic principles. And while he lost the contest to Douglas, he gained a national following. "The Republican principle—the unalterable principle, never to be lost sight of—is that slavery is wrong," he said in 1859.

With Lincoln emerging as one of the Republican Party's strongest men, the presidency now began to loom as a possibility. "I will be entirely frank," he wrote to a friend. "The taste *is* in my mouth a little."

Shrewdly he began to position himself for an assault on the high office. He arranged for his debates with Douglas to be published; they instantly became a national best-seller. And he traveled to New York to show Easterners firsthand his oratory and his fire.

In March 1860 he wrote a friend about his candidacy. "My name is new in the field; and I suppose I am not the first choice of a very great many. Our policy, then, is to give no offense to others—leave them in a mood to come to us, if they shall be compelled to give up their first love."

Lincoln's managers went to work repackaging their candidate. Instead of showing him as the prosperous, politically tough, at times corporate lawyer he was, he became "Abe Lincoln the rail splitter," the humble "man of the people." And in May 1860, following intense, behind-the-scenes politicking, Lincoln was chosen as the Republican Party's candidate for president. In November, when Lincoln won the election, Horace Greeley proclaimed, "Never 'til now has there been a time when the slave holders have not dictated the choice of a president." Lincoln admitted to a friend, "I then felt as I never had before, the responsibility that was upon me."

Despite his hatred of the institution of slavery, Lincoln was prepared to accept it where it already existed. In his inaugural address he pled with Southerners to remain in the Union. But he was not prepared to bargain with secessionists. Fortifying federal forts in the South, he stood by firmly until Confederates fired the first shots of war.

Lincoln called the Civil War "the great event." "All knew that slavery was somehow the cause," he said. But unlike more radical members of his party, who urged him to declare immediate emancipation for slaves, Lincoln's political instincts told him to bide his time. Free the slaves too pre-

Lincoln called it his "little brown cottage." He bought it in 1844 for the sizeable amount of $1,500, and here his four children were born. Now, in 1860, the "cottage" was seeing its most glorious day, as Springfield's first citizen reviewed the Republican parade, so long it took eight hours to pass the Lincoln home on its way to the fairgrounds. Lincoln had come to Springfield a humble, reticent nobody. Now he was getting ready to leave as a towering political force, and in the doorway of his home he was exactly that without even trying—eclipsing, in his white duster, each and every one of his adoring fellow citizens.

Lincoln was particularly proud of his height—six feet four inches in his stocking feet—and he made political hay of it whenever he could, either through humor, or through challenges to other tall men to measure against him, or by looming over those he debated or disagreed with.

The earliest known likeness of Lincoln was taken in 1846.

By the time Lincoln was forty-five, his face had lost its roundness.

He could look handsome and bland, as this ambrotype image shows.

He could also look horsy and ruthless, as he did here in 1860.

Beardless, his face could spark with intensity.

With whiskers, in 1861, the same face seems muted.

In need of a haircut, Lincoln has just arrived in Washington.

By late 1863, two and a half years of war have aged him.

Lincoln had a drooping eye that tended to make him look tired.

In this 1864 profile Lincoln still looks vigorous.

It may be that Lincoln had his hair cut short to prepare for a life mask.

In his last year of life, at fifty-six, Lincoln looked like an old man.

Lincoln was caught by at least thirty-one different camera operators on at least sixty-one separate occasions, making him the first heavily photographed president in American history. All the pictures before he was elected show him clean-shaven; in all the pictures after his election he wears a beard. Most of the time he looks stern or melancholy, not letting his face sparkle as it so often did. Friends said no photograph ever really captured him, that the complex movement of his facial muscles was so much a part of his looks that to freeze them only diminished him.

cipitously, he believed, and the border states would join the Confederacy. Delay too long, however, and a great opportunity would be lost.

"When the rebel army was at Frederick," he said in the late summer of 1862, "I determined, as soon as it should be driven out of Maryland, to issue a proclamation of emancipation. . . . I said nothing to anyone; but I made a promise to myself and . . . to my Maker."

In a political move designed to prepare public opinion and minimize disaffection, in August Lincoln outlined his position to the country. "My paramount object in this struggle is to save the Union, and is not either to save or destroy slavery. If I could save the Union without freeing any slave I would do it, and if I could save it by freeing all the slaves I would do it. . . . What I do about slavery, and the colored race, I do because I believe it helps save the Union."

He had chosen these words with immense care. He did not say his "sole object" was to save the Union, he said it was his "paramount object." And he had announced not only that freeing the slaves was within his power as president, but that if he decided to do so it would be unpatriotic to resist. In striking contrast to James Buchanan, Lincoln didn't avoid political conflict, he confronted it. And in doing so, he steered the nation toward a high moral purpose.

"Fellow citizens," he said in December, after issuing the preliminary Emancipation Proclamation. "We cannot escape history. . . . The fiery trial through which we pass, will light us down, in honor or dishonor, to the latest generation. . . . In giving freedom to the slave, we assure freedom to the free." And though Lincoln's proclamation applied to slaves only within the Confederacy, it changed the moral and military course of the war.

Throughout the war, Lincoln exercised political adroitness. He promised lucrative war contracts and government appointments in return for support and key votes. At times such patronage verged on out-and-out bribery. The editor of the *New York Herald* was offered the ministry to France in return for his paper's political support. "[My administration] distributed to its party friends as nearly all the patronage any administration ever did," Lincoln himself admitted.

But as time went on, Lincoln's actions became increasingly statesmanlike. His public addresses at Gettysburg and in Washington became masterpieces of healing and compassion. His sense of timing was extraordinary; he could somehow see society whole, and could distance himself enough from events to capture their meaning and then try to put that meaning into words at the right time to affect his national audience. His imagination bloomed. Then, when the Civil War neared its end, Lincoln extended his hand to the conquered South. "I hope there will be no persecution, no bloody work after the war is over," he said to his cabinet members. "Let them have their horses to plow with and, if you like, their guns to shoot crows with." "I want no one punished." "Blood cannot restore blood, and government should not act for revenge."

Unwilling to be inflexibly committed to any single plan of reconstruction, Lincoln steered his party on the course he had set. His presidency became a model for the higher possibilities of politics. And throughout it all he maintained an extraordinary humility. Once, before the end, Lincoln turned to his old friend Leonard Swett and said, "I may not have made as great a president as some other men, but I believe I have kept . . . discordant elements together as well as anyone could."

Out-of-doors Lincoln liked to add to the effect of his height by wearing a high, stovepipe hat. He loved his rare opportunities to get away from Washington and from the constant intrigues of his cabinet members, who sometimes tried to gang up on him.

In the spring of 1861, to help protect the city of Washington from a Confederate attack, Lincoln's newly named minister to Russia, Cassius M. Clay, put together a company of volunteers made up of his friends and associates. Seen here shouldering arms on the south side of the White House, the "Clay Battalion" helped guard the city until troops finally arrived from the north.

Lincoln devoured newspapers, often going out in the street in front of the White House to hail newsboys.

Some musings of a president:

I hold myself without mock modesty the humblest of all individuals that have ever been elevated to the Presidency.

I happen temporarily to occupy this big White House. I am a living witness that any one of your children may look to come here as my father's child has.

For the time being, [I] am at the head of a nation which is in great peril.

The last ray of hope for preserving the Union peaceably, expired at the assault upon Fort Sumter.

No choice was left but to call out the war power of the government; and so to resist force . . . by force.

It is very strange that I, a boy brought up in the woods, and seeing as it were but little of the world, should be drifted into the very apex of this great event.

I have thought a great deal about the relation of the war to slavery.

If slavery is not wrong, nothing is wrong. I cannot remember when I did not so think, and feel. And yet I never understood that the Presidency conferred upon me an unrestricted right to act officially upon this judgment and feeling.

I was, in my best judgment, driven to the alternative of either surrendering the Union, and "with it" the Constitution, or of laying hands upon the colored element.

The policy of emancipation, and of employing black soldiers gave to the future a new aspect. . . . In my judgment they have aided and will further aid, this cause for which they were intended.

There have been men who have proposed to me to return to slavery the black warriors . . . to conciliate the South. I should be damned in time in eternity for so doing. The world shall know that I will keep my faith to my friends & enemies, come what will.

Whenever [I] hear any one arguing for slavery, I feel a strong impulse to see it tried on him personally.

I expect to maintain this contest until successful, or till I die, or am conquered, or my term expires, or Congress or the country forsakes me.

I claim not to have controlled events, but confess plainly that events have controlled me.

It is not merely for to-day, but for all time to come that we should perpetuate for our children's children this great and free government, which we have enjoyed all our lives. I beg you to remember this.

The Gettysburg Address was conceived in such spiritual words no one could mistake it for mere politics. Here, Lincoln is surrounded by dignitaries and marshals on the platform that has been erected in the Gettysburg cemetery. The ceremonies are about to get under way. When it finally came time for the President to speak, what he said was so short people were just beginning to listen when it was over. Lincoln's 271 words were clocked at two minutes and fifteen seconds.

Mary Todd Lincoln

Left to Lincoln, the White House was not about to change much; he cared little for entertaining and had no eye for finery. But Mary Lincoln caught the decorating bug. Although she had run a thrifty house in Springfield, once in the White House, with her best friend in the world suddenly sealed off from her by his work and cares, Mary began spending. From G. S. Humphrey & Co. in New York came 320 yards of fancy matting. From Wm. H. Carryl & Bro. in Philadelphia came $7,500 worth of draperies and furniture. Rooms were papered. The East Room was newly carpeted in green velvet. Portraits and mirrors and chandeliers were cleaned and repaired. A. P. Zimandy of Washington provided glassware to the tune of $1,500. E. V. Haughwout & Co. billed $3,195 for a porcelain dining service with the Arms of the United States on each of the 190 pieces. Pretty soon Mary Lincoln's refurbishing added up to $26,000, $6,000 more than Congress had allotted. When Lincoln was asked to approve a request for additional funds, the overworked President finally took notice. "It can never have my approval," he exploded. "It would stink in the nostrils of the American people to have it said that the President . . . had approved a bill overrunning an appropriation of $20,000 for *flub dubs* for this damned old house, when the soldiers cannot have blankets!"

These two photographs are the only ones of Lincoln in his White House office. In the process of helping the artist Francis B. Carpenter get material to paint a giant portrait of the reading of the Emancipation Proclamation to the cabinet, the President is showing Brady's camera operator, Anthony Berger, how he looks sitting, then standing.

MUSIC TO HIS EARS

Lincoln couldn't carry a tune, yet he loved music of all sorts, from high opera arias to low-down banjo tunes, from *La Traviata* to *Blue Tail Fly*. He loved theater, too, especially the plays of Shakespeare—the haunting poetry was music to his ears. In Washington he watched Shakespeare performed by the foremost dramatic actors of the American stage, even critiquing their delivery, for he was a kind of actor himself—a born story-teller, a devastating mimic, a laugh-getter in any gathering, and with his prodigious memory he knew most of the great Shakespearean soliloquies by heart and would reel them off with professional skill.

Touring artists had first been welcomed into the White House in the 1840s, under Presidents Tyler, Polk, and Taylor. Under Lincoln, taste in entertainment broad-ened. He had been in the Executive Mansion less than a month when the first of many entertainers performed for him— an American Indian named Larooqua whose "melliflous voice" gained her praise as the "aboriginal Jenny Lind." A few months later a young local soprano named Meda Blanchard became the first opera singer ever to entertain in the White House.

Lincoln's favorite group of singers was the Hutchinson family. They had greatly helped his election efforts with their hearty campaign songs through the West. On January 7, 1862, their voices joined to fairly rock the White House.

Even had he wanted to, Lincoln could not have escaped the music of the times. The skies resounded with "Yes, we'll rally round the flag, boys, we'll rally round again," "Yankee Doodle," "The Battle Hymn of the Republic," and "Dixie," which Lincoln called for as the war ended, saying the Union had captured it back. And how could he escape from "Hail to the Chief," the royal strains of which he heard on the Capitol steps on March 4, 1861, at his first oath of office, and then, finally, after innumerable renditions in between, one last time, on April 14, 1865, as he entered Ford's Theatre to a standing ovation.

At the end, Lincoln is beyond politics; he sits regally, alone, knowing the war is all but over. Six days after General Lee's surrender to Ulysses S. Grant, Lincoln would be dead, the first president to be assassinated. He himself seemed to understand the massive public grief that would be unleashed. "The death of . . . [a] president may not be without its use," he had written years earlier, "in remind-ing us, that we, too, must die. Death . . . is the same with the high as with the low; but . . . we are not so much roused . . . by the fall of many undistinguished, as that of one . . . well-known name. By the latter, we are forced to muse, and ponder."

This rare glimpse of the Lincoln East Room shows no signs of the military use to which the room was placed in 1861. For weeks prior to the fortification of the capital city, soldiers actually slept here on the carpeted floor. Lincoln's secretary, John Nicolay, wrote to his fiancée in April, "The White House is turned into a barrack."

LYNDON B. JOHNSON

1963–1969

The Art of Political Bluster

Acentury has passed," Lyndon Johnson once said boldly, "since . . . Abraham Lincoln . . . signed the Emancipation Proclamation. . . . And yet the negro is not equal. . . . The time of justice has now come." It was the opening salvo of a personal war fought by one of the most ambitious professional politicians in the history of the nation.

Lyndon Baines Johnson was raised near Austin, Texas, in the years before the Great Depression. From early on he developed a deep and genuine compassion for the poor and the oppressed. "My first job after college," he later recalled as president, "was as a teacher in Cotulla, Texas, in a small Mexican-American school. . . . My students were poor and they often came to class without breakfast and hungry. And they knew even in their youth the pain of prejudice. . . . I never thought then, in 1928 . . . that I might have the chance to help the sons and daughters of those students and to help people like them all over this country. But now I do have that chance. And . . . I mean to use it."

Johnson could identify with the disenfranchised of society, for all his life he saw himself as an underdog, a poor boy who would have to do big things in order to prove himself. And to compensate for a deep sense of insecurity, he developed a burning need to excel. In 1934, he married Claudia Alta Taylor. Nicknamed "Lady Bird," she became Johnson's closest adviser and his financial supporter when he entered politics.

As a congressional aide and then a congressman himself, Johnson put in twelve hours a day, seven days a week, demanding the same effort from his entire staff. He soon became recognized as a political genius. After a failed run for the Senate in 1941, he turned his 1948 Senate campaign into the most extraordinary political event in Texas history. Using the methods of large traveling circuses, he sent advance men, musicians, and entertainers to lure people to his rallies. And his own dramatic arrival by helicopter, a rare sight in those days, ensured plenty of local media coverage. When he won the election by just eighty-seven votes, some probably obtained by illegal ballot-box stuffing, his opponents derided him as "Landslide Lyndon."

LBJ was already becoming larger than life. He had a huge, unappeasable hunger to be loved, and a huge desire to manipulate everybody. And in the Senate, his career skyrocketed. In 1951 he became majority whip, and soon after, minority leader. In 1955, the forty-six-year-old Texan became the youngest majority leader in the Senate's history.

Lyndon Johnson's twentieth-century hero was FDR, but it was Lincoln whom he idolized from the century before.

During his presidency, political cartoons often depicted Johnson with sly, squinting eyes; immobile features; thick, oversize ears; and a touch of evil to his mouth. Actually his face was strong and mobile, exuding energy and confidence.

During his 1941 campaign for Congress, LBJ talks to a wagonload of his kind of folks.

Lyndon with his teddy bear in 1909

Fledgling cowboy in 1915

Star of his 1928 college debating team

In 1937 with his hero FDR

Campaigning in 1941

LBJ and Claudia Taylor Johnson on their honeymoon in Mexico, November 1934

But that same year, just as Johnson was being widely touted as the next president, he suffered a massive heart attack. For the first time in his life this chain-smoking, food-shoveling workaholic was forced to slow down. Unable to regain his political momentum fully, Johnson lost his 1960 bid for the presidency to John F. Kennedy. It was then, for the first time in his life, that Lyndon Johnson lowered his political sights and agreed to serve as Kennedy's vice presidential running mate. In November they won a narrow victory in the national elections. "I wouldn't contend that any Vice President is ever fully informed of what the President is doing and thinking," LBJ later asserted. "I do believe that a Vice President . . . must be ready to step in and take over if something should ever happen to the President."

On November 22, 1963, Johnson traveled with the President to Texas on a political visit. Following in a car behind the Lincoln convertible in which the Kennedys rode, Johnson heard clearly the rifle shots that took the President's life. Just hours later, at 2:30 P.M., aboard Air Force One, with Jacqueline Kennedy by his side, LBJ took the oath of office. Five days later he addressed Congress as president. "All I have I would have gladly given not to be standing here today," he said. "The greatest leader of our time has been struck down by the foulest deed of our time. . . . An assassin's bullet has thrust upon me the awesome burden of the presidency." And then Johnson gave a simple pledge. "On the 20th day of January, in 1961, John F. Kennedy told his countrymen . . . 'let us begin.' Today, in this moment of new resolve, I would say to all my fellow Americans, 'let us continue.'"

But Lyndon Johnson was not content to simply continue what Kennedy had begun. Here, finally, was his chance to put all his ideals into action. In his State of the Union address to Congress seven weeks later, he did what no other president has ever done—he declared an "unconditional war on poverty" and pledged to end the long legacy of American racism. "This is not merely an economic issue," he said, "or a social, political, or international issue. It is a moral issue." He called his vision of America's future "The Great Society."

When Johnson became president in his own right in 1964, his ambitions rose with the opportunity he saw. Setting out to rid his home country, the South, of segregation, he wanted, as well, to literally end poverty in America. And he wanted to pass legislation at every opportunity. The endeavors exposed a well of idealism deep inside him. They also exposed a lack of restraint. No presidential leverage went unexploited. Johnson doled out public works projects, prized appointments, and photo opportunities to those who cooperated, and withheld them from those who did not. His tactics reinforced his image as the quintessential arm twister.

"I was on the phone with individual Senators way into the night, day and day after day," LBJ acknowledged. "A president is a political leader and

Sweet-talking a supporter in 1948

Making a point as minority leader in 1954

John Kennedy's vice presidential choice

Cross-country campaigning in 1960

Sworn in as president on Air Force One in 1963

he can never be above politics." If nothing else worked, Johnson knew how to shame a person into compliance, as he did when powerful Senator Richard Russell tried to avoid serving on the Warren Commission. "Don't tell me what you can do and what you can't," Johnson barked at Russell on the other end of a telephone, "because I can't arrest you, and I'm not going to put the FBI on you, but you're goddamn sure going to serve, I'll tell you that."

His political powers might well have gained Lyndon Johnson recognition as one of the country's most effective presidents ever, if it had not been for Vietnam. As the conflict in Southeast Asia escalated into an undeclared war, Johnson was determined not to let it divert Congressional attention away from his domestic legislation. So he escalated the war secretly, providing Congress with overly optimistic military reports in an effort to get complete support. As the death toll mounted to more than 500 American casualties each week, the country grew bitterly divided.

In Vietnam LBJ was faced with Ho Chi Minh, an opponent he couldn't master by his usual tactics of cajolery, persuasion, or intimidation. Faced by a war the President was unable to bring to a satisfying end, the people found their sentiments changing. They wanted a commander-in-chief and a man of temperate judgment rather than a politician. But Johnson couldn't change his style. There was not in Lyndon Johnson a saving moderation.

After the Democrats suffered a reversal in the 1966 mid-term elections, Johnson found his programs increasingly voted down in Congress. And the legislative skills by which he had forged strong coalitions in the past no longer seemed to work for him. On March 31, 1968, he abruptly pulled his name out of the upcoming presidential primaries. "I shall not seek, and I will not accept, the nomination of my party for another term of office as your President."

All his life Lyndon Johnson used politics to do big things. In civil rights, in education, in poverty programs, and in conservation, he changed the face of American society. But in the end, politics failed him, exposing an insecure side of Johnson's character—a side that he'd successfully covered up with political bluster all his professional life.

"Sometimes a President is prevented from achieving what he wants . . . by circumstances completely beyond his control," he said not long afterward. "The crucible of the White House brings out the best and the worst in men. . . . [But] a President is not elected to do what's wrong. His biggest problem is trying to find out what's right and doing it. . . . And that's a very big question mark in this very complicated world."

Finally president in his own right (above), Johnson would intensify his efforts to bring about the Great Society. He had already overcome the Southern filibuster to pass the Civil Rights Act of 1964. Now he would apply all his skills as a legislative tactician to help pass the Voting Rights Act of 1965. Among Johnson's many creations were VISTA, Head Start, the Job Corps, and Medicare.

Signing a new law was one of LBJ's most treasured rituals. He used special pens and handed them out afterward to those who he felt were the most deserving. Sometimes the signings took place in the Oval Office, sometimes the East Room, but often a new law merited a more symbolic delivery room. When he signed the 1965 Immigration Act, it took place beside the Statue of Liberty.

President Johnson couldn't bear not to be connected to the world. He walked around with a transistor radio held to his ear and constantly monitored the three-screen console in the Oval Office (right), or the duplicate setup in his bedroom. Also in his office stood AP, UP, and Reuters ticker tapes. "I think it is fair to say," Johnson declared, "that I was getting a wider variety of information . . . on a broader range of subjects than any man in or out of government."

As part of his bullying tactics Johnson made use of the White House swimming pool. In the midst of a meeting he might suddenly decide to take a swim, stalk to the pool, strip off his clothes, and dive in naked. Then he would badger his associates until they were embarrassed into following suit. He took special delight in mortifying loyal Kennedy staffers. His own men, like Jack Valenti (left), were hardened to LBJ's behavior.

Almost anything could remind LBJ of a story, and he told them in great detail, with plenty of hand-show and mimicry. It made little difference whether listeners sometimes recognized the facts of the stories to be incorrect; each and every member of his audience was expected to heed his every word, no matter how tall the story or how many times the President had told it before.

For LBJ, work never ceased. His office could
be anywhere—even his bedroom.

LBJ on the presidency:

I'm sure that the Presidents who stand out in our history and in our memory are those who led the nation through times of great trial and challenge: . . . Washington, Jackson, Lincoln, Wilson, Roosevelt, Truman. On the other hand, these very same Presidents would not be regarded now as great if their reactions and their responses had been weak, or if they had failed to achieve some of their major goals or if they had run away from the challenges. . . . Greatness is an elusive thing and the judgment of history is sometimes different from that that is made when a President's in office or just after he leaves office. Wilson died a broken and disappointed man because he failed to win approval of the League. Yet history has judged that he was right in that fight and the willful men of the Senate who opposed him were wrong. . . . There are a great many misconceptions about the Presidency. . . . Some people think the President is a man who welcomes visitors to our country, who signs the laws that Congress sends him, who occasionally makes a speech about one of our problems, a kind of a father or figurehead. Others see him as a manipulator or as an arm twister who is interested in power and how to use it. Others see him as a solitary figure surrounded by yes men, insulated from all [counselors], isolated from the real world. But very few people have any idea of the long and tedious and grinding work that goes into every presidential day. . . . I doubt that there was a single day of the Presidency, Sundays included, that I didn't give two or three hours to just solitary reading. There was hardly a night that I was President that I didn't read two or three hours. Even if it were a State dinner or dancing . . . when I retired for the evening, I would have two hours of night reading ahead of me. . . . No President in history has been able to do all the things that he or the people hoped he could accomplish at the time of election. But that doesn't mean that the job is impossible and that doesn't mean it's doomed. It is doable.

Johnson dominated. He got up so close, especially to members of his staff, it was uncomfortable. Bodies actually touched. Breath intermingled. Who could stand up to him, his six feet four inches bent forward like a weapon, his laughter so intimate that the staffer would never forget it and from that moment on would always feel he owed the President something.

The great furrowed face could strike terror in the heart of an enemy but it also could convey tenderness and concern to a friend.

IN HIS OWN WORDS

Just seven weeks after the death of John F. Kennedy, Johnson delivered a State of the Union address to Congress, in which he revealed goals going far beyond those of any previous president:

Unfortunately, many Americans live on the outskirts of hope—some because of their poverty, and some because of their color, and all too many because of both. Our task is to help replace their despair with opportunity. This administration today, here and now, declares unconditional war on poverty in America.

Fourteen months later, in the spring of 1965, LBJ spoke movingly to Congress and the nation:

This is the richest, most powerful country which ever occupied this globe. The might of past empires is little compared to our[s]. But I do not want to be the President who built empires, or sought grandeur, or extended dominion. I want to be the President who educated young children . . . who helped to feed the hungry . . . who helped the poor to find their own way and who protected the right of every citizen to vote in every election.

On the night of March 31, 1968, Lyndon Johnson stunned the country with another address:

This country's ultimate strength lies in the unity of our people. There is division in the American house now. There is divisiveness among us all tonight. And holding the trust that is mine, as President of all the people, I cannot disregard the peril to the progress of the American people and the hope and prospect of peace for all people. . . . With America's sons in the fields far away, with America's future under challenge right here at home. . . . I do not believe that I should devote an hour or a day of my time to any personal partisan causes. . . . Accordingly, I shall not seek, and will not accept, the nomination of my party for another term as your President.

She had been called Lady Bird ever since she was a child, but still she was his Lady Bird. Loving companion and constant adviser throughout LBJ's long career, here she does some final editing on the speech in which her husband renounced his bid for reelection. Before saying those final, fateful words, he glanced at her, looking, possibly, for a signal to turn back. It did not come.

AN INDEPENDENT CAST OF MIND

CHAPTER FOUR

Is independence of mind an admirable trait for a president or can
extreme self-reliance work against the office?

Rutherford B. Hayes

Jimmy Carter

The presidency as it was first created was meant to stand above all political factions and serve in the general public interest, an ideal first incarnated in George Washington. Independent-minded yet conciliatory, both a leader and a listener, Washington successfully held the young nation together. "You cannot shield yourselves too much against the jealousies . . . which spring from [faction]," he warned his fellow Americans. "They tend to render alien to each other those who ought to be bound together by fraternal affection."

But disagreements between Washington's secretary of the treasury, Alexander Hamilton, and his secretary of state, Thomas Jefferson, eventually led to a political rupture, exactly what Washington had warned against. To be politically successful by the late 1790s meant to be thoroughly aligned with one or the other of two national "parties," the Federalists or the Democratic-Republicans.

John Adams was one of those few who was never so aligned. Though

Like his father, John Quincy Adams stubbornly contended he was a free man with obligations to nobody.

Southerner Andrew Johnson tried to remain independent by remaining loyal to the North but ended up reviled by everyone.

nominally a Federalist, he despised Alexander Hamilton, whom he saw as personally ambitious and as biased toward the wealthy. But he also deeply distrusted Thomas Jefferson, whom he considered naive for his belief in unfettered democracy and for his enthusiasm for the French Revolution. Attempting to mark out his own pathway, but lacking Washington's extraordinary abilities, Adams ended up politically isolated and unsuccessful.

John Adams became the archetype of the independent chief executive —the president above party attempting to govern in isolation. Few would match the extremes of his audacious and stubborn posture, but the archetype would continue through American political history.

John Adams's eldest son, John Quincy Adams, was cut from the same cloth as his spirited father—brilliant and principled, but also cantankerous and inflexible. Like his father he wanted to recover the Constitutional ideal of a president unattached and unbeholden to others, independent in his judgment and thus free to pursue the common good. But that ideal belonged to an era that was fast vanishing, replaced by an ever-increasing demand for political engagement. When John Quincy ran for reelection in 1828 against the supremely political Andrew Jackson, the voters deserted him.

The selection of William Harrison in 1840 was the Whig attempt to counteract the Jackson Democratic avalanche. Harrison was presented as a war hero, like Jackson, but even more tellingly as a citizen statesman in the independent tradition of George Washington. And Harrison just might have exercised a healing function in the country had he not died only a month after assuming office. He left as his successor John Tyler, a man so independent of his newly adopted Whig Party he might as well have been still a Democrat. Chosen exclusively to help balance the presidential ticket, he quickly revealed himself as opposed to virtually all his party's programs. And when he went on to use his veto power repeatedly to thwart Whig legislation, he was eventually expelled from the party.

Just four years later came Zachary Taylor, a stubborn-minded old fighting man fresh from the Mexican War. Taylor's extreme independence, combined with political naivete, ended up undermining what everyone expected would be a precarious presidency.

Democrat Andrew Johnson was a contrarian all his life. The only Southern senator to remain loyal to the Union, he had been rewarded by President Lincoln with the 1864 vice presidential nomination, in which the unlikely pair ran on the independent "Union party" ticket. Once elevated to the presidency by John Wilkes Booth's bullet, Johnson became despised by Republicans and Democrats alike. He was unable to arouse public sympathy and, left politically isolated, he would escape conviction in an 1868 impeachment trial by a single vote.

The idea of independence as a positive trait was revived in the late nineteenth century, when President Rutherford B. Hayes attempted significant civil service reform and stood up forcefully to an overly dominant Congress. Hayes criticized what he called the country's "counterfeit statesmen" and pleaded for the return of "the genuine article which were produced in good measure a hundred years ago."

Even strong presidents, however, can be done in by their independent-mindedness. Woodrow Wilson, whose dream was to revive government by party caucus, began his presidency well connected to the men in Congress, and he dominated domestic affairs as few presidents before him. But by the end of his second term, he was beset by a string of illnesses that culminated in his massive stroke of 1919. Much like Grover Cleveland following his bout with cancer, the Wilson who emerged was stubborn and inflexible and unwilling to compromise. His refusal to bargain with Senate Republicans in 1920 was responsible, at least in part, for the failure of the United States to join the League of Nations. His was the independent cast of mind as a medical condition.

With the growth of the White House staff and the development of the executive office in the twentieth century, the institution of the presidency assumed an increasingly independent status. This, when in combination with a president of an independent cast of mind, led to situations that ran amok, as they did under Richard Nixon. For Jimmy Carter, independence took on a popular tinge; it was not just antiparty, it was in some ways antigovernment.

An independent president has long had the ability to go over the heads of both Congress and party and appeal for support to the American people. With the advent of radio, and even more important, of television, presidents could turn ever more directly to the public. Jimmy Carter might have been able to maintain his outsider status had he developed a more effective personal use of the media. But unable to rally the country to his own high standards, he ended up alone and at the mercy of a hostile Congress. In sharp contrast was the performance of his successor, Ronald Reagan, who became known because of his mastery of the media as "the great communicator."

At its best, the independent cast of mind produces admirable qualities. Presidents like Adams and Taylor and Hayes and Carter each stood for important principles and could point to meaningful accomplishments. Each was able to rise above petty partisanship, and set a standard of decency for others to follow. But when independence takes the place of working effectively with others, problems inevitably arise. In an era of divided government, independence can mean irrelevance, the inability to forge connections and bridge divisions. To be truly effective in the presidency, one cannot in the end downplay politics. And yet the promise of independent leadership, of those who will put national interest above partisan politics, survives. And the model of an independent executive can set an example for every president to chart his own moral course.

In his second term, Grover Cleveland's vaunted independence turned rigid and intractable.

Richard Nixon was a loner all his life. By the time he was forced to resign from office he had virtually no support left within his own political party.

Pennsylvania Avenue.

From the very beginning of the government's move to Washington, D.C., the presidency and Congress were separated geographically, at opposite ends of Pennsylvania Avenue. But independent-minded presidents who ignore their fellow politicians on Capitol Hill have often made the distance seem much greater.

Going It Alone

John Adams was in many ways the deepest thinker of his generation, an idealist whose calling card was his extraordinary independence. "I must be independent as long as I live," he once said. "The feeling is essential to my existence." He was a man of opposites—a brilliant and courageous visionary on one hand; vain, suspicious, and irascible on the other. Thomas Jefferson praised him as "profound" and "amiable" but also called him "irritable and a bad calculator of [others'] motives."

The roots of Adams's lonely integrity lay in his Puritan heritage in rural Massachusetts. "I was born and bred in the ancient town of Braintree, now called Quincy," he wrote. "There I began to love my books." Though his parents hoped he would enter the ordained ministry, the idea soon came to rankle the young Adams. "I had some faculty for public speaking," he later wrote, "and determined that I should make a better lawyer than divine."

He rose to become Boston's foremost attorney, often standing alone and taking on controversial causes. His successful defense of nine British soldiers arrested after the "Boston Massacre" was unpopular, but it reinforced a reputation for sticking to his own principles. "The object of all my wishes, and of all my politics," he said, "is the triumph of stubborn independence."

America in the 1770s consisted of two and a half million British citizens whose relationship to England was steadily worsening. Following the Boston Tea Party, in 1773, the British shut down the port of Boston. From his farm in Quincy, John Adams wrote, "The die is cast."

"Swim or sink, live or die, survive or perish with my country was my unalterable determination."

In June of 1774, thirty-eight-year-old Adams was elected a Congressional delegate to a meeting of the thirteen colonies to take place in what would become known as Independence Hall in Philadelphia. Converted to the Patriot cause by his fiery cousin Samuel Adams, he became one of the earliest proponents of revolution. And he was a tireless worker, serving eventually on some fifty committees, and chairing twenty-five of them. His contemporaries soon called him the "Atlas" of independence. But he also made enemies. Always convinced he was right, he refused to compromise and called people "fools" to their faces when they disagreed with him. "I would quarrel with every individual before I would prostitute my pen," he wrote. "I am determined to preserve my independence, even at the expense of my ambition."

War erupted in 1776, and John Adams was placed in charge of a committee to draft a declaration of independence. As Adams later remembered

A newly married lawyer when the above painting was made in 1764, young John Adams was already passionately committed to American independence. His respect for the law and for justice was so strong, however, that six years later he refused to jump onto the colonial bandwagon following the so-called Boston Massacre (below). Instead he defended the British soldiers in court.

John Adams was extraordinarily learned but also prone to fits of temper. "Human society, like the ocean, [needs] commotion," he once said, "in order to keep it from putrefying."

On his role as a founding father of the nation:

I knew Great Britain was determined on her system, and that very determination determined me on mine . . . . I had passed the Rubicon, swim or sink, live or die, survive or perish with my country, was my unalterable determination.

Last night 3 cargoes of Bohea tea were emptied into the sea. . . . There is a dignity, a majesty, a sublimity, in this last effort of the patriots, that I greatly admire.

The Revolution was effected before the war commenced. The Revolution was in the minds and hearts of the people.

Yesterday the greatest question was decided, and a greater perhaps, never was, nor will be, decided among men. A resolution was passed without one dissenting colony "that these united colonies are to be free and independent states." You will see in a few days a "declaration" on setting forth "the cause."

The history of our Revolution will be one continued lie . . . that Dr. Franklin's electrical rod smote the earth and out sprung General Washington. That Franklin electricized him with his rod—and henceforward these two conducted all the policy, negotiation, legislation and war.

I . . . have been sent into life at a time when the greatest lawgivers of antiquity would have wished to live. How few of the human race have ever enjoyed an opportunity of making [a] . . . government.

The institutions now made in America will not wholly wear out for thousands of years. It is of the last importance, then, that they should begin right.

Between his service in the Continental Congress and his vice presidency Adams spent ten years in Europe as a foreign minister. Critics said these years changed him from an ardent Republican patriot into a quasi-monarchist, out of touch with the play of American politics. "You'd be surprised to see your friend," Adams himself wrote to wife Abigail. "He is much altered."

This painting, by the painter-historian J. L. G. Ferris, shows three members of the Declaration committee at work. From left are Benjamin Franklin, John Adams, and Thomas Jefferson. Adams recalled: "Jefferson proposed to me to make the draught. I said I will not. . . . Reason first—You are a Virginian, and a Virginian ought to appear at the head of this business. Reason second—I am obnoxious, suspected and unpopular. You are very much otherwise. Reason third—You can write ten times better than I can."

it, rather self-servingly, the committee then appointed him, along with the young Thomas Jefferson, to draw up the text of the declaration. Claiming a key role in the discussions that preceded composition, Adams said he then requested his eloquent junior to do the actual writing. And so it was the tall, charismatic Jefferson who became the author of the Declaration of Independence, leaving John Adams to regret it for the rest of his life. "Jefferson ran away with . . . all the glory of it," he wrote.

Adams continued to work for American independence, in missions to France and then England, where he helped negotiate an end to the Revolutionary War. And in 1788, after nearly a decade abroad, he finally returned to a new house in Quincy, where he planned to retire. But retirement didn't lie within Adams's power, for just one year later he was elected the country's first vice president and was forced to leave his beloved Quincy once again. Most of Adams's eight years serving under George Washington were spent in Philadelphia's Congress Hall. And during that time he came to detest the vice presidency. "My country has in its wisdom contrived for me the most insignificant office that ever man contrived," he wrote, "a mere mechanical tool to wind up the clock."

In 1797, in an orderly transfer of power that astonished the world, Adams became the nation's second president. But if he had looked to the office to give him the same power George Washington had wielded, he soon found that the office itself didn't provide it. And his superior attitude eventually put him on a collision course with nearly everyone in government. Though Adams retained George Washington's entire cabinet, he was suspicious of their loyalties and largely ignored them. "When the people have chosen their Presidents," he wrote, "they ought to expect they will act their own independent judgments."

As president, all too often his independence was counterproductive. When Congress met to debate whether to establish an alliance with France or England, Adams stubbornly refused to commit himself to either side. He saw it as his moral duty to stand apart from and above all others. "Two parties existed in this country headed by men of the most determined ambition," he wrote, "the one inclined to France and the other to England. It was my destiny to run the gauntlet between these two factions."

Though Adams was himself a Federalist, what he really wanted to be was above both the Jeffersonian Republicans and the Hamiltonian Federalists, in the same way that George Washington had been above them. But there was no way that Adams could accomplish this; he simply did not possess Washington's immense stature or his ability to hold divergent factions together. And failing to cultivate support on either side, he ended up with little support from either.

As the country's first vice president, John Adams witnesses the inauguration of the country's first president. Detesting his position, Adams came to call the vice presidency "the most insignificant office that ever man contrived."

By the time John Adams moved in on November 1, 1800, the outside of the President's House was finished as this contemporary sketch of the north side shows. But the inside of the mansion was still in disarray. Fires still smoldered in some of the thirty-nine fireplaces in an attempt to dry the plaster walls; much of the flooring was unfinished; and the grand staircase-to-be was nothing but a gaping hole. Annoyed at having to undergo these inconveniences, Adams's attitude seems to have softened after his first night's sleep in the house. In a letter to his wife Abigail that next morning he wrote the sentiment shown at right, a prayer for future occupants. During the Kennedy administration the words would be carved into the mantel of the State Dining Room.

Before I end my Letter I pray Heaven to bestow the best of Blessings on this House and all that shall hereafter inhabit it. May none but honest and wise Men ever rule under this roof.

Abigail Adams

As a boy the squat, young Adams loved to skate and wrestle and fly kites and shoot marbles, to hunt in the fields and forests, and he could hardly keep his eyes off the girls. "I was of an amorous disposition . . . from ten or eleven years of age," he remembered. "If I look upon a book, my eyes tis true are on the book, but Imagination is at a tea table seeing that hair, those eyes, that shape, and hearing sense divine come mended from her tongue." Later, while wrestling with constitutional dilemmas as a young attorney, John was courting a remarkable parson's daughter named Abigail Smith. "Miss Adorable," he wrote her, "By the same token that the bearer hereof sat up with you last night, I hereby order you to give him as many kisses, and as many hours of your company after 9 o'clock as he shall please to demand." The two were married in 1764 and gloried in each other for the next fifty-four years, even though Adams was separated for long periods from his "dear girl" and "best friend" helping run the war and later as a world diplomat. It was during these many years apart that Abigail found her calling as a correspondent. Her letters to her husband describing life at home in Quincy, Massachusetts—her role as a mother, farmer, barterer, her wide reading, newsy asides, her manifold interests, and profound patriotism—have given her, since their publication by a grandson, a high place in American letters. They have also given us insight into her strange, brilliant, affectionate, often impossible husband. "His rule through life," Abigail claimed, "has been to vote and act independent of party, agreeable to the dictates of his conscience." When the long trip to Philadelphia and responsibilities at the farm kept Abigail away from the President, Adams solved the problem by simply governing from Quincy. He was miserable without her. After the presidency he lived for eighteen more years with his adored wife, followed by seven more without her.

Adams's presidency became consumed by an international crisis, triggered by France, which was harassing American ships at sea. After failed diplomatic efforts, the President pushed through the creation of a new Department of the Navy, and ordered the rapid buildup of American naval forces. But as war fever raged across the country, Adams suddenly reversed his initial tough position. His new stance, in favor of revised peace efforts, turned the Hamilton faction of his own party against him, and led to a full-scale cabinet revolt. "Hamilton . . . intends to drive the country into war with France," Adams wrote. "He is a man devoid of every moral principle," he added. "Either he is stark mad or I am."

As the crisis mounted, Adams turned to George Washington for help, asking him to resume his old duties as commander of the armies. But in doing so Adams compromised his own presidency, undermining his standing as commander-in-chief. Ignoring his increasing political isolation, Adams worked alone on a plan for a peace mission to France. Then in the midst of a political storm he retreated to his farm in Massachusetts, where he insisted he would govern in isolation. And there he remained for the next eight months of his presidency. Even his friends called it an "abdication."

"The people elected me to administer the government, it is true," he responded, "and I do administer it, here at Quincy."

Toward the end of his term in office, Adams became the first president to live in the new Executive Mansion in the capital city of Washington. And there, the man who chose not to be an ordained minister offered a simple prayer for future presidents. "I pray heaven to bestow the best blessings on this house and on all that shall hereafter inhabit it. May none but honest and wise men ever rule under this roof."

Adams finally did establish peace with France, but not in time to help restore his popularity. During his final year in office, he was publicly criticized as a man of "vanity" and "egotism," who was "unfit" for the office of chief executive. "It was utterly impossible that I could have lived through one more year of such labors and cares," he wrote. "It is a sad thing that simple integrity should have so many enemies in the world."

In 1800, Adams lost his bid for reelection to Thomas Jefferson. And on March 4, 1801, he refused to take part in his successor's inauguration. Instead, he quietly slipped out of town early that morning. "I left Washington on the 4th," he wrote, "and arrived at Quincy on the 18th having trotted the bogs five hundred miles. . . . I found about a hundred loads of seaweed in my barnyard, and I thought I had made a good exchange—honors and virtues for manure."

Adams lived on for twenty-five more years, long enough to reconcile his differences with his longtime political adversary, Thomas Jefferson and to witness his son John Quincy become the country's sixth president. But when a neighbor tried to offer his congratulations about John Quincy, the older Adams grew cynical. "No man who ever held the office of President," he muttered, "would congratulate a friend on obtaining it." Toward the end, when he was described publicly as a man with few friends, the old sage became furious, and then grew wistful. "I fear the information is too true," he said. "It is impossible that any man should run such a gauntlet as I have, and have many friends at the last." Or, as he had written years before as he first came to understand his own nature, "A man who discovers a disposition to be independent seldom succeeds."

Shown here in his last portrait, by Gilbert Stuart, John Adams grew old gracefully, presiding over a bountiful table where boiled cornmeal pudding was always served first to stem the appetite. "Mr. Rotundity," as he was called behind his back, kept his wig off now during the hot summers, yet his opinions were still strong and straight. "I shudder when I think of the calamities which slavery is likely to produce in this country," he offered. "If the gangrene is not stopped, I see nothing but insurrection of the blacks against the whites." Adams died at age ninety-one on the fiftieth anniversary of the Declaration of Independence, just hours after the death of his old friend Thomas Jefferson.

ZACHARY TAYLOR

1849–1850

"Old Rough and Ready"

Zachary Taylor's greatest victory during the Mexican War took place on February 22–23, 1847 at Buena Vista. Below, American cavalry line up at Minon's Pass in the mountains just north of Buena Vista. This image, taken from a daguerreotype by an unknown photographer, is one of the earliest pictures ever made of war under way.

In 1849 there rose to the nation's highest office a sixty-four-year-old fighting man who was so politically inexperienced he had never even voted. As had been true for John Adams, his presidency offers a cautionary tale about bringing too much independence into the White House, for Zachary Taylor's crusty independence and complete disdain for the maneuvering of politicians would eventually put him in conflict with almost everyone in government. "On the subject of the presidency . . . I do not care a fig about the office," he once said. "I [would] be . . . as well contented in a cabin as in the White House."

He had grown up in a log cabin, even though he sprang from one of Virginia's most aristocratic families, which boasted the famous Lees and Madisons as relatives. After the Revolutionary War his father had emigrated to the Kentucky wilderness, where he had hacked a plantation out of the Kentucky badlands, then known as the "Dark and Bloody Ground." At night "Little Zack" helped barricade the front door against Indians. By day he played soldier, devising mock maneuvers.

Taylor entered the U.S. army in 1808 and not long after was ordered west into Indiana Territory where he would assume the command of Fort Harrison. During the War of 1812 his qualities of leadership became evident. Standing just five feet eight inches and weighing 170 pounds, he was self-reliant and decisive and completely fearless, with a deep loyalty to his men and concern for their safety. Once he repulsed a massive Shawnee attack with only a handful of soldiers. "Although the Indians continued to pour in . . . an innumerable quantity of arrows," he reported, "during the whole time the attack lasted . . . I had but [two men] killed."

But it was in the late 1830s, during the second Seminole War, in Florida, that he earned his nickname "Old Rough and Ready." There, during the ferocious battle of Lake Okee-cho-bee, Taylor's toughness helped him prevail against severe attacks.

He became known as the finest Indian fighter in the Army, and the fairest—meticulously sticking to treaties and preventing whites from spreading into Indian lands. When he captured runaway slaves who were fighting alongside the Seminoles, Taylor angered his fellow Southerners when he refused to return them to their owners. But all his life he was a man of contradictions and he remained, like his son-in-law Jefferson Davis, an ardent supporter of slavery. "So far as slavery is concerned," he said in the 1840s, "we of the South must . . . defend our rights . . . to the last . . . [with] the sword, if necessary."

In the year of his election, Taylor poses for a typical jut-lipped, frowning daguerreotype. His secret was that no one knew where he stood on any major issue. The General talked in patriotic generalities, intoning personal promises of high principle.

Taylor at Buena Vista

Taylor was not an especially gifted tactician. His military success lay in the fact that his men would do almost anything for him. They liked how Old Zack looked, how he kept a flag up outside his tent to show he was home, how he loved hominy grits, the simplest of foods. They even liked the fact that on horseback he looked "like an old toad." Artists converged on Taylor's camp and tried to capture his laid-back, unorthodox, seat-of-the-pants style. But in pictures the romance was lost. Bowlegged and squinting through nearsighted eyes, big-boned, thick-necked, long-nosed Zachary Taylor didn't look very heroic. Still, the stocky, little, unconventional general, who wore civilian clothes and an old straw hat to battle, fired the imagination of the citizens back home. "You are surrounded by twenty thousand men," the Mexican leader Santa Anna had informed him, "and cannot avoid being cut to pieces. Surrender!" How could the voters resist the man who calmly replied, "I beg leave to say I decline," and went on at Buena Vista to one of the greatest victories in U.S. history.

Taylor's craggy profile

In 1846, President James K. Polk ordered Zachary Taylor and a small army to enter territory disputed between Texas and Mexico. This led to the outbreak of the Mexican War, where decisive victories by Taylor turned him into a national hero. It was the first time that the telegraph was used to report day-to-day battle progress to newspapers, and the American public was entranced. Even before the war was over, Zachary Taylor was being mentioned as a presidential candidate.

"My repugnance for being a candidate has been frankly made known," Taylor responded. "My . . . thoughts . . . are now occupied in bringing this war to a speedy and honorable close."

But at the White House, the general's sudden popularity was perceived as a political threat. President Polk wrote, "Taylor is no doubt brave and will fight, but he is a man made giddy with the idea of the presidency. He is wholly unfit for the chief command." And in 1846, Polk transferred most of Taylor's troops to another general.

"I [have] been stripped of nearly the whole of the regular force & more than one half of the volunteers," Taylor reported. "It seems to me the great object . . . is to keep me as much in the dark . . . as . . . possible."

But nothing could stop Zachary Taylor from fighting. Outnumbered four to one at Buena Vista, Mexico, Old Rough and Ready refused to surrender. Through pure grit and determination, he pulled off one of the most astonishing military victories in America's history. "By pursuing the course I did," Taylor wrote, "I saved the administration, [and] preserved . . . the national honor and our glorious flag from being trailed in the dust."

The imagination of the people back home was fired by newspaper accounts of the stocky general who did things his own way—how he wore civilian clothes and an old straw hat in action, took bullets through his sleeve, and fought on the front line alongside his men. In Washington, a "Taylor for President" club was formed, led by a group of Whig congressmen that included a young Abraham Lincoln. And in an age when generals were more revered than politicians, Taylor was actively pursued by three national parties. "I was nominated by . . . Whigs, Democrats, and Natives, in separate and mixed meetings," he explained. "I resisted them all."

Part of Taylor's appeal lay in the fact that no one knew what political party he belonged to, or where he stood on any major issue. Persuaded that he had to be connected to a specific party, Taylor finally announced that he was a Whig, but then cautioned, "not an ultra Whig."

"Near forty years of my life have been passed in the military," Taylor wrote, "in the camp, the field or . . . in the Indian country. I . . . have had but little time to . . . investigate political matters."

In November 1848, Zachary Taylor's independent spirit and ambiguous politics helped get him elected the country's twelfth president. "My triumphs and trials have commenced," Taylor wrote. "In the discharge of my duties, my guide will be the Constitution."

In the White House, Taylor looked as disheveled as he had in the field. Neither a drinker nor a smoker, he was a confirmed tobacco chewer, and visitors said he had perfect spitting aim, never missing a sand-filled box across his office. "I will commit many blunders there can be no doubt," he once exclaimed. "But I flatter myself they will . . . be attributed to the head & not to the heart."

From the start, Taylor seemed to go out of his way to alienate fellow Whigs. He virtually ignored his own cabinet members, as well as such influential senators as Henry Clay and Daniel Webster. And determined to communicate with all political parties, he bypassed the established Whig press and set up his own administration newspaper.

Just twelve years before the Civil War, the major issue of Taylor's presidency centered on the institution of slavery. By the Mexican War, the United States had gained vast new Western territories, including what would become the states of California and New Mexico. The issue now was whether they would become slave states or free. Everyone assumed that the slave-owning president would see to it that the institution of slavery was extended. "I was represented as a southern slaveholder . . . in favor of the extension of slavery," Taylor wrote, "[and as a man who] trafficked in human flesh."

But in his annual message to Congress, Taylor revealed that above all else he was a confirmed Unionist, and was in favor of the admission of the new states even if they first banned slavery. Southerners were stunned, and called the President a "turncoat." Speaking on behalf of his fellow Southern congressmen, an exasperated Alexander Stephens confronted Taylor in the White House and threatened secession if he didn't change his policy. The old general grew furious. "I informed [him] that if they were taken in rebellion against the Union, I would hang them with less reluctance than I had hung deserters and spies in Mexico!"

With the country hurtling toward civil war, a national debate now raged in Congress, attempting to find a compromise between North and South. But in the White House, Zachary Taylor dug in his heels, refusing to cooperate with anyone. Threatening to veto any effort at congressional compromise, even if that meant risking civil war, he said he would personally take charge of the Army if necessary, and that he was determined to do what he thought right, no matter what the consequence. "I esteem the President," bemoaned fellow Whig Daniel Webster, "but the administration is doomed, and the Whig Party doomed with it."

This is the earliest known photograph of a president and his cabinet. The daguerreotype was probably taken by Mathew Brady in April 1849. Standing in the center is President Taylor. Seated, starting at far left, are William M. Meredith, secretary of the treasury; Thomas Ewing, secretary of the interior; John M. Clayton, secretary of state; William B. Preston, secretary of the Navy; George W. Crawford, secretary of war; Jacob Collamer, postmaster general; and Reverdy Johnson, attorney general.

No president was ever elevated as fast as Taylor was to the big job, and no president had less preparation for it. His childhood in Kentucky had limited his learning to the home. His early letters show an unorganized, fragmented, and repetitious mind. Later, his letters on politics were rambling and confusing, whereas he had proved he could be very clear when talking about farming and raising animals. His home was in Baton Rouge, Louisiana, but he held land in both Kentucky and Mississippi as well. Whenever he was home, he made sure his slaves were well cared for and he always referred to them as servants, never slaves. Taylor was an easygoing man with a good sense of humor. He liked to joke about marriage, possibly because his was so uncertain, besieged by poor health. He was devoted to his "Peggy" even though she was too weak to act as his hostess in the White House. Taylor had a healthy temper. He got mad at the Army when it failed to promote him fast enough. He got mad at the Senate for withholding brevet nominations. He got mad at the government for allowing so much red tape to dominate military life. He got mad at President Polk for withdrawing support in Mexico, and at General Winfield Scott "after his acting so low and contemptible towards me, doing all in his power to cut my throat." During his presidency he especially got mad at Southerners who talked secession if they didn't get their way on slavery in the new states. He was a poor speaker, often stammering, and unable to put together a string of ideas. But he was a man who always acted decisively, usually wisely, and he knew how to get right to the point. After being felled by gastroenteritis, he said, "In two days I shall be a dead man." And he was right.

This was the chaotic state of affairs in America when the country paused to celebrate its seventy-fourth Independence Day. Just sixteen months into office, an exhausted President Taylor sat under a roasting sun for hours during a Fourth of July observance. Then he downed large quantities of tainted milk and raw fruit and vegetables. Stricken by acute gastroenteritis, the invincible hero was confined to his bed—eating ice, taking quinine, being bled. His condition, made worse by the efforts of his doctors, would lead to his death in less than a week.

On July 9, 1850, Vice President Millard Fillmore prepared to assume office and inherit the unresolved crisis Taylor was leaving behind. And for one brief moment the entire nation, both Northerners and Southerners, united in sorrow. It was a fitting tribute to the man who had stubbornly clung to his independence throughout a mounting political storm. Taylor's last words were to his family, grouped around his bed. "The storm, in passing, has swept away the trunk. . . . I expect the summons soon. . . . I regret nothing."

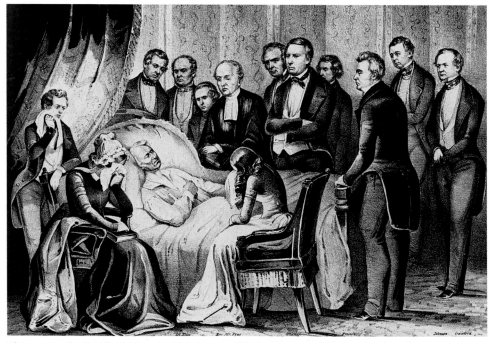

The scene in the President's House at 10:35 P.M. on July 9, 1850, saw Old Rough and Ready breathe his last while attended by his son (far left), his wife, and his daughter. Aides, cabinet members and the Reverend Mr. Pyne hover about as Vice President Millard Fillmore, with crossed arms, waits to become the thirteenth president.

This daguerreotype of Zachary Taylor—the last Whig elected to the high office—was taken during his sixteen-month-long, embattled presidency. It shows how much he aged over the course of his administration.

The Capitol, as it looked during the Taylor administration, and as photographed for the first time ever by John Plumbe, Jr. When the federal city was being conceived, a contest had been held for the best design for a House of Congress. The winner was William Thornton, originally from the British Virgin Islands, who had studied medicine in Scotland. Thornton's turtle-shell dome would be replaced in the 1860s with a much higher and more imposing crown.

RUTHERFORD B. HAYES

1877–1881

"No Fondness for Political Life"

The blossoming young lawyer and his wife Lucy had their first child in 1853. Hayes himself had grown up knowing that his only brother, Lorenzo, had drowned while skating on a pond. Coming to grips with his fears, Hayes made himself learn how to skate. It was the beginning of a lifelong commitment not to be intimidated by anything or anyone.

The Presidential mania . . . makes mad every man who is at all prominent in Washington," once wrote Rutherford B. Hayes. "It never seemed to me worth . . . the cost of self-respect, of independence."

All his life, Hayes was hardworking, methodical, and impeccably honest—so pristine, James Garfield once said, "no nickname can be pinned to him." He saw himself as nothing more than a nonpartisan public servant, intent on cleansing the taints that had infected his own party during the Grant administration.

Like Adams, Hayes traced his lineage back almost to the *Mayflower*. His great-grandfathers had all served in the Revolutionary War, and for decades his family had been associated with Ohio. As his father had died before he was born, Hayes was raised by his mother. His lifelong commitment became not to be intimidated—by anything or anyone. "[I discovered that] my chiefest obstacles were in myself," he wrote in college; "[that] if I could *master myself*, all other difficulties would vanish."

At Harvard Law School, Hayes rose to the top of his class. And once back in Ohio he became known as a lawyer of unquestioned integrity. He was a devoted reader of Ralph Waldo Emerson, whose belief in self-reliant individualism helped shape Hayes's personal philosophy.

In 1852 he married Lucy Webb and settled down to have eight children and to lead what Hayes hoped would be a quiet and disciplined life. But on April 12, 1861, Fort Sumter was attacked by South Carolina troops, and Hayes's orderly life came to an abrupt end.

"My feelings . . . were . . . that this was a just and necessary war," Hayes wrote, "and that I would prefer to go into it [even] if I knew I was to . . . be killed, . . . than to live through and after it without taking any part in it."

Hayes rose rapidly through the ranks to brigadier general, and during the course of the war he was wounded five times. "My first wound—a shell fragment hit the right knee. *I feel it yet,*" he wrote. "[But] I never enjoyed any business or mode of life as much as I [did the] . . . marches and campaigns in the hills of western Virginia."

His leadership qualities got him noticed. When he was approached during the war to campaign for public office, Hayes exclaimed, "an officer who at this crisis would abandon his post to electioneer for a seat in Congress ought to be scalped!" Despite his objections, he was elected while still

At the height of his powers, Hayes exhibited a basic decency, high intelligence, and deep loyalty. His few minor flaws included a tendency toward self-righteousness.

In the Civil War, Hayes rose to the rank of brevet major general. He loved the male camaraderie the Army provided, and although he suffered multiple wounds, he treated war as a cheerful adventure.

A lover of books, with his own large private collection, Hayes became known as a scholarly congressman and then was elected to three terms as Governor of Ohio. Appealing to reformers, Republican Party regulars, and Civil War veterans, in 1875 he was pushed forward for the presidency.

fighting in Virginia, and after the war served in Congress. He went on to be elected three times as governor of Ohio.

By 1876, state Republicans were pushing their "favorite son" toward the presidency, even though Hayes was for the most part unknown outside Ohio. One East Coast observer called him "a third rate nonentity." But at the Republican National Convention in Cincinnati, when other more prominent candidates failed to secure majorities, the delegates turned to Hayes. Reform-minded liberals, Republican Party regulars, and Civil War veterans all rallied 'round. And on the seventh ballot Hayes was nominated. "I . . . discouraged rather than encouraged 'the Hayes movement,'" he wrote. "[But] I shall show a *grit* that will astonish those who predict weakness."

In November, Hayes's Democratic opponent, Samuel Tilden, narrowly won the popular vote. But the electoral count in three Southern states was called into question, so the dispute was laid before an Electoral Commission. As party leaders argued and bargained, Hayes refused to make any political concessions. But after nearly four months of stalemate, Southern Democrats were secretly assured that if Hayes was named president, he would end Reconstruction and pull federal troops out of the South. With that assurance, it was announced that Hayes, not Tilden, was the country's nineteenth president. His political enemies labeled him "Rutherfraud" B. Hayes. "I . . . never had any misgiving about my success in 1876," Hayes wrote later. "There had been crimes against the ballot box, . . . [and] we were . . . entitled to . . . a decided majority of the popular vote."

Hayes took office under a terrible cloud. And he went on to put an end to Reconstruction as promised. "My judgement was that the time had come to put an end to bayonet rule," he wrote, "to wipe out the color line, to abolish sectionalism and bring peace. . . . [And] to restore confidence in . . . a Republican Administration. The army was withdrawn [from the South] because I believed it . . . a wise thing to do."

But Hayes's ending of Reconstruction came at a cost. Pledges he had received from Southern Democrats to protect the rights of black citizens proved worthless, and the civil rights revolution that Hayes had inherited would be stalled until the twentieth century.

From the start of his presidency, Hayes firmly established his independence, and acted as he saw fit, vindicating himself by his sheer rectitude. Fellow Republicans were soon outraged at his choice of a cabinet, which included a Democrat, David M. Key, who had once been a Confederate officer. "For the first time in our history a gentleman who had opposed the election of a President was by that President invited into his Cabinet," Hayes wrote proudly. "I was ready to . . . risk my own standing and reputation with my party."

Increasingly distraught over corporate greed, Hayes spoke out against big business and on behalf of working-class Americans. "The vast wealth and power is in the hands of the few . . . who represent or control capital," he once blasted. "This is a government of the people, by the people and for the people no longer. It is a government of corporations, by corporations, and for corporations."

Hayes's independent views eventually pitted him against nearly every politician in Washington. He stood up to railroad companies, called out federal troops to suppress a national railroad strike, became an early environmentalist, and risked political capital when he vetoed a bill that he saw as prejudicial to Chinese Americans. And he got himself cordially detested by members of Congress for vetoing their pet projects in order to prevent raids on the treasury. Most difficult for fellow Republicans to take was his attack upon the long-standing system of political patronage—especially when he went after the bastion of the party machine, the New York Customhouse.

In the 1870s, the Customhouse was the center of national party politics. Responsible for collecting three-quarters of the revenue of the federal government, it had become rife with corruption. Hayes fired its top three officials, including the Collector himself, future President Chester A. Arthur. And despite strong resistance by the Senate, he stood firm, ordering that no federal employee engage in any political activity. "The great success of [my] Administration . . . was in getting the control of the New York custom House," Hayes wrote, "and in changing it from a political machine for the benefit of party leaders into a business office for the benefit of the public."

At the White House, Hayes was a diligent chief executive. A religious man who never missed his morning prayers, he met with callers every afternoon and often late into the night. Hayes had the first telephone installed in the White House and placed his first call to Alexander Graham Bell. And he became the first president to travel to the West Coast while in office.

His greatest asset, he liked to say, was his wife, Lucy, who was the most esteemed White House hostess since Dolley Madison. Nicknamed "Lemonade Lucy" for her barring of alcohol from White House functions, she was the first to be widely referred to as "The First Lady." "[Lucy's] large, warm heart and lively sympathy for . . . all around her . . . have made her wonderfully popular," he said.

Hayes found himself increasingly appreciated by the American public. His independent spirit, his habits of hard work, and his basic decency were refreshing in Washington. He had promised upon entering office that he would seek one term only, thus freeing him, he said, to be thoroughly independent in his actions. When friends tried to convince him to run for a second term, he adamantly refused even to consider it. "I never had an overweening fondness for political life," he insisted. "My periods of public employment were merely episodes—parentheses—in my private life, my citizen's life."

In retirement Hayes became more active in social causes than any previous former president. He worked principally in the area of education, in particular on behalf of poor black children in the South. And he was conspicuous in the prison reform movement. Above all, he was glad no longer to be president.

"[It was my] equanimity of temper which . . . enabled me to bear the vexations and anxieties . . . which [have] broken down so many of my predecessors," he wrote. "Now [that] I am back where I belong, I mean to stay there. . . . While I am not . . . wealthy, . . . I am, happily, independent."

LEMONADE LUCY

Lucy Webb Hayes with her children, Scott and Fanny, in the White House Conservatory

"Lemonade Lucy" the press called her, alluding to the fact that no liquor or wine was served in the Hayes White House. To foil complaints that there were not even after-dinner cordials, the President and First Lady would rise from the dinner table and lead a procession of guests on a tour of the conservatory, where the two, both knowledgeable gardeners, would discourse on their leafy treasures. The tour ended up at the foot of the grand staircase, where Hayes and wife would say goodnight, leaving no room for thirsty grievance. The couple had first met when Rutherford was at Harvard Law School. At first, Rutherford paid little heed to the fifteen-year-old. "A bright sunny hearted little girl not quite old enough to fall in love with —and so I didn't," Rutherford told his diary afterwards. A few years later he was changing his mind. "Her low sweet voice is very winning, her soft rich eye not often equaled; a heart as true as steel, I know." His analytical mind kept working. "Intellect she has, too, a quick sprightly one, rather than a reflective and profound one. She sees at a glance what others study upon." Finally he had convinced himself. "By George! I am in love with her." When she moved into the White House at forty-five, Lucy was the first college graduate First Lady. Hugely popular, she kept her strong feelings about temperance, women's suffrage, and feminism in general to herself, believing that the man of the marriage made those pronouncements and it was her duty to support him.

BRADY,   WASHINGTON, D. C.

Despite ridicule for her strict temperance rules at the White House, Lucy Hayes became the best-loved wife of a president since Dolley Madison.

785 BROADWAY, N. Y.

By his stubborn disregard for politics-as-usual, Hayes reversed the downward spiral of executive influence and ushered in a new era of presidential strength.

This is what a Hayes family dinner looked like in the 1880s. The aging ex-President, his single term well behind him, sits at right.

Priding himself always on being a man first and only second a politician, Hayes nurtured his private life within the pages of a vast, unfolding, multi-volumed diary, begun at age twelve and kept up to within days of his death, at seventy. His sounding board, his retreat, his personal taskmaster, and viewed almost as a friend, the diary taught him to trust his own insights and maintain his independence. Of all our presidents, only John Quincy Adams and James K. Polk kept a comparable daily record. What follows is part of Hayes's entry for March 18, 1878, a meticulous description of his presidential routine.

As President . . . I rise about 7 A.M. [and] write until breakfast. . . . After breakfast, prayers—i.e. the reading of a chapter in the Bible, each one present reading a verse in turn, and all kneeling repeat the Lord's Prayer. . . . From 10 to 12 . . . members of Congress [have] preference of all visitors except Cabinet ministers. Callers "to pay respects" are usually permitted to come in to shake hands whenever the number reaches about a half dozen waiting. Twelve to 2 P.M., on Tuesdays and Fridays, are Cabinet hours. . . . At 2 P.M., lunch. I commonly invite to that cup of tea and biscuit and butter with cold meat—any gentleman I wish to have more conference with than is practicable in hours given to miscellaneous business. After lunch the correspondence of the day, well briefed, and each letter in an envelope, is examined . . . then I drive an hour and a half. Returning I . . . take a fifteen or twenty minutes' nap, and get ready to dine at 6 P.M. After dinner, callers on important business occupy me until 10:30 to 11:30 P.M., when I go to bed. . . . There is not enough exercise in this way of life. I try to make up by active gymnastics before I dress when I get up, by walking rapidly in the lower hall and the greenhouse after each meal for perhaps five to ten minutes, and a good hand rubbing before going to bed.

Lucy died of a stroke at fifty-seven. Rutherford followed her three and a half years later, shortly after visiting his wife's grave. "I know that I am going where Lucy is," Hayes told his doctor. "I am not unhappy; my life is an exceptionally happy one."

A natural aristocrat, admired for his intellect and moral fiber, Hayes had an almost childlike love of the outdoors, in all seasons. Each summer of his administration, to his great delight, tropical plants were carried from the presidential greenhouses and placed in a circle around the outdoor pool (left), whose fountain now boasted 500 tiny nozzles that turned its waters to mist.

The Outsider

Of all the Presidents who came after Hayes, the man who most resembled his personal style was a Southern governor who hated politics-as-usual. In the aftermath of Watergate, Jimmy Carter promised to bring a sense of decency back to the presidency. "I was the first president in more than 125 years elected from the Deep South," he once said, explaining how he felt as a Washington outsider. "I was a governor who had not been involved in any way in Washington. When we arrived at the White House at what should have been a glorious reception, I remember the cartoons about me insinuating that I had an IQ of about 50. They had a picture of my mother, barefooted—of outhouses with moons cut in the door, straw coming out of our ears. I felt that I was an outsider and I didn't want to be, but I think it was almost inherent in my background as a lonely Georgian farmer who was reaching out for personal support."

James Earl Carter, Jr., was born into a peanut-farming family in 1924. From his father, he acquired a lifelong belief in discipline and hard work. From his mother, he inherited a compassion for the poor and a commitment to civil rights. "We had a good life," he remembered. "We lived, along with everyone else, with no money and no electricity and no running water, hard work, and things of that kind. Our family was run with a strictest possible discipline. I mean, there was no concept in my family of disobeying a direct order of my father. If you had asked me when I was five years old or eight years old, What do you want to be when you grow up? it was always, I want to go to Annapolis and be a naval officer. And until I was thirty years old, my only ambition was to be a successful naval officer."

With a degree in nuclear engineering from Annapolis, Carter served in the Navy for seven years working as an aide to Hyman Rickover, the father of the "nuclear navy." With his wife Rosalynn he started a family and they thrived on their independent life in the North, far from the small-town world of Plains, Georgia. But in 1953, after the death of his father, Carter was forced to change careers abruptly and return to run the family peanut business.

"It was one of the worst things that I have ever done," Carter remembered. "I prayed about it. I labored over it and I was afraid to tell Rosalynn that I was even considering it. When I finally told her that, it almost broke up our marriage. We have never had a more serious confrontation. When I finally resigned from the Navy, we had three little boys. We drove from Sch-

From a very young age Carter's goal in life was a high school and college education. He was a natural reader, and in third grade he won a prize for reading the most books. By the eighth grade he had thought out some good mental habits and written them down in his scrapbook. "If you think in the right way you will develop: (1) the habit of accomplishing what you attempt, (2) the habit of expecting to like other people, (3) the habit of deciding quickly what you'd like to do and doing it, (4) the habit of sticking to it, (5) the habit of welcoming cheerfully all wholesome ideas and experiences, (6) a person who wants to build good mental habits should avoid the idle daydream; should give up worry and anger; hatred and envy; should neither fear nor be ashamed of anything that is honest and purposeful."

Jimmy Carter shows the wear and tear of four tough years in office.

On a short leave from the Naval Academy twenty-year-old Jimmy found a seventeen-year-old Plains girl named Eleanor Rosalynn Smith, kissed her on their first date, and decided she was for him. Shy, uncertain Rosalynn said no at first, but something about the man in the white uniform was too much for her and the couple were married on July 7, 1946, soon after his graduation from Annapolis. This is their wedding picture.

To Rosalynn's disappointment and outright anger, after his father died Jimmy quit the Navy and moved back to Plains to run the family peanut business. A friend described the precipitous move this way: "It was almost like a medieval idea, that one man, his father, was responsible for the souls in the town of Plains, Georgia . . . [that] without his father those 1,500 people were not going to have any means to live. . . . He was just torn over the obligation to those people and the idea that he [had been] picked to be chief engineer of the *Sea Wolf*."

enectady, New York, where I was working on a nuclear submarine, back to Plains. She hardly said a word to me on the way home. And for six months after we got back to Plains, she didn't cooperate in many ways. She was devastated. The first entire year I was home, our income was less than $300. But we stuck it out and I never [since] have really had doubt that I made the right decision in going back home."

Entering first local, then state politics, Carter built a reputation for strict honesty and idealism. But he also became known as a man who distanced himself from his colleagues. His 1966 bid for the governorship of Georgia failed in part because of his political isolation. "I was disillusioned then about God's purpose for my life," Carter said. "I thought my political life was over in 1966. I was doomed to just growing peanuts for the rest of my existence." It was his sister, Ruth Stapleton, an evangelical minister, who encouraged him to see his setback as a chance for personal renewal.

In 1970 Carter ran for the governorship again and this time he won, in part because of his appeal to working class voters. Then, just two years later, he set his ambitions even higher.

"I began to plan secretly to run for president—only about five or six of us knew it," Carter remembered. "And then by the time I announced in 1974, nobody cared. Nobody thought I had a chance. But I was confident. It wasn't until the final returns came in from the state of Mississippi that I went over the top."

When Jimmy Carter came into office in 1977 he refused to engage in party politics. Distancing himself from fellow Democrats, he so outraged the National Committee that it formally rebuked him. But Carter was determined to maintain his independence in the White House as he tackled as many problems as fast as he could. He pushed a series of major energy bills through Congress, including the deregulation of natural gas and oil prices; and he dominated nuclear energy technology. He wanted to do so many things in his presidency—to advance disarmament, altogether alter the nation's energy policy, and bring a national health care system into being. But for a president to accomplish important large goals, he has to develop coalitions, not only in Congress but within the interests outside of Congress. And he has to bring public opinion to bear on Congress. Carter's passionate, do-it-yourself approach to new legislation often failed to gain congressional support.

"I never lost an hour of sleep while I was president worrying about what had happened or what might happen," Carter said. "I did the best I could. And with my self-confidence and my religious faith I accommodated disappointments and really enjoyed being president."

He seemed particularly adept at foreign affairs, successfully completing normalization of relations with China including the exchange of ambassadors, and he raised human rights as a vital concern of foreign policy.

"I think the best time was probably dealing with the Middle East issue at Camp David," he said, "and even better I think was the peace treaty that came along six months later. I made a very difficult decision over the almost unanimous opposition of my cabinet and my staff to take the initiative and to go to Egypt and to go to Israel to try to get Begin and Sadat to agree on a peace treaty. And when they did sign—both of them signed the agreement—I guess that was probably my best moment."

Carter put enormous effort and intensity and sense of purpose into bringing the Egyptians and the Israelis together. It was a brilliant piece of personal work. But that attention to detail, that careful pursuit of it, left too many other things unattended to at the same time, including the deteriorating regime in Iran. And when fifty-two Americans were taken hostage in Iran, he was to pay a terrible price. "There was a time of great stress for me," Carter remembered, "and that's while the hostages were being held, when I was obsessed with preserving their lives and bringing them back home safely. I would meet personally with the families of the hostages and try to reassure them of my interests. So that was a very bad time."

Jimmy Carter's presidency was undone by the hostage crisis in Iran, by a national oil crisis, and by soaring inflation. But perhaps more than anything else, it was his independent-mindedness that left him alienated from both Republicans and Democrats.

"Well I have to admit, not very proudly, that I didn't ever put party loyalty at a very high level in my list of priorities," Carter said. "As a matter of fact, I had more political trouble with the liberal Democrats than I did with the Republicans. Even when I got the renomination in 1980, it was after a bitter battle with Ted Kennedy and his supporters, and he almost refused even to shake hands with me on the platform of the Democratic Party. We never did heal those wounds within the party."

In retirement Carter became an energetic humanitarian, working, as Rutherford Hayes had, on numerous charitable ventures. And he became active, as well, as an international trouble-shooter, known for his tough but always fair-minded negotiations. His basic decency had survived his years as president, and he became widely admired across America and around the world. "I went to the White House with my own ideas about what ought to be done," Carter recalled. "And I never did fit in really with the Washington environment much. But I think that I did have an independent set of mind."

Showing his handshaking form, Jimmy presses some political flesh in the 1966 campaign for the governorship of Georgia.

Running for president in 1976, Carter shows the confidence in himself that never wavered. The year before "was a lonely existence. I visited 135 cities in Iowa . . . and I would rarely get on radio, and never on television, but I just went from one town to another and would go and speak to college classes—maybe twenty people would come. I remember once I went to Des Moines and spent a lot of money to have a big reception . . . and two people came."

On his childhood: My playmates were black kids. And the standard salary then for a day worker was a dollar a day. Little kids, under teenage, were twenty-five cents a day. And that meant that you went to the barn in the dark. You got to the field, hooked up your mule, and when it got bright enough that the mule wouldn't plow up any cotton, you started plowing and you didn't stop until sundown.

On running for governor: I lost the first campaign in 1966. And the reason I felt bad was that the avowed and very proud segregationist Lester Maddox was the eventual winner. And I couldn't understand how the Georgia people would choose him instead of a fine young man like me. I couldn't understand how God would permit something like this to happen.

On help from his sister: Ruth Carter Stapleton was a very famous evangelist. And she came down to our place after I was defeated. I told her that my political life was over. I was doomed to be just growing peanuts for the rest of my existence, that God had no interest in the future of my life. She convinced me that those kinds of tragedies or setbacks should be the foundation for a greater life, for renewed vigor and confidence and purpose, for reassessment of what we have done, and were not a cause for despair. . . . So I began to campaign again, and in 1970 I was elected.

On fair elections: We're the only nation in the world that doesn't give equal free time to all candidates. And it means that anyone who wants to be a viable candidate for president, or even for Congress, has to have enormous financial wealth, personally, or appeal to special interest groups to finance a very expensive campaign. It's an unrecognized blight on the democratic nature of our country.

On human rights: I think the recognition of the worth of an individual is a basic premise on which human rights have to be founded. . . . The thrust of it, the vitality of it, was derived on my own experience in the Deep South, as someone who grew up in segregation years, who had to struggle through that ordeal of change, and who saw the burden of segregation being equally heavy on white people as it was on our African-American neighbors. It was a millstone around our neck. . . . I said that if I am elected, human rights would be a foundation stone for the building of our foreign policy.

All things seem possible as the Carters, having left their limousine, joyfully join the parade down Pennsylvania Avenue on Inauguration Day.

This picture and the three to the right show Carter's frank press conference style. Sometimes amused, sometimes severe, it was usually no-nonsense, with a press that seemed at times out to get him.

Writing late into the night in the Cabinet Room, Carter works on his energy plan. Like all the rest of the country's most independent-minded presidents, he would not be elected to a second term.

Early on January 20, 1981, the last morning of the Carter presidency, Jimmy Carter and Vice President Walter Mondale were still trying to work out the final details in the negotiations that would free the hostages in Iran. In a noontime ceremony this day Ronald Reagan would be sworn in.

Advice to the next president: We are now the only superpower in the world. . . . I would like to see our nation exemplify all the characteristics of a superpower. I'd like to see every person in the world look on the United States as a foremost proponent of peace, so that every time there is a dispute upon the earth the U.S. would devote a major portion of its great political and economic and even military strength to bringing the disputing parties together. . . . I'd like to see our country be the champion of basic human rights in a broad sense so that people would turn to America for correction of human rights abuses, and we would not be guilty of human rights abuses ourselves. I'd like for our country to be looked upon as a foremost proponent and protector of liberty, freedom, and democracy. So every time there is an election held in the world in a troubled, transitional country, the United States would be in the forefront of making sure that the election was fair and honest and trusted by both sides as a means to perpetuate what might be a fragile peace. I'd like to see our country be unselfish for a change. We are now the most selfish developed nation in the world. We give three-tenths of one percent of our gross national product to healing the wounds of people around the world. Whereas a country like Norway gives twenty times as much [proportionately] for the same purpose. So I would say peace and human rights and freedom and alleviation of suffering are the characteristics, in my opinion, of a great nation and we don't exhibit those. And I think they would be both politically attractive and inspirational and that they would accurately mirror the characteristics of the American people. That would be my advice to the next president.

Cradled in the grip of Carter's left hand is a pile of appendages that could spell peace in the Middle East. Egypt's Anwar Sadat (left) and Israel's Menachem Begin had spent thirteen arduous days at Camp David with Carter, and the treaty they had just signed was the President's crowning achievement.

PART THREE

A MATTER OF DESTINY

Washington, D.C., in the 1890s

John Quincy Adams

Benjamin Harrison

FAMILY TIES

CHAPTER FIVE

Coming from a powerful political lineage can give a candidate a special cachet—
and it doesn't hurt if there has already been a president in the family.

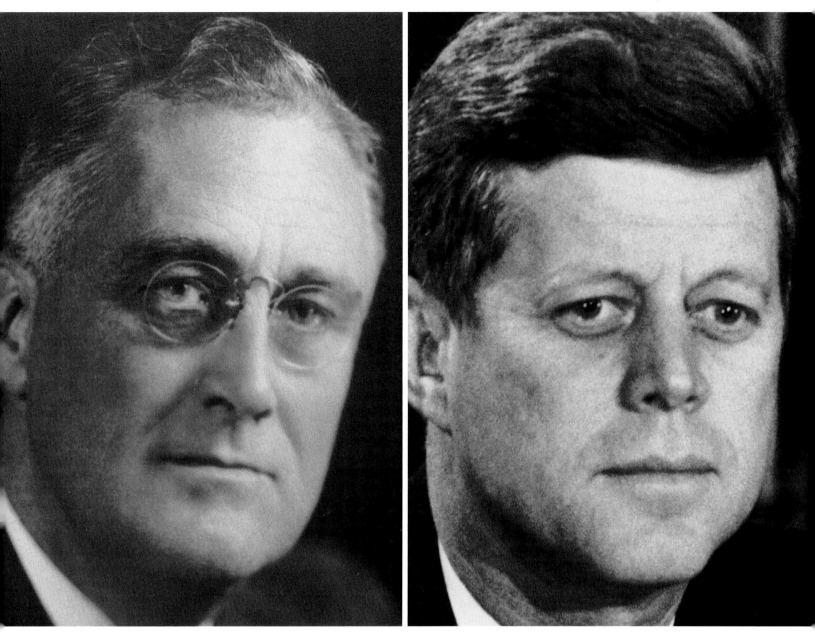

The American presidency, though it retains some of the aura of kingship, is a republican office with no bloodline. Presidents, for the most part, have arisen from ordinary American families, sometimes even from backgrounds of extreme poverty and ignorance. But throughout our history there have been certain prominent, well-to-do families that have been fertile nurturing grounds for presidents. Cultivating a strong ethic of public service at home, and fostering it from generation to generation, they have fashioned themselves into American political dynasties.

In a way, it is surprising that there have not been more of such families. The first five presidents are often perceived as a kind of original American aristocracy, but in fact not one of them arose from a distinguished family. Though George Washington was a direct descendant of King Edward III, by the time he was born, in rural Virginia, his family ties to British royalty had been totally forgotten. His grandfather was, in fact, an impoverished Virginia frontiersman who had slowly worked his way up into the minor gen-

John Adams, the country's second president, fully expected his son to follow in his footsteps. The pressure started early. John wrote his stern, loving, ambitious wife, Abigail, "Let our ardent anxiety be to improve the minds and manners of our children. Let us teach them not only to do virtuously, but to excel."

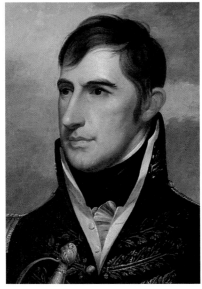

The ninth president, William Henry Harrison, had been a leading western general during the War of 1812. His famous name continued to have a hero's glow to it, which naturally radiated to his grandson Benjamin.

try, and his father was the restless and ambitious owner of 10,000 acres, but he was hardly the progenitor of a great family dynasty. And Washington never begot children of his own.

James Monroe was also a descendant of King Edward III, and thus a distant relative of George Washington's. But he too arose from undistinguished American roots and owed his later stature to his political friendship with Thomas Jefferson.

The Virginian with the greatest claim to a powerful family heritage was the tenth president, John Tyler. Born at "Greenway," the family homestead, he was the son of Virginia's governor and the grandson of a high official in the old colonial court system. But he was leader of one of the most volatile administrations in American history—his family legacy did little to help him and was not carried on by his descendants.

Four American presidents hailed from truly remarkable families and brought to the office a keen sense of their heritage and its responsibilities. John Quincy Adams was born to a life of public service. His father, John Adams, had established a tradition of family excellence, transforming himself from a farmer's son into one of the leading figures of his day. Married to the highly literate and strong-minded Abigail Smith, he possessed a brilliant if curmudgeonly intellect and was independent-minded to a fault. He and Abigail passed on their ideals to their son John Quincy, who became the second Adams to achieve the presidency. They were the only father and son to have each served as president. And the family tradition did not end with John Quincy. Charles Francis, his son, became a congressman from Massachusetts and was appointed Abraham Lincoln's minister to Great Britain. And Charles Francis's son Henry Adams became one of America's finest historical writers. Though other members of the family didn't fare as well, and a stain of tragedy darkens the family history, the Adamses remain one of the greatest political dynasties America has produced.

Between John Quincy Adams and Benjamin Harrison, sixty years later, Americans elected presidents from a variety of backgrounds. Andrew Jackson was the first man born in poverty to attain the presidency. The son of a Scotch-Irish immigrant who labored as a subsistence farmer, he blazed the trail for a host of later presidents, including the most famous poor-man-made-good, Abraham Lincoln. Millard Fillmore, Andrew Johnson, and James Garfield each had a deprived and obscure childhood. In fact, well before the time of Benjamin Harrison in the 1880s, humble origins were considered an attractive asset for presidential contenders, while family privilege was often perceived as a political handicap. In his bid for the presidency, Harrison downplayed his famous grandfather, William Henry Harrison, as well as his eminent family legacy. He rarely spoke of his great-grandfather, Benjamin, who had been a signer of the Declaration of Independence, or even of his father, John, who had served as a U.S. congressman. Few families have passed on the ideal of public service for more generations than did the Harrisons. And few presidents have made less out of their family connections than did our twenty-third president, Benjamin Harrison.

Just the opposite was the case with Franklin D. Roosevelt. The fifth cousin and nephew-by-marriage of President Theodore Roosevelt, FDR reveled in his family connections and used them to advance his career. Unapologetic about his family money and high place in society, he represented a new kind of American aristocrat on the national scene. A graduate of Groton School and Harvard, he possessed a sense of noblesse oblige, the belief that with privilege comes responsibility for public service. And though he became a member of a different political party from his famous relative, he advanced many of the same progressive ideas as had Theodore before him. Unlike Adams or Harrison, FDR adored the presidency and was totally at home in the White House. Believing almost literally that he had been born for the job, he came to think of the entire country as his patrimony.

The Kennedy family, with its Irish Catholic origins, was entirely different from the Roosevelts. But it too had its all-important progenitor. Joseph Kennedy created an American dynasty that has come closest to approximating American royalty. And through his powerful connections and campaign financing, he helped obtain the presidency for his second son, John. After John F. Kennedy's assassination in 1963, his brother Robert became a U.S. senator and presidential contender himself. And John's youngest brother Edward, throughout his political career as a senator from Massachusetts, stayed in the political forefront longer than any other member of the family.

The twentieth century has produced two other presidential dynasties. William Howard Taft was born of a prominent Ohio political family; his father was Ulysses S. Grant's attorney general and later served as ambassador to Austria-Hungary and Russia. And following William Taft's presidency, his eldest son, Robert, went on to become a U.S. senator and a leading conservative Republican. The other notable family line of the twentieth century belongs to George Bush, the son of U.S. Senator Prescott Bush, and the father of two sons who have assumed prominence within the Republican party. One of them, Governor George W. Bush of Texas, seemed destined, like his father, for presidential politics.

But despite the occasional family success story, most American presidents still come from humble origins. Bill Clinton was the son of an itinerant salesman; Ronald Reagan, of a shoe salesman; Jimmy Carter, of a peanut farmer. Gerald Ford was the adopted son of the owner of a paint store. Richard Nixon's father owned a gas station and family market; Dwight Eisenhower's managed a small gas company; Harry Truman's was a small farmer and livestock salesman. Americans trust leaders who have come up the hard way, even though running for president now requires access to a small fortune. Ever since Andrew Jackson, Americans have wanted presidents who are "of the people."

Still there is the other tradition: of a kind of American royalty—represented by the Adamses, the Harrisons, the Roosevelts, and the Kennedys, and in most recent times by the Bush dynasty— which offers something appealing to the American public. Provided native aristocrats know how to conduct themselves in office and have a popular touch, as did FDR and Kennedy, there is something exciting and reassuring about political dynasties. And once or twice in a century, America seems to raise to the presidency successive members of powerful and prominent families.

The name Roosevelt first swept the land as Theodore Roosevelt performed his exploits at the beginning of the twentieth century, encouraging Americans to live hard and love life. Coming on the scene only a generation later, his distant cousin Franklin benefited from the memory of his relative's zestful presidency.

There was no president in the family tree of John F. Kennedy, but a force equally as commanding lurked just behind the dashing young candidate—his father, Joe, who wagered his fortune and power to produce an American president with the Kennedy name.

JOHN QUINCY ADAMS

1825–1829

This miniature portrait by John Ramage shows what John Quincy Adams looked like in his mid-twenties. As a boy he had traveled widely with his father, gaining knowledge of the world, and now, in 1794, he had been appointed by President Washington as American minister to Holland. "I still find myself," he confessed, "as obscure . . . as the most indolent or the most stupid of human beings."

Twenty years later, to help end the War of 1812, John Quincy headed the American delegation at the peace conference in the Belgian city of Ghent. Here, on Christmas Eve 1814, he shakes hands with Britain's Lord Gambier at the signing of the Treaty of Ghent.

His Father's Son

John Quincy Adams once wrote, "I cannot escape my destiny. . . . I am bound to my parents by more than ordinary ties." He was the only son of a president ever to rise to the presidency, and he did so almost in spite of himself. A recluse by nature, always more respected than loved, he described himself as a "cold" and "silent animal." "I well know that I never shall be a popular man," he wrote. "I have none of the honey which is the true fly-catcher."

Adams was raised at the family homestead in what would later be known as Quincy, Massachusetts. With his famous father off helping run the country during the Revolutionary War, his mother became the dominating influence in his early life. When, at age eleven, he accompanied his father on a diplomatic mission to Europe, she tried hard to maintain her maternal control over him. "[My son] must never disgrace his mother," Abigail Adams wrote in a letter. "For dear as you are to me, I had much rather you should have found your grave in the ocean . . . than see you an immoral profligate or a graceless child." John Quincy's father also put enormous pressures on him to succeed. "You came into life with advantages which will disgrace you if your success is mediocre," he once lectured. "And if you do not rise to the head of your country, it will be owing to your own laziness and slovenliness."

In his twenties, in part to please his parents, John Quincy accepted an appointment as America's minister to Holland. While abroad, he met and proposed marriage to Louisa Johnson, the daughter of the U.S. Consul in London. He himself admitted that he was marrying the wealthy heiress in part to support him in his literary pursuits once back in America. But when Louisa's family declared bankruptcy in 1796, the stiff-lipped young ambassador went through with the marriage anyway. "I have done my duty—rigorous, inflexible duty," he wrote. "I am as happy as a virtuous, discreet and amiable woman can make me."

John Quincy's methodical approach to life served him well in his work. In time President Washington called him "the most valuable public character we have abroad." And when John Adams became president in 1797, his son was elevated to the position of minister to Prussia.

In 1801, with his father's retirement from the presidency, John Quincy returned to the United States to settle down on the family homestead. "I never can find contentment . . . at a distance from my parents," he wrote. "I

John Quincy Adams, shown here in an 1843 daguerreotype, looked back on his White House years with distaste. "Make no mistake about it," he wrote acidly, "the four most miserable years of my life were my four years in the Presidency."

Abigail Adams

No matter how good a letter writer and observer of the passing scene, Abigail Adams had her failings as a mother. She wanted to possess her "Johnny," to forge his every move, to drive him in the path of righteousness. If her discipline was severe enough, maybe her son would be saved from the fate of her own brother, who had deserted his wife and family for loose women and easy drink, eventually to die an alcoholic. When Johnny accompanied his father to Paris, he was followed by a chain of letters warning him to avoid worldly temptations. Back home again, the passionate young man fell in love, but try as he might to keep his infatuation quiet, the suspicious and dictatorial Abigail sniffed the situation out and put a swift end to it. "Never form connections until you see a prospect of supporting a family," she wrote in one of her withering letters. John Quincy was emotionally destroyed; he was never quite the same person again, and the cold, austere man who would later be so famous now started to appear. He developed a disdain for women and began seeking out common streetwalkers in Boston for sexual adventures. His appointment as American minister to Holland helped launch his independence and allowed him to meet and pursue his future bride in England. But it wasn't until Abigail heard of the romance and tried to squash this one, too, that he finally charged into marriage. When his own children arrived, he could not keep himself from acting toward them very much as his mother had toward him, and, even though secondhand, a new generation was to feel Abigail Adams's severe manner of parenting. None of this seemed to affect John Quincy's lifelong adoration for his mother, who when she died at seventy-four, was "beloved and lamented more than language can express." He neglected, however, to attend her funeral.

feel an attachment to these places more powerful than to any other spot upon earth."

While he was away, tragedy had struck the family. John Quincy's younger brother Charles had succumbed to alcoholism. An angry John Adams had refused even to visit his dying son, branding him "a mere buck and beast" and utterly renouncing him. Unable to live up to the family ideal, Charles had become its first victim.

Fearing the pressures that had destroyed his brother, John Quincy vowed he would never enter politics—he would rather "clean filth off the streets." But the family destiny proved impossible to resist. Elected to the upper house of the Massachusetts legislature in 1802, one year later he won a seat in the U.S. Senate. And in 1809, he was named minister to Russia by Republican president James Madison.

It was John Quincy, widely recognized as the country's most skillful diplomat, who negotiated the close of the War of 1812. In recognition of his accomplishments after eight years overseas, he was named James Monroe's secretary of state.

He proved himself to be brilliant in this role, perhaps the finest secretary of state in American history, toiling over complex negotiations involving boundary disputes and the acquisition of Florida. And he became the chief architect of the Monroe Doctrine. "Of the public history of Mr. Monroe's administration," he wrote, "all that will be worth telling to posterity has been transacted by the Department of State. . . . I might confidently say by me."

In 1823 Adams's name was put forward as a candidate for president. When no victor emerged in the electoral college, John Quincy, who had run second to Andrew Jackson in the popular vote, was named president by the House of Representatives.

He was one of the brightest men ever to enter the high office and his administration was marked by its bold initiatives. He advocated federally funded roads, canals, river widenings, and harbor works. And in a visionary program far ahead of its time, he called for the creation of a national observatory. In foreign affairs, he became known for his patient negotiations, concluding more commercial treaties than any president prior to the Civil War.

But Adams's basic independence and arrogant manner overshadowed his many achievements. Over his years in office, he became vilified as one of the country's most unpopular presidents ever. "[I am] reproach[ed as] a gloomy misanthropist [and] an unsocial savage!" he wrote. "But I am not formed to shine in company, nor be delighted with it. . . . I have no powers of fascination."

In early July 1826, Adams received a letter from Massachusetts, announcing that his father's health was rapidly sinking. The President reached the family homestead on July 13, six days too late for his father's funeral. Dazed, he wandered through his father's house. "Everything about the house is the same," he wrote. "I was not fully sensible of the change til I entered his bed-chamber. . . . That moment . . . struck me as if it had been an arrow to my heart. . . . The charm which has always made this house to me an abode of enchantment is dissolved; and yet my attachment to it . . . is stronger than I ever felt it before."

John Quincy descended into a profound depression, and the remainder of his presidency was desperately unhappy. Two years later, the hugely popular "people's candidate," Andrew Jackson, defeated Adams by a large majority. "My own career is closed," John Quincy wrote dejectedly. "The sun of my political life sets in the deepest gloom."

His hopes now focused on his own children, all three of whom he had largely ignored during the past two decades. "My sons have not only their own honor but that of two preceding generations to sustain," he wrote.

For years, though, he had had troubles with his offspring, none of whom had distinguished himself academically. "I had hoped that at least one of my sons would have been ambitious to excel," he had written. "[But] I find all three coming to manhood with indolent minds. . . . [It is a] bitter disappointment." When he learned that his oldest son George had begun drinking heavily, as well as gambling and womanizing, he wrote, "I have been horror struck at your danger. May I remind you of the blood from which you came." But when he demanded that George come to talk over his life, his confused and despairing son leapt to his death from aboard a steamboat. "Oh! My unhappy son!" Adams wrote. "What a paradise of earthly enjoyment I had figured . . . as awaiting thee and me. It is withered forever."

A year later Adams was still depressed. "No one knows . . . the agony of mind that I suffered," he wrote. "[It was like] roasting to death by a slow fire." It was his religious faith that finally brought him around. That, and a distinct honor awarded him in 1831 by the people of Massachusetts, who elected him as a representative to the U.S. Congress. He became the only ex-president ever to serve in the House of Representatives. "No election or appointment ever gave me so much pleasure," he wrote. "My election as president was not half so gratifying."

And so commenced the final chapter in John Quincy's long life. He served in Congress for the next seventeen years, becoming the most passionate and respected liberal voice in Washington. He spoke out on Indian rights, on the advancement of science, on freedom of speech, on the evil of slavery. But in his family life, problems continued. In 1834 his second son, John, died, also from alcoholism. That left only his youngest son, Charles Francis. "All my hopes . . . in this world are now centered upon him," Adams wrote. "[I would] die despondent if I were under the conviction that no remaining drop of my father's blood transmitted through me would survive." The family name would continue on through Charles Francis, who would go on to become a U.S. congressman.

John Quincy once swore he would die in the pursuit of duty, and in 1848 he received his wish, suffering a fatal stroke on the floor of the House of Representatives. To the end, it was his family that had kept him going. That, and a lifelong ambition that destroyed so many other Adamses—to have earned the right to be called his father's son.

John Quincy's eldest son, George Washington Adams, took to gambling, womanizing, and drink, before finally committing suicide.

Unhappiness consumed Adams's second son, John, who also died of alcoholism.

Only the youngest son escaped; Charles Francis Adams would become a congressman, and later, minister to England. He saw "the scourge of intemperance" in the family as emanating from the forebears of Abigail.

Through his life Adams kept an extraordinary diary, using it in part to analyze himself and point out his own failings. Here, in 1805, as a senator, he has taken part in a floor debate and finds himself lacking as a speaker.

On this occasion . . . I felt most sensibly my deficiency as an extemporaneous speaker. In tracing this deficiency to its source, I find it arising from a cause that is irreparable. . . . It is slowness of comprehension—an incapacity to grasp the whole compass of a subject in the mind at once with such an arrangement as leaves a proper impression of the detail—and incapacity to form ideas properly precise and definite with the rapidity necessary to give them uninterrupted utterance. My manner, therefore, is slow, hesitating, and often much confused. Sometimes, from inability to furnish the words to finish a thought commenced, I begin a sentence with propriety and end it with nonsense.

His diary was also a forum for his beliefs. Here, in 1841, as a member of the House of Representatives, he makes a passionate entry on the slave trade.

The world, the flesh, and all the devils in hell are arrayed against any man who now in this North American Union shall dare to join the standard of Almighty God to put down the African slave-trade; and what can I, upon the verge of my seventy-fourth birthday, with a shaking hand, a darkening eye, a drowsy brain, and with all my faculties dropping from me one by one, as the teeth are dropping from my head—what can I do for the cause of God and man, for the progress of human emancipation, for the suppression of the African slave-trade? Yet my conscience presses me on; let me but die upon the breach.

His diary also gave Adams an outlet for his vivid, often mean-spirited reactions to others. Here, in 1844, he describes Stephen A. Douglas of Illinois, who has addressed the House.

His face was convulsed, his gesticulation frantic, and he lashed himself into such a heat that if his body had been made of combustible matter it would have been burnt out. In the midst of his roaring, to save himself from choking, he stripped and cast away his cravat, unbuttoned his waistcoat, and had the air and aspect of a half-naked pugilist. And this man comes from a judicial bench, and passes for an eloquent orator!

Trying to rise from his chair in the House of Representatives, Adams topples into the arms of fellow congressmen. For two days the eighty-year-old, self-described "relic of the past" lay half-conscious in the speaker's private chamber before he expired. To both friends and enemies he would ever be remembered as the "Old Man Eloquent" of the U.S. Congress. At right, this daguerreotype portrait of John Quincy Adams was made by Edward Anthony, probably in 1848, the year of the sixth president's death. "There is no passion more deeply rooted in my bosom," Adams once wrote, "than the longing for posterity . . . to support my own and my father's name."

BENJAMIN HARRISON

1889–1893

"Nobody's Grandson"

Ben had grown up on his father's 2,000-acre estate along the Ohio River. After college (above), he chose the law over the ordained ministry, married his sweetheart, and moved to Indiana.

In the Civil War, "Little Ben" raised his own regiment and ended up a brigadier general. A tough disciplinarian who ran his own prayer sessions in camp, he did not hesitate to fill in for his overworked surgeons after a battle.

No politician ever made less use of his family heritage than Benjamin Harrison, grandson of President William Henry Harrison. All his life he had a desire to be his own man. "He will not build high who has not built for himself," he once told a crowd of his grandfather's admirers. But he also had a burning need to prove himself his grandfather's equal. "I [will] show all," he once wrote privately, that "[my] family . . . name is . . . safe in my keeping."

Harrison was a disciplined, dispassionate, proper individual and one of the finest lawyers in Cincinnati. But the very qualities that made him excel —his methodical approach, his absorption in logic and detail, his unwillingness to delegate—turned him into an overefficient workhorse with little sense of fun. "I do the same things every day—eat three meals, sleep six hours and read dusty old books the rest of the time," he wrote. "My life is about as barren of anything funny as the Great Desert is of grass."

Only once was his orderly life turned upside down, when in 1862, he left his wife and two young children to fight for the Union during the Civil War. His letters home were as personal as he ever got. "I am thinking much of you and the dear children," he wrote. "Many earnest prayers will I send up to God this night, should you lose a husband and they a father in this fight."

Because of his grandfather's reputation as a successful general, much was expected of Harrison during the war. Intent on proving himself worthy of his heritage, he fought in more battles in six months than his grandfather had in a lifetime. And serving under Sherman during the 1864 campaign in Georgia, Harrison distinguished himself for his bravery.

Returning to his law practice after the war, he became a force in Republican politics. His ascent was typically methodical: in 1876 he made an unsuccessful but politically important run for the Indiana governorship; in 1881 he won a seat in the U.S. Senate, a perfect position for increasing his visibility; and in 1888, four years after first being mentioned for the job, he won the Republican nomination for president. He told his party he wanted a low-key campaign, with as little emphasis placed on himself as possible, and with no mention at all of his famous ancestry.

"My ambition is for quietness rather than for publicity," he wrote. "I want to avoid everything that is personal. . . . I want it understood that I am the grandson of nobody."

But against his wishes, Harrison's managers insisted on making the connection to his famous grandfather. Campaign posters referred to

During Harrison's single term in office, nothing happened to the country that might have encouraged great deeds, brave moves, or grand moral decisions, from which might have emerged a great president.

Teeming rain at Harrison's inauguration was responsible for this long black ribbon of umbrellas.

Caroline Scott Harrison hardly ever saw her husband during his early law career, he worked so hard and long. During the war he vowed to change all that, a subject that "has been on my mind on the march, on my cot, and even in my dreams," he wrote his "Carrie."

Widowed in his last year in office, Harrison returned home to Indianapolis and married Carrie's niece. Their baby Elizabeth brightened Harrison's old age.

"Tippecanoe." "Keep the ball rolling" had been William Henry's campaign theme; now the giant ball of his grandfather's day was re-created so that the grandson could also push it to victory. And to Benjamin Harrison's great embarrassment, mock log cabins were set up as his campaign headquarters to evoke the spirit of the first Harrison candidacy and to symbolize his grandfather's supposed humble origins.

"[Oh] the noise and tinsel [of] . . . an American political canvas," Harrison lamented. "You know of course that while one part of [my grandfather's] house was a log cabin, that it had been weatherboarded outside and plastered within so as to conform to the rest of the house which was an ordinary frame. You could only find logs by going in through the closet."

The only time in the campaign Harrison spoke at all of his family was when a delegation of his grandfather's troops, now old men, arrived in a downpour. "I know . . . the respect, and even affection . . . which you bore to my grandfather," Benjamin spoke plaintively. "May I not . . . now say that . . . you have since created a modest . . . respect for me?"

Throughout the campaign Harrison stayed home. Nearly 300,000 people came out that summer to catch a glimpse of the presidential candidate, and he gave more than ninety speeches from the front porch of his house. "I fear I am making an impression that I am garrulous!" he commented. "But the truth is that there is no man in the country that dislikes to make a speech so much as I do."

Harrison's victory was a close one. Coming in second to Grover Cleveland in the popular vote, he won in the Electoral College and was pronounced the twenty-third chief executive. But right from the start Harrison found the presidency frustrating. His reclusive personality was not suited for the office, especially the part of the job involving people. And they came to see him in droves. "I am worked to the verge of despair in receiving callers," he wrote. "It is [a] frightful ordeal . . . filling the offices in the country. . . . The applicants . . . are generally respectable and worthy men and many of them are personal friends. . . . But . . . the President cannot aid . . . every needy person. . . . [And] I made myself unpopular."

With blue eyes and a graying red beard, at five feet six inches Harrison was only slightly taller than the shortest president, James Madison. Critics claimed he could never fill the hat of his famous grandfather, and that a microscope was needed to examine so insignificant a figure. And as the criticism intensified, the White House began to seem more like a prison to Harrison. "It is an office and a home combined—an evil combination," he wrote. "[It] is open to visitors from 10:00 A.M. to 2:00 P.M. . . . without card or introduction. . . . The grounds . . . are practically a public park. . . . There is not a square foot of ground, not a bench nor a shade tree, that the President or his family can use in privacy. . . . Until screens were placed in the windows of the private dining room it was not an unusual incident for a carriage to stop in front of them while the occupants took a gratified view of the President and his family at their breakfast or lunch."

Unwilling to delegate responsibility, Harrison tried to do the job single-handedly. He overshadowed his cabinet officers, outraged deserving politicians by ignoring them, had little to say, and assumed an annoying superior manner. "It is a rare piece of good fortune . . . if the President gets one wholly uninterrupted hour at his desk each day," he wrote. "Thoughtlessness is the root of all this. [Each one says,] 'I want only five minutes.'"

Outside for a stroll, Harrison would walk with his eyes on the sky to avoid having to acknowledge well-wishers. He never addressed even close associates by their first names. Once, when a friend pleaded, "for God sake be human," he answered, "I tried it, but I failed. I'll never try it again."

Having assumed the presidency without a popular majority, and with a Democratic Congress after 1890, there was little that Harrison was able to accomplish. His own personal philosophy was "to govern best is to govern least." Ever cautious, when electric lights were installed in the White House in 1891, he refused to touch the switch for the rest of his term, fearing he might be shocked. As the 1892 election approached, his prospects for a second term appeared dim. Running against him was Grover Cleveland—making it the first time ever that both candidates had been president.

In the midst of the reelection campaign, Harrison's wife Caroline developed tuberculosis. Dropping presidential obligations, Harrison nursed her himself, spending whole nights by her bedside in the White House. Observers said he was red-eyed from constant weeping, his lifelong coolness suddenly discarded under the pressure of his wife's illness. Just two weeks before the election Caroline died, and with her went the remainder of Harrison's ambition. "After the heavy blow of the death of my wife," he wrote, "I do not think I could have stood re-election."

When Grover Cleveland beat him handily, the fifty-nine-year-old President didn't seem to care. All he wanted was to return to his empty house in Indianapolis.

In retirement, Harrison attempted to rebuild a family, marrying his wife's young niece three years after leaving office. In doing so, he became permanently estranged from his grown children. "It is natural that a man's former children should not be pleased . . . with a second marriage," he wrote, "But . . . a home is life's essential to me." When a baby was born to the couple the following year, Harrison became a doting older father.

For the rest of his life the former President remained detached from the memory of his famous grandfather, routinely turning down requests for interviews about him. "I have not been a student of family history," he wrote one inquirer. "I suppose there is hardly a member of the family who is less informed." Nor was he inclined to answer requests for personal memories about his presidency. "I have sometimes thought that the life of the President is like that of the policeman in the opera—not a happy one," he wrote. "For nearly sixty years of my life I was driven by work. I want hereafter to do the driving myself."

WHY HE WAS SO FORGETTABLE

Two Benjamins in 1894

The "Gilded Age" of the nineteenth century wandered benignly toward its conclusion, but the serenity of the times was not the only reason Americans were not bowled over by their twenty-third president. In true Whig fashion, Harrison did not believe that the president should actively "do" things. As long as the honor of the flag was observed, the sacredness of the Constitution upheld, and the prosperity of the people nourished, the chief executive was performing his job. But even more to the point, Harrison lacked any kind of charisma. He had been a fine lawyer, one of the best to ever hold the top office, but the many qualities that made him excel at the bar—his absorption in detail, his fear of the cult of personality—were not rewarding traits for the presidency. Hard to excite, Harrison supposedly only used profanity twice in his life, once toward a Confederate soldier on a Civil War battlefield, and again, years later, when he discovered his father's body had been stolen from its grave and sold to the Ohio Medical School for dissection. Harrison took his quiet, civil demeanor to extremes—he could not bring himself to be familiar with people; he even addressed his law partners as Mister. And his high opinion of his own abilities left his colleagues cold. One adviser was stunned to hear him exclaim after his election, "Now I walk with God." This rigid, reserved, reliable, religious intellectual who could speak extemporaneously for hours and who liked to ponder each decision, no matter how slight, was completely unable to light up the White House. No wonder that Harrison's quiet, single term, sandwiched between Grover Cleveland's separated and more conspicuous two terms, was forgotten almost before it had ended.

With its half circle of mighty pillars, the south front of the White House looms over a parade of stylish visitors during the Harrison administration (left). Before 1910 the only government-supplied staff members for the White House residence were a steward, an usher, and nine doorkeepers, some of whom strike a casual pose for a camera (above). All other servants had to be paid for by the president.

BENJAMIN HARRISON'S WHITE HOUSE

Harrison details the White House staff, and a typical day in the presidency.

The office force of the White House is not large. The Private Secretary is at the head of it. His office is an important one, and discretion is the talent most in demand! . . . There is an Assistant Secretary, who carries and delivers the messages to Congress. . . . There are six clerks. . . . One of these is a stenographer . . . and has charge of the mail. One is a telegraph operator. . . . There is a doorkeeper for the President, and one for the Private Secretary. These, with four messengers, complete the office force proper.

Unless the President is very early, he will find some callers waiting for him as he passes through the Cabinet room to his office. . . . When the coming of the lunch hour has brought the morning reception to an end, one of the Cabinet officers appears by appointment, accompanied by a messenger with an armful or a basketful of papers—chiefly made up of petitions and letters relating to appointments. . . . A whole afternoon is often consumed in this way.

The day would not be a typical one without a call from one or more newspaper men. For routine business items, and for social news, the reporters deal with the Private Secretary, but when there are rumors of important public transactions . . . some of the more prominent of the newspaper men expect to have a few moments with the President.

The President's popular receptions begin the next day after his inauguration. . . . It has been suggested that a bow should be substituted for the hand-shake; but it would be quite as admissible to suggest a revision of the declaration of Independence. The interest which multitudes attach to a handshake with the President is so great that the people will endure the greatest discomfort and not a little peril to life and limb to attain it.

The President's daughter-in-law, Mrs. Russell Harrison, and two of his grandchildren

The President and Mrs. Harrison's bedroom

With the help of her staff, such as this duster named Jerry, Mrs. Harrison oversaw the first thorough cleaning of the White House in decades.

The cabinet room, just a short walk from the bedroom

The family's "private" dining room, on the first floor

A public day on the grounds. Harrison was convivial at first, but within a year he began to withdraw from the crowds.

The once tattered, now refurbished Harrison Blue Room

The White House family kitchen, with cook, Dolly Johnson

As president, Benjamin Harrison (above) deserves credit for his tireless efforts on behalf of conservation and the national park system. But true to his retiring nature, he closed off much of the White House to the public, with the notable exception of the East Room (right). Over the years, the décor of this greatest room in the White House changed often, in part due to constant wear and tear from the public and in part to reflect the different styles of the presidents. In sharp contrast to the French character of the other rooms, it took on a very American look under Andrew Jackson. Under Polk it became an imperialistic showcase, with its new ruby-colored carpeting decorated with eagles and stars. Under Pierce the room retained its essential spareness but also added an elaborate painted ceiling. Under Grant and the dawning of the Gilded Age, it came to look like the grand salon of a lushly appointed steamboat. And under Chester Arthur the room became even more plush and comfortable, with Turkish chairs and circular divans and new heavy, amber-colored window hangings. Serving as the dance floor for Grover Cleveland's 1886 wedding to Frances Folsom, the East Room was also the site for state funerals. William Henry Harrison's took place here in 1841, and in 1865, Abraham Lincoln's majestic ceremony. And when Benjamin Harrison's wife Caroline died in 1892, the President had her coffin placed in the East Room under the central chandelier, high up on a platform completely covered with pink flowers.

FRANKLIN D. ROOSEVELT

1933–1945

Possession by Right

Franklin Delano Roosevelt once said, "The Roosevelts have never felt that because they were born in a good position they could put their hands in their pockets and succeed. They have felt, rather, that there was no excuse for them if they did not do their duty."

An only child born to great wealth, Roosevelt grew up revering his aging father. His mother was much younger, and over the years she showered her delicate son with adoration. "I received a love and companionship that was rare between parent and child," he later looked back.

His world was a 900-acre family estate near Hyde Park, New York, on the banks of the Hudson River. It became his spiritual heart and center. Here, Sara Roosevelt was able to keep the real world far away from her beloved son. It wasn't until he attended Groton School, then Harvard, that he finally got away from his mother's watchful eye. Even then, family ties seemed to follow him everywhere. At college he became engaged to his fifth cousin, Eleanor. She was the favorite niece of President Theodore Roosevelt, who came up from Washington to give the bride away. Pulling Franklin aside he said, "There's nothing like keeping the name in the family."

When Franklin entered politics after college, he patterned his campaign style after his hero Theodore Roosevelt. It didn't matter that they belonged to different parties—family ties were far stronger than political ties. He told the same stories, peppered his speeches with the word "bully," and managed to take well-publicized hunting trips. A seat in the New York State Legislature came first; then seven years as assistant secretary of the Navy. It was the exact route to the presidency that his famous cousin had taken. Increasingly secretive, Franklin turned himself into a skilled and cagey politician. "I am a juggler and I never let my right hand know what my left hand does," he said.

Juggling his home life as well, he had six children with Eleanor over ten years. But in 1918 their seemingly perfect life fell apart when Eleanor discovered he was having an affair with her social secretary, Lucy Mercer. It would have led to divorce had not Franklin's mother stepped in, threatening to cut him off without a cent if he ever saw Lucy again. In turn, Eleanor agreed to support her husband publicly, but privately their relationship turned cool and purely professional.

Two years later, Franklin was badly beaten when he ran for vice president. At age thirty-nine he had come to a crossroads, both personally and

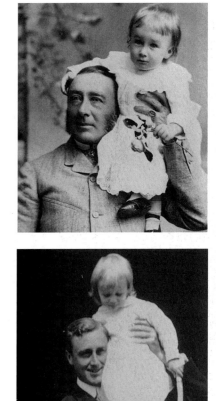

At midlife Franklin's wealthy, widowed father, James, married a woman half his age, one of the beautiful Delano girls. Sara's only child, Franklin, became the love of her life. At top, Franklin rides his father's shoulder in 1883, then, below, tries to duplicate the picture twenty-nine years later with his own son Elliott.

Beset by weariness and age, in October 1944 FDR still flashes his inspiring smile.

For 14 years Sara watched over every move her son made; she even picked his playmates. But at Groton School Franklin had to put up with rowdy classmates, tiny "cubicles" for living quarters, frigid showers upon rising, and incessant bells which marked a rigidly fixed schedule. Unaccustomed to the competition and the cruelties of youth, Franklin pretended to be happy but inside he seethed with uncertainty, craving to succeed. Too slight to excel at athletics, he hid his disappointment with bravado and sarcasm. To his parents he insisted nothing was wrong. When his hero TR came to school to speak, Theodore made Franklin a hero, too.

professionally, and he retreated to the solitude of Campobello, the family summer house on the Canada shore near Maine. There, he awoke one morning to find his legs would not work. Franklin had contracted polio, America's most dread disease. At first he denied there was anything permanently wrong. It took months, and a deep depression, before he was able to deal with his plight. "People who are crippled take a long time to be put back on their feet—sometimes years," he said.

In 1927 Roosevelt purchased an old resort in Warm Springs, Georgia, and opened a therapeutic center for polio victims. "This is really a discovery of a place," he wrote. "The mornings are taken up in the pool and the general exercise in the water is fine. The legs are really improving a great deal."

Slowly but surely—people close to him could see it—a remarkable transformation was taking place. The suffering Franklin was undergoing and his battle against despair were actually recasting him into a deeper, stronger, and more optimistic man. Refusing his mother's pleas that he come home to Hyde Park and spend the rest of his life as a comfortable invalid, with Eleanor's encouragement, Franklin decided to reenter politics.

In 1928, Franklin traced Theodore Roosevelt's course once again—running for and winning the governorship of New York. "Anyone who is governor of New York," he said, "has a good chance to be President with any luck."

To prevent his paralysis from being seen by voters as a sign of weakness, he surrounded himself with family members to help cover it up. Grabbing the strong arm of a son while bracing himself with a cane, he was actually able to make it appear as if he were walking. The great performer put on a mask of joviality and patience in the face of extraordinary frustration and pain.

By 1932, promising to restore prosperity in the midst of the worst depression the country had ever faced, Franklin Roosevelt was named the Democratic nominee for president. He was determined to show the country that his disability would never hold him back, and broke with tradition by going to the convention in Chicago to accept the nomination in person. "You have nominated me and I am here to thank you for the honor," he said. "I pledge myself to a New Deal for the American people."

As Franklin Roosevelt campaigned for the high office, a quarter of the labor force was unemployed and banks all across the country were closing. By Inauguration Day, the economy had hit bottom. All eyes were on the new President for desperately needed leadership. "I shall ask the Congress for one remaining instrument to meet the crisis," Roosevelt said boldly in his inaugural address, "broad executive power to wage a war against the emergency as great as the power that would have been given to me if we were in fact invaded by a foreign foe." And then, with eight simple words, he won the nation's heart, saying "we have nothing to fear but fear itself."

A grateful Congress granted FDR a mandate to lead such as few presidents have ever been given. In just fourteen weeks fifteen major bills were passed, shoring up the banking system, creating a huge public works program, and establishing financial safety nets for farmers and creditors.

Except for Herbert Hoover who had made halting attempts, it was the first time a president had tried to cure an economic crisis. "I knew that we must never let our economic system get out of joint again," he wrote, "and the only way . . . was to have a government with the power to cure the abuses." FDR's New Deal forced the country to take responsibility for its cit-

Soon after the death of his father, Franklin was secretly courting his tall, timid, toothy fifth cousin Eleanor Roosevelt. The alliance seemed odd, almost politically motivated, but Franklin proposed marriage anyway and an insecure Eleanor accepted.

Not long after they were married, Eleanor and Franklin began producing child after child. Here she holds James beside Franklin and Anna.

A state senator (above), then assistant secretary of the Navy, the dashing comer almost ended his marriage by an affair with Eleanor's young social secretary.

At age thirty-eight Roosevelt ran as the Democrats' vice presidential candidate, alongside Governor James M. Cox of Ohio (above left). Their defeat, by the Harding-Coolidge landslide, left Roosevelt's future uncertain. And then the unthinkable happened—he contracted polio.

Spending years out of the political limelight trying to face up to his physical problems, Roosevelt was transformed by his experience with polio. Shown here in 1929, at his newly opened therapeutic center at Warm Springs, Georgia, a forty-seven-year-old Roosevelt has a new look in his face. The years of depression and agony and having to learn a new way of life were turning the once shallow politician into a man of fortitude and compassion. Three years later, in 1932, he would run for president and win.

izens, ushering in unemployment relief, and eventually social security for millions of Americans. Roosevelt's visionary rescue measures reinvigorated a national spirit and changed the country's idea of what government should be about.

Like his cousin, Roosevelt ran the White House like a big informal boardinghouse, with its doors thrown open to family and friends. And he had the same command Theodore Roosevelt had had over the press. But now, because of radio, the President could do something his cousin could never do—talk directly to the American people, in what became known as his fireside chats. "It is your problem my friends, no less than it is mine," he said in one of them, talking as if he were in the same room with every member of his huge audience. "Together we cannot fail."

Embraced warmly by the American public, Roosevelt successfully campaigned for reelection in 1936. And in 1940, he went on to do what no other president has ever done—win election to a third term. With war now raging in Europe and Asia, Americans knew they couldn't afford to lose FDR's proven leadership in time of crisis. "We must try to prevent the domination of the world," Roosevelt said, "but I am not willing to fire the first shot. I am waiting to be pushed into the situation."

On December 7, 1941, Japan attacked the U.S. fleet at Pearl Harbor. Four days later Hitler declared war against the United States. And once again Roosevelt would have to rally the nation.

"We are now in this war," he said in one radio broadcast. "We are all in it. All the way. Every single man woman and child is a partner in the most tremendous undertaking of our American history."

With consummate skill, Roosevelt led the war effort, even at the expense of his own health. Forging an unbreakable alliance with Great Britain, and risking a wartime alliance with the Soviet Union, he became the acknowledged leader of the free world. British Prime Minister Winston Churchill called him "the greatest man I have ever known."

By the time Franklin Roosevelt was elected to an unprecedented fourth term, his face showed the signs of the toll of his twelve years in office. By now he had given everything he had. The strength and energy that had carried the nation were gone. Weak and in failing health, he asked that his fourth inauguration be held at the White House to make it easier on him. Just eighty-two days later, he collapsed of a cerebral hemorrhage. He would never see the end of the war, nor his dream, the United Nations, come into being, nor the new world order he had attempted to create. But he had made an indelible mark upon the world. On its editorial page the normally restrained *New York Times* wrote, "Men will thank God on their knees a hundred years from now that Franklin D. Roosevelt was in the White House."

Roosevelt's body was brought home to the shores of his beloved river, on the precious land of his ancestors. In death he rejoined the family heritage that had so influenced him in life. Once someone had asked him how, with the knowledge that he would never walk again, he ever got himself to sleep. "It's very easy," he said. "I coast down the hills in the snow, and then I walk slowly up, and I know every curve." And on another occasion he put it this way: "All that is in me goes back to the Hudson. . . . And to the days as a boy in Hyde Park."

Although he was seldom out of a wheelchair, Roosevelt saw to it that few pictures of him in one were ever taken. In this photograph at Hyde Park in 1941 he is joined by his Scottish terrier, Fala, and Ruthie Bie, a friend's granddaughter. Once, during the early years of his struggle, a visitor watched Roosevelt slip out of his wheelchair, crawl crablike across the room, grab a book and carry it back to the chair in his teeth. Why did you do that, he was asked? His answer was simple. "I felt I had to do it to show that I could."

FRANKLIN AND ELEANOR

The Roosevelts in 1941

FDR was a lonely man, a man afraid to express his inner feelings, a man made even more solitary as Eleanor became less and less the traditional wife. The woman who had called her servants "darkies" and "picaninnies" when she first moved to Washington was reshaping herself into the country's foremost defender of human rights. Freed of her marital obligations, she first set out to educate herself in politics and social justice. Then, with new self-confidence, new friends, and new freedom, she began traveling about the country as FDR's greatest ambassador, selling the New Deal to the people and fighting for the rights of oppressed Americans—especially blacks and women. So persistent and vocal was she about her causes that Eleanor once asked FDR if he minded her speaking out so. "No, certainly not," he replied. "You can say anything you want. I can always say, 'Well, that is my wife; I can't do anything about her.'" FDR threw open the White House door to his family, to cabinet members, to foreign visitors, to Eleanor's new friends. Sometimes his guests stayed for weeks, even months at a time. Part of FDR's daily ritual was cocktail hour. Work would stop in the late afternoon and whoever was around would gather in the President's study, where FDR mixed the drinks and led the conversation and the laughter. To the public his affliction remained hidden—a known fact, but so cloaked it seemed almost not to exist. To his family and friends he showed no embarrassment over his legs. When he tipped over something or fell, he just grinned or chuckled or said his favorite expression, "I love it." Despite Eleanor's absences she remained his closest adviser—he once called her "the most extraordinarily interesting woman he had ever met." Nor did he ever grow out of his attachment to his mother. When she died during the war, leaving him the family property at Hyde Park, Roosevelt ordered not a single stone on it be moved—he wanted it kept as a family shrine.

In the evening of December 7, 1941, the day Japan attacked Pearl Harbor, stunned citizens gathered in front of the White House behind the flow of traffic on Pennsylvania Avenue.

Presiding over the Great Depression.

January 17, 1930: The first duty of a State, and by that I mean a Government, is to promote the welfare of the citizens of that State. It is no longer sufficient to protect them from invasion, from lawless and criminal acts, from injustice and persecution, but the State must protect them, so far as lies in its power, from disease, from ignorance, from physical injury, and from old-age want.

April 8, 1931: It is high time to admit with courage that we are in the midst of an emergency at least equal to that of war. Let us mobilize to meet it.

July 2, 1932: I pledge you—I pledge myself to a new deal for the American people. Let us all here assembled constitute ourselves prophets of a new order of competence and of courage. This is more than a political campaign; it is a call to arms. Give me your help, not to win votes alone, but to win in this crusade to restore America to its own people.

March 4, 1933: This great nation will endure as it has endured, will revive and will prosper. So, first of all, let me assert my firm belief that the only thing we have to fear is fear itself—nameless, unreasoning, unjustified terror which paralyzes needed efforts to convert retreat into advance.

January 4, 1935: Governments can err—Presidents do make mistakes, but the immortal Dante tells us that divine justice weighs the sins of the cold-blooded and the sins of the warm-hearted in different scales. Better the occasional faults of a government that lives in a spirit of charity than the consistent omissions of a government frozen in the ice of its own indifference.

October 14, 1936: Four years ago . . . I came to a Chicago fighting with its back to the wall—factories closed, markets silent, banks shaky, ships and trains empty. Today those factories sing the song of industry—markets hum with bustling movement, banks are secure; ships and trains are running full. Once again it is a Chicago that smiles. And with Chicago a whole nation that had not been cheerful for years is full of cheer once more.

January 6, 1937: Ours was the task to prove that democracy could be made to function in the world of today as effectively as in the simpler world of a hundred years ago.

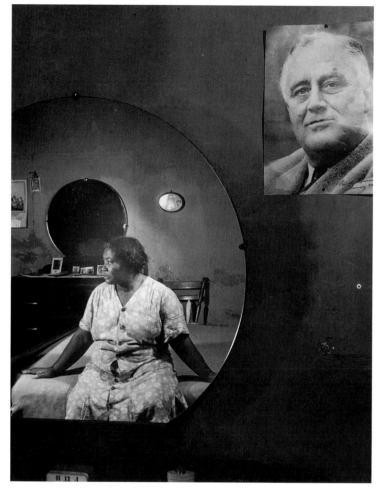

No president since Lincoln was so widely admired among African Americans as was Franklin Roosevelt. For his personal courage, for his strong support of blacks in the military (below), for his commitment to social justice, and for his compassion for the poor, FDR's picture adorned many a bedroom wall (above).

No one enjoyed being president more than FDR, shown here reviewing troops in Sicily in 1943.

The Big Three at Yalta, 1945. Roosevelt once told Churchill, "It is fun to be in the same decade with you."

This is probably the last picture ever taken of FDR. It is early April 1945 at Warm Springs, Georgia, and the President stretches his legs out on a wicker stool and either reads or nods off beside his work table.

On the morning of April 14, Roosevelt's black-draped caisson is drawn by six white horses from Union Station to the White House (above). Mourners line the streets along the way (right), many weeping, some saying prayers, all aghast at the loss of a beloved and extraordinary president.

Presiding over the beginnings of World War II

About three years ago we got the pretty definite information that there was in the making a policy of world domination between Germany, Italy, and Japan. . . . There are two ways to look at it. The first . . . is the hope that somebody will assassinate Hitler or that Germany will blow up from within; that somebody will kill Mussolini or he will get a bad cold in the morning and die. . . . The other attitude is that we must try to prevent the domination of the world. . . . This wild man . . . Hitler . . . believes himself to be a reincarnation of Julius Caesar and Jesus Christ.

This nation will remain a neutral nation, but I cannot ask that every American remain neutral in thought as well. Even a neutral has a right to take account of facts. Even a neutral cannot be asked to close his mind or his conscience.

I am not willing to fire the first shot. . . . I am waiting to be pushed into the situation.

Yesterday, December 7, 1941—a date which will live in infamy—the United States of America was suddenly and deliberately attacked by naval and air forces of the Empire of Japan.

Yes, the Nazis and the Fascists have asked for it—and they are going to get it.

This war is a new kind of war. It is different from all other wars of the past. . . . It is warfare in terms of every continent, every island, every sea, every air lane in the world. That is the reason why I have asked you to take out and spread before you a map of the whole earth, and to follow with me the . . . battle lines of this war.

Last night, when I spoke with you . . . I knew at that moment that troops of the United States and our allies were crossing the Channel. . . . And so, in this poignant hour, I ask you to join with me in prayer. Almighty God: Our sons, pride of our Nation, this day have set upon a mighty endeavor. . . . Lead them straight and true; give strength to their arms, stoutness to their hearts, steadfastness in their faith.

I hope you will pardon me for this unusual posture of sitting down during the presentation of what I want to say, but I know that you will realize that it makes it a lot easier for me not to have to carry about ten pounds of steel around on the bottom of my legs; and also because of the fact that I have just completed a fourteen-thousand mile trip.

JOHN F. KENNEDY

1961–1963

Vindicating the Irish

Seen here in costume at age six, John F. Kennedy came to rely on brains and charm in place of physical prowess.

In schoolboy years Jack Kennedy beams beside his father. Joseph P. Kennedy was convinced that his oldest son, Joe Jr., would one day be president of the United States. As for the bright but sickly second son: "Jack [is] going to be a university president."

The Roosevelts, like the Adamses and the Harrisons, were native aristocrats—part of America's Protestant establishment. But the next great political dynasty to produce an American president was Roman Catholic and had to seize its place in American history. It was the family of John Fitzgerald Kennedy.

At its head was Joseph Patrick Kennedy, of Irish immigrant roots, whose father had become successful in Massachusetts politics. Married to Rose Fitzgerald, the daughter of Boston's mayor, Joe had climbed his way up to become one of the richest men in America. For a summer home he chose the Wasp enclave of Hyannis Port, on Cape Cod, which would become the ground where the Kennedy family would stake its roots. Determined to break into the Protestant club of national government, Joe deliberately prepared his sons for greatness. "My father was very active in politics in our formative years," John Fitzgerald—also known as Jack— remembered. "And all the discussions at our table growing up were about government and political life."

Joe Kennedy became the architect of his children's lives. "We want winners," he told them. "We don't want losers around here." Home life was defined by constant verbal testing, competitive athletics, iron discipline, and no sympathy. Of all the children, Jack seemed the least like his father. He was detached and careless and more independent than his brothers and sisters. Unlike his robust father, he was sickly and frail, and suffered from spinal problems and asthma. And though he, like Franklin Roosevelt, attended Harvard, he was overshadowed there in everything he did by his older brother, Joe. "I was not very active in politics at Harvard," Jack said, "and I don't think that there was any indication that I was going to adopt it as a career."

Jack's luck changed in 1940 with the completion of his senior thesis on England's unpreparedness for World War II. Though his father strongly disagreed with its liberal democratic contents, Joe helped get it published and it was soon a best-seller. "I was always interested in writing," Jack later remembered. "[And] I wanted to teach for a while. So that if it hadn't been for what happened . . . I suppose I would have gone on with my original plans."

What happened was that his brother Joe was killed in World War II, an event which almost destroyed his father. Old Joe Kennedy had always intended that his eldest son be the member of the family who would ultimately make a run for the presidency and vindicate the much-maligned Irish

Joe Kennedy suffered a stroke during the last year of John Kennedy's presidency. The grandson of poor immigrants, he had earned his fortune in Hollywood and in the liquor business, then turned his attention to accumulating power. Whenever President Kennedy could get away from the White House for a weekend, he visited his father at the family compound on Cape Cod. On Monday morning, with the helicopters roaring on the compound lawn, Jack would bid goodbye with a gentle kiss to the man who helped make him president.

The skipper of a PT boat in the Pacific in World War II, Jack made the front page of the *New York Times* when a Japanese destroyer sliced his little craft in two.

In 1947, thin and tired-looking, the young congressman takes his desk in the Capitol.

They made a picture perfect political family—youthful Jack, radiant Jacqueline, adorable Caroline.

in the highest office in the United States. After Joe died, Joe Sr. convinced Jack to take his brother's place in the plan. "It was like being drafted," Jack later recalled. "My father wanted [me] . . . in politics; 'wanted' isn't the right word. He demanded it."

At first Jack rebelled. But as it had turned out for John Quincy Adams, his family destiny proved to be irresistible, and within a year and a half he was launched on a meteoric political career. "I ran in 1946 and was successful," Kennedy recalled. "And then . . . again in '48 and '50 and won then, and then again in 1952."

He seemed made for politics, and in Washington Jack Kennedy became a sought-after figure. His big family, his fortune, his sense of fun, his style and grace made him immensely appealing, especially to the young. And America's most eligible bachelor became even more popular when he married Jacqueline Bouvier in 1952.

Though he failed in 1956 to win the vice presidency, John F. Kennedy decided to make a run for the high office. As they had in each of his earlier elections, once again every member of the Kennedy clan would actively campaign, and it was joked that he was running on "the family plan." Joe Kennedy, the archconservative, stayed offstage but pulled important political strings from behind the scenes and provided all-important infusions of money. At a gridiron dinner in 1958, Jack was secure enough to make a crack about it. "I have just received the following wire from my generous daddy," he quipped. "Dear Jack—Don't buy a single vote more than is necessary—I'll be damned if I'm going to pay for a landslide." As it turned out it would be one of the closest elections in American history.

Jack Kennedy soon realized that he was not only running against Richard Nixon, he was running against widespread prejudice against his family's Irish Catholic roots. Though some advisers suggested he sidestep the issue, Kennedy decided to meet it head-on. He did so in September 1960, in an address to a group of Houston clergy that was televised across the country. "If this election is decided on the basis that forty million Americans lost their chance of being President on the day they were baptized," he said, "then it is the whole nation that will be the loser, in the eyes of Catholics and non-Catholics around the world, in the eyes of history, and in the eyes of our own people. . . . I am not the Catholic candidate for President. I am the Democratic party's candidate for President who happens to be Catholic."

His victory two months later, in November 1960, was a victory for all Roman Catholics, but it was a special vindication for the Kennedy family. At the inauguration ceremony the following January, one of every seven people on the podium was a Kennedy.

Jack's father had made just one request of the President-elect—that his brother Bobby, who had served as his campaign manager, be a member of his cabinet. "It's the only thing I'm asking for," he said, "and I want it." For Jack it meant taking a leap of faith; his brother Robert had never even practiced law. But against all the advice not to do it that poured in, Jack named his brother attorney general. Robert proved exceedingly effective in the job, and above all, he was devoted to his brother. He was not only a brother, he was a brother in an established hierarchy in a family that in some ways was an ancient Irish tribe. His loyalty could be counted on completely.

Initially, however, Jack Kennedy did not turn to his brother for advice. Instead, at the urging of a team of experts, including the director of the CIA, he approved a plan that had been hatched under Eisenhower—a secret inva-

Nineteen fifty-seven was the midpoint in John F. Kennedy's short, spectacular career. In the decade just past, he had won a congressional seat in the 11th Massachusetts District and held it for three terms before being elected to the Senate. He had met and married Jacqueline Bouvier. He had almost died of a back injury he received in the war, which required a three-hour operation to fuse the spinal disks. He had been afflicted with Addison's disease which caused his immune system to fail, and a staph infection had put the emaciated senator into a coma. He had published a best-seller, *Profiles in Courage*. And he had won national attention by losing a skirmish for the Democratic vice presidential nomination. By 1957, as he weighed running for the presidency in 1960, he had effectively distanced himself from his conservative father. "Look here, Dad," he had insisted while still a congressman. "You have your political vision and I have mine." As to foreign affairs, "We don't even discuss it," Jack said. "We're just so far apart, there's no point to it." But family ties for the Kennedys always ran deeper than political opinion, and Joe Sr. remained his son's strongest supporter. He campaigned behind the scenes and put to work his vast fortune, estimated to have reached $300 million. Rose Kennedy, too, joined the family efforts, claiming that the country needed her son in the White House. To this voracious clan, winning was first, but not far behind was family loyalty. "Just as I went into politics because Joe died," Jack announced, "if anything happened to me tomorrow, my brother Bobby would run for my seat. . . . And if Bobby died, Teddy would take over for him."

Like all the Kennedys, Ted, the youngest son, was on the road drumming up enthusiasm for his brother, who at this rally sits behind him bemused at the family spectacle.

After winning the nomination on the first ballot, Kennedy chose his former rival, Senate Majority Leader Lyndon Johnson, as his running mate. "It was the goddamnedest thing," Johnson said as he thought back to the fifties. "Here was a young whippersnapper, malaria-ridden and yellah, sickly, sickly . . . His growing hold on the American people was simply a mystery to me."

The Kennedy brothers—John, the candidate, and Robert, his campaign manager— brood and meditate at the 1960 Democratic convention.

Above, proud members of the Kennedy family, including Joe Sr. second from left, line up to greet the public following JFK's election to the presidency in 1960. During the campaign, Joe had stayed almost completely hidden from view, making few requests, even leaving the country for a time. But shortly after the election he hastened to the President-elect's Georgetown residence (below left) to make one firm demand—he wanted Bobby named to a position in Jack's cabinet. Not long afterwards JFK emerged (below right) to announce to the press that his brother Robert would be named attorney general.

sion of Cuba. It turned out to be a terrible mistake. Of the 1,450 soldiers who were landed at the Bay of Pigs, all but 150 were captured or killed. Kennedy vowed never again to be swayed by outside advisers and increasingly came to place his trust in family members and friends.

To those around him, his family seemed linked to everything he did. When he dealt with Soviet leader Nikita Khrushchev, he said it was like "dealing with Dad . . . all give and no take." Upon hearing that construction of the Berlin Wall had begun, Kennedy's first words were "go get Bobby." When he established the Peace Corps, he announced that his brother-in-law Sargent Shriver would run it. And he turned to his wife, Jacqueline, to transform the White House into a center of culture.

But it was Kennedy's own considerable skills at statecraft that marked his presidency. And in October 1962, all his faculties of judgment and leadership would be tested in what came to be known as the Cuban Missile Crisis. American reconnaissance had learned that the Soviets had moved nuclear missiles into Cuba, where they were capable of reaching any region in the United States. Military advisers were recommending a preemptive air strike. A wrong move at any point could provoke nuclear war.

This time Kennedy relied on his own cool judgment and on a penetrating analysis of the motives of the Soviets. This time his chief adviser was his brother Bobby, who was sent behind the scenes to open a direct line of communication with the Soviet Union. By direct contact and by perceptive bargaining, John Kennedy was able to defuse the single most dangerous confrontation of the nuclear age. By the following year the superpowers had established a direct hotline between Moscow and the White House and had signed the first nuclear weapons test ban treaty. No accomplishment, Kennedy said, gave him greater satisfaction.

In the summer before his assassination, which lurked just a few months away—on November 22, 1963—President Kennedy made a sentimental journey. His father would be unable to travel with him; having suffered a stroke, he was unable to walk or talk, unable to give any more advice. Now, Kennedy was off to his ancestral homeland, to Ireland, where he was mobbed by adoring crowds. Here he was, the first Catholic president of the United States, fulfilling his father's ambitions for him and for his entire family, indeed for all the Irish in America. Here he was being greeted by the entire population of the island as a hero. It was, in a way, a completing of the circle—a vindication of the Irish, who had struggled so long in their homeland and in America to achieve the recognition they deserved.

Like Franklin Roosevelt, Kennedy had a superb feel for the presidency and from the outset showed evident enjoyment of the office.

The new President ponders a decision at his desk in the Oval Office. As the first president to preside over a world fraught with nuclear dangers, Kennedy brought a new standard of performance to the job.

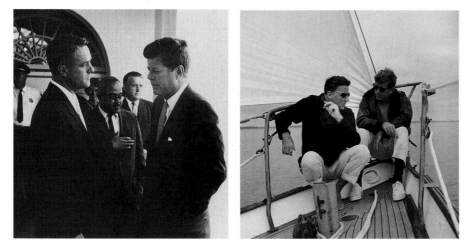

Family ties were always important to the President. Here he confers with his brothers-in-law Sargent Shriver (far left) and Peter Lawford (left).

At the U.S. embassy in Vienna the President and Soviet boss Nikita Khrushchev exchange their opposing views of the world in June of 1961.

JFK's private secretary Evelyn Lincoln is amused alongside two Johns—one short, the other tall.

The President confers with Secretary of Defense Robert McNamara at the height of the Cuban Missile crisis.

Whether manning the tiller or comforting Caroline on deck, Kennedy was always happiest when on the ocean. "We all came from the sea," he once said. "It is an interesting biological fact that all of us have in our veins the exact same percentage of salt . . . that exists in the ocean. And therefore, we have salt in our blood, in our sweat, in our tears. We are tied to the sea. And when we go back to the sea, whether it is to sail or to watch it, we are going back from whence we came." Thirty-six years later, John F. Kennedy, Jr. crashed his small plane into the same seas his father had once sailed, not far from the family homestead in Massachusetts.

At age forty-four John F. Kennedy was the youngest man ever elected president.

When Jacqueline Kennedy first inspected the White House, she said it looked as if it had been furnished from a discount department store. She went on to launch a complete redecoration. The first couple brought to the office an enchanting elegance and a conviction that all things were possible if tackled intelligently and hard. And then, suddenly, it was over. In November of 1963, they traveled to Dallas. There, in a motorcade through the city, President Kennedy was assassinated by a political malcontent with a 6.5 millimeter mail-order carbine. A devastated nation was led through an unforgettable televised funeral pageant by the indefatigable Jacqueline, who then, at the height of her grief, granted an interview to her friend the presidential historian Theodore White. "All I could keep thinking of is this line from a musical comedy," she told White of how her husband's favorite song had stuck in her head during the tragic hours. "Don't let it be forgot, that once there was a spot, for one brief shining moment that was known as Camelot." On publication of the interview, the Kennedy era took on a fairy-tale shimmer of knights and kings and romance and heraldry in the mists of which it has been cloaked ever since.

Inaugural Address, Jan. 20, 1961: Let the word go forth from this time and place, to friend and foe alike, that the torch has been passed to a new generation of Americans. . . . Let every nation know, whether it wishes us well or ill, that we shall pay any price, bear any burden, meet any hardship, support any friend, oppose any foe to assure the survival and the success of liberty. . . . If a free society cannot help the many who are poor, it cannot save the few who are rich. . . . All this will not be finished in the first one hundred days. Nor will it be finished in the first one thousand days, nor in the life of this Administration, nor even perhaps in our lifetime on this planet. But let us begin. . . . And so, my fellow Americans: ask not what your country can do for you—ask what you can do for your country.

On the Cuban missile Crisis, Oct. 22, 1962: Missiles in Cuba add to an already clear and present danger. . . . This secret, swift, and extraordinary buildup . . . in an area well known to have a special and historical relationship to the United States and the nations of the Western Hemisphere, in violation of Soviet assurances, and in defiance of American and hemispheric policy—this sudden, clandestine decision to station strategic weapons for the first time outside of Soviet soil—is a deliberately provocative and unjustified change in the status quo which cannot be accepted by this country, if our courage and our commitments are ever to be trusted again by either friend or foe.

On the presidency, Sept. 23, 1963: The American Presidency is a formidable, exposed, and somewhat mysterious institution. It is formidable because it represents the point of ultimate decision in the American political system. It is exposed because decision cannot take place in a vacuum: the Presidency is the center of the play of pressure, interest, and idea in the Nation; and the presidential office is the vortex into which all the elements of national decision are irresistibly drawn. And it is mysterious because the essence of ultimate decision remains impenetrable to the observer—often, indeed, to the decider himself.

Gentler and wiser with his children than his father had been with his, Kennedy loved to play with Caroline and John Jr., laugh with them, listen to them. He also liked to dream of what the future would be like.

John Tyler

Millard Fillmore

HAPPENSTANCE

CHAPTER SIX

Eight vice presidents have been thrust into the high office upon
the death of a sitting president. Often underqualified and ill prepared, they
became known in their times as "the accidental presidents."

Andrew Johnson

Chester A. Arthur

Harry S. Truman

James Madison's meticulous notes taken at the 1787 Constitutional Convention were not published in time to help inform the first successor presidents, but they made clear that the Framers never intended for the vice president to succeed to the presidency in full. The vice president was conceived as a temporary fill-in; in the language of the Convention's "Committee on Postponed Matters," he "shall exercise [the President's] powers and duties until another President be chosen." Madison himself went on record at the convention in support of specially called elections to follow presidential deaths or removals. But an unintended ambiguity in the final language of the Constitution, introduced by the so-called "Committee of Style," obscured the original intent of the Framers and laid open the possibility of misinterpretation.

At the same time, the Constitution, by the very method it outlined for selecting the president and vice president, tried to ensure the election of vice presidents of the highest caliber. Presidential "electors," to be appointed in

McKinley's second-term vice president, Theodore Roosevelt, signaled a turning point in how the nation viewed the second in command. Here the two pose together on McKinley's front porch in July 1900.

In the wings for Warren G. Harding (left) was the stubborn, enigmatic Calvin Coolidge, who not only went on to win his own term of office but also became so popular he probably could have won a second term too if he had chosen to run.

each state in accordance to its total number of senators and representatives, were to vote for two persons, one of whom had to reside outside his own state. The person with the most votes, if a majority, became president; the runner-up became vice president. "The process of election affords a moral certainty," wrote Alexander Hamilton, "that the office of President will seldom fall to the lot of any man who is not in an eminent degree endowed with the requisite qualification. . . . [And] as the Vice President may occasionally become a substitute for the President . . . all the reasons . . . for the one apply . . . to the manner of appointing the other."

At first the system worked extremely well, as proved by the election of George Washington and John Adams to the top two offices. But as presidential elections became increasingly politicized, unexpected developments began to occur. In the election of 1800, Republicans attempted to elect Aaron Burr as Thomas Jefferson's vice president. But the plan backfired when an unexpected tie threw the election into the House of Representatives, almost propelling the unsavory Burr into the highest office. A widespread call for reform arose, leading to the Twelfth Amendment, passed in 1804, which provided for the first time a distinct ballot for president and vice president.

But while the Twelfth Amendment solved one problem, it created another. The vice presidency, no longer filled by the runner-up for president, began attracting lesser men, often convinced to run merely to balance the presidential ticket. Monroe's vice president, Daniel Tompkins, spent much of his time in office fighting off charges of financial misdoings. Martin Van Buren's vice president, Richard Johnson, was so busy running a Maryland tavern, where he kept slave mistresses, he was rarely seen in Washington. The vice presidency was becoming increasingly degraded.

Then, fifty-two years into the history of the presidency, came the sudden death of the ninth president, William Henry Harrison, just weeks after his inauguration. With his death, the insignificant office of vice president, for the first time, took on compelling importance. John Tyler's forceful assumption of the presidency in full set a precedent that would be followed by all later vice presidents faced with a presidential death in office. But the Tyler presidency was an intensely volatile one. Having been chosen originally to balance the Harrison ticket, this former states'-rights Democrat was soon opposed by his entire cabinet. Though he vigorously fought to sustain his authority, Tyler was compromised in his ability to offer positive leadership. And this too became a precedent he bequeathed to others. All three of the remaining successor presidents of the nineteenth century—Millard Fillmore, Andrew Johnson, and Chester Arthur—were notably ineffectual and none was able to go on to win his own term in office. Each, in a way, was a fiasco of ticket balancing—Fillmore and Arthur represented Northern interests, while Andrew Johnson, a Southern Democrat, was utterly out of place within a postwar Republican government. None was a person of the highest stature; each seemed to deserve the title of "accidental president." Writing in 1888, the British observer James Bryce noted, "Very little pains are bestowed on the election of a Vice President. The convention . . . usually gives the nomination . . . to a man in the second rank. . . . And thus if the President happens to die, a man who may, like Tyler or Johnson, be of no great personal account, steps into the chief magistracy of the nation."

Beginning with the national tragedy of William McKinley's murder, however, a new kind of successor president emerged. By the sheer force of his personality and political will, Theodore Roosevelt enlarged the vision of what a successor president could be, and went on, as none of his predecessors had, to win his own term of office. His example seemed to benefit the successor presidents that followed. Calvin Coolidge, who succeeded Warren G. Harding after his death in office, also was able to win election in his own right, as was Harry Truman, following Franklin Roosevelt's death, and Lyndon Johnson, following the assassination of John F. Kennedy. Part of the success of these twentieth century successors may have been due to changes in the nominating process. And part of it lay in the increasing stature of the vice presidency itself, which in modern times began to attract far more able and gifted individuals.

In the end, none of the successor presidents was truly "accidental." Each was nominated by a national convention, with the full knowledge that he might inherit the presidential duties. What is accidental, and almost never prepared for, is how often presidents themselves end up dying while in office—which is why, finally, the Tyler precedent is so important. The framers of the Constitution may have seen things differently, but they lived in simpler times, when a hiatus during a special election of a new president could cause no real harm. Today, in a far more dangerous, fast-paced world, we require instantaneous succession, and a succession not just to the duties of president but to the full office itself.

The Twenty-fifth Amendment, passed in 1967, finally codified what had long been the nation's historical practice. Breaking with the Framers' original intent, and siding instead with the Tyler precedent, the amendment left no grammatical ambiguities about its meaning. "In the case of the removal of the President from office or of his death or resignation," it reads, "the Vice President shall become President."

Presidents and vice presidents have often not gotten along, partly because the vice president can so easily remind the president that he is mortal. And some ambitious men have settled for the second spot in hopes of one day succeeding to the first. But in times of national trauma caused by the death of a president, the succession of the vice president can be the key to the nation's stability.

Ready to take over from John F. Kennedy was Lyndon B. Johnson, one of the strongest legislators in the history of the country. Here he is shown with JFK at the 1960 Democratic National Convention, getting an earful from his running mate's mother.

Gerald Ford is the only vice president to have suddenly moved into the top spot for a reason other than death. He was elevated when Richard Nixon became the first president ever to resign from office. The two are shown here in the Oval Office on the day of the resignation.

Brady, N.Y.

JOHN TYLER

1841–1845

Establishing the Precedent

In many ways John Tyler seemed a natural for the high office. Raised on a 12,000-acre, forty-slave plantation on the James River, he had attended William and Mary College, following in the tradition of Jefferson and Monroe. And like his father before him, he had gone on to become governor of Virginia.

Tall and gaunt to the point of emaciation, with a prominent Roman nose that he joked about, he had a courtly bearing and a silvery voice, which he frequently utilized for impassioned oratory. It led him eventually into Congress and then the Senate, where he switched parties and became a Whig. Then, in 1840, he was chosen to run as William Henry Harrison's vice president. He was the "Tyler, too" to Harrison's "Tippecanoe," in the slogan the popular duo campaigned with to victory in November.

But on an early Sunday morning in 1841, just a month after their inauguration, John Tyler was awakened at his home in Williamsburg, Virginia with a message that President Harrison was dead. For the first time in the fifty-two-year history of the nation, the question of presidential succession would have to be faced.

The Constitution was anything but clear on the subject. It stated that "in case of the removal of the President from office or of his death, resignation, or inability to discharge the powers and duties . . . the same shall devolve on the Vice President." But what exactly did the words "the same" refer to? The office itself, or merely the duties of the office? And why did the Twelfth Amendment, passed in 1804, read that "the Vice President shall act as President . . . in the case of death," and not "shall become President"?

"I am under Providence made the instrument of a new test which is for the first time to be applied to our institutions," Tyler wrote.

Tyler himself was convinced he was already president in full. But when he reached Washington on the following morning, he found he was embroiled in a mounting controversy. The "Vice President, Acting as President," he was being called, or, worse still, "His Accidency." Furthermore, he was personally looked down upon by many. "He is a slave-monger whose talents are not above mediocrity," wrote John Quincy Adams. "No one ever thought of his being placed in the executive chair." When Tyler summoned Harrison's cabinet to meet with him at Brown's

After only a month in office, President William Henry Harrison (above) died of pneumonia. His vice president, John Tyler, didn't even know that Harrison had been ill. Tyler was at his home in Williamsburg, Virginia, when Daniel Webster's son officially brought him the shocking news (below). Suddenly, for the first time in the history of the republic, the vice presidency was a matter of supreme importance.

Though John Tyler (left, in a Mathew Brady portrait) assumed the presidency in full, for years afterward he was considered to be in a category of his own. John Quincy Adams persisted in referring to him as "His Accidency." And Tyler's successor, James K. Polk, officially the eleventh president, liked to describe himself as "the tenth President elected by the people."

In this 1844 silhouette, Tyler's Roman nose appears to be his most dominant feature. Tall and thin, he played the violin, loved horses and champagne, and composed poetry. And he was the most headstrong president since Andrew Jackson.

Hotel, he was told that all administration matters would have to be approved by them. But the cabinet members were not counting on what Tyler did next.

"I am very glad to have in my Cabinet such able statesmen as you," he told them. "But I can never consent to being dictated to as to what I shall or shall not do. . . . I am the President. . . . When you think otherwise, your resignations will be accepted."

John Tyler had laid claim to the presidency in full, with all its powers and authorities. Caught off guard by his bold stance, one after another the cabinet members backed down. Then, at the request of Secretary of State Daniel Webster, Tyler accepted a compromise to his position that he was already president; he agreed to be officially sworn into office. The oath taking would set a new precedent for the future, marking the moment a vice president becomes president. Three days later, as he prepared to move into the White House, Tyler issued a printed substitute for an inaugural address. "By a deplored event I was unexpectedly elevated to the Presidency," he wrote. "For the first time in our history the person elected to the Vice Presidency of the United States has had devolved upon him the Presidential office."

From the outset, Tyler's presidency came under ferocious attack. After vetoing a Whig bank bill that he believed unconstitutional, he was soon being called a traitor to the party. And less than half a year into his administration, five of his six cabinet members resigned in protest. When Tyler replaced them with former Jackson men like himself, a group of Whig leaders in Congress formally expelled him from the party ranks.

"From the moment of my assuming the helm . . . my ship [was] tempest-tossed," Tyler wrote. "A Vice President, who succeeds to the Presidency by the demise of the President . . . has no party at his heels to sustain his measures."

But Tyler refused to subordinate himself to his enemies, chief among whom was the ambitious Henry Clay. "I pray you to believe that my back is to the wall," he wrote a friend, "and that while I . . . deplore the assaults, I shall . . . beat back the assailants." When he perceived meddling in his cabinet appointments in 1843, he blasted, "My cabinet arrangements should be left to myself, and if anybody . . . shall choose to make that a topic of discussion, I can only regard it as proceeding from a spirit of mischief."

Tyler's cabinet became the most disrupted in presidential history, its six positions filled and refilled by a total of twenty-two different occupants. And when Tyler vetoed a tariff bill supported by both Daniel Webster and Henry Clay, the House of Representatives introduced the first impeachment resolution ever lodged against a president. Though the highly partisan effort was unsuccessful, Tyler was burned in effigy in a dozen different cities.

"I have been so rudely buffeted by the waves of party politics," Tyler wrote, "that I sigh for the quiet of my country residence, and look most anxiously to the . . . [time] when my connection with political life will expire."

Tyler's last act as president was once again opposed by many Whigs—his ardent support for the annexation of Texas. He himself produced the treaty specifying the transfer of Texas's sovereignty, which he insisted would be for the good of the entire nation. A spiteful Senate would delay acting upon it until Tyler was out of office, and James K. Polk would receive all the credit as well as his share of the shame. For Texas was soon seen as fertile new ground for slavery, which increasingly made support of annexation a

Painted in the second year of his turbulent presidency by artist G. P. A. Healy, Tyler poses coyly. His vetoes of Whig legislation had led him to be cut off by his party, and he became the first president faced with an impeachment movement in the House.

Tyler's beloved wife Letitia bore him seven children, but she was never well for long. Half paralyzed by a stroke in 1839, she could not function as first lady and only once made an appearance downstairs in the White House, on the occasion of the nuptials of her daughter Elizabeth. In 1842 Letitia died, making Tyler the first president to become a widower while in office (later Benjamin Harrison and Woodrow Wilson also became widowers during their presidencies.) Tyler's period of mourning lasted only a matter of months, cut short by the appearance in Washington of Julia Gardiner, a vivacious New Yorker thirty years his junior. After knowing her for a brief time, the aroused widower chased her around the rooms of the White House, kissed her, and proposed. Much later Julia recalled, "I had never thought of love, so I said, 'No, no, no,' and shook my head with each word, which flung the tassel of my Greek cap into his face with every move. It was undignified, but it amused me very much to see his expression as he tried to make love to me and the tassel brushed his face." Perhaps nothing permanent would have evolved between them had it not been for a fatal accident on board the naval vessel, the *Princeton*, which killed Tyler's secretary of state, the secretary of the Navy, and Julia's father. At the sudden, traumatic loss, Julia yearned for paternal comforting. "After I lost my father I felt differently toward the President," she remembered. "He seemed to fill the place and to be more agreeable in every way than any younger man ever was or could be." Secretly the unlikely couple was married in New York City. Tyler didn't even let his four daughters in on the news until after the wedding. "Well, what has been talked of . . . is consummated," he then wrote, "and Julia Gardiner, the most lovely of her sex, is my own wedded wife."

matter of Southern interests. "This last move chafed me more than the first," Tyler wrote, "for it substantially converted the Executive into a mere southern agency in place of being what it truly was, the representative of American interests."

On February 22, 1845, Washington bade farewell to Tyler at a gala White House party. Two thousand invitations had been sent out, and the East Room was lit by a thousand candles. Tyler managed one of the few witticisms of his presidency. "They cannot say now that I am a president without a party."

In the end, the hallmark of John Tyler's turbulent presidency was the stubborn and uncompromising manner in which it had begun. He had permanently established the pattern of vice presidential succession, a tradition that would ever afterward be known as the Tyler Precedent.

"I had . . . to follow the lights of my own judgment and the promptings of my own feelings," Tyler wrote. "A President, elected by the people, comes into office at the head of a triumphant party. Not so, however, with a Vice President, who succeeds to the Presidency by the demise of the President."

Tyler's romance with the young Julia Gardiner was sealed by this explosion. He described the scene: "The experimental ship, the *Princeton,* floated majestically on the . . . Potomac, and her . . . commander . . . had sent out cards of invitation for a fete on board. . . . The decks were soon crowded with a host of happy visitors. . . . The gallant commander . . . ascended to the deck, accompanied by a few friends . . . to witness the effect of a discharge from one of the guns. . . . A loud report is at length heard. . . . The upper deck is reached and there lies, sealed in death . . . two imminent secretaries and three other distinguished citizens."

Providing Tyler with seven additional children, Julia Gardiner never regretted having married an older man. On his sixty-second birthday she wrote him this affectionate poem, "Then, listen, dearest, to my strain—and never doubt its truth—Thy ripen'd charms are all to me,—Wit I prefer to Youth!"

In this daguerreotype portrait, attributed to J. M. Edwards and Edward Anthony, a defiant John Tyler shows the grit he was famous for.

Just a year or so after Tyler left office, the first known photograph of the White House was taken by the Welsh-born daguerreotypist John Plumbe, Jr.

MILLARD FILLMORE

1850–1853

"Called by a Bereavement"

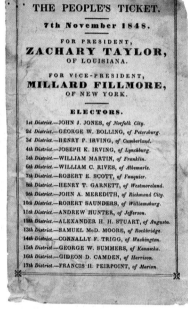

Zachary Taylor was a slaveholder from the deep South. In a classic case of ticket balancing, Whigs turned for his running mate to a northern moderate —Millard Fillmore (below).

Only five years after the close of Tyler's presidency, death once again struck down a sitting president, another aging Whig general, Zachary Taylor. This time the vice president waiting in the wings was as unlike John Tyler as a person could be. He was a self-made New Yorker known for his thoroughgoing commitment to the Union and to the Whig Party. He was Millard Fillmore.

"I was called to the executive chair by a bereavement which shrouded the nation in mourning," he wrote. "However much I may be oppressed by . . . the discharge of the duties, . . . I dare not shrink [from them]."

All his life Millard Fillmore had driven himself to succeed. Raised in dire poverty in western New York State, in the most desperate beginnings of any of our presidents, at fifteen he was apprenticed to a clothmaker. There, while working the carding machines, he taught himself to read. "I . . . bought a small dictionary," he later recalled, "and determined to seek out the meaning of every word . . . which I did not understand . . . and . . . fix it in my memory."

It was this kind of initiative that drove Fillmore to success, eventually as a lawyer and then in government service. In any job he took, he shone, whether as New York State comptroller or as a U.S. congressman. And in 1848 he was nationally recognized at the Whig convention in Philadelphia, where he was chosen as Zachary Taylor's presidential running mate.

But in Washington, Fillmore's vice presidency was not a happy one. His wife Abigail insisted on returning to Buffalo, and Fillmore lived alone in a single room at Willard's Hotel. To make matters worse, he soon found himself caught in the middle of a political firestorm. As settlers headed west to occupy new territories seized from Mexico, the burning question across the country was whether slavery would be permitted there. President Zachary Taylor argued that such Western territories as California and New Mexico be admitted to the Union as states without slavery. But his vice president was privately at odds with him and favored a position more conciliatory toward the South. In his role as president of the Senate, Millard Fillmore held the tie-breaking vote on the volatile issue. In early July 1850, Fillmore told Taylor he would be forced to vote against him. "I wished him to understand," Fillmore explained, "that it was not out of any hostility to him or his Administration, but the vote would be given because I deemed it for the interests of the country."

Just a few days later, on July 8, Fillmore was presiding over the Senate when a message was handed to him. President Taylor, who had been strick-

When Millard Fillmore was suddenly elevated into high office, not all Whigs were pleased. Fellow New Yorker William Seward remarked acidly, "Providence has at last led the man of hesitations and double opinions where decision and singleness are indispensable."

Millard Fillmore was widely considered one of the handsomest men of the era. Here his youthful good looks are captured in a pastel drawing by Thomas Sully.

B. M. BRADY,   WASHINGTON, D. C.

Zachary Taylor's little-known running mate, Millard Fillmore, was a civic-minded, friendly New York politician with impeccable credentials, chosen to help offset the fact that Taylor was a slaveholder from the Deep South.

IN HIS OWN WORDS

On his meager beginnings: At the time of my birth, my father and his brother Calvin, and their wives, occupied the same log house in the midst of the forest, having no neighbor nearer than four miles. . . . I had, like most boys, a great passion for hunting and fishing, but my father was very unwilling to indulge it. He used to tell me that . . . those employments were only fit for Indians. . . . There were no schools. . . . The first that I recollect was . . . in an old deserted log house, which had been furnished with a few benches without backs, and a board for writing upon. In this school I learned my alphabet, at the age of six or seven. . . . I learned to plow, to hoe, to chop, to log and clear land, to mow, to reap.

To General Zachary Taylor, after being named his vice presidential running mate: Although I have never had the pleasure of a personal acquaintance, nor can I flatter myself that you have ever heard of me before the late convention, yet as I feel quite acquainted with you from a general knowledge of your widely extended reputation, and as our fellow citizens have seen fit to associate our names for the next presidential contest, I take the liberty by introduction of enclosing a copy of my acceptance of the nomination. . . . I should be happy to hear from you.

His views on slavery before the election: I regarded slavery as an evil, but one with which the National Government had nothing to do—that by the Constitution of the United States, the whole power over that question was vested in the several states where the institution was tolerated. If they regarded it as a blessing they had a constitutional right to enjoy it, and if they regarded it as an evil they had the power and knew best how to apply the remedy.

On the key challenge of his presidency: You all know that when I was called to the executive chair by a bereavement . . . the country was unfortunately agitated from one end to the other upon the all-exciting subject of slavery. . . . I felt it was my duty to rise above every sectional prejudice, and look to the welfare of the whole nation. . . . The agitation which disturbed the peace of the country in 1850, was unavoidable. It was brought about by the acquisition of new territory, for the government of which it was necessary to provide territorial organizations. . . . Many noble patriots, Whigs and Democrats, in both Houses of Congress, rallied around and sustained the Administration in that trying time, and to them was chiefly due the merit of settling that exciting controversy. . . . I regarded the Compromise Measures of 1850 . . . as a "final settlement" of [the slavery] question. . . . I then thought that this . . . subject was put at rest.

To the Emperor of Japan, upon sending Commodore Matthew Perry to open up that country: Great and good friend: I send you this letter . . . to bear to you my greeting and good wishes, and to promote friendship and commerce between the two countries. . . . Our steamers . . . must pass along the coasts of your Empire; storms and winds may cause them to be wrecked on your shores, and we ask and expect . . . kindness for our men and protection for our property. . . . We wish that our People may be permitted to trade with your People, but we shall not authorize them to break any law of your Empire.

Inheriting a nation on the brink of civil war, Fillmore labored to keep the country together.

en by a stomach disorder, was dying in the White House. It was approaching midnight on July 9 when there came the dreaded knocking at Fillmore's door at Willard's Hotel. A note from the cabinet told him "Zachary Taylor is no more."

"I have no language to express the emotions of my heart," Fillmore responded. "The shock is so sudden and unexpected, I am overwhelmed."

The following morning Fillmore wrote out his first official contact with Congress as president-to-be. "I have to perform the melancholy duty of announcing to you that it has pleased Almighty God to remove from this life Zachary Taylor. . . . I propose this day at twelve o'clock . . . in the presence of both Houses of Congress, to take the oath prescribed by the Constitution."

In front of the wooden dome of the old Capitol building, Millard Fillmore followed the Tyler precedent and was sworn in as the nation's thirteenth president. Though a large inaugural ceremony took place in the House Chamber, Fillmore refused to make an inaugural address, setting a pattern that would be followed by the majority of successor presidents. "Neither the time nor the occasion appeared to require [it]," he explained. "The country was shrouded in mourning . . . and . . . grief."

Unlike Tyler, or General Taylor, Fillmore was a thoroughgoing party man, and he quickly swung his support behind the Congressional Compromise involving the Western territories. "The Compromise Measures of 1850, were not in all respects what I could have desired," he later wrote, "but they were the best that could be obtained after a protracted discussion that shook the Republic to its very foundation." At the heart of the discussion was the matter the future of slavery in the West. "God knows that I detest slavery," Fillmore insisted, "but it is an existing evil . . . and we must endure it, and give it such protection as is guaranteed by the Constitution."

The Compromise of 1850 helped calm the nation and made Millard Fillmore extremely popular for a while. "It was the last great effort," wrote journalist Walt Whitman, "to avert a rupture [in the nation] and go on peaceably." But as it turned out, the Compromise was only briefly effective. Southerners came to regret the many concessions they had made in it. And Northerners increasingly objected to a tough new fugitive slave law, which mandated harsh penalties for all harborers of runaway slaves. Caught in the middle, Fillmore would come to lament that he was misunderstood by both sides. "In the North I was charged with being a pro-slavery man, seeking to extend slavery over free territory," he would write, "and in the South I was accused of being an abolitionist. But I am neither."

Fillmore worked hard to implement the policies of his party, which he believed could alone prevent civil war, but he lacked the drive to go after the presidency in his own right. And though his supporters convinced him to seek the 1852 nomination, he was bypassed in favor of the Whig general Winfield Scott. After just two and a half years in office, he drifted back to Buffalo, where he lived on through the years of the Civil War, and beyond.

"I feel no regret . . . that I [was] relieved from [the] thankless task of administering this government," Fillmore wrote. "The agitation which disturbed the peace of the country in 1850 was unavoidable. . . . [It was] the muttering thunder and . . . the gathering storm [of an] . . . unholy rebellion."

"THE LIGHT OF THE HOUSE IS GONE"

Abigail: the first Mrs. Fillmore

Abigail Powers was a red-haired school teacher when Millard met her back in his youth, and it was Abigail who encouraged him to learn as much as he could and enter the law. They adored each other so much that Fillmore twice quit the House to be in Albany with his wife, who hated Washington. As his presidency ended, Fillmore was looking forward at fifty-three to a blissful retirement, but it was not to be. Before he could leave Washington, Abigail caught cold and died of pneumonia, throwing Fillmore

into an agony of depression. "I have felt no desire to do anything," he wrote a friend. "The light of the house is gone; and I can never hope to enjoy life again." A year later, life became even darker when his daughter followed her mother to the grave. Fillmore never intentionally looked for a second wife, but in the late 1850s he found one. Caroline Carmichael McIntosh was a wealthy childless widow of a railroad magnate who accepted his proposal of marriage but made him sign a prenuptial agreement first. Their union dispelled his worries about money and gave Fillmore some much needed companionship in the final years of his life.

Caroline: the second Mrs. Fillmore

Fillmore lived on after his presidency for twenty-one years, even making another attempt at the high office, as a third-party candidate. During the Civil War he donned a federal uniform as Captain of the Union Continentals.

Millard Fillmore first met the photographer Mathew Brady in the early 1850s when he sat for a daguerreotype. Later he was back in the Brady studio to be captured once again in this striking portrait.

Andrew Johnson's intractable stubbornness during a long fight
with Congress earned him the title of "The Grim Presence."

ANDREW JOHNSON

1865–1869

"Elect of an Assassin"

Never has happenstance played such havoc with the presidency as it did following the assassination of Abraham Lincoln. The vice president who would succeed him was Andrew Johnson, a stubborn white supremacist almost entirely lacking in Lincoln's political skills. "An inscrutable Providence saw proper to remove [Lincoln] . . . and I came into his place," Johnson quickly declared. "This is a country for white men, and by God, as long as I am President, it shall be a government for white men." One horrified contemporary wrote, "He is the elect of an assassin, and not of the people. . . . By murder most foul did he succeed to the Presidency."

His story began back in 1808 in a North Carolina shack where Johnson endured a childhood of squalor and ignorance. "If being poor was a crime . . . I was guilty," he wrote. "Yes, I have wrestled with poverty, that gaunt and haggard monster. . . . I have felt his withering approach and his blighting influence."

The son of an illiterate porter and a laundress in the little settlement of Raleigh, Andy Johnson never went to school a day in his life. Under an arrangement that indentured him for a period of eleven years, he was apprenticed to a tailor at the age of ten. The first time he heard words from books was when public-spirited men volunteered to read aloud to the apprentices as they stitched away. "A man named William Hill . . . used to come into the shop and read . . . extracts from . . . *The American Speaker*," he later recalled. "Oh how ardently I wished I could read like Bill Hill." Obtaining a book of great speeches, he stayed up late into the nights, and painstakingly taught himself to read.

Vice president for less than five weeks after the inauguration (above), Johnson was sworn in as president in the parlor of suite 68 of the Kirkwood House soon after Lincoln's death. Before two cabinet members and a few other exhausted dignitaries, the fifty-six-year-old Democrat from Tennessee followed the ceremony with some short remarks that used the pronoun "I" fifteen times but never mentioned Abraham Lincoln.

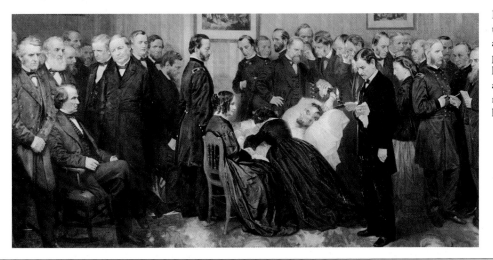

In this oil painting by Alonzo Chappel, the artist has Johnson seated at the left as Lincoln is dying. Actually, the vice president was back in his hotel room, having looked in on the deathbed scene a few hours earlier before quickly being removed when Mary Lincoln, who hated him, came into the room.

This daguerrian locket portrait of Andrew Johnson was taken when he was a freshman congressman in Washington, D.C., and given as a keepsake to his eldest daughter, Martha.

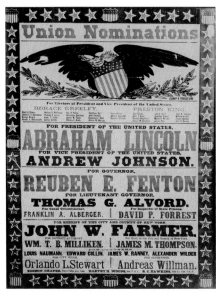

To broaden the presidential ticket in 1864, Republicans turned for the second spot to Tennessee Democrat Andrew Johnson, the sole senator from a seceding state to have remained loyal to the Union and an active supporter of Lincoln's Reconstruction program. Appearing on what was called the "Union ticket," Lincoln and Johnson went on to win the election by a landslide.

At age fifteen Johnson ran away from home and his apprenticeship. Three years later he surfaced in Greeneville, Tennessee, where he married a sixteen-year-old, Eliza McCardle, and opened his own tailor shop. It was Eliza who taught her husband to write. "If I had been educated in early life, I would have been a schoolmaster," he later mused. "But [I] feel proud that . . . I was . . . the proprietor of my own shop."

He soon became known as the tailor-politician, as he worked his way up from alderman and then mayor of Greeneville, to assemblyman, U.S. congressman, and eventually governor and U.S. senator. Committed to the principles of Jefferson and Jackson, the usually sullen Democrat came alive on the stump, with his own colorful and abusive debating style.

"I am a mechanic, a plebeian mechanic, and not ashamed nor afraid to own it," he declared. "I . . . speak for the working man regardless of the frowns, taunts, and jeers of an upstart aristocracy . . . an illegitimate, swaggering, bastard, scrub aristocracy."

But though he especially despised wealthy plantation owners, he was a firm believer in the institution of slavery, and he himself was a slave owner. "If you liberate the negro, what will be the next step?" he once asked in typically outrageous form. "It would place every splay-footed, bandy-shanked, humpbacked negro in the country upon an equality with the poor white man." "You can't get rid of the negro except by holding him in slavery."

As a politician, Johnson was strongest when standing in opposition. And in the great national crisis of 1860 and '61, he boldly stood up to his fellow Southerners and supported the Union. "I took decided grounds against secession," he later recalled, "because I knew that it would bring war and bloodshed. I said to the people, let us fight this battle in the Union and under the Constitution; let it be a battle of words and not of swords."

During the Civil War, Johnson became the only senator from a seceding state to remain in Washington to back the Union. "Damn the negroes," he explained to a Northern general; "I am fighting those traitorous aristocrats, their masters." The following year, even though he was a Democrat and Lincoln a Republican, the President rewarded his loyalty by naming him wartime governor of Tennessee. And in 1864, after Johnson publicly supported Lincoln's policy of emancipation, he was chosen to run on the Union ticket for vice president. On November 8, they won the election.

But the President soon had reason to regret his choice, for Johnson's behavior at the inauguration was a severe embarrassment. Having taken considerable whiskey to fortify himself from a recent illness, the swaying, stammering, beet-red Vice President called on each cabinet member by name, telling them in turn that they were plebeians—creatures of the people.

"I'm a-goin' for to tell you here today," he sang out. "Yes, I'm a-goin' for to tell you all, that I'm a plebeian. I glory in it. The people, yes, the people have made me what I am. And I am a-goin' for to tell you here today, yes, today, in this place, that the people are everything!"

"To think," said an editorial in the *New York World,* "that one frail life stands between this insolent, clownish creature and the Presidency."

In this photograph made in the Washington, D.C., studio of photographer Mathew Brady, the gruff President actually looks handsome. One of Johnson's problems in the presidency was his stubborn aloofness from his colleagues, described at the time as his "Tyler-izing." His generally supportive secretary of the Navy Gideon Welles wrote, "there is a . . . want of confidence in his friends. . . . It is a mistake, an infirmity, a habit fixed before he was President, to keep his own counsel."

Andrew Johnson had been in office just shy of seven months when the commander of the infamous Georgia prison camp at Andersonville was executed in the shadow of the Capitol. As in the earlier case of the Lincoln murder conspirators, Johnson had refused all pleas for mercy for Henry Wirz. When Alexander Gardner took this picture, Wirz's already lifeless body was swinging beneath the open gallows. He was the only Confederate officer to be tried for "war crimes."

He was all too often sullen, this tailor-politician from the South. But on the stump he came alive, as unlikely words blossomed from his lips to help form his surprisingly coarse but effective debating style. Single-minded, easily slighted, often called a boor and a demagogue, Johnson never shook off his deeply ingrained Southern conviction that blacks were inferior. Once in Washington, he spent his free time bettering himself at the Library of Congress, hiding his cultural shortcomings behind impeccable clothes and newly learned fancy phrases. A states-righter who fought against almost all forms of federal spending, he was a loner, hard to read, even harder to get to know. Few were taken into his confidence or asked for advice. Sometimes his gloom and anger took on lyrical flights and revealed his intense feelings of inferiority. "If I should happen to die," he once said about himself and his world of enemies, "I would bequeath the last dollar to some negro to take my dirty, stinking carcass out on some mountain-peak to be devoured by the vultures or make a fire that it might pass in smoke and ride upon the wind in triumph over the godforsaken and hell-deserving, money-loving, hypocritical, backbiting, Sunday-praying scoundrels."

With the improvement of photography in the late 1850s and early 1860s, including shorter exposure times and the ability to capture outdoor action, a new era of candid portraiture began to emerge. Outdoor candids of the famous and powerful were still uncommon—they usually insisted on carefully posed portraits they could control. But here and on pages 232-233 are some rare informal shots of Andrew Johnson as he went about his presidency. Trying to boost his standing with the public, Johnson made a whirlwind speaking tour in 1866 and was photographed on the rear platform of his railroad car (above) as a city turned out to greet him. He was also photographed that same year on a porch in New York State (left), along with his highly supportive secretary of the Navy, Gideon Welles, and the newly appointed commander general of the Army, Ulysses S. Grant. One month later, Grant wrote to his wife, "I have never been so tired of anything before as I have been with the political speeches of Mr. Johnson. . . . I look upon them as a national disgrace."

Little more than a month later, Lincoln was killed, and the fifty-six-year-old Democrat from Tennessee was sworn in as the seventeenth president. "I have been almost overwhelmed by the sad event," Johnson uttered in a brief statement from his hotel room after taking the oath of office. "I feel incompetent to perform . . . duties so unexpectedly thrown upon me."

From the beginning, everything in Johnson's presidency went wrong. Although he retained Lincoln's entire cabinet, he resisted calling upon their experience and wisdom. And instead of cultivating Republican leaders in Congress, he allowed his differences with them regarding the difficult problem of Reconstruction to set them off on a collision course.

Unlike the majority of Congress who wanted to hold the South accountable and safeguard black rights, Johnson was determined to remain faithful to what he saw as Lincoln's policy of leniency. On May 29, he announced a general amnesty to former Confederates, to be supplemented by presidential pardons for the top leaders of secession.

Bolstered by the President's strong support and sympathy, Southern states began reinstating many of their old leaders, acting as if the Civil War had never been fought. Four Confederate generals, five colonels, and even the former vice president of the Confederacy, Alexander Stephens, were elected to Congress.

Outraged, Congress refused to seat them. Instead, acting on what it called the true spirit of Lincoln, it passed a bill to provide federal aid to liberated slaves, which Johnson quickly vetoed, and then a sweeping civil rights bill declaring blacks to be full citizens of the United States. Johnson vetoed again. "I am right. I know I am right, and I am damned if I do not adhere to it," he insisted. When Congress, by a two-thirds vote, overrode this second veto, it became open war.

To seek support from the American people, Johnson launched a cross-country speaking tour. But his undignified harangues only increased his unpopularity. "Congress has undertaken to poison the minds of the American people," Johnson blasted. "This common gang of cormorants and bloodsuckers have been fattening upon the country for the past four or five years. . . . [They think] everybody is a traitor that is against them."

With Congress taking full control of Reconstruction, Johnson was now virtually ignored, referred to by one observer as "the dead dog of the White House." Former Congressman Isaac N. Arnold, in a letter to the President, wrote, "You have betrayed the great . . . party which elected Abraham Lincoln."

In March 1867, to further constrain him, Congress passed the Tenure of Office Act, forbidding the president to dismiss his top officials without the Senate's concurrence. In defiance Johnson ignored the law and fired Edwin Stanton, the secretary of war, claiming he was disloyal. Republicans became convinced that Johnson had committed a convictable crime, and in the following year, Congress voted to impeach. "Impeachment of me for violating the Constitution!" Johnson exclaimed. "Damn them! Have I not been struggling ever since I have been in this chair to uphold the Constitution which they trample under foot[?]"

In the embattled White House, Johnson wondered and waited, kept informed of the proceedings in the Senate chamber through eyewitness reports. And then, after more than a month, the day of decision arrived. In the end it all came down to one man's vote, that of Edmund G. Ross, a Republican senator from Kansas, to whom Johnson had promised that he

Photographed at an outdoor political picnic during his futile 1866 speaking tour, President Johnson sits shoulder to shoulder with General Grant and with Secretary of the Navy Gideon Welles.

Washington was in an uproar. Rumors and invective flew around the city. The President was called everything from "tailor" to "traitor." Charges and countercharges filled the newspapers. Illegal spying to determine who were the swayable senators was followed by arm twisting and even blackmail to force votes for removal from office. The betting was against Johnson to survive. In the embattled White House the old-time Constitutionalist President wondered and waited, acting now with statesman-like calm as he remained informed of the wild proceedings in the Senate Chamber through eyewitness reports from his secretaries, attorneys, and members of the cabinet. Johnson entertained at the White House as usual throughout it all, but never mentioned the impeachment proceedings to his guests. "Conviction?" the President once asked with contempt. "Conviction of what?"

Andrew Johnson's whole life was an act of defiance. Fierce, stubborn, driven, and opinionated, he seemed to thrive on lost causes and was always strongest when standing in lonely opposition. He lacked the ability for positive leadership, for building coalitions and accomplishing projects, and his passions were almost entirely negative ones. He was against government spending and government projects; against secession; against congressional Reconstruction. When his causes were good—such as his opposition to secession—Johnson shone brightly. After all, it was his courageous speaking out on behalf of the Union that had attracted Lincoln to him in the first place. But when his causes were essentially backward—for example, his callous disregard for the welfare of American blacks—Johnson was at his worst. Unlike Lincoln, the man he replaced, Johnson had no relevant vision for the country, no feel for history and its demands. He was best as a curmudgeon in the Senate, where his loud voice of opposition sometimes helped frame the debates. But in the role of president, he was a total failure.

would soften his opposition to congressional Reconstruction. "Not guilty!" Ross intoned. The news was run by foot to the White House, where on hearing it, the President wept.

"I intend to devote the remainder of my life," he said, "to the vindication of my own character."

Never before had two branches of the government been at such odds, or the office of the presidency been so diminished. And much of it—though not all—had been Andrew Johnson's fault. Stubborn and independent, at his best moments heroically so, he was also crude and uncompromising and lacking in any sympathy for black Americans. And he was unable to lead the country through the massive challenges of Reconstruction.

In November 1868, General Ulysses S. Grant was elected president, and after four months Johnson returned to Tennessee. "I have performed my duty to my God, my country, and my family," he would insist. "I have nothing to fear." Five years later, in an attempt to restore his reputation, Johnson ran for a seat in the U.S. Senate. When news of his victory in Tennessee reached him—making him the only former president ever to be elected to the Senate—the old fighter grew emotional. "I'd rather have this information than to learn that I had been elected president of the United States. Thank God for the vindication."

For more than a month, this was the hottest ticket in Washington.

In this composite group portrait are the seven members of the House "Board of Managers" chosen to prosecute Andrew Johnson in his trial before the Senate. In the front row, from left, are two radicals, Benjamin F. Butler and Thaddeus Stevens, and two moderates, Thomas Williams and John A. Bingham, who served as chairman. Behind are James F. Wilson, head of the House Judiciary Committee; George S. Boutwell, who introduced the first resolution of impeachment; and Illinois Republican and radical John A. Logan.

If Johnson had been ousted, the president pro tem of the Senate, Ohio's ultra-radical Ben Wade, would have become the country's acting president. On the outcome of the Senate trial, Johnson had this to say in a letter to a friend: "You allude to the vote on impeachment as a 'close shave.' It was not so close as most people think; for Senator Morgan of New York would have cast his vote against impeachment rather than to have seen Ben Wade succeed to the Presidential chair."

Entered according to Act of Congress by M.B. Brady & Co. in the year 1865 in the Clerk's Office of the District Court of the District of Columbia.

When Congress first acted to impeach a president, Washington was still a rural and swampy and primitive city, in which cattle, pigs, and sheep ranged freely.

CHESTER A. ARTHUR

1881–1885

"Gentleman Boss"

Chester Arthur at age twenty-nine (above) was an idealistic young lawyer with a passion for civil liberties. He had recently taken part in an important test case that led to the racial integration of New York City's streetcar system. After a stint as an engineer and then as a quartermaster general in the Civil War, Arthur turned to politics, where he quickly excelled. Not only did he come to serve as James Garfield's running mate in 1880, he was also the party boss in charge of much of the campaign.

JAMES A. GARFIELD
REPUBLICAN CANDIDATE FOR PRESIDENT

CHESTER A. ARTHUR
REPUBLICAN CANDIDATE FOR VICE PRESIDENT

If Andrew Johnson represented a nadir for the presidency, at least no one ever charged him with graft or corruption. But with the administration of Ulysses S. Grant, a new era, dominated by spoilsmen, began. And in 1880 the Republicans nominated for vice president a man many considered the epitome of corrupt politics—New York City's infamous former customs officer, Chester Arthur.

Raised as a preacher's son in northeastern Vermont, Chester Arthur as a young man was an idealistic lawyer whose chief interest was civil rights. After serving in the Civil War as a quartermaster general, in the mid-1860s he became active in New York City politics, home of some of the worst party corruption in the country. "It was customary to station 'heelers' in the lines of voters," Arthur related of the period before his arrival, "and these fellows would at a signal break up the lines. On one occasion these ruffians were provided with awls, which they prodded into the flesh of the majority, thus dispersing them. Ballot boxes were stuffed almost openly."

Arthur liked money and he liked power, and he climbed rapidly in the city's Republican organization, becoming a favorite of New York's new senator, Roscoe Conkling. Always impeccably dressed, Arthur found his darkening nature particularly suited to the spoils system. He was a smooth back-slapper, willing to follow orders and give up his nights to drinking with the boys in the assemblage of power. And he became especially noted for his loyalty. "I was always to be counted . . . on to stand by the friends who have for so long acted together," he once boasted.

It was President Grant who appointed Arthur to the highest-paying civil service job in the federal government—customs collector for New York City. Seventy-five percent of the nation's customs receipts came through the sprawling New York port, creating countless ways to siphon off money— from fixed scales and rigged measurements to out-and-out bribery. Though Arthur was never personally charged with bribery or payoffs, he tolerated the crookedness of others. And when this was pointed out to him by a friend, the portly spoilsman bridled. "You are one of those goody-goody fellows," he blurted out, "who set up a high standard of morality that other people cannot reach."

Civil Service reform swept in during the Hayes administration, and the Customhouse was accused of dishonesty from top to bottom. When

When Arthur became president (right), the historian Henry Adams was shocked. "Chet Arthur, President of the United States!" he exclaimed. "Good God! We are going to have a nasty chopping-sea in politics."

As a handsome young Easterner seeking opportunity in the West, Chet Arthur (above) exposed his passionate nature in a letter to his sweetheart, nineteen-year-old "Nell" Herndon. "I know you are thinking of me now. I feel the pulses of your love answering to mine. If I were with you now, you would go and sing for me 'Robin Adair' then you would come and sit by me—you would put your arms around my neck and press your soft sweet lips over my eyes. I can feel them now." Nell (below) came from Virginia and sang like a dream. The two married, but it was not long before Arthur's political career working for the Republican machine in New York City started interfering. Nell was ignored or left alone for most of their marriage and was on the verge of breaking up with her husband in 1880 when she suddenly died.

Arthur tried to stonewall the investigating commission, President Hayes fired him. But the "Gentleman Boss" Chester Arthur continued to oversee party strategy, and became the permanent president of New York's Republican Central Committee. When Grant lost the 1880 nomination to Ohio's Senator Garfield, Arthur made a successful bid for the vice presidential nomination.

Considered the shrewdest political manager in the country, Arthur assumed overall charge of the Republican campaign—raising money, booking speakers, and organizing publicity throughout the pivotal state of New York. Later, at a celebration dinner following the Garfield-Arthur victory, a partially inebriated Arthur all but admitted his orchestration of the ballot box. "I don't think we had better go into the minute secrets of the campaign because I see the reporters are present," he laughed. "If I should get to going about the secrets . . . there is no saying what I might say."

Only three months into his term as vice president, as he was debarking from a steamer from Albany, Arthur received the news that Garfield had been shot, by an assassin who claimed he did it to get Arthur into the White House. As rumors spread that Arthur had hired the assassin, a wave of panic swept across the nation. Though there was no truth to the rumors, for the next ten weeks, as President Garfield hovered between life and death, Arthur avoided a suspicious press. "I am overwhelmed with grief," he admitted privately. "The most frightful responsibility which ever devolved upon any one would be the casting of the Presidency upon me."

On September 19, 1881, a messenger brought Arthur the dreaded news of Garfield's death. "It cannot be," Arthur reacted. "I hope, my God, I do hope it is a mistake." Alone in his home in New York City, with his head on his desk and his face buried in his hands, Arthur wept.

Soon a telegram arrived from members of Garfield's cabinet. "It becomes our painful duty," it read, "to advise you to take the oath of office as President of the United States without delay. We will be very glad if you will come here on the earliest train tomorrow morning."

Arthur now made an all-important decision. He would put aside his past, and disown his old cronies. He wanted to go down in history as an admired president. Unlike Fillmore or Johnson, he went on to deliver an inaugural address designed to prove the seriousness with which he took his new position. "For the fourth time in the history of the Republic," he proclaimed, "its Chief Magistrate has been removed by death. . . . Men may die, but the fabric of our free institutions remain unshaken."

As president, Arthur surprised all by becoming a champion of civil service reform, though it took him two years to finally join the movement. In addition to signing the Pendleton Act of 1883, he put forward an array of thoughtful presidential actions. He argued for the establishment of a government for Alaska, for decent housing for the Library of Congress, and for a line item veto. He championed naval development and received praise for his sometimes courageous vetoes. And he took interest in the West, in particular the natural resources of that part of the country. "The conditions of the forests," he wrote in 1882, "and the wasteful manner in which their destruction is taking place give cause for serious apprehension."

But if Arthur became a creditable president, he also soon found he hated the office. Bored by the endless desk work and by matters of state, he routinely arrived late to the office and procrastinated on duties. He lived for his time off, and for his regular vacations, which he spent fishing or cruis-

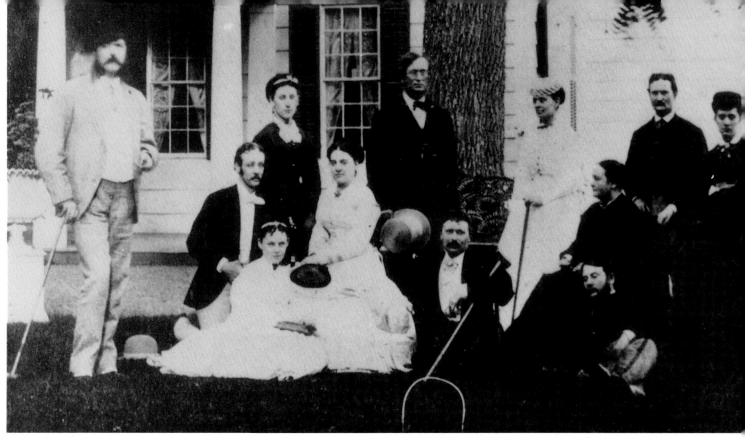

Nothing but the best suited Chester Arthur, whether wine, jewelry, clothes or swell places to visit. His wife, Nell, from an aristocratic family, was able to teach him about what she considered the finest things in life. Here in 1876, Arthur (at left) presides over a stylish game of croquet in Cooperstown, New York.

At the 1880 Republican Convention, Chester Arthur had worked diligently to get General Grant back in office. When Ohio Senator James Garfield won instead, his supporters approached Arthur about the vice presidency.

In 1882 Chester Arthur hired Louis
Tiffany, the thirty-four-year-old son
of the New York jeweler, to make an
elaborate redecoration of the interior
of the White House. His most stunning transformation was of an old cast
iron screen that had long divided the
entrance hall from the transverse hall
behind it. Filling the ten-foot-high
screen with dramatically colored and
shaped stained glass, Tiffany gave
what was considered an Islamic touch
to the White House.

ing on the presidential yacht. "I need a holiday as much as the poorest of my fellow citizens," he once said; "but it is generally supposed that we people at Washington do not want any rest."

What Arthur liked best was entertaining. To enhance the White House atmosphere, he refurbished its interior, hiring a New York decorator to make extensive alterations and adding an expensive Tiffany screen at the north entrance. Then he instituted weekly black tie state dinners at which as many as fourteen courses were served, along with eight varieties of wine.

Hidden from the public at Arthur's insistence was the fact that he was suffering from Bright's disease, a fatal kidney ailment that produced lethargy and depression. Diagnosed in his second year in office, the illness increased Arthur's distaste for the presidency, and led him eventually to oppose his own renomination. "I have been so ill," he confided to his son in early 1883, "that I have hardly been able to dispose of the . . . business . . . before me." And later he came out and said it plainly, "I do not want to be reelected."

Arthur's wife Nell had died shortly before his presidency. With no one now to share his retirement, and knowing that he was dying, the outgoing President had few plans for the future. "There doesn't seem anything for an ex-president to do," he told a friend, "but to go out into the country and raise big pumpkins."

Once out of office, Arthur's health deteriorated quickly. Consumed by worries about his early shaky history, and about his place in American history, the day before he died in 1886 he made sure that no damning evidence would be left behind. From his bedside, calling upon a friend, Arthur had all his private and public papers stuffed into garbage cans—and burned.

Arthur still looks healthy before he was afflicted with Bright's disease.

Like a surprisingly large number of American presidents, Arthur loved to fish.

An 1883 journey took the vacation-loving President to Wyoming.

No longer a lieutenant of the strong-armed New York senator Roscoe Conkling, Arthur achieved his finest hour in his inauguration address, a part of which follows:

For the fourth time in the history of the Republic its Chief Magistrate has been removed by death. All hearts are filled with grief and horror at the hideous crime which has darkened our land, and the memory of the murdered President, his protracted sufferings, his unyielding fortitude, the example and achievements of his life, and the pathos of his death will forever illuminate the pages of our history. For the fourth time the officer elected by the people and ordained by the Constitution to fill a vacancy so created is called to assume the Executive chair. The wisdom of our fathers, foreseeing even most dire possibilities, made sure that the Government should never be imperiled because of the uncertainty of human life. Men may die, but the fabrics of our free institutions remain unshaken. No higher or more assuring proof could exist of the strength and permanence of popular government than the fact that though the chosen of the people be struck down his constitutional successor is peacefully installed without shock or strain except the sorrow which mourns the bereavement. All the noble aspirations of my lamented predecessor which found expression in his life, the measures devised and suggested during his brief Administration to correct abuses, to enforce economy, to advance prosperity, and to promote the general welfare, to insure domestic security and maintain friendly and honorable relations with the nations of the earth, will be garnered in the hearts of the people; and it will be my earnest endeavor to profit, and to see that the nation shall profit, by his example and experience.

Though he was a diligent chief executive, Arthur avoided desk work when he could, much preferring to appear at functions in his greatcoat—he helped open the Brooklyn Bridge and spoke at the dedication of the Washington Monument. A night owl, he loved to entertain friends in his refurbished private dining room, which one White House staff member described as "snugly luxurious." Usually at ease in public, he bowed graciously to everyone, but his temper flared when confronted by the curious or the prying. "Madame," he once said, turning on a snoop, "I may be President of the United States, but my private life is nobody's damn business."

In the Chester Arthur era, a train passes by the back of the majestic Capitol amid plenty of empty real estate.

In 1949 the cocky President looked like this in St. Paul, Minnesota. "It takes men to make history," Truman wrote in his memoirs, "or there would be no history. History does not make the man."

HARRY S. TRUMAN

1945–1953

American Optimist

Harry Truman believed in the United States with an intensity that few today can quite understand. He profoundly believed, without ever articulating it, that nothing fundamentally bad could happen to this country, because the United States was God's country. It was a nineteenth-century belief from a twentieth-century Midwestern optimist. "Of course you've got to be an optimist if you're going to try to help the country go forward," he once said. "No pessimist ever did anything for the welfare of the world."

He was born and raised in western Missouri into a hardworking farm family. "My mother was naturally the one who took care of the youngsters at home and saw that they came up the right way," he recalled. "When I was ten . . . [she] gave me a little blackboard on the back of which was a column of four or five paragraphs on every President up 'til that time, which included Grover Cleveland. And that's where I got interested in the history of the country." His father wanted Harry to become a farmer, and he exercised tough discipline on the studious boy. "If he didn't like what you did," Truman remembered, "he'd hit you with a hickory cane—and that was an Andrew Jackson descendent."

Except for a few years when he served as a bank clerk, Truman worked on the family farm until he was thirty years old. He despised the work; "corn-shucking," he said, was "a job invented by Satan." And when his father died in 1914, Truman broke free. He tried his hand at a series of speculative ventures but failed at everything he attempted. Those who knew him said that these repeated business failures left him with an inner anger that he never completely lost.

By 1918 Truman, a strong believer in Woodrow Wilson and in the cause of the Allied Powers, was swept into World War I. He served overseas as a combat artillery captain, and emerged a war hero, returning home a more confident man. The first thing he did was marry his longtime sweetheart Bess Wallace. And to make a living, he became a shopkeeper in Kansas City, opening a men's furnishing store on West Twelfth Street. When, as one of the little businessmen, Truman went bust, he said this final failure in business left him utterly broke and convinced him to try his luck in politics. "I had to have a job," he later recalled. "I had a lot of good friends in Jackson

Newly selected as the running mate for FDR, a spry Harry Truman lunches at the White House with his frail boss (above). Seven months later Roosevelt was dead. Truman had come a long way from his farmhand beginnings which involved driving a plow on the Grandview farm in 1912 (below). For almost the whole decade of his twenties, he "tried to dig a living out of the ground," but he never felt quite right about the profession. "No man that's any good would be a farmhand," he once said.

At an early age, Harry was found to have malformed eyeballs. Here he is at age thirteen with his thick, expensive eyeglasses. "Without my glasses I was blind as a bat, and to tell the truth I was kind of a sissy," he once told a group of children at the Truman Library. "If there was any danger of getting into a fight, I always ran. I guess that's why I'm here today."

Faking an eye exam and shedding his glasses for a 1918 military ID card picture, Truman insisted on being part of World War I, even though he was past draft age. "I was stirred in heart and soul by the war messages of Woodrow Wilson. . . . I thought I ought to go. . . . I felt that I was a Galahad after the Grail. . . . I rather felt we owed France something for Lafayette."

County and was kin to nearly everyone in that part of the county; and so I ran for Eastern Judge."

Backed by the notorious and powerful Kansas City boss Tom Pendergast, Truman was elected over the next decade to a series of increasingly important county offices. Though his sponsor developed ties to organized crime, Truman himself was incorruptible. And he became known for his commitment to the workingman, especially during the years of the Great Depression. "During that period," he remembered, "I had to make work projects and build roads and buildings . . . to keep enough people employed in the county so nobody would starve."

By 1934, Harry Truman was elected to the U.S. Senate, where he became known for his plain talk and his colorful use of profanity. He would later be nicknamed "Give-'em-hell-Harry," and his refreshingly honest style made him one of the most popular men in Washington. Elected to a second term, he also became one of the most powerful, serving as chairman of a special Senate investigative committee—which became known as the Truman Committee—charged with uncovering Defense Department waste and fraud. Saving the country hundreds of million of dollars, it put Truman's name on the map. In 1943, *Time* magazine named him Man of the Year. And at the Democratic National Convention in 1944, he was selected to be President Roosevelt's running mate. The Roosevelt-Truman ticket swept to victory in the 1944 election.

Truman was hoping to serve a single term as vice president and then return to his work in the Senate. But just seven weeks after the inauguration, President Roosevelt collapsed. Truman later recalled the terrible day: "On April 12, 1945, I had been presiding over the Senate in my capacity as Vice President. When the Senate recessed about five o'clock in the afternoon . . . I was told . . . to come over to the White House as quickly as possible. . . . When I arrived Mrs. Roosevelt told me the tragic news. . . . President Roosevelt had died." An insecure and unprepared Harry Truman was

In June 1919, Harry married his former classmate and longtime sweetheart, Bess Wallace (left). Bess had wanted to marry him before he left for war, but Harry had told her no by letter. "You may be sure that I'll be just as loyal to you as if you were my wife. . . . Bess, this is a crazy letter but I'm crazy about you and I can't say all these nutty things to you without making you weep. When you weep, I want to [too] . . . and a weeping man is an abomination unto the Lord."

Truman holds still for the camera in his haberdashery shop located on the ground floor of a five-story building in the business and entertainment center of Kansas City. Selling men's underwear, socks, shirts, belts, hats, and collars and specializing in silk shirts and kid gloves, the venture never quite made it—Truman was able to pay himself only $40 a week. The shop's failure drove him into another profession: politics.

immediately sworn into office, becoming the seventh of the nation's presidents by happenstance. "It was a terrible thing to have to take over," Truman later said. "[But] maybe that made me work harder."

Less than a month after he took office, Germany surrendered and Truman proceeded to give all his attention to the Pacific, where the war against Japan was taking a terrible toll. With an estimate that as many as 100,000 more American lives would be lost before Tokyo could be conquered, Truman decided, if necessary, he was willing to use the newly developed top-secret atomic bomb. On July 26, acting in concert with the British and the Chinese, Truman issued Japan a final ultimatum. Though no specific mention was made of the A-bomb, Truman promised utter destruction to the Japanese if they did not surrender unconditionally. "Let there be no mistake," he publicly declared, "we shall completely destroy Japan's power to make war. If they do not now accept our terms, they may expect a rain of ruin from the air the like of which has never been seen on this earth."

On August 6, at 8:11 A.M. Japanese time, an atomic bomb was dropped on Hiroshima, killing 75,000 Japanese, almost all of them civilians. When no word of surrender came forth after the attack, a second bomb was dropped on Nagasaki three days later. Five days after that, Emperor Hirohito surrendered. In the years ahead Truman was severely criticized for dropping the bomb on Japanese citizens. But to the end of his life, he never doubted his decision. "The greatest part of the President's job," he said, "is to make decisions—big ones and small ones, dozens of them almost every day. . . . The President—whoever he is—has to decide. He can't pass the buck to anybody."

Throughout his presidency, Truman kept to the same routine. He awoke at 5 A.M. and began the day with morning exercise, usually a one- or two-mile walk around the streets of Washington. Returning home, he took a shot of bourbon, had a rubdown, and ate a light breakfast. He was in the Oval Office by seven o'clock.

On April 12, at 7:09 P.M. I was sworn in as president by Chief Justice Stone in the Cabinet Room. Things were happening fast in those days. The San Francisco conference to organize the United Nations had been called for April 25. I was asked if that meeting would go forward. I announced that it would. That was my first decision. . . . On May 7, Germany surrendered. The announcement was made on . . . my sixty-first birthday. The war against Japan was still going on. I made the decision that the atomic bomb had to be used to end it. . . . I suppose that history will remember my term in office as the years when the "Cold War" began to overshadow our lives. . . . And always in the background there has been the atomic bomb. . . . The first crisis came in 1945 and 1946, when the Soviet Union refused to honor its agreement to remove its troops from Iran. So we took our stand . . . and the Soviet troops were withdrawn from Iran. Then came the Marshall Plan which saved Europe; the heroic Berlin airlift; and our military aid programs. We inaugurated the North Atlantic Pact, the Rio Pact, binding the Western Hemisphere together, and the defense pacts with countries of the Far Pacific. Most important of all, we acted in Korea. . . . It was not easy to make the decision to send American boys again into battle. . . . The decision I believe was the most important in my time as President of the United States. . . . As I have thought about our worldwide struggle with the Communists these past eight years—day in and day out—I have never once doubted that the people of our country have the will to do what is necessary to win this terrible fight against Communism. As the free world grows stronger, more united, more attractive to men on both sides of the Iron Curtain—and as the Soviet hopes for easy expansion are blocked—then there will have to come a time of change in the Soviet world. Nobody can say for sure when that is going to be, or exactly how it will come about, whether by revolution, or trouble in the satellite states, or by a change inside the Kremlin. I have not a doubt in the world that a change will occur.

Truman's domestic policies were innovative, with new commitments to civil rights and to social programs he called "The Fair Deal." But throughout his presidency, foreign affairs predominated. When the Soviets broke their Yalta agreements and moved to consolidate their hold over Eastern Europe, Truman insisted that the United States stay active on the world stage and work to contain the spread of Communism. This policy came to be known as "The Truman Doctrine," backed up by the Marshall Plan, in which billions of American dollars were committed to the rebuilding of Western Europe.

But it was also the start of the Cold War, and of a nuclear arms race with the Soviet Union. And as foreign dangers multiplied, Truman's presidency came under increasing attack. Following stunning defeats for the Democrats in 1946, his popularity dropped so low that he was urged by his party not to run for reelection. He seemed destined to fade away. But unlike so many of his nineteenth-century predecessors-by-happenstance, Truman refused to allow himself to be submerged. Rekindling the enthusiasm of Democrats for New Deal–style reform, he won the Democratic nomination and campaigned against a "do-nothing" Republican Congress. His surprise victory over Thomas E. Dewey in the November 1948 elections was one of the great upsets in presidential history, and put an end to his reputation as an "accidental president."

In Truman's second term, major structural problems were uncovered in the White House. Earlier he had built the "Truman balcony." Now he would be forced to move out of the mansion during a massive renovation—the most significant since the rebuilding after the War of 1812. "We were across the street in Blair House," Truman recalled, "[and it] was not as convenient as living in the White House. The secret service wouldn't let me walk across the street, so I had to get in a car every morning to cross the street to the White House offices, again at noon . . . for lunch, and finally take an automobile at night to return to Blair House."

Truman's second term was dominated by the Korean War and was made worse by the eruption of McCarthyism. Afraid that a Congressional declaration of war would seem too much like the onset of World War III, Truman tried to run the Korean campaign himself under his authority as commander-in-chief. But when the war lengthened, it came to be seen as Truman's War. Congress disassociated itself, and Truman got all the political fallout.

When he fired the immensely popular General Douglas MacArthur, his popularity plummeted to 23 percent, four points below Richard Nixon's low before the resignation. On March 29, 1952, as the war in Korea continued to drag on, Truman surprised the nation and announced that he would not seek another term in office. "I have served my country long and I think efficiently and honestly," he said. "I do not feel it is my duty to spend another four years in the White House."

When Harry Truman returned home to Independence, Missouri, he took genuine pleasure in the fact that he was once again an ordinary citizen. And he lived long enough to see his reputation restored. The common touch he'd brought to the office and his decisive style of leadership made him stand out as the finest of all the "accidental presidents."

In one of the only photographs of them together, Truman and Missouri machine boss Tom Pendergast share smiles at the 1936 Democratic National Convention. Truman depended on Pendergast backing to get him into office and keep him there, but for that he paid a high price. He could never really shake the reputation of being soft on crime and a Pendergast minion.

Truman had been selected by FDR as his running mate in 1944. Here the two are pelted by rain as they ride in an open car in a victory parade in Washington. Roosevelt was trying to make people feel he was still strong enough for a fourth term when actually death was closing in.

With everyone still numb from FDR's sudden death that afternoon, Truman takes the oath of office as his distressed wife and daughter look on. "When Franklin Roosevelt died," Truman said, "I felt there must be a million men better qualified than I to take up the presidential task. But the work was mine to do, and I had to do it."

Before the Potsdam Conference begins, Churchill, Truman, and Stalin entwine hands. "Churchill was one of the most agreeable men I ever met," Truman thought. "He's a hard bargainer. He likes to argue about everything, but when it comes right down to brass tacks, he's always on the right side." As for Stalin, "[he] made a very agreeable impression on me."

No one thought Harry Truman could beat Tom Dewey in 1948—no one, that is, except Harry Truman, who told it like it was in 356 speeches across the country, shook countless hands, and insisted that the people would "throw the Galluping polls right into the ashcan—you watch 'em." Truman went to bed election eve convinced premature results indicating a Dewey victory were mistaken. They were.

What better place to be than at Harry Truman's White House on the day World War II ended—August 14, 1945.

HARRY TRUMAN'S WHITE HOUSE

Truman's desk in the Oval Office
during the summer of 1950

The country can thank Harry Truman for what he did to the White House. And not just the controversial but well-enjoyed balcony built on the south side in 1947, but his total reconstruction of the mansion's interior. Actually, he had little choice; the place was literally falling down. Pipes dripped, plaster crumbled, walls shifted and collapsed, and there were unsettling vibrations in some of the floors. It was impossible just to polish the old house up once again. So the Truman family moved out in the fall of 1948, and for three years the country was run from the Blair House close by. Mantels, paneling, floors, fixtures, and furnishings were boxed up and stored in warehouses as the White House was literally gutted. The only things left after demolition were the original outside walls of stone, leaving a huge, cavernous void inside them. With the underpinnings shored up, sixty-six tons of steel were used in the construction of a skeleton that would bear the entire weight of the interior of the house, leaving the stone walls to hold up only themselves. Those walls were inviolate; Harry Truman wouldn't let an opening be carved in them to let a big tractor through. Instead the tractor had to be taken apart, carried inside piece by piece through an existing passageway, and reassembled. Even though the Korean War had begun, Truman found time to study plans, haunt the catwalks, and make decisions as the new interior walls went up. By 1951, the stored mantels, wood floors, and paneling returned. The historic rooms, although brand new now, were replicas of what they had been before; the service areas, however, resembled those of a fine, modern hotel. Eighteen painters worked through the winter of 1952, and on March 27 Harry and Bess moved back in. He had administered the making of a completely new house, safe in structure now and fireproofed, yet in many ways the old house still, reincarnated.

Against a thicket of steel braces, the subbasements of the White House (top) are excavated in 1950. Truman's complete overhaul created the White House of today. Above, Truman and Eisenhower look each other over just before Ike's inauguration. At right, back in Independence, Missouri, Harry Truman, just plain "citizen" again, approaches home at 219 North Delaware Street, showing a part of himself familiar to photographers—his back.

PART FOUR

EXECUTIVE VISION

Washington, D.C., in 1904

Thomas Jefferson

Calvin Coolidge

THE AMERICAN WAY

CHAPTER SEVEN

Many presidents have had a passion for what America is to be about;
some have raised this to a matter of principle.

Herbert C. Hoover   Ronald Reagan

Ｆrom the beginning, American national identity has been less a condition than a set of ideas—the values and virtues and purposes and ideals that have served to unite us as a people. Through our history, the president has been in a unique position to help articulate these basic values—and as a source of ideas that have defined America, Thomas Jefferson remains unrivaled. His principal accomplishment, the Declaration of Independence, has attained the status of an American creed, and his lifelong struggle to make his vision a reality for the nation has affected American history right up to the present.

At the heart of Jefferson's vision lay his belief in "the people," and their ability, if unencumbered, to work out their own destiny. Even though repeatedly warned about the potential tyranny of majorities, Jefferson held firm to this basic faith in the people. It was a faith he saw compromised during John Adams's presidency, with its enlarged executive powers and its practice of keeping a standing army. Worst of all, to Jefferson, was its incur-

Andrew Jackson's vision of the American way was the most broadly democratic yet, and his government would be the first to include hundreds of ordinary Americans.

With his extraordinary rise from the backwoods to the White House, Abraham Lincoln seemed to embody the American Dream. He spoke about a country where all would have an equal chance, and in his presidency, by ending slavery, he brought that vision a giant step closer to reality.

sion into civil liberties, the most glaring examples of which were the Alien and Sedition Acts. Passed in 1798 in preparation for an anticipated war with France, the Acts tightened restrictions on citizenship and made anti-government speech illegal for all Americans. For Jefferson, it added up to a dangerous drift away from fundamental principles.

When Jefferson sought the presidency in 1800, he cast himself as a revolutionary outsider, and promised to restore America's republican simplicity. His vision of the American way was, indeed, a rather simple one: stand firm for Americans' liberties and keep government small and unobtrusive. In some ways it was an eighteenth-century vision, of an America remaining primarily rural. Jefferson called farmers "the chosen people of God," and attributed to them a "substantial and genuine virtue." Urbanites, on the other hand, played little part in his vision. "The mobs of the great cities add just so much to the support of pure government," he once wrote, "as sores do to the strength of the human body."

And yet despite these aspects of his philosophy, Jefferson's belief in what he called "an empire of liberty" was at its essence forward-looking. America, for Jefferson, represented something new in history—a giant leap forward from the old ways of other countries. America was to be built upon enlightened individualism and self-government. It was to be a vast domain of liberty, filled with essentially equal people. In contrast to Europe, with its impoverished, landless hordes, Jefferson's America was to be built around a constellation of small property owners. "It is not too soon to provide by every possible means," he wrote in the 1780s, "that as few as possible shall be without a little portion of land." It was the beginnings of what would be called "the American Dream," which at its heart is a Jeffersonian dream. "Above all," he later wrote, demonstrating his belief in fundamental equality, "I hope the education of the common people will be attended to."

When Andrew Jackson became president in 1829, he called himself a dyed-in-the-wool Jeffersonian. In some ways he resembled his hero only slightly—he was intolerant and prone to rages, whereas Jefferson had been enlightened and rationalistic. But Jackson's vision of America had a driving power that in some ways took it far beyond the Jeffersonian revolution. Jackson saw a future more complex than Jefferson's, in which ordinary Americans, rural and urban, controlled their own destiny and took part in the political process. That future came to be called the "democratic" vision, and though it still excluded women and blacks and Native Americans, it represented a genuine broadening of participatory government.

Twenty-five years after Jackson came Abraham Lincoln, with his own passionate belief in the American Dream. At its core was a belief in the right of each person to elevate himself in society, a belief that became, over time, Lincoln's way into the slavery issue. For if anything undermined a person's basic right to self-betterment, it was the long-entrenched institution of slavery. Neither Jefferson nor Jackson had been willing to take slavery on, even though it made a mockery of their belief that all men were created equal. But by the 1850s, Lincoln was insisting that slavery was wrong, and it became a major issue in his 1860 quest for the presidency. "One of the reasons I am opposed to slavery is just here," he said. "I want every man to have the chance—and I believe a black man is entitled to it—in which he can better his condition."

Lincoln's Gettysburg Address, delivered in 1863, was a profound revisioning of Jefferson's Declaration of Independence. Highlighting the "all equal" clause and insisting that the Civil War was being fought to test its viability, Lincoln gave new meaning and life to the American creed itself.

Other presidents continued in the Jeffersonian tradition. Some, like Calvin Coolidge and Herbert Hoover, emphasized Jefferson's critique of large government and the importance of individual and community effort. Others, like Theodore Roosevelt and his cousin Franklin, emphasized civil liberties and equality and democracy. As the American dream widened out to include more and more of the previously disenfranchised, the Jeffersonian vision became increasingly universalized.

Ironically, Franklin Roosevelt, in his belief that big government should help solve the nation's problems, represented in some ways the antithesis of the Jeffersonian message. And yet FDR successfully appropriated Jefferson's blessing for his federalist agenda, in part by presiding over the dedication of the Jefferson Memorial in Washington.

Unlike Jackson or Lincoln or either of the Roosevelts, Ronald Reagan did not push the Jeffersonian vision into new horizons. Instead, he romanticized the American past, especially the prosperous era of Calvin Coolidge. He called Coolidge "one of our most underrated presidents," noting that "instead of raising taxes, he cut the tax rate and government revenue increased." One of Reagan's first acts as president was to bring Coolidge's portrait out of storage and to hang it in the Cabinet Room, where it could inspire him. He drew heavily as well upon Herbert Hoover, and on Hoover's belief in volunteerism and charity as an alternative to government welfare. Most of all he was inspired by Thomas Jefferson, whom he seemed to quote more than he did any other president. When he said, "We should each pluck a flower from Thomas Jefferson's life and wear it on our soul forever," his rhetoric seemed overblown, but Reagan shared Jefferson's vision of America as an "empire of liberty" that would stand as a beacon of light to the rest of the world. His vast military buildup, expansion of the federal debt, and entanglement in the affairs of Central America marked him in key ways as an opposite of Thomas Jefferson. And he possessed none of Jefferson's immense intellectual curiosity. Yet in other ways Reagan and Jefferson were similar. They stood up for the American ideal against the "evil empires" of their day. They shared a quality of expansiveness that included an infectious optimism and a belief in human nature, and each helped to restore a lagging American spirit. In Reagan's case, his belief in individual effort and in American capitalism helped launch a powerful new era of economic expansion. This was his own contribution to the American way.

No one loved America more than Theodore Roosevelt, whose passionate nature embraced the entire continent. A populist, a reformer, a conservationist, a family man, he was a promoter of the American way like few presidents before him.

Franklin Roosevelt's immediate predecessor, Herbert Hoover, called him a dangerous experimenter whose New Deal would "destroy our American system." But in his belief that federal government should be involved in solving the nation's problems, and in his faith in the American people to overcome, it was Roosevelt who more deeply defined the American way.

THOMAS JEFFERSON

1801–1809

His "Empire of Liberty"

Estranged from his mother and barely a teenager when his father died, Jefferson recollected that he was alone in the world "without a relation or friend qualified to advise or guide me," and that for a time he ran with "bad company." "I am astonished I did not turn off with some of them and become as worthless to society as they were." Instead he became an obsessive student, training his remarkable intellect and insatiable curiosity to master a remarkably wide variety of knowldege. One early biographer described him as someone "who could calculate an eclipse, survey an estate, tie an artery, plan an ediface, try a cause, break a horse, dance a minuet, and play the violin."

From his mountaintop estate of Monticello, Thomas Jefferson loomed over his age as its most brilliant and influential figure. Omnivorously curious, he was proficient in a dozen subjects, from agriculture, science, history, and languages to religion, political philosophy, architecture and music. "There is not a sprig of grass . . . uninteresting to me," he once wrote, "nor anything that moves."

Though he could be physically awkward and lacked oratorical abilities, he was also, in his time, the most politically effective man in America, with an uncanny ability to inspire those around him. And he was an impassioned believer in the American way. "The first object of my heart is my own country," he proclaimed. "This solitary republic of the world [is] the only monument of human rights, and the sole repository of the sacred fire of freedom."

Perhaps above all else he was a dreamer and a rebel, who had early on come under the influence of Virginia's fiery orator Patrick Henry. "Henry's talents as a popular orator . . . were great indeed," he remembered, "such as I have never heard from any other man. He appeared to me to speak as Homer wrote."

Elected at age twenty-six to Virginia's House of Burgesses, Thomas Jefferson became known as a political radical who strongly supported independence from Britain. When he published his first work, "A Summary View of the Rights of British America," he was recognized by his colleagues as a gifted writer. At the Continental Congress in Philadelphia in 1776, he was given what turned out to be the most important commission of his life—to serve on a drafting committee as the chief writer for a declaration of independence.

In his second-floor lodging in a brick house in Philadelphia, Jefferson applied himself to his task. Sitting in a Windsor chair and using a portable writing desk he himself had designed, he spent just days writing the words that would make his name immortal.

At the heart of Jefferson's masterpiece lay fifty-six key words (later slightly amended): "We hold these truths to be self–evident; that all men are created equal; that they are endowed by their Creator with inherent and inalienable rights; that among these are life, liberty and the pursuit of happiness; that to secure these rights, governments are instituted among men, deriving their just powers from the consent of the governed." Here were the core articles of what would become the American creed—Jeffersonian words that would shape the rest of American history.

Charles Willson Peale painted Jefferson's portrait when Jefferson was George Washington's secretary of state.

A Declaration by the Representatives of the UNITED STATES OF AMERICA, in General Congress assembled.

When in the course of human events it becomes necessary for one people to dissolve the political bands which have connected them with another, and to assume among the powers of the earth the separate and equal station to which the laws of nature & of nature's god entitle them, a decent respect to the opinions of mankind requires that they should declare the causes which impel them to the separation.

We hold these truths to be self-evident; that all men are created equal, that they are endowed by their creator with inherent & inalienable rights; that among these are life, liberty, & the pursuit of happiness; that to secure these rights, governments are instituted among men, deriving their just powers from the consent of the governed; that whenever any form of government

The brilliant young squire had his life figured out. He would bring his twenty-three-year-old bride to his wild Virginia mountaintop, and withdraw to a private world of books and beauty, farms and philosophy. But he had not counted on the other side of his nature, which soon was drawing him like a magnet to the hotbed of colonial dissent. And so it was that a tall, elegant redhead who hummed under his breath and bowed to whomever he met arrived in Philadelphia attended by three servants in formal attire.

Jefferson was reporting for duty as a delegate to the Continental Congress. In an era of orators, Jefferson wasn't much good as a public speaker, but writing was something else. When Congress finally decided to make its permanent break from England, the unthinkable had to be justified in writing, and the thirty-three-year-old Virginian was chosen to compose the manifesto. So was born the Declaration of Independence, a rough draft of a portion of which, in Jefferson's hand, is shown above (containing at least one of

the several changes asked for by fellow committee members John Adams and Benjamin Franklin). Below, in John Trumbull's highly symbolic painting, Jefferson is a head taller than the other four members of the drafting committee as the declaration is presented for signing, supposedly on July 4. Actually, the presentation took place on June 28, and a week of intensive congressional debate and editing preceded final approval on the fourth, after which the "signing" took place in stages throughout the long summer.

"[My aim was] not to find out new principles or . . . to say things which had never been said before," Jefferson explained with overdue modesty, "but to place before mankind the common sense of the subject. . . . It was intended to be an expression of the American mind."

Jefferson went on to serve in the House of Delegates, and then as governor of Virginia, where he became friends with James Madison. After the war he retired to Monticello. "I rested all prospects of future happiness," he wrote, "on domestic and literary objects." But in 1782, when his beloved wife Martha died following childbirth, Jefferson's dream of domestic bliss was shattered. "A single event wiped away all my plans and left me a blank which I had not the spirits to fill up," he wrote. Two years later he accepted a commission overseas, to serve as an American minister to France. In Paris he joined Benjamin Franklin and John Adams to make a triumvirate of American diplomacy never equaled before or since.

While Jefferson quickly fell in love with all things French—the architecture, the culture, the famous vineyards, the food—his years abroad actually helped focus his American vision, and in a deep sense, made him more truly American. "[In] Europe . . . I find the general fate of humanity . . . most deplorable," he wrote, "compare[d] with that degree of happiness which is enjoyed in America, by every class of people."

Returning to Monticello after five years overseas, he began laying plans for a longed-for retirement. "I had rather be shut up . . . with my books, my family and a few old friends, dining on simple bacon, and letting the world roll on as it liked," he had written, "than to occupy the most splendid post, which any human power can give."

But early retirement was not meant to be. In 1790 Jefferson was approached by President Washington to accept the position of the nation's first secretary of state. Though he at first recoiled, he finally came round. "It is not for an individual to choose his post," he wrote a friend. "A good citizen should take his stand where the public authority marshals him."

Jefferson's revolutionary viewpoints soon shaped the beginnings of a profound split in American politics. On one side, centering on the figure of the secretary of the treasury, Alexander Hamilton, were those favoring big federal government, a strong presidency, and ties to England. On the other side, centered on Thomas Jefferson, were those favoring small national government, a limited presidency, and ties to revolutionary France. "The spirit of 1776 is not dead," Jefferson warned. "[But] we are likely to preserve the liberty we have obtained only by unremitting labors and perils."

Eventually his beliefs led Jefferson into his own quest for the presidency. In 1796 he came in second to John Adams and became vice president. But four years later, after a rupture in his relations with Adams, he ran again, and this time he won. He would later call his victory a "revolution." "The Revolution of 1800 . . . was as real . . . as that of 1776," he proclaimed; "not effected indeed by the sword . . . but by the rational and peaceable instrument of reform, the suffrage of the people."

On March 4, 1801, in a deliberate act of republican simplicity, President-elect Jefferson walked to the Capitol and his inauguration. It was the beginning of his effort to demystify the presidency. As chief executive he did away with the pomp and ceremony of his predecessors, eliminating the state carriage and all formal court appearances. He gave up delivering the State of the Union address in person because it seemed too much like the British monarch's Address to Parliament. Rejecting protocol, when the British Min-

Although he wrote and accomplished much in the fifty years left to him, Jefferson came to realize that he had reached his peak in 1776.

Second from right in this rendition of the country's first cabinet, Jefferson carefully studies George Washington (left) and Alexander Hamilton (standing).

On George Washington:

Perhaps the strongest feature in his character was prudence, never acting until every circumstance, every consideration, was maturely weighed; refraining if he saw a doubt, but, when once decided, going through with his purpose whatever obstacles opposed. His integrity was most pure, his justice the most inflexible I have ever known, no motives of interest or consanguinity, of friendship or hatred, being able to bias his decision. He was, indeed, in every sense of the words, a wise, a good, and a great man. His temper was naturally irritable and high-toned, but reflection and resolution had obtained a firm and habitual ascendancy over it. If ever, however, it broke its bonds, he was most tremendous in his wrath. . . . His heart was not warm in its affections, but he exactly calculated every man's value and gave him a solid esteem proportioned to it. . . . On the whole, his character was, in its mass, perfect, in nothing bad, in few points indifferent; and it may truly be said that never did nature and fortune combine more perfectly to make a man great.

On Alexander Hamilton:

The room being hung around with a collection of the portraits of remarkable men, among them were those of Bacon, Newton, and Locke, Hamilton asked me who they were. I told him they were my trinity of the three greatest men the world had ever produced, naming them. He paused for some time: "The greatest man," said he, "that ever lived was Julius Caesar." . . . Hamilton was, indeed, a singular character. Of acute understanding . . . and honorable in all private transactions, amiable in society, and duly valuing virtue in private life, yet so bewitched and perverted by the British example as to be under thorough conviction that corruption was essential to the government of a nation.

ister was officially presented at the White House, Jefferson appeared in rumpled clothes and old slippers. And the Minister's wife was insulted when the President refused to take her on his arm. "We have told him that the principle of society . . . with us is equality of the individuals composing it," Jefferson wrote to James Monroe. "If his wife perseveres, she must eat her soup at home."

Determined to cut back what he considered a bloated federal government, Jefferson set to work to reinvent America. In an extraordinary move he eliminated all internal taxes, abolishing the Internal Revenue Service. And he made his number-one priority the retiring of national debt, which he partly accomplished within his first four years. To pay for it all, he made radical cuts in the Army and Navy, and proposed closing down American embassies abroad. "I am for free commerce with all nations; political connection with none; and little or no diplomatic establishment," he said.

The great paradox of Jefferson's first term was the Louisiana Purchase, one of the most decisive executive actions in United States history. As Jefferson knew, the Constitution makes no mention of acquiring territory, only of admitting states to the Union. Transforming himself into an almost monarchical president, Jefferson claimed it was his duty to break the rules sometimes for the good of the nation. "In seizing [Louisiana I] . . . have done an act beyond the Constitution," he said. "[But] it is incumbent on those . . . who accept great charges, to risk themselves on great occasions." Louisiana not only doubled America's size, but it stretched the nation's horizons, and offered an area for settlement and agrarian development of precisely the sort in which Jefferson profoundly believed.

Jefferson's first term was one of the most successful in presidential history. Despite his belief in limited executive power, he had no inhibitions in serving as the leader of his partisans. In an era before standing committees had come into existence, he encouraged the House to create a Congressional caucus of all like-minded followers and created a floor leader as his personal representative. Then, through consultation in small groups and through the work of the floor leader, he dominated all decisions of the House. But his dominance was as party leader, and not as president, and this was very

important to Jefferson. It demonstrated, he said, that the people were in charge and that it was indeed a revolution from the way George Washington and John Adams had endeavored to carry on the government.

In Jefferson's second term his perennial good luck ran out. Faced with British attacks on American commercial ships at sea, he called for the Embargo Act of 1807, closing American ports to all foreign trade. This final effort to free America from European power and turn the national sights inward on a new path of development ended up all but crippling the American economy and nearly led to the secession of heavily affected New England. To enforce his embargo, Jefferson had to resort to federal policing, an action contrary to his basic philosophy of small government and civil liberties. He grew increasingly unpopular and unhappy in the presidency, and he finally decided he had had enough. "I determined to withdraw at the end of my second term," he said. "General Washington set the example. . . . I shall follow it."

On March 4, 1809, Jefferson left Washington for good and returned home to his mountaintop in Virginia. Here on his thousands of acres served by more than a hundred slaves, he reimmersed himself in agriculture and intellectual pursuits. "Nature intended me for the tranquil pursuits of science, by rendering them my supreme delight," he explained. "The enormities of the times in which I have lived . . . forced me to take a part in . . . them."

To the end he was a man of profound contradictions: monumentally learned, he could also be extraordinarily naive; friendly, he remained aloof; a believer in the people, he was at heart an aristocrat. And the great proponent of human equality remained a lifelong slave owner who saw no future for blacks in America. "Nothing is more certainly written in the book of fate than that these people are to be free," he once wrote. "[But] the two races . . . cannot live in the same government. Nature, habit, opinion has drawn indelible lines of distinction between them." Ironically, though he especially warned against miscegenation, recent evidence suggests he may have secretly fathered a child with his longtime personal slave Sally Hemmings.

In spite of blind spots and human shortcomings, Jefferson was the preeminent visionary of American liberty, who foresaw a great country populated by essentially equal people. It was a vision he had placed at the heart of the Declaration of Independence, a vision which in the end was much bigger than Jefferson himself.

A color lithograph (above) shows the soft-spoken, optimistic Jefferson at midlife. "I am among those who think well of the human character generally," he wrote. "I consider man as formed for society, and . . . I believe . . . that his mind is perfectible to a degree of which we cannot as yet form any conception."

"I cannot live without books," once wrote Thomas Jefferson, whose private library was the most important in the country and included, among its 10,000 volumes, the books shown above. Following the British burning of the Library of Congress in 1814, Jefferson promptly offered his collection as a replacement. "I have been fifty years in the making it," he wrote. "Eighteen or twenty wagons would place it in Washington in a . . . fortnight." Congress accepted.

Jefferson was a fine amateur architect. At left is his original rough sketch for Monticello before work began. In the engraving of the finished building (above), a dome has supplanted the peaked roof.

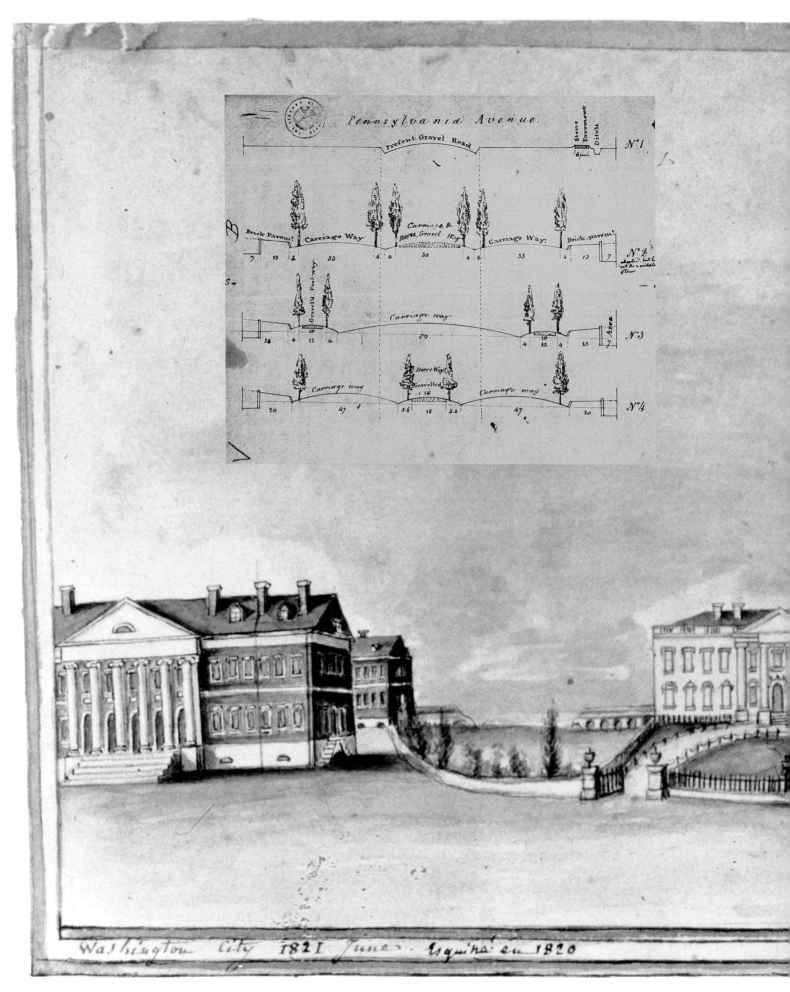

When Thomas Jefferson became president in 1801, he disbanded the capital commission established under George Washington and appointed a single city architect—Benjamin Latrobe—answerable only to himself. Jefferson set up a drafting table in a corner office of the Executive Mansion, surrounded himself with books, plants, and pets, and began producing hundreds of rough sketches and architectural plans, which he turned over to Latrobe for execution. Included was a sketch of four options for the improvement of Pennsylvania Avenue, which as yet stopped short of the president's residence (far left). Below, in a watercolor of the White House painted eleven years after Jefferson's presidency, evidences can be seen of Jefferson's impact on the property. There are the circular stone walls that enclose the property, seen here facing out in the direction of what will soon be Pennsylvania Avenue. And there are the two low-lying wings stretching out from either side of the mansion, part of Jefferson's plan to connect the house with the executive buildings on either side. In late 1806, during final construction of the east wing in cold weather, its central arch collapsed, never to be rebuilt. To some the ruin seemed eerily symbolic of Jefferson's increasingly troubled second term.

APHILOSOPHIC COCK

Even in his own day there were accusations of a clandestine relationship between President Thomas Jefferson and his slave Sally Hemmings, who is pictured at left as a turban-wearing hen beside the "philosophic cock" of Monticello. DNA testing established that Jefferson, or someone closely related to him, was the father of one of Sally's children.

IN HIS OWN WORDS

On the Revolution:
May it be to the world what I believe it will be, . . . the signal of arousing men to burst [their] chains . . . and to assume the blessings and security of self-government.

On John Adams:
He is vain, irritable and a bad calculator of the force and probable effect of the motives which govern men. That is all the ill which can possibly be said of him. . . . He is profound in views . . . accurate in his judgment . . . [and] so amiable that I pronounce you will love him.

On religious and intellectual freedom:
I have sworn upon the altar of God, eternal hostility against every form of tyranny over the mind of man.

On the people:
The people . . . can be trusted with their own government, . . . whenever things get so far wrong as to attract their notice, they may be relied upon to set them to rights.

On the presidency:
The second office of this government is honorable & easy, the first is but a splendid misery.

On the dangers of slavery:
I tremble for my country when I reflect that God is just: that his justice cannot sleep forever: that . . . a revolution of the wheel of fortune, an exchange of situations, is among possible events: that it may become probable by supernatural interference!

Deep prejudices entertained by whites, ten thousand recollections, by the blacks, of injuries they have sustained; new provocations; the real distinctions that nature has made . . . will divide us into parties, and produce convulsions that will probably never end but in the extermination of one or the other race.

On the future:
We can no longer say there is nothing new under the sun. For this whole chapter in the history of man is new. The great extent of our Republic is new. . . . The mighty wave of public opinion which has rolled over it is new.

There are indeed . . . gloomy and hypochondriac minds . . . disgusted with the present and despairing of the future; always counting that the worst will happen, because it may happen. . . . My temperament is sanguine. I steer my bark with Hope in the head, leaving Fear astern.

JEFFERSON'S INCONSISTENCIES

Thomas Jefferson has long baffled the world with the many apparent contradictions between his life and his thought. What he said and what he did were often at odds. The most glaring example was his stance on slavery. In 1776 he authored the Declaration of Independence, stating unequivocally that "all men are created equal." And for a time afterward Jefferson was one of the leaders in the antislavery movement. Yet throughout his life he owned slaves, and unlike George Washington, did not set them free at his death. Instead some were sold to help pay off his considerable debts. For Jefferson "all equal" was never meant to include blacks, just as it never included women or Native Americans. It took later generations to stretch Jefferson's vision so that it properly embraced everyone within the American creed.

Jefferson's elusive, contradictory personality surfaced in many forms. He was friendly, yet aloof. He was an aristocrat, yet he believed in the people. He was a strict constitutionalist, yet he was willing to flout the Constitution for the Louisiana Purchase. He took his daughter, Patsy, to France to clothe her with culture and to stay close to her, yet he shut her away in a convent. He championed farming, yet he personally disliked it. He abhorred industry, yet he started a factory on his property. And though he called racial intermixture a great evil, he is believed to have carried on a clandestine relationship with his slave Sally Hemmings, and may have been the father of one of her children. These incongruities and many more will probably never be adequately explained, and Thomas Jefferson will remain America's most glorious puzzle.

In 1805, in the middle of his presidency, Jefferson was painted in his fur collar by Rembrandt Peale.

CALVIN COOLIDGE

1923–1929

Preacher of Prosperity

John Calvin Coolidge grew up on the family farm in Vermont, working so hard he was left with little time for himself. Often lonely as a boy, he also feared being left alone, and meeting strangers was an agony that never left him. "When I was a little fellow," he recalled, "I would go into a panic if I heard stranger voices in the house. . . . The hardest thing in the world was to have to go through the kitchen door and give them a greeting. . . . By fighting hard I used to manage to get through that door."

Losing his beloved mother at age twelve, he came increasingly under the influence of his taciturn, puritanical father, who ran a general store, and to whom he would retain a lifelong devotion. "My father . . . had the strong New England trait of great repugnance at seeing anything wasted," he later wrote. "He regarded waste as a moral wrong."

Calvin, too, saw to it that he wasted nothing. As he saw it, reading for pleasure, anything musical, dancing, playing a sport, indulging in a hobby, having a sweetheart all squandered precious time and energy. Even talking itself could be a form of waste. "He who gives license to his tongue," he once wrote, "proclaims his lack of discipline . . . and self-respect."

After graduating from Amherst College, Coolidge entered the law and then turned to politics, mixing the religious philosophy of his favorite teacher with a belief in progress and prosperity. Dealing his cautious, conservative hand in the state of Massachusetts, he worked slowly but steadily up the political ladder, eventually becoming mayor of Northampton and finally governor of Massachusetts. When he was thrust into national prominence by the Boston police strike, to which he took a strong contrary position, Governor Coolidge's name was suddenly on the nation's lips. "I stated among other things that 'there is no right to strike against the public safety by any body, any time, any where,'" Coolidge recalled. "This phrase caught the attention of the nation."

A quickly published collection of Coolidge's writings increased his national stature and assisted his reelection as governor. Then, at the 1920 Republican convention, his name was put forward for president. Though he lost to Warren G. Harding, Coolidge was nominated for vice president, and in the fall he and Harding won a stunning victory. "So long as I am in that position [of vice president]," Coolidge vowed, "it is my duty to uphold the policies and actions of the administration one hundred percent. . . . When I

Calvin Coolidge (above, at age three) was born on the 4th of July, 1872. New England virtues of thrift were stressed from the beginning. "While in theory I was always urged to work and to save," he wrote, "in practice I [did] . . . my share of playing and wasting. My playthings often lay in the road to be run over, and my ballgame often interfered with my filling the wood box. I have been taken out of bed to do penance for such derelictions." At Amherst (below) "it was not until senior year that an opportunity came to belong to [a fraternity] that I wished to accept. It has been my observation in life that, if one will only exercise the patience to wait, his wants are likely to be filled."

Riding an immense wave of popularity during the roaring twenties, an imperturbable Calvin Coolidge poses on the south lawn of the White House. "He was the incarnation of New England horse sense," wrote Herbert Hoover, "endowed with certain Puritan rigidities that served the nation well."

Above, John Coolidge, Calvin's father, relaxes in his general store in Plymouth Notch, Vermont, adjacent to the five-room cottage in which Calvin grew up. With him at left is Calvin's uncle John Wilder. Below, a crowd of well-wishers presses in to hear half of the Republican ticket lambaste the opposition at a whistle-stop in 1920.

cannot conscientiously agree with them it is then my duty to keep silent." It was the beginning of his national nickname of "Silent Cal."

Two and a half years into his vice presidency, Coolidge made a visit to his father in Plymouth Notch, Vermont. There, on the night of August 3, 1923, he was jarred awake from a deep sleep. "I was awakened by my father coming up the stairs calling my name," he recalled. "I noticed that his voice trembled. . . . I knew that something of the gravest nature had occurred. . . . He placed in my hands an official report and told me that President Harding had just passed away."

A Republican poster for the 1920 election.

Coolidge dressed and then knelt in prayer. In the sitting room, by the light of a kerosene lamp, with his mother's Bible on the table beside him, he was sworn into office. "The oath was administered by my father in his capacity as a notary public," Coolidge later wrote. "I do not know of any [other] case in history where a father has administered to his son the qualifying oath of office which made him the chief magistrate of a nation."

And so for the sixth time in American history, a vice president found himself unexpectedly presiding over the nation. Americans quickly took to this unpretentious New England original. Holding more than five hundred press conferences over the course of his administration, he was photographed more often than any preceding president, and despite his taciturn nature he delivered radio broadcasts that were heard by millions of Americans. "It was my desire to maintain an attitude of simplicity," he said, "and not engage in anything that had an air of [pretention]."

Coolidge represented in his own person many of the virtues of traditional New England. He was pithy, terse, upright, and honest. He kept his word and expected other people to keep theirs. He didn't speak unless he had something to say, and then he was always specific and to the point. All these classic virtues were appreciated by the general public. In many ways he was the perfect president in an era when people were intent on pursuing their own futures, disillusioned with large internationalist ideals, and uninterested in large governmental enterprises.

A doffed hat and a wicked smile were uncharacteristic for President Coolidge. Photographers were more likely to encounter the dour farmer's face, below, that one person said made him look like he'd been "weaned on a pickle."

But there was also a sour side to Calvin Coolidge that led him to be disliked by some who saw him when out of the public eye. Longtime White House usher Irwin Hoover, who had adored working for Woodrow Wilson and others, wrote, "President Coolidge was different from the rest. He seemed to be always watching, suspicious lest something be 'put over' on him." Even his humor had a terseness to it. Once, a dinner partner told him she had made a bet she could engage him in conversation for five minutes. His answer consisted of two words: "You lose." When asked why he attended so many luncheons and dinners, he allowed three words—though one not quite a word—for his answer: "Gotta eat somewhere." And when someone once requested a new photograph of him, he said slyly, "I don't know what you want another for; I'm using the same face." And then there was tragedy, stark tragedy, in the sudden death of his younger son, Calvin. Coolidge blamed himself for it: "If I had not been President he would not have raised a blister on his toe . . . playing lawn tennis on the South grounds . . . which resulted in blood poisoning. . . . When he went, the power and the glory of the Presidency went with him."

As president, Coolidge made some fine appointments, including Harlan Stone as attorney general and Herbert Hoover as secretary of commerce. And he deliberately emulated Thomas Jefferson, by making his top priority a commitment to fiscal economy. When asked if he intended any internal

Describing the neighbors and the environment of his youth in the Green Mountains of central Vermont, Coolidge wasn't just talking about the past, he was waving his own personal flag.

The neighborhood around The Notch was made up of people of exemplary habits. Their speech was clean and their lives were above reproach. They had no mortgages on their farms. . . . The break of day saw them stirring. Their industry continued until twilight. They kept up no church organization . . . but they were without exception a people of faith and charity and of good works. They cherished the teachings of the Bible and sought to live in accordance with its precepts. . . . They drew no class distinctions except towards those who assumed superior airs. Those they held in contempt. They held strongly to the doctrine of equality. Whenever the hired man or the hired girl wanted to go anywhere they were always understood to be entitled to my place in the wagon, in which case I remained at home. This gave me a very early training in democratic ideas and impressed upon me very forcibly the dignity and power, if not the superiority of labor. It was all a fine atmosphere to raise a boy. . . . It was all close to nature and in accordance with the ways of nature. The streams ran clear. The roads, the woods, the fields, the people—all were clean. Even when I try to divest it of the halo which I know always surrounds the past, I am unable to create any other impression than that it was fresh and clean.

Coolidge was only too happy to don costumes for the photographers (above), but his own farming uniform (below) was something else again: "When news pictures began to be taken of me [at the farm], I found that among the public this was generally supposed to be a makeup costume, which it was not, so I have since been obliged to forego the comfort of wearing it. In public life it is sometimes necessary in order to appear really natural to be actually artificial."

improvements to the nation he answered, "I am exceedingly interested in reducing . . . the national debt. That would constitute . . . the very largest internal improvement that it would be possible to conceive."

His personal heroes were men like Andrew Carnegie and Charles Schwab, self-made multimillionaires who represented unfettered capitalism. Protection of their interests was a major part of Coolidge's vision of the American way. "A man has a right to make as much money as he can, and the more a man makes, the more he can pay his workmen," he once said. "The fostering and protection of large aggregates of wealth are the only foundation on which to build the prosperity of the whole people." Here was the core of Coolidge's American philosophy. "The chief business of the American people is business," he liked to say. "If we have any destiny we have found it in that direction." He felt toward industry what Jefferson had felt toward agriculture. "The man who builds a factory builds a temple," he once said. "The man who works there worships there."

Corporate America responded robustly to Coolidge's philosophy, and during the Coolidge years the economy boomed, leading to the greatest wave of prosperity the country had ever known. Coolidge, who continued on his own Spartan lifestyle, insisted that prosperity was a great good, but not just as an end in itself. "Men struggle for material success," he said, "because that is the path . . . to the development of character." In Coolidge's vision private wealth was meant to undergird all the idealistic purposes of the American nation.

But in contrast to such active predecessors as Theodore Roosevelt and Woodrow Wilson, Coolidge refused to be a leader for those idealistic purposes. His legislative program put forward in Congress mostly involved subsidies for business-related activities. Though he successfully balanced the budget and reduced the deficit, his only positive social program was a minor expansion of the federal role in road building. All his other social policies were negative, including his refusal to work on behalf of black Americans and their civil rights, and his strict and discriminatory immigration policy. "Those who do not want to be partakers of the American spirit," he once said, "ought not to settle in America. . . . America must be kept American." Like Jefferson, he was a strict constructionist of the Constitution and did not think it was the federal government's business to take care of the downtrodden. Virtually off his radar screen were the millions of American poor—elderly, urban blacks, and American farm workers, people who needed government help but didn't find it under Calvin Coolidge. He was a president, it was declared, for the "haves," and not the "have-nots."

Despite Coolidge's stance as an economic wizard, he in fact knew little about the workings of the modern economy. His small-town Vermont background and his simplistic, self-help philosophy were inadequate to the rigors of the twentieth century. Nor did he bring in outside experts who might have helped him understand the problems. Though signs of trouble in the stock market were evident by the late 1920s, Coolidge did nothing to avert a looming financial crisis. Instead, at the last moment, he announced his decision not to seek a second full term.

In retirement he would watch as the economy came apart during the presidency of his successor, Herbert Hoover. And as the Coolidge prosperity went out the window, the preacher of the American way had little left to say. "I am no longer fit for these times," he told a newspaperman. "We are in a new era to which I do not belong."

Although no fisherman, Coolidge poses with the sport's paraphernalia, but his suit and tie and hat give him away. He was a Puritan living in an industrial age, holding to an ideology of self-reliance in an era of increasing interdependencies. "[He] was a real conservative," summed up his successor Herbert Hoover, "probably the equal of Benjamin Harrison."

Coolidge poses with his wife, Grace, and younger son, Calvin (above). Everybody agreed that it was Grace Coolidge who made her husband presentable. A charming first lady, she accepted his blue funks and his rages, his hypochondria, his suspicious nature, and his dry, cutting humor. Never allowed to intrude on his work or asked for advice, Grace smoothed over his rudenesses and tried to explain him to the world. "For almost a quarter of a century," Coolidge finally acknowledged, "she has borne with my infirmities, and I have rejoiced in her graces."

At right Calvin Jr. appears at his father's right shoulder along with his older brother, John, standing with his hands behind his back. This picture was taken shortly before young Calvin's sudden death at sixteen from blood poisoning. Coolidge blamed himself and his presidency. "When he went the . . . glory of the Presidency went with him," he wrote. "I do not know why such a price was exacted for occupying the White House."

Coolidge promoted the American way in part through his own homespun aphorisms. They not only reveal his essential parsimony, they also help describe his experience in the presidency.

One of the greatest mysteries in the world is the success that lies in conscientious work. It is not industry but idleness that is degrading.

The chief business of the American people is business.

So long as wealth is made the means and not the end, we need not greatly fear it.

What I have ever been able to do has been the result of first learning how to do it. I am not gifted with intuition.

My folks are happy and contented. They belong to themselves, live within their income, and fear no man.

The political mind is the product of men in public life who have been twice spoiled. They have been spoiled with praise and they have been spoiled with abuse. With them nothing is natural, everything is artificial.

In the discharge of the duties of the office [of president] there is one rule of action more important than all others. It consists in never doing anything that someone else can do for you.

You have to stand every day three or four hours of visitors. Nine-tenths of them want something they ought not to have. If you keep dead-still they will run down in three or four minutes. If you even cough or smile they will start up all over again.

If you see ten troubles coming down the road, you can be sure that nine will run into the ditch before they reach you and you have to battle with only one of them.

Don't hurry to legislate. Give administration a chance to catch up with legislation.

Perhaps one of the most important accomplishments of my administration has been minding my own business.

A taciturn man all his life, Coolidge (at right) found speechmaking difficult. "I always knew there was some water in my well," he once said, "but that I had to pump to get it. It is not a gushing fountain." Another time he declared, "The Coolidges never slop over." In the White House Coolidge preferred nibbling to talking. He couldn't keep away from sweets or nuts, liked to slather crackers with preserves and build hearty cheese sandwiches. He once said to Will Rogers that he kept fit in the presidency "by avoiding the big problems."

Thrifty Calvin Coolidge was appalled when he was told the White House needed an estimated half million dollars' worth of work. At first he opted to do nothing. He later changed his mind when the ceiling of the second-story family quarters started to buckle. In 1927 the Coolidges moved out from March until August as construction took place on a new roof and extensive remodeling took place beneath it.

HERBERT C. HOOVER

1929–1933

American Individualist

Herbert Clark Hoover was the son of a small-town Iowa blacksmith and a kindly Quaker mother, whose simple, humane faith would become an important influence in his life. At age nine he was orphaned and forced to grow up quickly when he was shipped off to Oregon to be the ward of a country-doctor uncle. "He was one of many Quakers who do not hold to extreme pacifism," he later recalled. "One of his expressions was, 'Turn your other cheek once, but if he smites it, then punch him.'"

Graduating in Stanford's pioneer class with a degree in geology, the shy, tactless Hoover headed for Nevada City, where he worked seventy hours a week pushing ore carts in a gold mine. Eventually he was hired by the British firm Bewick Moreing, and sent to Australia to evaluate mines through sampling, surveying, and analysis. One of his most valued qualities was his toughness under inhospitable conditions. "Coolgardie is three yards inside the borders of civilization," he wrote, "a place of red dust, black flies, and white heat." It is "among the hottest and driest and dustiest places on this earth. The temperature was over 100 degrees at midnight."

By his ability to recognize promising mines, Hoover made millions for his company and rose rapidly in its ranks. Named chief engineer for a major mining project in China, in 1899 he headed there with his new wife, Stanford geology major Lou Henry. "I want a man who loves the mountains, the rocks and the ocean like my father does," Lou had written before ever meeting her new husband. And in Hoover she had found exactly that type of man. But in China their mutual love of the outdoors was curtailed when they became targets of the Boxer Rebellion. "Their avowed purpose was . . . to root out every foreign thing . . . [and] they believed they had supernatural protection from foreign bullets," Hoover wrote. "[We were] a group of civilian men, women and children, fighting for very life against a horde of fanatics with modern arms." During a month-long siege on his settlement, Hoover became the recognized leader, showing courage under fire and superb organizational skills. When they were finally rescued by American marines sent in by William McKinley, he decided to leave China for good.

Over the next decade, Hoover circled the globe five times, first as a partner in his firm, then as a freelance international mining consultant. He bought personal stakes along the way in a series of profitable mines, and by the end of this period he had become a multimillionaire. "[If a man] has not made a million dollars by the time he is forty he is not worth much," he later boasted. A major text written by Hoover at this time on the principles

It was hard for the energetic, high-strung Hoover to stay still for formal portraits.

In Stanford University's very first class, Bert Hoover sits at the left in the surveying squad of the Geology Department. After graduation, Hoover got a job in the Nevada City gold mines. "Among [my] instruction[s] was how to keep warm in a wet level when the smoke of blasting cleared. It was done by curling up in a steel wheelbarrow heated with several candles underneath."

Working for a British firm that sent him to Australia, the young bachelor's job was to evaluate mines. Shown here standing, the fledgling engineer did not buckle under adverse conditions, which included choking dust and temperatures well over 100 degrees.

From Australia in 1898, Bert proposed by telegram to Stanford geology major Lou Henry. When the athletic, bright outdoors-lover said yes, he returned to California for the wedding. Here he sits beside Lou, whose Iowa father is partially obscured by her hat.

At the time this picture was taken, the baby-faced mining mogul was already a multimillionaire. Living in London Hoover didn't always look this neat; usually his shoes were scuffed, his collar askew, and his studs missing.

As head of the Food Administration during World War I, Hoover practically commuted to Europe. Here the Great Engineer and his second son Allan share the deck of a liner crossing the Atlantic.

of mining established him as a serious scholar and a force to reckon with.

In 1914 Hoover turned his enormous energy and talents to public service. World War I had just begun, and Belgian citizens, caught by the German invasion, were on the verge of starvation. Taking charge of a giant relief effort spearheaded by the officially neutral United States, Hoover set out to feed and clothe the Belgians and to prevent their slaughter as well. Never before in the history of war had a humanitarian project this large and bold been tried. "We are turning barren neutrality into something positive," Hoover wrote.

Hoover's American Commission for Relief in Belgium acted as a country unto itself, establishing neutrality, making its own rules, crossing borders at will, and raising money and gathering food in any way it could. Hoover's 1914 German passport stated, "This man is not to be stopped anywhere under any circumstances." Extending his work throughout the war years and beyond, Hoover became known around the world as the "food czar." Saving millions of European and Russian men, women, and children from starvation, he was an American offering friendship and service to the world. "Our free feeding of . . . millions of undernourished children . . . was American," he proclaimed. "European governments had nothing to do with it."

His years abroad gave Hoover a new perspective upon America and a strong belief in American volunteerism and generosity. Returning to the country he encapsulated his views in a book entitled *American Individualism*.

In contrast to the glitzy stars of the roaring twenties, Hoover projected an image of public-spiritedness and morality and, above all, competence. In 1921 he was named President Harding's secretary of commerce, a post to which he was reappointed by Calvin Coolidge. He was soon being described as "Under-Secretary of everything else," as he staked out claims to many aspects of other departments. Working on problems of aviation and farming and child hygiene and the regulation of the airwaves, he seemed to be almost everywhere at once. When massive flooding occurred along the Mississippi River, it was Hoover who personally oversaw the relief effort. Letters addressed simply to "The Miracle Man, Washington, D.C.," invariably got delivered. And when Coolidge chose not to run again in 1928, it was almost inevitable who would be the next president. "I am convinced that this country needs a few officials," Hoover wrote, "who will not be seeking public honors for having done their simple duty!"

As president, Hoover set out to implement his ideals and his growing belief in a public–private partnership. In a far more subtle and balanced approach than that of Calvin Coolidge, he called for volunteerism backed up by governmental programs and support. "[I believe] we are passing from a period of extreme individualistic action into a period of associationalism activities," he wrote. In the progressive tradition of Theodore Roosevelt, he worked on behalf of child welfare, conservation, civil liberties, and public education. And he was a strong advocate of the rights of Native Americans. Tireless, unselfish, and committed to the public good, he seemed capable of solving almost any problem. "I have no dread of the ordinary work of the presidency," he once remarked. "What I do fear is the exaggerated idea that people have conceived of me. They have a conviction that I am a sort of superman, that no problem is beyond my capacity. . . . If some unprecedented calamity should come upon the nation . . . I would be sacrificed to the unreasoning disappointment of a people who expected too much."

Just seven months into his presidency, the stock market crashed. For the first time in his life, Hoover was faced with a force over which he had no control. As the Great Depression shouldered its way in, the country sank into a spiral of despair. On top of immense unemployment and spreading hunger, a great drought turned a large part of the country to dust. But as American suffering grew ever deeper, the world's greatest humanitarian and most brilliant social organizer seemed stymied about launching a federal response. "I am opposed to any direct or indirect government dole," he declared. "Where people divest themselves of local government responsibilities, they at once lay the foundation for the destruction of their liberties."

Hoover's belief that the Depression could be battled by a public-private cooperation was simply inadequate to the unprecedented emergency. Local governments could not cope with the immensity of the crisis, and private volunteerism, contrary to his expectations, failed to materialize. On top of this, the President himself was changing. The decisive leader of European relief during World War I was becoming more passive and distant. At one point he blurted out that what the country needed most was a good joke or "a big laugh" to make people "forget about the Depression." In the spring of 1930, he showed a failure to grasp the crisis when he declared, "I am convinced we have passed the worst; . . . we shall rapidly recover." And when the millionaire President made the public statement that "nobody" in the country "is actually starving," the American people turned against him. In time, his very name began to spell hate and hunger to millions. Poverty-stricken shantytowns became known as "Hoovervilles"; newspapers that homeless men slept under were called "Hoover blankets"; and broken-down automobiles pulled by mules—an increasingly common sight—were dubbed "Hoover wagons." Seeing the President as uncompassionate and out of touch with reality, the country began to look to Franklin Roosevelt as a new kind of political leader.

"I had little hope of reelection in 1932 but it was incumbent on me to fight it out to the end," Hoover wrote. "One of Roosevelt's most effective campaign issues was . . . to allege that I had made the depression and then done nothing about it."

As secretary of commerce for Presidents Harding and Coolidge, Hoover transformed the department from a network of small technical bureaus into a massive guidance system for the U.S. economy. Radio and its regulation was one of the many areas that fell under Hoover's jurisdiction. Here he tests the airways.

This stereo card was taken in 1924 and mass-produced during Hoover's Commerce days. *The New Republic* wondered "whether in the whole history of the American government a Cabinet officer has engaged in such a wide diversity of activities or covered so much ground."

Above, gazing fixedly at a poster of himself, Hoover addresses the delegates at the Republican National Convention in Kansas City in 1928. He won 837 out of 1,089 votes on the first ballot. His most memorable statement at the convention was "Shall prosperity in this nation be more thoroughly distributed?"

Below, President Hoover addresses a joint session of Congress. A poor speaker who mumbled his dry words in a monotone and delivered them through an assortment of sour expressions, Hoover resolutely refused to be something he was not.

In the final year of his presidency, Hoover initiated a series of important federal measures to provide food for hungry Americans and to shore up the banking system. But to his critics it was too little, too late. Just fourteen weeks before the national election, thousands of unemployed veterans, with their wives and children, descended upon Washington seeking an early payment of a war bonus. When the Senate failed to pass such a bill, the so-called "Bonus Army" initiated a siege.

Led by the California figure of Roy Robertson, who wore a high leather brace to protect his once broken neck, the protestors staged a "death march" around the Capitol building. Congressmen, trapped inside and fearing for their lives, had to escape through subterranean tunnels. When a riot erupted, and the protestors turned toward the White House, President Hoover authorized the U.S. Army to intervene.

To young Colonel Dwight Eisenhower's horror, General MacArthur ignored the President's request that he use peaceable means, and instead sent in cavalrymen with drawn swords, and infantry with bayonets and tear gas. With their temporary huts set on fire, the protesters were run out of the city. When Franklin Roosevelt heard of the rout he said, "This will elect me."

A bitter Hoover never got over his crushing defeat that year. "Democracy is not a polite employer," he commented. "The only way out of elective office is to get sick or die or get kicked out."

And so Herbert Hoover, as he had done at regular intervals all his life, went fishing. Fly fishing was his cherished pastime and a favorite metaphor for American democracy. "All men are equal before fishes," he liked to say. "I am for fish. . . . But it is too long between bites."

In more ordinary times, his philosophy of American volunteerism might have helped make him a great president. And to the end of his long life, which lasted into the 1960s, his faith in America never dimmed. "Within the soul of America is freedom of mind and spirit," he said. "Here alone is human dignity, not a dream, but an accomplishment. Perhaps it's not perfect, but it's more full of its realization here than in any other place in the world."

Hoover's cherished pastime was trout fishing. "The Declaration of Independence," he once wrote, "is firm that all men (and boys) are endowed with certain inalienable rights . . . which obviously includes the pursuit of fish." Fly fishing restored and nourished his soul, he said, and whenever he was near a rushing stream, out came his creel and tackle and waders.

In June 1929, four and a half months before the stock market crash, the country still felt good about itself. Here a host of citizens admire their flag-draped Capitol. Few paid attention to Hoover's warning about market speculation or the facts that car sales were dropping and the building industry was growing increasingly sluggish.

President Hoover gives a speech to a "talkie," takes a horseback ride, plays with his dog (far right), and waves from a White House balcony along with his wife, Lou (below). Below left, in a picture taken early in his presidency, Hoover poses with Lou and their two sons, Herbert Jr. and Allan (at the right), while young Herbert's wife Margaret stands in the middle.

First press conference: Absolute freedom of the press to discuss public questions is a foundation stone of American liberty.

On the dangers of 1929: The only trouble with capitalism is capitalists. They're too damned greedy.

During the spring of 1930: I am convinced we have passed the worst and with continued effort we shall rapidly recover.

After an untrue newspaper story: I have not in my experience in Washington seen anything so rotten in an attitude of the press towards the President of the United States.

On Federal relief in the Depression: Where people divest themselves of local government responsibilities they at once lay the foundation for the destruction of their liberties.

Lecturing at Valley Forge during the Depression: [Valley Forge] is our American synonym for the trial of human character through privation and suffering, and it is the symbol of the triumph of the American soul. . . . If those few thousand men endured that long winter . . . what right have we to be of little faith?

On selling short: Men are not justified in deliberately making a profit from the losses of other people. . . . These operations destroy public confidence, and induce a slowing down of business.

On income taxes: My view is that we should raise the upper brackets . . . to 45 percent, as compared to the present 23 percent.

RONALD REAGAN

1981–1989

The handsome, youthful, good-natured Ronald Reagan already radiated the message that would later make him president—that everything was going to be all right. At twenty-five he was a Midwestern radio sportscaster (above). On a trip to California he got himself a screen test and was signed by Warner Bros. at $200 a week. He made twenty films over the next three years. In *Knute Rockne, All American* Reagan played the part of Coach Rockne's great halfback, George Gipp (below).

An American Dreamer

Ronald Wilson Reagan was born in 1911 in Tampico, Illinois, the second son of Jack and Nelle Reagan. He had a difficult childhood. His father was an itinerant shoe salesman and an alcoholic. And in school his undiagnosed nearsightedness held him back until a writing teacher named B. J. Frazier brought out Reagan's native talent. "I was always called on to read [my papers]," Reagan remembered. "Maybe that's where the 'ham' began." Public speaking became Reagan's passion, combined with his own brand of humor and optimism, which helped him overcome his troubles. The caption beneath his high school yearbook picture read, "Life is just one grand sweet song, so start the music."

In 1937, after an initial career as a radio sportscaster, he took a screen test at Warner Bros.' Studio, which led to a seven-year contract. In Hollywood he was cast as the All-American boy, a role he played so many times that he became identified with it. Eventually he appeared in more than fifty feature films, and by 1941 Warner Bros. reported that only Errol Flynn received more fan mail than Ronald Reagan.

During World War II, Reagan served in the army's motion picture unit, narrating training films. But after the war, his film career fizzled and he was increasingly relegated to the nightclub circuit, which he hated. When his wife, the actress Jane Wyman, divorced him in 1948, he entered the lowest period of his life. But Reagan was not Reagan unless he was upbeat. Four years later he married another actress, Nancy Davis, who became his greatest ally and friend. Then, "like the cavalry to the rescue," he said, came a new opportunity—he was offered the job as host of the weekly television program *General Electric Theater*. Under Reagan it climbed to be the number-one show in its time slot, making him one of the most recognizable men in America. And when he became a part owner of the series, it also made him rich. Selected to serve as the company's national spokesperson, Reagan began traveling to GE factories around the country, where he spoke to employees and at corporate banquets, gaining a valuable political apprenticeship. His speeches were part patriotism, part pro-business pep rally. And though he was a Democrat, his message was becoming increasingly conservative. "I began to talk more and more," he remembered, "of how government had expanded and was infringing on liberties and interfering with private enterprise. . . . It finally grew to the point that one day I came home

At his first inauguration, in January 1981, Ronald Reagan strikes his winner's pose. That day he told the country "to believe that together with God's help we can and will resolve the problems which now confront us. And, after all, why shouldn't we believe that? We are Americans."

In 1955 Ronald and Nancy Davis had been married three years (above). Not a typical Hollywood type, Reagan was a loner who didn't drink or swear or chase women. The kind of part he usually played in the movies was what he was—a wholesome, nice guy. His first wife, movie actress Jane Wyman, had decided she found him boring. Despondent and bitter, Reagan trusted no one until he met Nancy, also an actress, who insisted on giving up her career for her husband.

Elected governor of California in 1966, with Nancy by his side Ronald thanks his supporters at his inaugural ball in Sacramento.

from a speaking tour and said to Nancy, 'I go out there and make these speeches which I believe—they are my own speeches —and then every four years I find myself campaigning for the people who are doing the things that I am speaking against.' And I said, 'I am on the wrong side.'"

In 1962 Reagan switched political parties and began a rapid ascent in Republican party circles. His televised speech for Barry Goldwater two years later drew more contributions than any political speech in American history. And it established Ronald Reagan as a political force in his own right, with strong support in the business community in southern California. "When I was beset in 1965 by a group that insisted that I had to seek the governorship against the incumbent governor," he later said, "I fought like a tiger not to. Finally, I couldn't sleep nights, and Nancy and I said yes."

Reagan served as governor of California for eight years, making his mark as an aggressive and popular conservative and slowly building a strong financial and political base from which to make his own run on the high office. In his quest for the presidency in 1980, Reagan cast himself as a revolutionary outsider—a crusader out to restore the American way of life.

The country in 1980 was in a profound state of gloom. For more than a year Jimmy Carter had struggled unsuccessfully to free a group of fifty-two American hostages held in Iran. And with the economy in trouble and inflation in double digits, Carter's repeated calls for sacrifice and for lower expectations had left many Americans pessimistic about the future. Ronald Reagan saw his job as teaching Americans how to dream again.

To Reagan, much as it had been to Calvin Coolidge, big government was the enemy of the American way. Reagan's vision was one of individual enterprise and a return to what he called the self-confident spirit of the founding fathers. When he won the election by an electoral landslide, he called it "the Reagan revolution of 1980."

Reagan brought to the presidency his well-known sense of humor and the charm that people called "the Reagan magic." Following an era when Americans had felt threatened and small, Ronald Reagan made them feel big again. Following the release of the American hostages at the very start of his presidency, Reagan turned to his campaign promise to revolutionize American government. He established a strong bond with Congress and obtained impressive legislative victories, including cuts in domestic spending and, at the same time, large-scale tax cuts. And in a striking departure from Jeffersonian policy, he called for an increase in military spending, eventually achieving the largest peacetime buildup in the history of the nation.

Less than three months into his term, in a scene so dramatic it seemed as if out of one of his own movies, Reagan was fired upon and critically wounded by a crazed gunman. The President's bravery and good humor in the wake of the shooting impressed the nation, and his popularity soared. A sympathetic Congress, acting with bipartisanship, swiftly passed the remainder of his economic policies. But his lengthy recuperation isolated him from the hard work of the presidency. At the White House, staff members began to notice a lack of concentration. Reagan's workday was limited to nine-to-five, and included an extended midday personal break. National Security Council briefing sessions were kept as short as possible and the President began regularly neglecting his official reading. Reagan saved his energy for what he called "the big picture" and for important public performances, which he pulled off to perfection. Again and again in televised speeches he promoted his vision of the American way—free markets, free-

Two years after winning the governorship of California, Reagan ran for president for the first time. Despite a spirited Reagan demonstration (above), the Republican National Convention nominated Richard Nixon on the first ballot. Even so, Reagan had his foot in the door, making the country realize that a Hollywood actor could be in the running.

"We must balance the budget, reduce tax rates and restore our defenses," Reagan announced, summing up his platform during the presidential race in 1980 (below). But it wasn't just his message that made so many people respond to him. It was his skill at projecting wholesomeness, patriotism, and morality into any performance he was called upon to make.

The President had just made a lunch-hour speech at the Washington Hilton. As he moved outside with his small entourage, a fusillade from a gunman twelve feet away sprayed the scene. One of the bullets hit the President. Nancy arrived at the hospital only moments after her husband and prayed through the operation that removed the bullet from his lung. Four days later Reagan was up and smiling (above).

Returning to Dixon, Illinois, to celebrate his seventy-third birthday in 1984, Reagan waves to admirers from his motorcade. It was here at Dixon High School, in school plays, that he first learned about acting.

dom from government, personal freedoms in general. The antithesis of all this, in Reagan's mind, was Communism, and in particular this meant the Soviet Union. "Let us be aware," he said in a 1983 speech, "that they are the focus of evil in the modern world."

When he pushed for an elaborate, antimissile space shield to protect America from Soviet missiles it became known as Star Wars. "The Strategic Defense Initiative has been labeled Star Wars," he said, "but it isn't about war, it's about peace. It isn't about retaliation, it's about prevention. It isn't about fear, it's about hope. And in that struggle, if you'll pardon my stealing a film line, the force is with us."

Reagan won reelection in 1984 by a landslide. But his second term was plagued with problems. At seventy-three, he was now the oldest president in American history. His hearing was poor, he was battling cancer, and his memory was not what it had been. Then, just three months after his second inaugural, Islamic terrorists hijacked TWA Flight 847 and took thirty-nine Americans hostage. It was Jimmy Carter's nightmare all over again. Working successfully to obtain their speedy release, Reagan ended up approving a secret deal: the sale of U.S. missiles to Iran in exchange for seven previously captured hostages. It was a direct contradiction of his publicly stated policy not to bargain with terrorists, and when news of it leaked out, Reagan flatly denied it. "The charge has been made that the United States has shipped weapons to Iran as ransom payment for the release of American hostages in Lebanon; that the United States undercut its allies and secretly violated American policy.... Those charges are utterly false.... We did not, repeat, did not trade weapons or anything else for hostages, nor will we."

But as his own diary proved, Reagan had authorized the sale. To make matters worse, some of the money raised by selling arms was then illegally funneled to the anticommunist Contras in Nicaragua—a cause Reagan believed in but had been unable to get Congressional support for. When the situation, now called "Iran-Contra," led to a Congressional investigation, for the first time in his political life the American public did not believe Reagan's word. It was Nancy who finally persuaded her husband to go back on television and admit the truth.

"A few months ago I told the American people I did not trade arms for hostages," he said on March 4, 1987. "My heart and my best intentions still

In 1982 the President speaks to senior citizens, many younger than he. With seven years left to his presidency, Reagan was already the oldest man ever to serve in the White House, having just edged out Dwight Eisenhower, James Buchanan, and Andrew Jackson. By the time he left office, just shy of seventy-eight, he was thirteen years older than George Washington had been at the end of his second term. But despite his age and an unnerving faulty memory, Reagan gave off a feeling of youthfulness, and said repeatedly he wanted to make America "feel young again."

tell me that's true, but the facts and the evidence tell me it is not. What began as a strategical outreach to Iran deteriorated in its implementation into trading arms for hostages. This runs counter to my own beliefs, to administration policy, and to the original strategy we had in mind. There are reasons why it happened, but no excuses. It was a mistake."

Ronald Reagan was able to put the scandal behind him. And although by the time he left office the national debt had tripled and the gap between rich and poor had greatly widened, a soaring stock market and economic good times for many helped him regain much of his lost popularity. Critics charged he had betrayed Jimmy Carter's finest legacy—a foreign policy committed to human rights. But others pointed out that the threat of his "Star Wars" program actually helped force a diplomatic breakthrough in U.S.–Soviet relations. President Reagan and Soviet Premier Mikhail Gorbachev held a total of five summits, which culminated in the signing of a historic agreement, the first actual reduction in each side's nuclear arsenals. It marked the beginning of the end of the Cold War, and it stands as Reagan's most enduring achievement.

On January 11, 1989, just shy of his seventy-eighth birthday, President Reagan gave his farewell address to the nation. In a way, it was a variation of what he called "The Speech," the same message he had been giving since his days working for GE. He spoke once again of America as "a shining city," and described himself a "citizen politician" who had tried to put government back into the hands of the people. "It's been the honor of my life to be your president," he said. "They called it the Reagan Revolution. Well, I'll accept that, but for me it always seemed more like the great rediscovery, a rediscovery of our values and our common sense. The way I see it, there were two great triumphs, two things that I'm proudest of. One is the economic recovery . . . the other is the recovery of our morale. America is respected again in the world and looked to for leadership."

After some pointers from professional golfer Raymond Floyd, President Reagan sinks a long one on a White House carpet. His favorite White House activity was watching movies— "golden oldies" were what he usually requested.

At the 1984 Republican National Convention, President Reagan wields the gavel in gleeful anticipation of a landslide victory in November.

At his desk before giving a televised speech on the successful U.S. invasion of Grenada, Reagan keeps his composure as he is surrounded by photographers.

Insiders in the Reagan White House knew of the President's ability to comfort. Here he consoles a mother of one of the 241 Marines killed in the 1983 bomb blast in Beirut.

President Reagan holds his own with Mikhail Gorbachev in a Washington meeting in 1987. The treaty they signed eventually did away with almost 2,700 U.S. and Soviet middle-distance nuclear missiles.

Reagan's closest foreign ally and friend was Britain's Prime Minister Margaret Thatcher. Here they wish each other goodbye after a 1985 meeting in West Germany.

America is too great for small dreams. There was a hunger in the land for a spiritual revival; if you will, a crusade for renewal. The American people said: Let us look to the future with confidence, both at home and abroad. Let us give freedom a chance.

The heart of America is strong; it's good and true. The cynics were wrong; America never was a sick society. We're seeing rededication to bedrock values of faith, family, work, neighborhood, peace, and freedom—values that help bring us together as one people.

People everywhere hunger for peace and a better life. The tide of the future is a freedom tide.

How can we not believe in the greatness of America? How can we not do what is right and needed to preserve this last best hope of man on Earth?

I wasn't a great communicator, but I communicated great things, and they didn't spring full bloom from my brow, they came from the heart of a great nation—from our experience, our wisdom, and our belief in the principles that have guided us for two centuries. They called it the Reagan Revolution. Well, I'll accept that, but for me it always seemed more like the great rediscovery, a rediscovery of our values and our common sense.

In this land of dreams . . . no victory is beyond our reach, no glory will ever be too great.

Reagan was a master of quips and short answers. The following are a sprinkling from throughout his presidency:

There are those who question the way we choose a president, who say that our process imposes difficult and exhausting burdens on those who seek the office. I have not found it so.

I have always stated that the nearest thing to eternal life we'll ever see on this earth is a government program.

I never found that Wall Street is a source of good economic advice.

When I was governor and wanted to return a tax surplus to the people, my finance director said, "It's never been done." And I said "Well, you've never had an actor up here before either."

And believe me, [my movie] *Bedtime for Bonzo* made more sense than what they were doing in Washington.

They still won't believe us, but we are going to balance this budget by 1984.

I did not come here to balance the budget—not at the expense of my tax-cutting and defense programs. If we can't do it in 1984, we'll have to do it later.

A recession is when your neighbor loses his job. A depression is when you lose yours. And recovery is when Jimmy Carter loses his.

You'd be surprised how much being a good actor pays off.

It's true hard work never killed anybody, but I figure why take the chance?

In 1974, having become a millionaire earlier through a series of land deals, Reagan paid half a million dollars for his 688-acre Rancho del Cielo in California's Santa Ynez Mountains. Here he takes a morning ride.

Over his two terms as president, Reagan spent a total of 345 days at the ranch, clearing brush, cutting wood, and heaving saddles.

The President allowed only his closest friends and colleagues to visit at the ranch. "This place has a spell," he said, "and people feel it when they come here."

Ronald Reagan gets his last bird's-eye look at the Capitol as a Marine helicopter lifts him to Andrews Air Force Base and the flight back to California as a citizen.

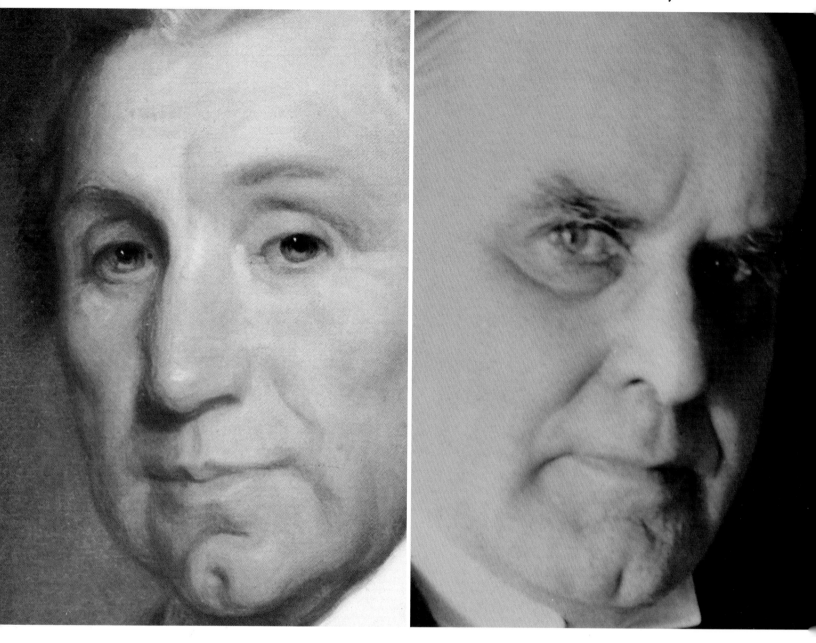

James Monroe

William McKinley

THE WORLD STAGE

CHAPTER EIGHT

Who is in charge of foreign policy, the president or Congress? As the
world sped up, the nation came to favor a single, swift voice.

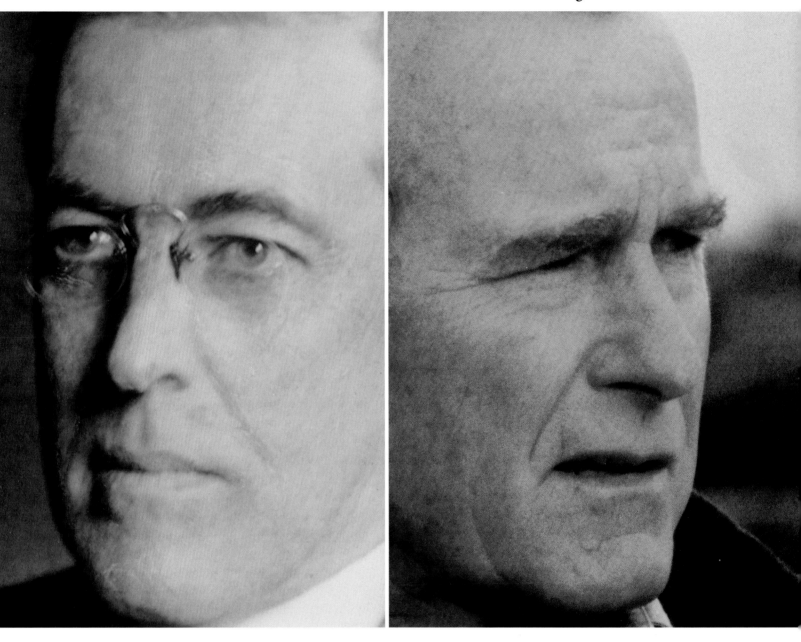

Woodrow Wilson   George Bush

It has been said that there are actually two presidencies, one involving matters inside the country, the other, America's relationship with the rest of the world. And while presidents often find their domestic powers frustratingly limited, it is in the second presidency, involving foreign affairs, that they have had the most freedom to use their powers and make their mark on history.

The Constitution actually granted the president few unilateral powers for conducting foreign affairs, intending a collaborative effort between the president and the Senate. The president was authorized to make treaties and appoint ambassadors, but in each area he was required to seek senatorial advice and consent. And though the president was named commander-in-chief of the armed forces, he was denied the all-important power to declare war. The only autonomous role granted the president was that of receiving foreign ambassadors—a role envisioned chiefly as a ceremonial function.

But early presidents were not willing to serve as mere executive clerks

Among other presidents who loomed large on the world stage was Franklin Roosevelt. His close alliance with Winston Churchill helped FDR guide America into the leadership of the free world.

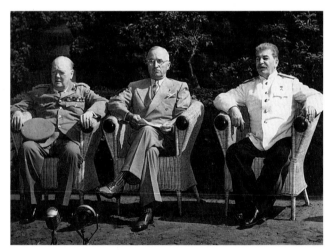

Harry Truman's turn on the world stage began during secret WWII meetings with Churchill and Stalin. The Truman Doctrine followed, the Marshall Plan, the Berlin Airlift, the Korean War. Truman preferred domestic affairs but he was forced into becoming an internationalist.

to Congress or simply as ceremonial heads of state. Acting alone, and prior to any congressional approval, George Washington proclaimed his own controversial policy of neutrality in the war between Great Britain and France. A reluctant Congress supported him a year later with the Neutrality Act of 1794. Five years later the Supreme Court ruled on the issue of who could represent the interests of the United States abroad when Chief Justice John Marshall wrote that the president was the "sole organ of the nation in its external relations and its sole representative with foreign nations."

Even though he had long opposed an overly powerful executive, in 1803 Thomas Jefferson pushed through a presidential act that went beyond any power outlined in the Constitution: the purchase of French-owned Louisiana. Stretching from the Mississippi River to the Rocky Mountains, Louisiana doubled the size of the United States. Congressmen then began to recognize the president's unique advantages—how, unlike their branch of government, he was always in session, and how, as a sole agent, he could act far more swiftly and decisively than they could during foreign crises. By 1816 even the Senate's Foreign Relations Committee had to admit the president's supremacy in foreign affairs.

If the first four presidents of the United States had to struggle for the very survival of the young Republic, buffeted as it was between the superpowers of France and Britain, after the War of 1812 the United States entered a new era. And the president who presided over it and all its opportunities was Thomas Jefferson's former minister to France, James Monroe. An idealist like Jefferson, Monroe labored to expand the national boundaries. And believing that America should be a beacon of liberty to others, he stood up forcefully on behalf of the new Latin American republics. His famous pronouncement of 1823, the Monroe Doctrine, became for the young Republic a stunning debut on the world stage; it would guide American policy for the remainder of the century.

But as the United States pursued its continental expansion, it increasingly turned its back on the rest of the world. By 1885, even though the United States had surpassed Great Britain in manufacturing, it was still not considered a great world power. And lacking interest in foreign affairs, the nation's presidency had lost its luster. Writing in 1884, a young graduate student named Woodrow Wilson claimed that the presidency was no longer of any real importance, and that the nation was now run by a "Congressional government." But what Wilson hadn't counted on in his initial study of American politics was the extraordinary reemergence of United States' involvement in foreign affairs, and with it the resurgence of the presidency itself.

In the 1890s, while an aging Spanish empire was losing its hold on its colonies, four great powers dominated the world scene—Great Britain, France, Russia, and Germany. With Britain and France fast moving into Africa, and Russia and Germany competing for influence in the Far East, many in the United States began to hunger for superpower status for their own nation, amidst a rising new spirit of "manifest destiny." At the same time, powerful American industrial and banking groups were in search of overseas markets, and of Pacific coaling stations and naval bases that would help make the U.S. competitive in Asia. And then came the fateful year of 1898, and with it the Spanish-American War. Marking the nation's first intervention in the great power conflicts of the twentieth century, the war became a turning point in U.S. history. In a new book revising his earlier thesis Wilson wrote, "The war with Spain . . . changed . . . the balance [in U.S. history]. . . . Foreign questions became leading questions again as they had been in the first days of the government." Impressed by the bold leadership of William McKinley, Wilson wrote, "The President of the United States is now . . . at the front of affairs, as no President, except Lincoln, has been since the first quarter of the nineteenth century."

As Wilson's own presidency proved thirteen years later, the twentieth century would be an era of vastly expanding American influence abroad. Wilson argued for a new internationalism and for the broadest interpretation of the Monroe Doctrine. But Wilson was a president ahead of his time, and American isolationism reasserted itself after World War I. It was under FDR—once Wilson's assistant secretary of the Navy—that the country sloughed off its isolationism for good and boldly stood up to the new German quest for world dominance. Guiding the country into a new role as the leader of the free world, FDR launched an era of presidential forcefulness. With the exception of Wilson, presidents prior to World War II had rarely reached out directly to other world leaders. FDR changed that with a series of trips overseas to confer personally with Allied leaders. And this new precedent was followed by his successor, Harry Truman. By 1948, presidential prestige in foreign affairs had become so strong that Truman could say, "I make foreign policy." His statement was only a slight exaggeration.

With the spread of the Cold War and the increasing nuclear threat, the president's dominance over foreign affairs grew even stronger, symbolized by his control of the nuclear "button." Through the "Eisenhower Doctrine," Congress granted the president vast new powers to conduct military reprisals, and the Tonkin Gulf Resolution did the same for Lyndon Johnson. Even with the resurgence of Congressional power after Watergate, and the War Powers Resolution of 1973, which limited presidential use of troops overseas to a maximum of sixty days, presidents continued to find ways to get what they wanted.

No modern president had been as knowledgeable in foreign affairs as Richard Nixon, but it was Ronald Reagan who best exemplified the tradition of James Monroe and Woodrow Wilson. Believing that history was on the side of the Western democracies, and that Communism was doomed to ultimate failure, he initially appeared to make the Cold War even colder when he blasted the Soviet Union as an "evil empire." But when he personally met with Mikhail Gorbachev at a superpower summit at Reykjavik, Iceland, he made more progress in U.S.–Soviet relations than any president before him. And not long afterward, the Cold War ended.

In the post–Cold War era, as the influence of other nations has grown, the United Nations has assumed a greater role in world events, and presidents have had to learn to act in concert with it. George Bush, who once served as the U.S. ambassador to the U.N., took its mandates seriously; he also built his own relationships with dozens of top world leaders, taking presidential diplomacy in a new direction. The United States, which had begun as a minor player on the world stage, and then expanded its role until it came to lead the free world, now was taking its place as a power among others, committed to inhabiting what was being called "a new world order."

John F. Kennedy was so entranced with foreign affairs that he devoted his entire inaugural address to the subject. Though he stumbled early on in his foreshortened presidency, his masterful handling of the Cuban Missile Crisis helped bring the world back from the brink of nuclear war. Here he meets Soviet Premier Nikita Khrushchev in Vienna in 1961.

Few presidents have had more knowledge of foreign affairs or more understanding of geopolitical realities than Richard Nixon. And only Theodore Roosevelt had traveled so much abroad. Nixon's trip to China in 1972 marked the high point of his presidency, part of an initiative that helped end two decades of cold war hostility.

A Vision for the Hemisphere

James Monroe's most lasting contribution, the "Monroe Doctrine," was imbedded in his 1823 Annual Message to Congress, the opening page of which is shown above. Conceived with the help of his brilliant secretary of state, John Quincy Adams, the message was a declaration to the "old world" powers of Europe that the "new world" of the Americas was henceforth off-limits to colonization and that it would stand united against outside aggression.

Throughout our history there have been presidents who possessed an almost religious belief in the principles of the United States and who sought ways to extend America's influence on the world stage. That was certainly the case for our fifth president, a passionate visionary and lifelong diplomat named James Monroe. One of the first to believe that the world was bound to move in a democratic direction, he saw the country much more in relation to the world and its development than had many of the leading citizens of the older generation, who had simply wanted to keep the ex-colonies safe by keeping them as isolated as possible.

Monroe's revolutionary politics were shaped during war, when he served as an officer under George Washington. But it was Thomas Jefferson who became his lifelong mentor, tutoring him at Monticello in the law and in democracy. With Jefferson's help Monroe ran successfully for the Virginia Assembly. He then bought land directly adjacent to Monticello, 2,500 acres that he named Ash Lawn. "Mr. Jefferson proposed to have a house built for me on my plantation near him," Monroe wrote to their mutual friend James Madison. "I have agreed."

In 1790 Monroe was elected to the U.S. Senate. And four years later George Washington ordered him to cross the Atlantic and serve as his minister to France. "The proposition surprised me," Monroe wrote privately to Jefferson, "for I really thought I was among the last men to whom it would be made. . . . [But] the President was resolved to send a republican character to that nation." It was the beginning of Monroe's training in foreign affairs, which would become the dominant theme of his career. From the beginning he found it demanding but exhilarating.

"My . . . mission . . . to the French Republic was [when] ... the French Revolution was at its height," he wrote. "I found our affairs ... in the worst possible situation. . . . It was suspected we were about to abandon them for a connection with England."

Monroe was full of enthusiasm for the French Revolution, seeing it as a successor to the American Revolution, which he believed would someday overtake the monarchies of the whole continent. But in Paris, he allowed his unrestrained enthusiasm for the French to undermine his country's official policy of neutrality. And in 1796, President Washington abruptly issued a recall. Monroe was mortified. "I was charged with a failure to perform my duty," he wrote, "and recalled from it and censured." But if Washington had supposed that Monroe would submit in silence, he was mistaken. In a private letter Monroe called Washington "insane." Then he wrote a fiery 407-

To Rembrandt Peale, Monroe looked like this at the end of his second term as president. Even with his $25,000 salary, when Monroe left the White House he was heavily in debt from the high cost of his political life and was forced to sell off his land and slaves in order to regain solvency.

In 1803, under instructions from President Jefferson to try to buy New Orleans and West Florida from the French, special envoy James Monroe (center) and Ambassador Robert Livingston (right) are pleased when France decides the United States can have all the land between the Mississippi and the Rocky Mountains if she'll pay for it. Marquis François de Barbe-Marbois shows on a map some of the 828,000 square miles his country will turn over for a mere $15 million.

At right, Monroe strikes a global pose, appearing to signify the coming expansion of the American nation. To the President's far right is Secretary of State John Quincy Adams, the chief architect of what would become known as the Monroe Doctrine.

John Vanderlyn painted this portrait of Monroe in 1821, showing his hand resting on a map of Florida, territory that the United States was wresting from Spain. To Monroe's left is one of the thirty-eight chairs made in France for the oval drawing room in the newly rebuilt White House.

page defense of himself, charging Washington with incompetence in foreign affairs. Many believed that by publishing this angry outburst, Monroe had signed his political "death warrant." But his tough stance impressed his fellow Republicans, and in 1799, he was elected governor of Virginia. Just three years later, his mentor Thomas Jefferson, who was now president, appointed him to negotiate the purchase of New Orleans from France.

Monroe outdid himself, helping to orchestrate the Louisiana Purchase, which doubled the size of the United States. His vision of a vastly expanded America was taking hold, and his diplomatic triumph helped position him for higher office. In 1811 he became secretary of state under James Madison. And during the late days of the War of 1812, as the only man in government who had fought in the Revolution, he was also named the country's secretary of war. "When I took charge of it," he later wrote, "the enemy were menacing, with an immense force from Europe. . . . This city was still smoking, its public buildings in ruin. . . . [F]or the first month at least, I never went to bed. . . . I had a couch . . . from which, even in the night, I was called every two hours." Helping lead his country to a successful resolution of the war, Monroe was then catapulted into the presidency.

Elected in 1816, he became the fourth chief executive from Virginia, and the last to spring from the Revolution. Monroe took the oath of office in front of the burned-out Capitol destroyed by the British in the recent war. "It is particularly gratifying to me," he said in his inaugural address, "to enter on . . . these duties at a time when the United States are blessed with peace."

Monroe eventually moved his family into the Executive Mansion, which had also been burned by the British and was still under reconstruction. With a coat of white paint to help cover the fire's scorch marks, it was now widely referred to as "The White House."

Even in his day, Monroe looked old-fashioned. He wore his hair long and tied back with a black ribbon, and he dressed in Revolutionary War–era knee britches. But in his presidential actions he was anything but old-fashioned, becoming an aggressive expansionist at every opportunity. He pushed the nation's frontier 1,500 miles westward to the Yellowstone River. And he allowed American troops to invade Spanish-owned Florida.

"This is not a time to think of repose," he wrote his general, Andrew Jackson. "Great interests are at stake." Interpreting this as presidential approval, which Monroe later denied, Jackson ripped through Florida, capturing Spanish forts and conquering Spanish towns. Though his actions were nothing short of a military invasion, it led to the signing of the Transcontinental Treaty, transferring Florida to the United States and consolidating the young nation's hold on the continent. "In great emergencies a nation must

support its character," Monroe wrote. "An overcautious policy often risks more than a bold one."

By 1823 there was need of a formal statement of policy, a definition of America's relationship to the world. In a carefully worded message composed by his brilliant secretary of state, John Quincy Adams, Monroe announced a bold new national policy: America would no longer tolerate any European effort to move into the Western Hemisphere.

"The American continents . . . are henceforth not to be considered as subjects for future colonization by any European powers."

His policy would come to be known as the Monroe Doctrine, the guiding principle of the country in its relationship to the world stage. It not only asserted America's authority in the hemisphere, but it proclaimed the United States as the chief protector of republican principles throughout the Americas. Thomas Jefferson heralded it as "the most momentous [pronouncement] which has been . . . offered . . . since that of Independence. That made us a nation. This sets our compass and points the course."

"We owe it . . . to . . . those powers," Monroe explained, "to declare that we should consider any attempt on their part to extend their system to this hemisphere, as dangerous to our peace and safety."

In spite of Monroe's successes in foreign policy, his second term was not a happy one. He was accused of corruption, of accepting a large loan in return for political favors. His secretary of the treasury, William Cranford, actually raised his cane at the President and called him a scoundrel. Seizing the tongs from a nearby fireplace, Monroe ordered him out of the White House. It was a sign of the end of the "era of good feelings."

"I have . . . treat[ed] every attack . . . with contempt," Monroe wrote. "I shall . . . be happy when I can retire beyond their reach in peace to my farm."

In 1825 Monroe retired to an estate outside Washington he called Oak Hill. Increasingly obsessed with his own privacy, he destroyed all his personal papers. Six years later he died. The last of the original Virginia presidents, he possessed none of Thomas Jefferson's eloquence, or James Madison's genius, or George Washington's stature. But James Monroe had presided over a vast expansion of the American empire. He had spoken out as if the United States were a world power, and as he did so, it began to become one.

Even into the 1820s James Monroe wore his revolutionary-era knee britches and buckled shoes, reminders of the days when he had fought in the Revolutionary War under George Washington. Less intellectual than any of his four extraordinary predecessors, Monroe was an excellent administrator, with a profound interest in America's role on the world stage.

In 1829 the seventy-one-year-old Monroe had been ill. Instead of showing him as an infirm old man, artist Thomas Sully idealized him as strong and dynamic.

On fighting alongside George Washington at the Battle of Trenton; written by Monroe in the third person: The night was tempestuous, as was the succeeding day, and made more severe by a heavy fall of snow. . . . At the dawn of the day our army approached, with the Commander-in-chief at its head. . . . A general alarm then took place among the troops in town. The drums were beat to arms, and two cannons were placed in the main street to bear on the head of our column as it entered. . . . [After the captain was wounded] the command then devolved on Lieutenant Monroe, who advanced in like manner at the head of the corps, and was shot down by a musket ball which passed through his breast and shoulder. He . . . was carried from the field. . . . In the great events of which I have spoken Mr. Monroe, being a mere youth, counted for nothing in comparison with those distinguished citizens who had the direction of public affairs. . . . It was a school of instruction in the knowledge of mankind, in the science of government, and what is of still great importance, for inculcating on the youthful mind those sound moral and political principles on which the success of our system depends.

From Paris, a letter to his friend James Madison: There are many things here which I think would suit you. I beg you to give me a list of what you want, such as clocks, carpets, glass, furniture, table linen, &ca.— they are cheaper infinitely than with you considering I have advantages of the exch'ge.

On being recalled from France by George Washington [to Secretary of State Timothy Pickering]: If you supposed that I would submit in silence to the injurious imputations that were raised against me by the administration, you were mistaken. I put too high a value upon the blessing of an honest fame . . . to suffer myself to be robbed of it.

On George Washington's policies: Most of the monarchs of the earth practice ingratitude with other powers but Mr. Washington has the merit of transcending, not the great men of the ancient republics, but the little monarchs of the present day, in preaching it as a public virtue. Such a collection of vain, superficial blunderers were never before placed at the head of any respectable state. . . . Our national honor is in the dust; we have been kicked, cuffed and plundered all over the ocean; our reputation for faith scouted; our government and people branded as cowards, incapable of being provoked to resist, and ready to receive again those chains we had taught others to burst. Long will it be before we shall be able to forget what we are, nor will centuries suffice to raise us to the high ground from which we have fallen.

On the War of 1812: Had we yielded to G. Britain, without a struggle, our govt. would have received a wound from which it would most probably never have recovered. As it is, our national reputation has risen considerably abroad, and if we succeed, as I trust we shall, the best effects will result from it.

On the sanctity of the Western Hemisphere: In the wars of the European powers in matters relating to themselves we have never taken any part. . . . With the movements in this hemisphere we are of necessity more immediately connected, and by causes which must be obvious to all enlightened and impartial observers.

On the death of his wife in 1830: After having lived, with the partner of your cares, in so many raptures of life, so long together, and afforded to each other, comforts which no other person on earth could do, as both of us have done, to have her snatched from us, is an affliction which none but those who feel it can justly estimate. . . . We have spent long and happy years together and I await the summons to follow her.

Painted two years before Monroe's death, Chester Harding's portrait is considered to be the closest likeness of the retired President.

WILLIAM McKINLEY

1897–1901

Reluctant Apostle

One of the most self-confident men ever to rise to the presidency, William McKinley once told a reporter, "I cannot subscribe to the idea that luck had very much to do with making me President of the United States. I have never been in doubt since I was old enough to think intelligently that I would sometime be made President." It was a self-confidence that would prove immensely valuable in what would turn out to be a watershed presidency.

McKinley was born in 1843 in Niles, Ohio, in an unpainted clapboard house on Main Street, the seventh of nine children. His father, a staunch abolitionist, worked in the blast furnace business. The chief influence in his life was his mother, a devout Methodist, but it was against her wishes that he signed up for duty in the Civil War. During the Battle of Antietam in 1862, while serving as a commissary sergeant, McKinley risked his life driving a mule-drawn wagon through the line of fire to bring hot food and coffee to the front lines. He called it his greatest day and was later cited for bravery in the field.

After the war McKinley returned to private life and began practicing law in Canton, Ohio. In 1871 he married Ida Saxton, the daughter of Canton's most prominent family. Five years later he was elected to Congress.

In Washington he served a total of six terms, and is best remembered for the McKinley Tariff, which helped protect American industry, then growing rapidly, from foreign competition. Patient and courteous, he became a beloved figure in Washington; it was said that he was the only man in Congress who had no enemies. But even his closest colleagues recognized that he kept his private life completely closed off. Having lost two daughters, his only children, he devoted every moment he could to his invalid wife, who suffered from severe depression and frequent seizures. Once at the table, at a rare public function together, when a bad seizure gripped her, he quietly spread his napkin over Ida's face. When the episode was over, he gently removed it and the conversation went on as if nothing had happened.

When McKinley failed in 1890 to obtain a seventh term in Congress, he ran instead for Ohio's governorship, and won. And by the mid-1890s, his name was put forward as a candidate for president. He launched what became known as his "front porch campaign," a tradition of letting the voters come to him first used eight years earlier by fellow Midwesterner Benjamin Harrison. During the summer of 1896, three-quarters of a million people made the pilgrimage to Canton to hear McKinley speak. And in November, buoyed by the support of big business and by an unprecedented advertising campaign, his victory was by a landslide.

McKinley entered the presidency during an economic depression, which had undermined the administration of his predecessor, Grover Cleveland. Because he was concerned primarily with effecting a domestic recovery, the last thing McKinley wanted as president was foreign complications. What he got was much worse: an international crisis. It began shortly after he took office, in nearby Cuba. For centuries the island had been part of the Spanish Empire, but now Cubans were fighting for their independence. To crush the rebellion, Spain had sent hundreds of thousands of troops to the island, unleashing a reign of terror upon the population. McKinley was sympathetic to the Cuban cause, but he was intent on avoiding being drawn into a war. So he allowed the American battleship the *Maine* to anchor off Havana and simply observe.

On February 15, 1898, the *Maine* mysteriously exploded, killing more than 250 on board. When news of it reached the United States, war fever broke out across the nation. A sensationalist press fanned the fires, but McKinley refused to overreact. Instead, he appointed a naval court of inquiry to determine the cause of the explosion. "The United States [should] never enter upon a war," he explained, "until every effort for peace has been exhausted."

Critics accused him of cowardice and indecision, and under the stress of the crisis the President grew haggard. Sleepless, he paced the White House by night. "I was one of those who held back to the last moment," he wrote.

Although later evidence would show that a mechanical problem in the ship's boiler was the most likely cause of the explosion, in late March

With gout-ridden outgoing President Grover Cleveland looking on, President McKinley delivers his inaugural address. "We want no wars of conquest," he says. "We must avoid the temptation of territorial aggression."

Even though his cigar and jaunty pose make him look like a tough guy, the youthful McKinley was described by his Latin teacher as owning "a winsome personality."

Taken just prior to his military service, this photograph of McKinley shows why his penetrating, hypnotic eyes were famous. "I was but a school boy when I went into the army," McKinley said. "I only knew that the Union was threatened with overthrow."

The war behind him, instead of joining other veterans who set off for the West to seek their fortunes in gold mining, McKinley practiced law in Canton, Ohio, got married, and ran for Congress.

the naval court ruled that the *Maine* had been destroyed by an external device. And one month later McKinley asked Congress for a declaration of war. "On the 25th of April," the President recorded, "the United States sounded the call to arms. Our country, after an interval of half a century of peace with other nations, found itself engaged in [a] deadly conflict with a foreign enemy." Once committed, McKinley threw himself into the job of commander-in-chief, transforming a corner office in the White House into the first modern war room. The first target of the war was Manila Bay in the Philippines, where Admiral George Dewey rapidly destroyed Spain's Pacific fleet. "The effect of this remarkable victory upon the spirit of our people and upon the fortunes of the war was instant," McKinley wrote. "A prestige of invincibility attached to our arms."

This victory was followed by a massive attack against the Spanish Navy in Cuba, where in less than three hours, on July 3, all the Spanish ships were destroyed. McKinley wrote that he saw "the hand of God" in the ordeal.

McKinley took an active role in negotiating the Treaty of Paris, and forcefully stood up to the Speaker of the House, who opposed it. By so doing, he established the modern presidency as the preeminent force in American national government.

With its victory over Spain, the United States became Cuba's protector, and took possession of Puerto Rico and Guam. In a final protest before relinquishing its Caribbean islands, Spain declared, "This . . . strips us of the . . . last memory of a glorious past, and expels us . . . from the Western Hemisphere." With the addition of its new "colonies," the United States emerged for the first time as a world power. "It is no longer a question of expansion with us," McKinley boasted. "We have expanded. . . . It is manifest destiny."

But when McKinley tried also to take control of the Philippines, America was accused of becoming the new oppressor. Angry Filipinos called for "Death to the tyrants. War to the false Americans who have deceived us." And on February 4, 1899, fighting broke out. "Nothing is left for us to do but to put down the rebellion," McKinley said in a speech in Ohio. "That territory is ours . . . and we mean to carry our civilization there."

It became America's first overseas guerrilla war, and atrocities abounded. In the heat of battle, captured Filipinos were forced to dig their own graves; then many were lined up and shot. Whole villages were set on fire, exterminating innocent men, women, and children. One American general wrote, "It may be necessary to kill half the Filipinos in order that the remaining half be advanced to a higher plane of life."

McKinley was anguished by news of such atrocities. But he couldn't admit what later Americans would realize, that the war in the Philippines was a contradiction of the deepest principles that America stood for. To the end, he insisted that America's unwanted presence there would eventually prove to be a blessing to all. "Our flag in the Philippines [is] not the banner of imperialism, or the symbol of oppression," he wrote. "It is the flag of freedom, of hope, of civilization."

With military successes abroad and a return of prosperity at home, in 1900 McKinley was overwhelmingly reelected, alongside Theodore Roosevelt, the hero of the war in Cuba. The first Republican to be elected by both Northerners and Southerners, he saw his victory as a historic reuniting of the country.

"I am no longer called the President of a party," he wrote. "I am now the President of the whole people."

Supported by a war chest thirteen times that of the Democrats, McKinley directed his 1896 presidential campaign from his front porch in Canton. In just four and a half months he spoke to three-quarters of a million people in front of his home. The picket fence was reduced to splinters by souvenir seekers, and the lawn it formerly guarded looked as though, as someone said, "a herd of buffalo had passed that way."

Fastidious in his dress and grooming, the prudish McKinley rarely drank liquor but smoked from fifty to one hundred cigars each week, usually among friends, and never in front of his wife, for fear of upsetting her. He was the only clean-shaven president between Andrew Johnson and Woodrow Wilson.

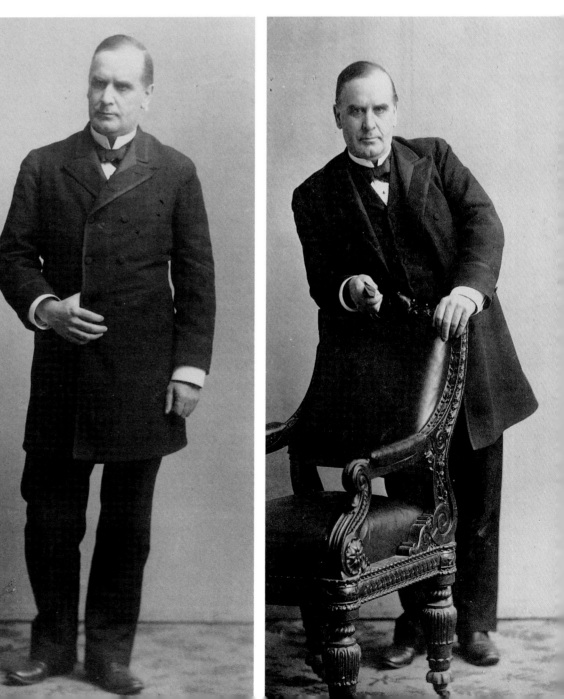

For his bureaucratic efficiency during the Spanish-American War—and for his forceful involvement in the passage of the Treaty of Paris—William McKinley is often considered the first "modern" president. Yet in many ways he belonged to an earlier era, symbolized by these horses and carriages lined up in front of the White House. Though better organized than past White Houses, McKinley's White House was still served by a very small staff—a steward, an usher, and nine doorkeepers were the sole government employees. All other servants and staff were paid for by the president himself, including the all-important private secretary (George Cortelyou), who served as McKinley's speech writer, press secretary, and political advisor, as well as overseeing all clerical matters.

Ida Saxton McKinley in the White House Conservatory.

One of the reasons the country was so entranced with McKinley was his almost saintly behavior toward his wife. An epileptic given to depression and "fits," she remained the center of his life and his beloved throughout her long, downhill journey. "Oh, if you could have seen what a beauty Ida was as a girl," McKinley often said. "Ida was the most beautiful girl you ever saw." The slide had begun early, in the years following their marriage in Canton, as first one daughter, then a second died, their only children. Never thereafter was Ida free of the terrible sadness that enveloped her, threw her into a sickbed, darkened her mind, and filled her with self-pity and an obsessive love for her husband. She hung his portrait next to her bed so his would be the last face she would see each night, the first each morning. She was jealous and quick-tempered whenever another woman even looked at her William. Through it all McKinley lavished love and patience on his besieged wife. If he had to work late, he never failed to send her the same message: "Receive my evening benediction of love." He would always try to lunch with her; and when Ida couldn't gather the strength to make it downstairs, they'd dine in her room. When she couldn't be near him she'd sit staring blankly, or busily occupy her needles at slippers, one of five thousand pairs she made over the years for charity. The devotion between the birdlike eccentric and her understanding husband was an inspiration for all of Washington. Said Ida's best friend, Jennie Hobart, wife of McKinley's first vice president, "The relationship between them was one of those rare and beautiful things that live only in tradition."

Two hundred sixty men perished when the *Maine* blew up in the Havana harbor. Here the flag-draped coffins have been assembled for burial at Arlington Cemetery.

In the summer of 1901, McKinley left on a victorious six-week tour across the American continent. Mingling freely with the crowds, he was the last chief executive to do so without Secret Service protection. "If it is in the mind and heart of anybody to kill me, he will do so," he said, "for plenty of opportunity will be offered him."

On September 6, McKinley attended an exposition in Buffalo, New York. There, without warning, an assassin took aim and fired twice, hitting the President in the chest and stomach. Operated on at a small hospital on the fairgrounds, McKinley was then moved to a private home in Buffalo, where a badly shaken Ida McKinley was waiting.

"My wife—be careful how you tell her," he said to his attendants. "Oh be careful!"

At first it looked as if the President would survive. The nation's hope rose with each passing day. But a gangrenous infection soon set in, and within a week McKinley's condition was determined to be fatal. His last words were spoken eight days after the shooting. "Goodbye. Goodbye to all. It is God's will. His will, not ours, be done."

He was the third American president to be assassinated, and his coffin would rest in the White House East Room during a period of intense national mourning. As America's first modern president, he had presided over an era of great international expansion. The new president, Theodore Roosevelt, spoke for the nation when he called him "the most widely loved man in all the United States."

"All a man can hope for during his lifetime [is] to set an example," William McKinley had once said, "and, when he's dead, to be an inspiration for history."

The warfare America waged against the Filipinos in the name of civilization led to appalling scenes like this.

In McKinley's war room, the first war room ever for the White House, telegraph operators send messages in 1898.

McKinley meets with his cabinet in 1899. Starting at the President's left, clockwise, are Lyman Gage, John Griggs, John D. Long, James Wilson, Ethan A. Hitchcock, Charles E. Smith, Elihu Root, and John Hay.

Although McKinley was a man of peace, he could not escape war.

I have been through one war. I have seen the dead piled up, and I do not want to see another.

It isn't the money that will be spent nor the property that will be destroyed, if war comes that concerns me; but the thought of human suffering that must come into thousands of homes throughout the country is almost overwhelming.

On the 25th of April . . . the United States sounded the call to arms. . . . Our country thus, after an interval of half a century of peace with all nations, found itself engaged in [a] deadly conflict with a foreign enemy.

The faith of a Christian nation recognizes the hand of Almighty God in the ordeal. . . . Divine favor seemed manifest everywhere.

The truth is, I didn't want the Philippines, and when they . . . dropped into our laps I confess I did not know what to do with them. . . . One night late it came to me. . . . We could not give them back to Spain; . . . we could not turn them over to France or Germany; . . . we could not leave them by themselves—they would soon have anarchy. There was nothing left to do but to take them all, and to . . . civilize and Christianize . . . the Filipinos.

I have had enough of it. . . . I have had . . . responsibilities enough to kill any man.

Every red drop, whether from the veins of an American soldier or a misguided Filipino, is anguish to my heart. . . . But this territory came to us in the Providence of God. . . . It is ours . . . and we mean to carry our . . . civilization there.

Isolation is no longer possible or desirable. . . . The period of exclusiveness is past.

Having already spoken at the Pan American Exposition in Buffalo, President McKinley (far left) returned the next afternoon for a pleasant reception and more sightseeing after having visited Niagara Falls in the morning. As he approached his destination (left), he did not seem to care that security at the Hall of Music where he was to appear was lax; McKinley refused to take precautions, tossing off remarks such as, "If it were not for Ida, I would prefer to go as Lincoln went." A few minutes after 4:00, a Bach sonata accompanied the President's handshakes as McKinley greeted a young man with a bandaged right hand. McKinley was reaching out with his left hand when two pistol shots resounded through the hall and two bullets entered the President's midsection. Astonished, McKinley rose on his tiptoes and looked at the smoking bandage.

Behind bars, the assassin Leon F. Czolgosz was vacant-faced as he awaited his trial (left). On Oct. 29, 1901, the anarchist was strapped into the newly perfected electric chair at New York's Auburn Prison. Fearful that angry mobs would dig up his body, authorities doused it with sulfuric acid before its secret burial. Below, the dead chief executive lies in state at the Capitol, watched over by another assassinated president people said McKinley resembled.

On the day of the funeral in Washington, umbrellaed crowds stand silently in the rain outside the Capitol. One biographer said: "Even the heavens seemed to weep."

Woodrow Wilson, photographed straight on and in profile in the East Room of the White House on June 14, 1918

WOODROW WILSON

1913–1921

American Idealist

Woodrow Wilson presented an austere public personality, and all his life was careful to cover up deeply felt passions. "My constant embarrassment," he once said, "is to restrain the emotions that are inside of me." As a young man he became known as an intense and hardworking scholar. His first book, written while he was still a graduate student, was acclaimed as "the best critical writing on the Constitution since the Federalist Papers." A day-dreamer since boyhood, and prone to impulsiveness, in 1883 he proposed marriage to Ellen Axson on the fourth visit after meeting her. "You did a most dangerous thing, young lady, in capturing me," he wrote to her. "Some day you will know what a vital, insisting, obtrusive thing my love is."

He went on to a series of teaching positions, finally landing at Princeton University, where he was widely recognized not only as a gifted and inspiring lecturer, but as a political scientist of the highest order. "I have a passion for interpreting great thoughts to the world," he wrote. "It is my heart's dearest desire that I may become one of the guides of public policy."

In 1902 he was elected Princeton's president, and he was soon making his mark as an educational reformer. But under the stresses of his public role, and with his health beginning to suffer, Wilson's private life gradually began to unravel. In 1907, during a doctor-ordered rest in Bermuda, he met Mary Hulbert Peck, an American divorcée. Their affair, which began the following year, and which ran intermittently until early 1910, ended only after his conscience finally got the better of him. By then he had become caught up in a rancorous controversy at Princeton, in which the board of trustees failed to support his leadership. "My inclination is to resign and leave them to their own devices," he wrote angrily. But even before he had made his decision whether or not to quit, he was approached by local Democrats to run for the governorship of New Jersey. Wilson leapt at the chance.

As a politician he cut a strange figure—bookish and austere, and with a touch of arrogance. But in a day of rampant political corruption, he possessed an astonishing freshness, with his eloquence, his commitment to high principle, and an almost contagious belief in himself. And in November 1910, he was elected New Jersey's new governor.

After serving less than two years in the governor's office, Wilson was nominated for president. And in the fall of 1912, after a three way race for the presidency, he won the election. "It is a fine system," he wrote jokingly, "where some remote, severe schoolmaster may become president of the United States."

Like McKinley, Wilson had campaigned exclusively on domestic issues.

At Princeton, then named the College of New Jersey, undergraduate Woodrow Wilson was known as Tommy, and found his experience there "magical."

As president of Princeton, Wilson added the formal study of political science to the curriculum.

As governor of New Jersey Wilson was popular with the press but was considered too independent-minded and idealistic by the political bosses.

And in his inaugural address he did not even mention the subject of the world stage. "It would be an irony of fate," he mused privately, "if my administration had to deal chiefly with foreign affairs."

In the White House he launched into a grueling work schedule, insisting on hand-typing all his own letters and speeches. His principal aim would be an overhaul of the national banking system, including the creation of the Federal Reserve Board. And he assembled one of the most effective cabinets in the history of the presidency. His "New Freedom" programs to regulate industry and for social welfare would anticipate by twenty years FDR's New Deal. And though he was slow to become an advocate of the 19th Amendment, he would eventually gain the widespread support of American women. Throughout it all, his strongest supporter was his wife Ellen, for whom he had rediscovered all his earlier adoration. "You have been so loyal, so forgiving, so self-sacrificing," he wrote. "How bright you make my way through every test and trial."

But in the spring of 1914 Ellen collapsed with a fatal kidney ailment, and on August 14 she died of Bright's disease. Wilson wrote, "God has stricken me almost beyond what I can bear." He descended into a near-crippling depression. But Wilson would not be granted the luxury of despair. Almost precisely at the same time as Ellen's death, World War I erupted in Europe. The president who had planned to focus on domestic affairs alone was now forced to enter upon the world stage.

Wilson resisted armed intervention for two years, even though it brought him considerable criticism. Theodore Roosevelt denounced him as a traitor and a coward. But Wilson was horrified by what was happening to Europe. He knew that hundreds of thousands of soldiers were being killed off in battles that had no real result. And he wanted to spare his country.

Even after the Germans torpedoed and sank the British passenger liner the *Lusitania,* and then the *Sussex,* resulting in American casualties, Wilson insisted on working for peace. "I will not be rushed into war," he insisted, "no matter if every damned congressman and senator stands up on his hind legs and proclaims me a coward." But he was a tough-minded diplomat, who used the threat of American involvement to force Germany to end its unrestrained submarine warfare.

In the spring of 1915 Wilson met Edith Galt, a Washington widow. They were married later that same year. "She seemed to come into my life . . . like a special gift from Heaven," Wilson wrote. "I have won a sweet companion who will soon make me forget the intolerable loneliness and isolation of the weary months since this terrible war began."

In 1916 Wilson won reelection, hailed as "the man who had kept the country out of war." Then, just two months into his second term, everything changed. The Germans, who had begun committing atrocities against the Belgians, resumed their all-out submarine warfare. On April 2, 1917, Wilson appeared before Congress and delivered one of the greatest speeches of his life, declaring that "the world must be made safe for democracy." Wilson presented the war to the American people as a moral crusade, as a clear struggle of right against wrong. "We entered it not because our material interests were directly threatened," he wrote, "but only because we saw . . . free government everywhere imperiled."

Two million American soldiers were eventually sent to Europe, assuring Allied victory. And when victory finally came, it also assured America's permanent position on the world stage.

But Wilson had a higher goal in mind. He wanted to shape a new world order in which world wars such as this would never again happen. On January 8, 1918, he outlined fourteen points for a lasting peace. And he proposed establishing what he called a "League of Nations," in which law-abiding countries would pledge to protect one another in the future. "Our task is to set up a new international psychology," he proclaimed.

On December 3, 1918, with his popularity and prestige at an all-time high, Wilson left for Europe to take part in the Allied peace talks. It was the first time an American president had ever visited Europe while in office, and in France hundreds of thousands poured out to see him. To wartorn Europeans he had become the recognized moral leader of the free world and a symbol of idealism. "Before this war Europe did not believe in us," Wilson wrote. "But when they saw that America not only held the ideals but acted the ideals, they were converted to America."

But the Paris peace talks quickly degenerated into greedy quarreling, with Wilson alone standing up for the highest principles. "He is the only great, serious statesman here," wrote one observer. "He is a titan struggling with forces too great even for him." When the final treaty was signed at Versailles, it was far less idealistic than what Wilson had argued for. But it included his idea for a "League of Nations." As the President headed home, he knew it was now up to him to convince the U.S. Senate to consent to it.

To build up public support for the treaty, Wilson launched on a cross-country tour. At issue was the future of world peace, he insisted, in speeches that were filled with a prophetic fire. "We cannot turn back. We can only go forward, with lifted eyes to follow the vision. America shall in truth show the way."

But on September 25, in Pueblo, Colorado, an exhausted President Wilson stumbled on the speakers' platform, and that night complained of a piercing headache. It was decided to cancel the rest of the tour and the stricken President was rushed home to Washington. One week later he suffered a severe stroke, paralyzing him on his left side. Even after he was able to resume some of his duties, Woodrow Wilson was never the same again. The stroke permanently damaged his sense of judgment and allowed his intense passions to go unchecked. As the Senate debated the League of Nations, Wilson irrationally refused to compromise on any point. And when the Senate rejected the treaty, Wilson's great dream for a new world order was shattered. "I have given my vitality, and almost my life, for the League of Nations," Wilson wrote. "If I were not a Christian I think I should go mad."

For seven months the president was a near recluse in the White House. His disability was the longest lasting crisis the presidency had ever faced, as his cabinet carried on the business of government. Finally in 1921 he left office, an idealist who had lived ahead of his time.

In the end history would redeem him. His dream of an American-involved League of Nations became reality under Franklin Roosevelt and Harry Truman with the formation of the United Nations. And, virtually every great foreign policy of the modern era would owe its lineage to Woodrow Wilson. "I do not mean any disrespect to any other great people," Wilson wrote toward the end, "when I say that America is now the hope of the world."

In his 1912 presidential campaign, Wilson emerged as a skillful political animal.

With President Taft at his side, Wilson rides to his inauguration.

Wilson delivers his inaugural address in 1913.

Washington photographers during the Wilson administration take a moment in 1918 to emerge from behind their cameras and pose on the South Lawn of the White House.

Tall and thin, with a look of determination, Wilson seemed a hybrid of Abraham Lincoln and a medieval scholar. Many found him forbiddingly solemn, but close friends and family knew his silly side, how he loved to make puns and clown around. He was considered homely, but his face took on a riveting magnetism when he talked or lectured or gave a speech. A simple man, Wilson disliked the White House cooking, with its French sauces, saying he couldn't "see any sense in wrapping food up in pajamas." He drank herbal tea instead of coffee, liked his eggs boiled for thirty minutes, was a fast dresser, and refused to be shaved by his barber, preferring to do it himself. He loved golf and tennis and shooting pool, and he hated walking. A loner, he thrived on his privacy, which allowed him to accomplish enormous feats of thinking and writing. He had a photographic memory; he could memorize an entire address and give it as if spontaneously. Wilson never seemed content in any one career. In 1894, in the midst of his highly successful Princeton professorship, he found himself "hungry—too hungry—for reputation and influence." Though a scholar by nature, he was also an activist, never really content with the life of the academic cloister. On the other hand, when he turned to politics, there was always the academic side to him in evidence. He once referred to himself as "a high-brow president." Everything about him seemed intense and overcharged—his mind, his sensitivities, his industry, his libido. "All my passions are upon so terrible a scale of power," he once wrote. "What other severe and serious statesman of the twentieth century would call to his . . . [wife], "My love! My love! . . . I think when I get you in my arms again I cannot let you go till I have kissed you out of breath and consciousness."

After the death of his first wife, Wilson woos his soon-to-be-second.

Wilson's first cabinet was a collection of gifted men, mostly progressive, heavily weighted with Southerners. Sitting in the foreground is Wilson's controversial appointee as secretary of state—William Jennings Bryan. Bryan had twice been the Democratic nominee for president, and his support of Wilson had been key to Wilson's victory. He would resign from the cabinet in 1915 over Wilson's strong protest of the German sinking of the *Lusitania*.

Wilson is blindfolded so he can impartially pick the first men to be drafted for World War I.

The high point of Wilson's presidency began when the formerly German, now American ship *George Washington* edged into the harbor at Brest, France, carrying the first family of the United States. The reception the president was to receive, in both numbers and ardor, first in France, then in England and Italy, surpassed the welcome any human being in history had ever before been afforded.

On December 14, 1918, French soldiers lead the presidential motorcade in the rue Madeleine. For Europeans sick of war, Wilson seemed to personify peace, and kings and leaders of Europe came to honor a man from America.

After the treaty signing, Wilson tours Europe.

Wilson on war and peace:

Jan. 29, 1915: The allies on both sides have seemed to turn to the United States as to a sort of court of opinion in this great struggle, but we have no wish to be the judges; we desire only to play the part of disinterested friends who have nothing at stake except their interest in the peace of the world.

April 2, 1917: With a profound sense of the solemn and even tragical character of the step I am taking and of the grave responsibilities which it involves . . . I advise that the Congress declare the recent course of the Imperial German Government to be in fact nothing less than war against the government and people of the United States.

May 30, 1917: There are times when words seem empty and only action seems great. Such a time has come, and, in the Providence of God, America will once more have an opportunity to show to the world that she was born to serve mankind.

June 27, 1919: My fellow-countrymen: the treaty of peace has been signed. If it is ratified and acted upon in full and sincere execution of its terms it will furnish the charter for a new order of affairs in the world . . . . It ends, once for all, an old and intolerable order under which small groups of selfish men could use the peoples of great empires to serve their own ambition for power and dominion. It associates the free governments of the world in a permanent league in which they are pledged to . . . maintain peace by maintaining right and justice.

On a month-long tour of the West to sell the peace treaty and the League of Nations to the American people, Wilson leans down from his special car, the *Mayflower,* to help convince a citizen. Making major addresses sometimes twice a day, Wilson used all his powers to convey his message. "There seems to me to stand between us and the rejection or qualification of this treaty, the serried ranks of those boys in khaki—not only those boys who came home but those dear ghosts that still deploy upon the fields of France." Outside Pueblo, Colorado, Wilson collapsed from exhaustion.

With Wilson away in Europe for long stretches negotiating the peace treaty in person as no other president had ever done, sheep had grazed on the White House lawn. Now, as Wilson suffered an incapacitating stroke, the message that had been sent him in Europe—to hurry home, the sheep had no shepherd—seemed even more poignant.

Suddenly all the glories of Paris had vanished; a major stroke had left Wilson a broken man. But as he slowly improved, it was clear to the few who watched him that a different man was emerging. When an amateur photographer caught Wilson on a drive, the world started to realize, too, that only a shadow of the great fighter remained. Without his leadership, an increasingly conservative Senate soon rejected America's involvement in the League of Nations.

While Americans were pulling for Wilson to recover, life went on as usual outside the White House. Here, the public does what it has always done—poses outside the White House gates.

335

Personal Contact

The youngest Navy pilot in World War II, Bush fills out a flight log in 1944.

Polite, youthful, and appealing, George Bush lays his charm on "the people" during his 1992 campaign to be reelected. "I resisted people trying to make me something I wasn't," he said. "Wear this! Do your hair with a bouffant do! There's too much of that. And yet, I think had I done it all better, I mean, who knows?" One thing not in question was Bush's ability, during the Gulf crisis, to call upon an enormous network of international friends carefully built up over the years. "In dealing with Gorbachev, in dealing with the Chinese even, and in dealing, certainly, with great friends like Thatcher and John Major, Brian Mulrooney, and Helmut Kohl, personal contacts help."

George Herbert Walker Bush was raised in privilege in suburban Connecticut, in a family that cared deeply about international issues. "People say I was a man of privilege and by that they mean money," Bush reflected. "But I was privileged in the question of values—a mother and father who were determined to help their kids be good people."

His mother, Dorothy Walker Bush, had a lifelong influence on him; he said she was still instructing him even when he was in the White House. His father, Prescott Bush, was a successful businessman who went on in later life to become a Senator. Bush credited him with passing on his core values: "Tell the truth, be honest, work hard, try to see the other guy's point of view while sticking to your own principles. These were truisms, you might say, that my three brothers and my sister and I had inculcated into us growing up."

His values were affirmed at the private school Andover Academy. But it was his experience as a Navy pilot, shot down in the Pacific, that left the deepest imprint on him. It forced him, he said, to count his blessings.

Returning home after the war, Bush married Barbara Pierce, and upon his graduation from Yale, they left for Texas, where he would make his fortune in the oil business. Then he and Barbara were struck by a personal tragedy—the death from leukemia of their four-year-old daughter, Robin. "We thought, why, dear God, why does this child have to die?" Bush said. "The epitome of innocence to us—beauty, everything else. And there's no explanation. But all these things contribute to your life, maybe your character, to what you stand for, and that was a maturing happening. But it hurt, badly."

It was then that Bush began to grow increasingly interested in Republican politics. "I ran in 1964, with a spectacular lack of success, for the U.S. Senate," he recalled. "And maybe Dad's experience, though I was way out in west Texas while he was Senator, had something to do with my desire to be in elective politics."

In 1966 he won a seat in the U.S. Congress. And over the next two decades, international affairs would become the main focus of his life. He served as ambassador to the United Nations, then as U.S. envoy to China, and in 1975 as director of the CIA. "The U.N. was fabulously important in terms of contacts, knowing people around the world," he remembered. "The CIA, equally as important in terms of issues."

Shortly after leaving the CIA, Bush had his first ambition to go after the presidency. "Jimmy Carter had been elected," he said. "I went home to Texas and I started thinking, 'Well why not? I'd like to think I can help make

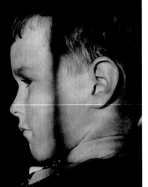

George Bush around age six

A star first baseman at Andover

The Bushes at Yale in 1945

With daughter Robin

Winning a congressional seat

George and Barbara at their wedding in 1945

things better, here and abroad.'" He ran against Ronald Reagan in the GOP primaries, but Reagan trounced him. It was after that that he agreed to run as Reagan's vice president. "Reagan, at the last moment, put me on the ticket," Bush remembered. "He was so good to me in every single way. And so the pluses of the vice presidency far outweighed any of the confines of the vice presidency."

When he ran for the presidency in 1988, George Bush promised to turn the country into a "kinder and gentler" nation. But he also made a promise that would come back to haunt him. "Read my lips," he told a campaign crowd. "No new taxes."

As President, Bush's principal focus became foreign affairs, the area in which he was best prepared and in which presidents have the most liberty to exercise their powers. In an important link back to the hemispheric perspective of James Monroe, Bush became involved in the affairs of Latin America. Following the killing of an American soldier in Panama in 1989, he personally ordered troops to invade the country and to capture Panama's dictator, Manuel Noriega. Encouraged by an elected government that Noriega had suppressed, he saw his presidential invasion as in keeping with the spirit of the Monroe Doctrine. He called it "Operation Just Cause."

Bush saw his chief task in foreign policy as overseeing an end to the Cold War. "I hoped it would end but I wasn't sure it would end that fast," Bush later recalled. "I wasn't sure the [Berlin] wall would come down. I wasn't sure Germany would be unified. I wasn't sure that the Soviet Union would have dramatically imploded as it did."

Following in the footsteps of Ronald Reagan, Bush developed a relationship with Soviet Premier Mikhail Gorbachev. His personal access to the top Soviet leader became the key to his ensuing successes in diplomacy. "I believed in Gorbachev," Bush said. "I believed in his word. Some were very skeptical of that. But I think history will be very kind to Mikhail Gorbachev."

The collapse of Communism and the end of the Cold War left America for the first time in decades without a clear mission in world affairs. But then came Iraq's invasion of Kuwait, and the United States involvement in the Persian Gulf War. Critics claimed the real motive for fighting was oil. George Bush insisted it was a matter of principle.

"The evil against the good was so clear," he said, "it made it very easy for me. It didn't make it easy for a lot of the American people at the outset. Didn't make it easier for those congressmen that fought me almost unanimously on the other side of the aisle when I asked for the authority to

U.N. ambassador in the 1970s

With father, Prescott, in 1972

Director of the CIA in 1975

Reagan's vice president in 1987

Finally, as president, in 1990

do what the U.N. said we should do. But it was an easy call for me on principle."

Using the telephone for personal diplomacy like no president before him, Bush placed personal calls to dozens of world leaders, and brought together a coalition of nations to oppose Iraq. Then he carefully held that coalition together throughout the war. "We used the U.N. in the best way since its founding," Bush said. "We could do that because of our relationship with Gorbachev, and our convincing Gorbachev that he should join us and not stand with his traditional ally, Iraq." It was an example of what Bush called the beginnings of "a new world order," in which peaceful nations could stand united against rogue states and against terrorism. "A hundred generations have searched for this elusive path to peace," he said in a speech in 1990. It was a vision in keeping with that of Woodrow Wilson, and many years before him, of James Monroe. And when the Gulf War was won, in large part because of George Bush's efforts, he reaped an extraordinary political benefit. "I think Desert Storm lifted the morale of our country and healed some of the wounds of Vietnam. I'm sure of it," he said.

Bush's conduct of the Gulf War, his carefulness about objectives, and his success in coalition building left him with the highest approval ratings of any president in the history of the Gallup polls. By most accounts, that should have given him a second term. But it didn't. And it didn't because the economy had weakened and the voters took their frustrations to the ballot box. In his 1992 campaign for reelection, Bush was cast by critics as a tired relic of the Cold War who had neglected the home front and broken his pledge not to increase taxes. Competing in a three-way election against Bill Clinton and Ross Perot, in November he received the lowest percentage of votes of any sitting president in eighty years.

"It hurt a lot," Bush later admitted. "But the minute we got back to Houston, Texas, and were welcomed by our neighbors, and went into that little house with two dogs and Barbara and me and nobody else, we began to say, 'Hey, life's pretty good. And I think some of the reason that I'm very happy is I think we upheld the honor of the presidency; because I did feel the majesty of the office. And you wanted to keep it. You wanted the kids to have stars in their eyes when they went through the White House or looked at the West Wing, looked at the Oval Office. Maybe it's old-fashioned but I have great respect for the dignity of the office, and for the presidency itself." When asked what he wanted historians finally to say about his presidency, George Bush answered simply, "He did his best. Did it with honor."

Forty years after their wedding, they dance again.

General Colin Powell (left) advises the President in one of the daily huddles that Bush employed for assistance in making his decisions. Directing the agenda is Chief of Staff John Sununu (right). "I had great confidence in the intelligence I was given," says Bush. Standing is General Brent Scowcroft; Secretary of Defense Dick Cheney sits with his back to the camera.

Wherever the action was, Bush wanted to be there. Here, in 1991, he greets servicemen returning from Operation Desert Storm at a welcome-home rally in Sumter, South Carolina. "I wanted to show the flag," Bush said, "the flag of the Commander-in-Chief."

During the Gulf War, the Bushes say prayers for U.S. troops in action in Operation Desert Storm. "The hardest part is when you have to send someone's kid into battle," Bush said. "That's the hardest part by far."

On world cooperation: By itself, America can do much. Together with its friends and allies, America can do much more for peace and justice.

On the dual presidency: People really basically want to support the President on foreign affairs, and partisanship does, in a sense, stop at the water's edge. Whereas on domestic policy, here I am with Democratic majorities in the Senate and Democratic majorities in the House, trying to persuade them to do what I think is best. It's complicated.

On leadership: Some see leadership as high drama, and the sound of trumpets calling. And sometimes it is that. But I see history as a book with many pages—and each day we fill a page with acts of hopefulness and meaning. The new breeze blows, a page turns, the story unfolds.

On foreign policy: When you get a problem with the complexities that the Middle East has now and the Gulf has now, I enjoy trying to put the coalition together and keep it together and work toward what I think is a proper end.

On U.S. responsibility: The U.S. has a disproportionate responsibility for the freedom and the security of various countries. And a lot of what is at stake in the Gulf relates to that. Not that we have to do it just so the U.S. preserves its position. People are looking to us for leadership.

On a new world order: Out of these troubled times a new world order can emerge from the threat of terror, stronger in the pursuit of justice and more secure in the quest for peace. An era in which the nations of the world, east and west, north and south, can prosper and live in harmony. A hundred generations have searched for this elusive path to peace, while a thousand wars raged across the span of human endeavor.

On the death of his daughter: I was told that when a family loses a child, that they often drift apart—the parents. It was the opposite in our case . . . but if Barbara and I were anything we were closer because of having shared this experience, and I had more respect for her, watching her hold this baby in her arms until the day the baby died.

On Barbara as a wife: Barbara started off as a conventional wife, as did most of the wives of the veterans with whom we went to college, her first responsibility being to her children. Being sure they could read, being sure they did their homework, being sure they were well. She was a great example. And then she started getting into being one of a thousand points of light, doing her charity work and all. And then she became . . . convinced the biggest problem facing the country is the fact that so many people can't read. So she pledged herself to do something about family literacy. And today she's a shining example. I think I'm married to the most popular woman in the United States of America.

On privilege and parents: We are privileged. I've never denied that. I never considered it a great liability as some people tried to make it in the political wars. But I was blessed by privilege. But blessed more by privilege that comes from having parents that teach you values.

On the Oval Office: I think I went there as a tourist one time way back somewhere in the sixties . . . and I felt this overwhelming sense of awe. . . . It wasn't just awe. It was excitement and respect for that office. And that's why when anybody was there, I would not ever go in there and have meetings with neckties gone and plastic cups, because I, and maybe it's old-fashioned, but I have great respect for the dignity of the office and for the office of the presidency itself.

On Ronald Reagan: There was a kindness there that taught me a good lesson— don't get to be a big deal, don't bawl out the airline stewardess, don't throw your weight around. Contain your anger. Smile a lot. Laugh. Be kind to people. Those values I learned from Ronald Reagan. He was a beautiful, beautiful man in that sense.

George and Barbara Bush, beside the grand columns of the White House, bid farewell on the last morning of Bush's presidency.

Out from behind one of the immense columns of the South Portico steps President-elect Bill Clinton to greet the outgoing president. With him is his wife, Hillary, and their daughter, Chelsea. Just a few hours later it will be their White House.

Alongside "Ladybird" Johnson, the widow of LBJ, three former first couples pose playfully for the camera—George and Barbara Bush, Gerald and Betty Ford, and Jimmy and Rosalynn Carter.

Like only a handful of other American political dynasties, the Bush family has produced three generations of high public leadership. Here, during the Bush presidency, the family spreads out beside their Kennebunkport mansion in Maine. From left: Neil Bush holding Lauren, with wife Sharon; George W. Bush, his wife Laura, and their twins Barbara and Jenna; behind Barbara and George is Margaret Bush, holding Marshall, with husband Marvin. Next, Bill LeBlond and Dorothy with their son Sam. Finally, George P. Bush, Jeb holding Jebby, and Columba, behind Noelle.

George Bush's Oval Office gets torn apart to make way for new wiring and fresh curtains for Bill Clinton, as well as the desk John F. Kennedy had used, especially requested by the next occupant.

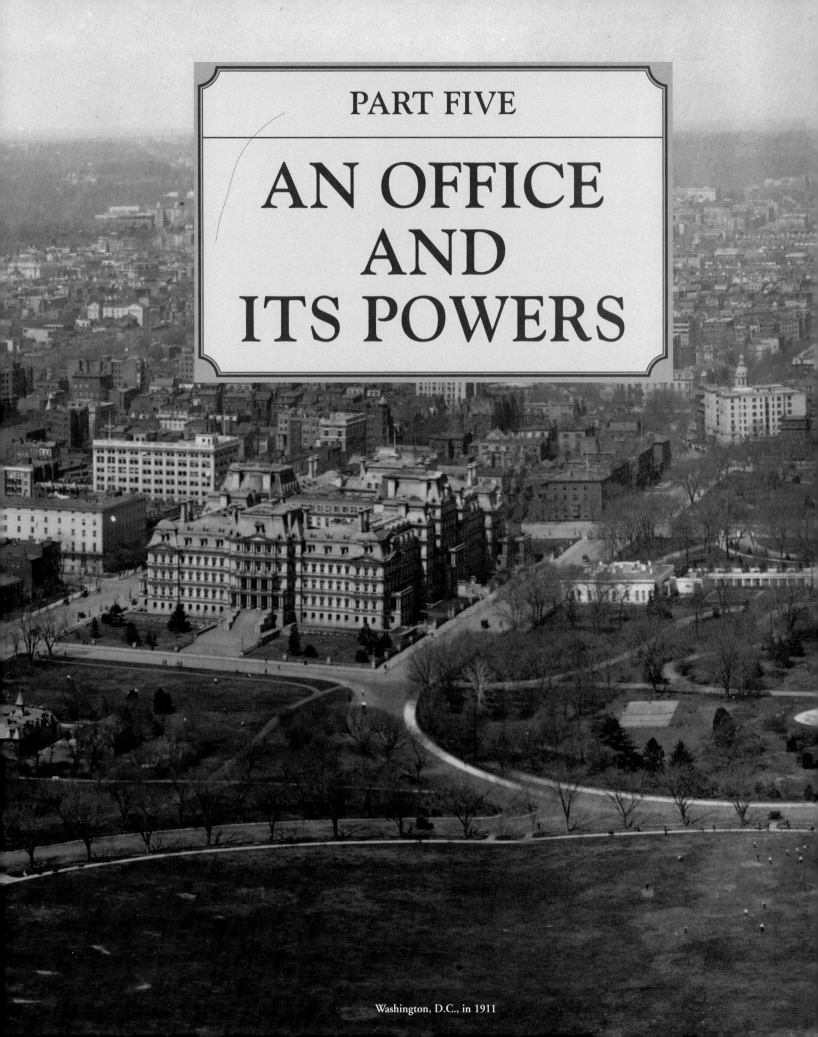

PART FIVE

AN OFFICE AND ITS POWERS

Washington, D.C., in 1911

Andrew Jackson

Grover Cleveland

EXPANDING POWER

CHAPTER NINE

How much power should the chief executive have?
A considerable amount, the founding fathers said. But certain bold
presidents have appropriated even more.

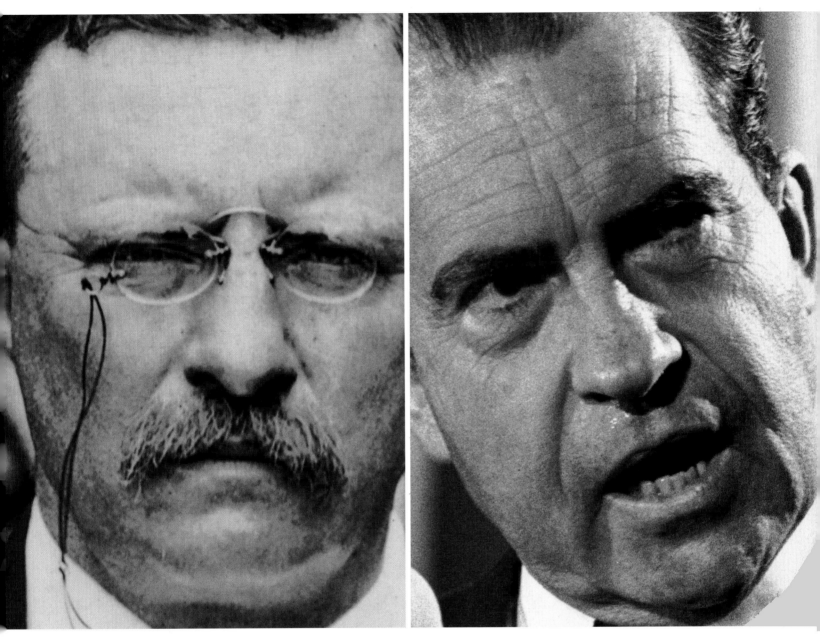

Theodore Roosevelt

Richard M. Nixon

The Constitutional Convention of 1787 was divided between advocates of a strong and a weak presidency. Some delegates were so wary of creating an American monarchy, they wanted the chief executive power to reside in a committee. Others, seeing the inadequacies of government by consensus, and remembering the problems during the war due to a lack of congressional leadership, wanted to reimpose at least some of the trappings of kingship. The fateful decision to empower an individual as chief executive was made in part because of the extraordinary person everyone expected would become the first president—the immensely trustworthy George Washington. But this was committed to only after certain powers had been stripped from the presidency and granted instead to Congress—above all, the kingly power to declare war. Though the president was vested with the formidable power of the veto, it was to be subject to overriding by a two-thirds vote of Congress. And though the president was granted the important power of appointment, allowing him to name

Though he professed belief in a weak executive, Thomas Jefferson was one of the strongest. Through behind-the-scenes political mastery he virtually controlled Congress, and in foreign affairs he took one of the boldest presidential actions in U.S. history —the Louisiana Purchase.

The crisis that unleashed Abraham Lincoln's huge executive power was the Civil War and the issue of slavery behind it. Invoking the commander-in-chief clause of the Constitution, Lincoln stretched his powers further than any previous president, becoming a virtual dictator during the war years. An era of presidential weakness followed.

key federal officers, it was a power to be shared at least in part with the Senate, which was charged with the duty of confirmation. To render the president even less monarchical, he was limited to an elected, though renewable, four-year term of office, and made subject to impeachment in the case of "treason, bribery, or other high crimes and misdemeanors."

And so the new nation's history began with a carefully constrained presidency and a carefully constrained Congress. The next two hundred years would witness enormous power struggles between these two branches, resulting in profound changes in the profile of the executive.

Though both Washington and Jefferson were strong presidents, the first major expansion of presidential power didn't occur until the 1830s, under the formidable figure of Andrew Jackson of Tennessee. The first Westerner to assume the presidency, Jackson saw himself as a "tribune of the people," and was determined to exercise all the potential power in the office. Above all, he made vast new uses of the veto power, establishing the president's right to enter vigorously into the legislative process. And he invaded the dominion of the Supreme Court too, insisting he had the authority to judge matters of constitutionality. Possessing a brilliant and ferocious personality, he became the archetype of what has since been known as the "strong," or "Jacksonian," presidency.

To confront and oppose the strong presidency and restore the standard of a dominant Congress, the Whig Party was formed in 1834. And with the exception of James Polk, an aggressive Jacksonian Democrat, the next quarter century saw a succession of weak presidents. Ironically, it was a Whig-turned-Republican, Abraham Lincoln, who presided over the most dramatic expansion of presidential power to date. Without asking for Congress's approval, Lincoln mobilized troops, waged war, suppressed newspapers, and emancipated slaves. His critics came to call him an outright dictator. But Lincoln's powers were emergency powers only—"war powers," he called them—meant to help protect the very future of the nation. And in the Civil War's aftermath, Congress seized back its traditional authority and created another era of presidential weakness. With the impeachment and near removal of Andrew Johnson and the scandal-ridden administrations of Ulysses S. Grant, the presidency entered upon a period of profound decline. By the 1880s some, including the young scholar Woodrow Wilson, were even predicting the presidency's demise as an institution.

The president's library in the White House as it looked around 1880

But then came the three strongest presidents since Lincoln: Grover Cleveland, William McKinley, and most notably, Theodore Roosevelt. Claiming Lincoln and Jackson as executive role models, Roosevelt forged a bold and aggressive new kind of presidency. He cast himself as a "steward of the nation," and insisted he alone represented the entire country, and thus must "actively do all he could for the people." And though his successor, William Taft, disapproved of the trend, the twentieth century belonged to this new breed of president. Wilson was one of this new breed—he was visionary, stubborn, and immensely powerful as president. But it was Theodore's cousin, Franklin Delano Roosevelt, who assumed the most wide-ranging new powers, in coping with the Great Depression and with World War II. And once these powers were institutionalized, they were passed along to subsequent presidents.

Embarrassed by its unpreparedness at Pearl Harbor in 1941, Congress granted successive presidents new scope in the area of defense and defense budgeting. And with the onset of the nuclear age, these powers continued to expand. Harry Truman was able to wage full-scale fighting in Korea without ever asking Congress to declare war. And during the Vietnam War, under Presidents Johnson and Nixon, Congress allowed presidential war powers to grow even greater. With vastly expanded White House staffs at their disposal, by 1970 presidents had reached the pinnacle of their power.

But with increased power comes increased danger, as the nation's founders once predicted. And the delicate balance of power of the American system was finally brought to a testing point in the 1970s during the presidency of Richard Nixon. Nixon's unauthorized bombings in Cambodia, followed by revelations about the Watergate break-in by Nixon's campaign operatives, led Congress finally to reassert its leadership. And in the decades since, as the Cold War has ended, the Constitutional branches have vied with one another in an uncertain balance.

"Power is poison," wrote the historian Henry Adams. But when power is well used, it is one of the essential ingredients of effective leadership. Strong presidents have always pushed their power to the limits. Andrew Jackson did it using his fearsome personality and by a decision to make vast new uses of the veto. Grover Cleveland threw all his massive weight and personal integrity into a fight with the Senate over the autonomy of the presidency. Theodore Roosevelt led the country by sheer exuberance, and by doing anything he wanted within lawful limits. Richard Nixon, who worked so hard to shape a new world order, overstepped those "lawful limits" and broke faith with the nation and with his oath of office.

"Nixon's breach of faith," says presidential scholar Richard Neustadt, "is not remembering what the White House has become over the years. The White House is to Americans in general a shrine. It is the place every president since Jefferson has lived. It's where Mr. Lincoln paced the floor. To forget that is, I think, to break faith. It's to forget that you are at some level, and in some part, the elected priest. You are supposed to be guarding the shrines. And to commit crimes in the People's House is unforgivable."

The president of the United States is not a monarch; he is an officer within a constitutional government. A half century ago the presidential scholar Clinton Rossiter described it this way: "The President is . . . a kind of magnificent lion who can roam widely and do great deeds so long as he does not try to break loose from his broad reservation."

Franklin Roosevelt ushered in a new era of presidential power. An unstoppable force, he was elected to office four times, and during the crises of the Great Depression and World War II Congress granted him almost unlimited license. Under Roosevelt the Executive Department and White House staffs ballooned, giving rise to modern "institutional presidency."

Lyndon Johnson's Great Society was the most ambitious social program ever attempted in U.S. history. Stretching presidential power even further than Roosevelt, Johnson inaugurated the era of "The President's Program," in which presidents are expected to set the national agenda.

ANDREW JACKSON

1829–1837

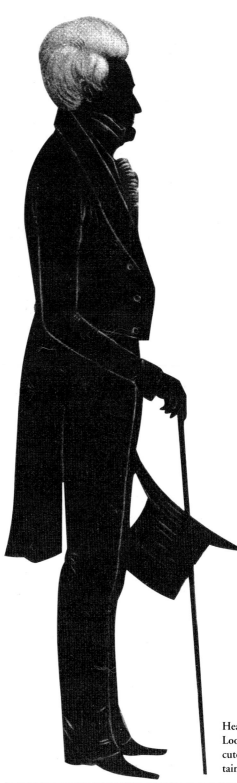

The Power of the People

Like all presidents who have won important power struggles, Andrew Jackson was a fighter. He was in fact the most violent-tempered man ever to rise to the presidency. Thomas Jefferson once said, "His passions are terrible. He is a dangerous man." John Quincy Adams called him, simply, "a barbarian."

"I am denounced as a man of revengeful temper," Jackson wrote upon arriving in Washington in 1824, "with a tomahawk in one hand and a scalping knife in the other. . . . Many conceive me to be a ferocious animal." Others recognized different dimensions to the old warrior: his tenacious intelligence, his belief in the common man, and what one surprised observer called his "mysterious charm wrought upon old and young." And Jackson used all these qualities, especially his ferocity, to transform the presidency.

Unlike the six presidents before him, Jackson was born poor, and his humble beginnings in South Carolina forged a lifelong toughness. Heading west to Tennessee as a young man after the Revolutionary War, he rose to become a major general in the state militia, a Superior Court judge, and Tennessee's first U.S. congressman. But he also became known as a man not to cross. Anyone who insulted him was challenged to a duel. On one occasion, his opponent fired first, lodging a bullet in Jackson's chest. As blood filled his shoes, Jackson calmly took aim and shot the man dead. "Of all ideas, to me it is the most humiliating to be thought to cringe to power," Jackson later wrote. "My reputation is dearer to me than life."

Becoming one of Tennessee's most renowned citizens, he settled with his wife Rachel on a large estate near Nashville, which they named "the Hermitage." Jackson turned it into a working plantation, and it was the only place where he appeared content and able to relax.

But with the War of 1812, his fiercer personality once again surfaced, and he left home to battle Indians in the backwoods of Tennessee. "The cry was raised from East to West for permission to carry a war into the Creek nation," he wrote. "The object was to exterminate them." In a series of brutally successful campaigns, Jackson earned his Indian nickname, "Sharpknife."

A war against Indians escalated into a war with England, and Jackson was ordered south to defend the mouth of the Mississippi. His victory at the

Heavy suits and padding disguised Jackson's slim frame, but nothing could hide his blunt views. Looking back over his administration, he once said his chief regret was that he had failed to execute Vice President John C. Calhoun for treason. "My country," Jackson said, "would have sustained me in the act, and his fate would have been a warning to traitors in all time to come."

Once he had lived through the War of 1812, it was inevitable that Jackson would become the most heroic figure of his time.

Indian fighter in his forties

First try for the White House

Before his second campaign

During his presidency

Back home at the Hermitage

Battle of New Orleans turned him into America's greatest living hero, and from that point on, it was assumed he would one day become president.

In 1824 Jackson ran for the presidency, losing to John Quincy Adams in an election so close it was thrown to the House of Representatives to decide. Jackson had actually won the popular vote, and thus saw himself as the people's choice. But when Speaker of the House Henry Clay threw his support to John Quincy Adams, it sealed the election for Adams. Soon afterwards Clay was named secretary of state. Convinced that a corrupt bargain lay at the heart of Adams's victory, Jackson determined to topple the old Eastern establishment. His struggle, he said, was over the very nature of the presidency. Did it belong to the privileged few, as it had almost de facto from the beginning, or did it belong, as he believed, to a much wider America? In 1828, four times as many voters as ever before came out to cast their ballot. And this time Jackson won by a landslide, gaining more than two-thirds of all the electoral votes in a stunning overturn of the aloof Easterner, Adams. As the seventh president of the United States, Jackson promised to turn over government to the common man.

Jackson was sworn in at what was called "the people's inaugural." And for the first time ever, the White House was opened wide to the public, with thousands of ordinary Americans swarming in to celebrate their hero. In the once elegant East Room, Jackson installed twenty spittoons.

At six feet one inch, and weighing less than 140 pounds, Andrew Jackson cut a strange figure in the presidency. He wore thick coats to lend the illusion of substance, and he was often sick in the White House, coughing up blood caused by the old dueling bullet still lodged near his heart. To ease his pain he sometimes bled himself, using his penknife to open the veins.

Washington society, however, soon learned how charming he could be, and he surprised many with his honesty and his thoughtful intelligence. But as he began to wield power, Jackson also demonstrated just how fierce he still was. In an effort to gain more than 100 million acres for the Southern states, Jackson insisted on the removal of Native Americans to territory beyond the Mississippi River. "Those tribes cannot exist surrounded by our settlements," he wrote. "They have neither the intelligence nor the moral habits. . . . Established in the midst of a superior race, they must disappear." Even after the Supreme Court upheld the Indians' treaty right to their Southern homeland, Jackson pressed ahead with his removal program. "It is as much the duty of the President to decide the constitutionality of any bill as it is the Supreme Judges," he later wrote. "The Supreme Court must not be permitted to control the Executive." The Cherokees would come to call the forced expulsion their "trail of tears." Daniel Webster declared it a glaring example of Jackson's abuse of power.

Throughout his presidency, Andrew Jackson picked fights, just as he had done all his life. When Vice President John C. Calhoun proposed that his state of South Carolina could annul the federal tariff on cotton, helping initiate what became known as the nullification crisis, Jackson violently opposed him, threatening to send in federal troops. And when Calhoun went on to advocate secession, Jackson blurted out, "He ought to be hung." Among others, Abraham Lincoln would be deeply influenced by Jackson's forceful standing up for the integrity of the Union.

Seeing himself as the people's man in government, the only officer elected by the populace at large, Jackson labored to increase the power of the office. And in one legendary duel with the Senate, he made his single most ferocious bid to do so. The fight was over the future of the America's national economy, which since the early days of the Republic had been controlled by the giant, and increasingly corrupt, Bank of the United States. Jackson wanted to democratize the system, so that small banks could compete across the country. But with the U.S. Bank granting cheap loans to congressmen and senators to keep them friendly, it was as entrenched an institution as any in the country. Jackson called it "the hydra-headed beast," and said he intended to slay it. "Until I can strangle the hydra I will not shrink from my duty," he wrote. "Unless the corrupting monster should be shraven of its ill-gotten power, my veto will meet it frankly and fearlessly."

Presidents prior to Jackson had rarely used the veto, and never in order to direct national policy. Jackson came to see it as a great untapped resource and a weapon that could underscore the independence of the executive branch. He would eventually veto more bills than all his predecessors combined, declaring it a president's right to kill a bill for almost any reason. His veto of the federal bank's early recharter has been called the most significant veto in U.S. history, setting a permanent new course for America's economy. His opponents called it the act of a willful tyrant.

But Jackson was not finished. When he was elected overwhelmingly to a second term, he claimed a mandate from the people to continue his attack on the bank, which still had three years left to its charter. In an effort to cripple it, he ordered the withdrawal of all federal deposits. Then, when his secretary of the treasury refused to comply, Jackson fired him and appointed a secretary who would. Nothing was going to stop him, he said, from "defanging the monster." In response, an irate Senate passed a "resolution of censure" against him, an action never taken before or since. Jackson fired back that a president was not responsible to the Senate, but solely to the American people. "The people are the sovereign power," he insisted. "The officers are their agents."

In the end, Jackson won his fight with the bank, and the censure resolution was officially expunged. This result demonstrated an extraordinary power shift—that by wielding the veto like a weapon, the president could become the chief power in government.

Jackson was a man of terrible contradictions—of deep prejudices against Native Americans, blacks, and those whom he considered his political enemies. But in part because of his simple roots, he was the first president to stand up for working-class Americans and help the nation become more of a true democracy. Through his difficult and often frustrating efforts during eight years in office, he helped define what would become the modern presidency.

In 1837, Andrew Jackson returned home to his beloved plantation. "Strange as it may appear," he wrote not long after, "my nerves are as steady as they were forty years gone by." Eight years later, shortly before his death, seventy-eight-year-old Andrew Jackson begrudgingly agreed to sit for a daguerreotype portrait. He was frail and didn't feel well; and when he saw his image on a silver-coated copper plate, he said simply, "Humph! Looks like a monkey." But etched into the face that was captured for all time were the battle scars of frustration—the result of one of the most intense fights ever to occur between the Senate and the White House. His entire life had been an attempt to use power for big purposes. "It is possible that friends are overawed by power," he once wrote. "It cannot overawe me."

Veto of the Second National Bank, July 10, 1832:

It is to be regretted that the rich and powerful too often bend the acts of government to their selfish purposes. Distinctions in society will always exist under every just government. Equality of talents, of education, or of wealth can not be reproduced by human institutions . . . but when the laws undertake to add to these natural and just advantages artificial distinctions . . . to make the rich richer and the potent more powerful, the humble members of society . . . the farmers, mechanics and laborers . . . have a right to complain of the injustice of their Government.

Nullification Proclamation, December 10, 1832:

The ordinance is founded, not on the . . . right of resisting acts which are plainly unconstitutional and too oppressive to be endured, but on the strange position that any one State may not only declare an act of Congress void, but prohibit its execution. . . . If this doctrine had been established at an earlier day, the Union would have been dissolved in its infancy. . . . I consider, then, the power to annul a law of the United States, assumed by one State, incompatible with the existence of the Union, contradicted expressly by the letter of the Constitution, unauthorized by its spirit, inconsistent with every principle on which it was founded, and destructive of the great object for which it was formed.

Farewell Address, March 4, 1837:

My own race is nearly run; advanced age and failing health warn me that before long I must pass beyond the reach of human events. . . . I thank God that my life has been spent in a land of liberty and that He has given me a heart to love my country with the affection of a son.

By 1835 when this portrait was painted by Asher B. Durand the handsome young redhead commander with the stunning blue eyes was at the height of his presidential powers and had turned majestic.

"The people's inaugural" was followed by "the people's reception." Previously used for entertaining only the elite, the White House had never seen anything like this. Rich, poor, old, young, black, white, male, female—the mobs poured in, climbing over the furniture, ripping curtains, breaking glasses, muddying carpets. Men fought. Women fainted. The orderly ways of previous presidents were tossed to the winds as Jackson's army of fellow Americans joined raucously in celebration.

ANDREW JACKSON'S WHITE HOUSE

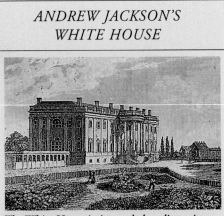

The White House in its newly bucolic setting, about 1830

Since the rebuilding of the burned-out White House after the War of 1812, the interior of the East Room had never been finished. It sat there—a huge, dark, vacant, unpainted barn. For Jackson, who would give two enormous public receptions each year, beautification and the lighting of this cavern became a top priority. In 1829 the great room's walls were finally covered with elegant, lemon-yellow wallpaper, the high windows hung with yellow-and-blue curtains, and the floor covered with complementary carpet. Overhead, suspended from the twenty-two-foot ceiling and nine feet above the floor, were three monumental crystal chandeliers, each lit by eighteen oil lamps with glass shades. The soot they left on the ceiling was whitewashed over each year thereafter. Jackson's White House also saw the arrival of running water. Up until then, buckets had to be drawn from a well and hauled to the kitchen, to the laundry, and upstairs to the bedrooms. A plan that had been conceived back in 1816 but shelved as too fanciful was now executed. Water would run underground from a spring, through hollowed-out logs, to a little reservoir on the White House grounds, from which it would be hand-pumped to key locations inside. A bathing room for men was installed as well, offering hot and cold tubs and a shower. The most visible innovation of the Jackson period was the elaborate landscaping of the White House grounds, with extensive ornamental plantings. One new addition didn't smell quite so sweet. In 1835 a present of a 1,400-pound cheddar cheese arrived drawn by twenty-four gray horses. For two years it sat in the entrance hall. Then, just before leaving for good, the General asked the public in to eat it. The eating took two hours, but it was said that the stain the gift left on the entrance floor lasted for years.

Ailing from dropsy, old age, and bad temper, seventy-eight-year-old Andrew Jackson rose from his sickbed at the Hermitage on April 15, 1845, dressed himself up, and posed for a daguerreotypist—probably the New York–based Edward Anthony—who tucked a supporting pillow behind the old man for at least one of the exposures (bottom). Late in life the far more celebrated New York photographer Mathew Brady claimed it was he who had sent an operator south, to have Jackson's image "taken barely in time to save his lineaments to posterity." Brady made sure to include a wet-plate copy of one of the pictures taken that day in his gallery of famous Americans (top). In a separate sitting, attributed to the Nashville daguerreotypist Daniel Adams, Jackson donned his glasses for the most stunning portrait of them all (far right). In one of his last letters, Old Hickory chronicled his final decline. "Gasping for breath . . . I am swollen from my legs to my abdomen & in bandages to my hips. My whole system a jelly. You can run a finger half a inch into the liver and the impression will last for minutes. . . . What my affliction will end in God only knows." By June 1845, the seventh president was dead.

Early in the Jackson era the White House still looked like a mistake, an enormous, unfinished edifice amid farmland. President Jefferson had ordered up the stone wall and the rail fence that hemmed in the house on five acres of the sixty available for grounds. A couple of shanties still remained from the reconstruction work after the War of 1812. To the far right is the Capitol, the only other monumental structure in the still primitive Washington City.

GROVER CLEVELAND

1885–1889 1893–1897

During his presidency Cleveland
was photographed numerous
times at his desk, where he could
usually be found, exhibiting his
frugal and obstinate nature.

"Ugly Honest"

Sworn into office on March 4, 1885, Stephen Grover Cleveland was the first Democrat to become president in twenty-four years. To many he seemed like a new Andrew Jackson; he had the same toughness and incorruptibility, and the same courage to stand up to any obstacle. And as with Jackson, Cleveland's power struggle as president would be with the Senate. His weapon was his enormous, stubborn integrity, a quality that was instilled in him as a youth.

"I remember well my early days," Cleveland once wrote. "I have always felt that my training as a minister's son has been more valuable to me than any other incident of my life." Reared in the strictest form of Presbyterianism, Cleveland spent most of his life laboring in obscurity, holding down low-level political offices in Buffalo, New York. He was a man of the people, whose passion for food and beer turned him over time into a 200-pound powerhouse. And as a loyal and hardworking Democrat, he became known for his high ethical standards.

"A Democratic thief is as bad as a Republican thief," he once said as he attempted to describe himself. "I am a sound, plain, uncomplaining Democrat."

While assistant district attorney and while sheriff of Erie County, one of his nicknames was "Ugly Honest," and by the 1880s his popularity had become contagious. He was elected Buffalo's mayor, then New York's governor. And just a year after that, in 1884, the forty-seven-year-old bachelor was running for president.

But his reputation was challenged during the campaign, when he was

Plenty of prodigious eating and beer drinking and little exercise transformed the young Cleveland, shown in the rare 1864 photograph at the left, into the bulky President at the right. Although he did not like having his size referred to by the press, Cleveland didn't mind family members calling him "Uncle Jumbo," after P. T. Barnum's famous elephant.

accused in the press of consorting with prostitutes. "I am shocked and dumbfounded by the newspapers," Cleveland wrote to a friend. "I have never seen a woman whom I have had any reason to suspect was in any way bad. I am at a loss to know how such wicked lies can be invented."

The most damning attack came in a Buffalo newspaper, in which Cleveland was accused of having fathered a child in the 1870s and having abandoned both mother and son. Throughout the uproar, Cleveland refused to deny paternity, even though it was rumored that he was actually covering up for the real father, a married friend. Cleveland's extraordinary dignity under fire eventually put an end to the ridicule he suffered. But the incident changed him. Though he won the election in November, he arrived in Washington feeling bitter not only toward the press but also toward the presidency itself.

"I look upon the four years to come," he wrote, "as a dreadful self-inflicted penance for the good of my country."

Cleveland began his presidency determined to clean house and to reward deserving Democrats with jobs. What he hadn't counted on was the depth of subordination to Congress to which the presidency had fallen over the two decades since Abraham Lincoln. As he began suspending government bureaucrats and appointing new public officials, the Senate simply refused to confirm them. Instead, they asked to see Cleveland's confidential files pertaining to his suspensions. A ferocious power struggle had begun.

"It was perfectly apparent that the issue was between the President and the Senate," Cleveland later wrote in a book on the subject. "The question was whether or not the Executive was invested with the power to suspend officials without interference."

The Senate had underestimated Grover Cleveland. Asserting an early form of what would become known as "executive privilege," the President refused to comply with the Senate's requests. "These suspensions are my executive acts," he wrote, "based upon considerations addressed to me alone. I am not responsible to the Senate, and I am unwilling to submit my actions to them for judgement." The American public, long starved for leadership, voiced its approval of Cleveland's strong stance. And intimidated by the outpouring of public approval, the Senate realized it had met its match. Cleveland's appointments were confirmed. And just one year later, the law that had curtailed presidential appointment power, the Tenure of Office Act of 1867, was stricken from the books. Cleveland later summed up his extraordinary victory: "The President became again the independent agent of the people, invested with powers not to be surrendered but used."

In the White House, Grover Cleveland became one of the hardest-working presidents ever, doing his own paperwork and routinely working past midnight, often until two or three in the morning. He paid his own expenses, dispensed with luxuries such as the presidential yacht, cussed openly, and bemoaned the fancy White House cooking. "I must go to dinner," he wrote one evening in disgust, "and I wish it was to eat a pickled herring, Swiss cheese and a chop instead of the French stuff I shall find."

For the rest of his term in office, Cleveland continued to use his powers liberally. Andrew Jackson had been criticized for his unprecedented twelve vetoes; Cleveland used the veto nearly six hundred times. But all too often the pieces of legislation he vetoed were bills that were popular with the people, and gradually he lost their support. In 1888 he failed in his bid for reelection, losing to the Republican Civil War hero Benjamin Harrison.

At first Cleveland claimed to be relieved that he had lost. "The question 'What shall be done with ex-Presidents?' is not laid to rest," he joked. "I sometimes think 'take them out and shoot them' is worthy of attention." But Cleveland wasn't ready to retire, and just four years later the Democratic Party convinced him to run again. Winning the election in November, he became the only president ever elected to nonconsecutive terms.

Just two months after Grover Cleveland's second inaugural, the stock market crashed, sending the country into the worst depression ever felt to that time. At the height of the nation's financial emergency, Cleveland faced a personal crisis that would undermine his strength for the remainder of his second term. For years he had been a heavy smoker. Now he was diagnosed with a malignant tumor of the mouth.

"Whatever developed found its opportunity in the weakened walls of my constitution," he wrote. "I have learned how weak the strongest man is."

Lest news of the President's plight lead to new waves of financial panic, Cleveland traveled to New York City, purportedly to begin his summer

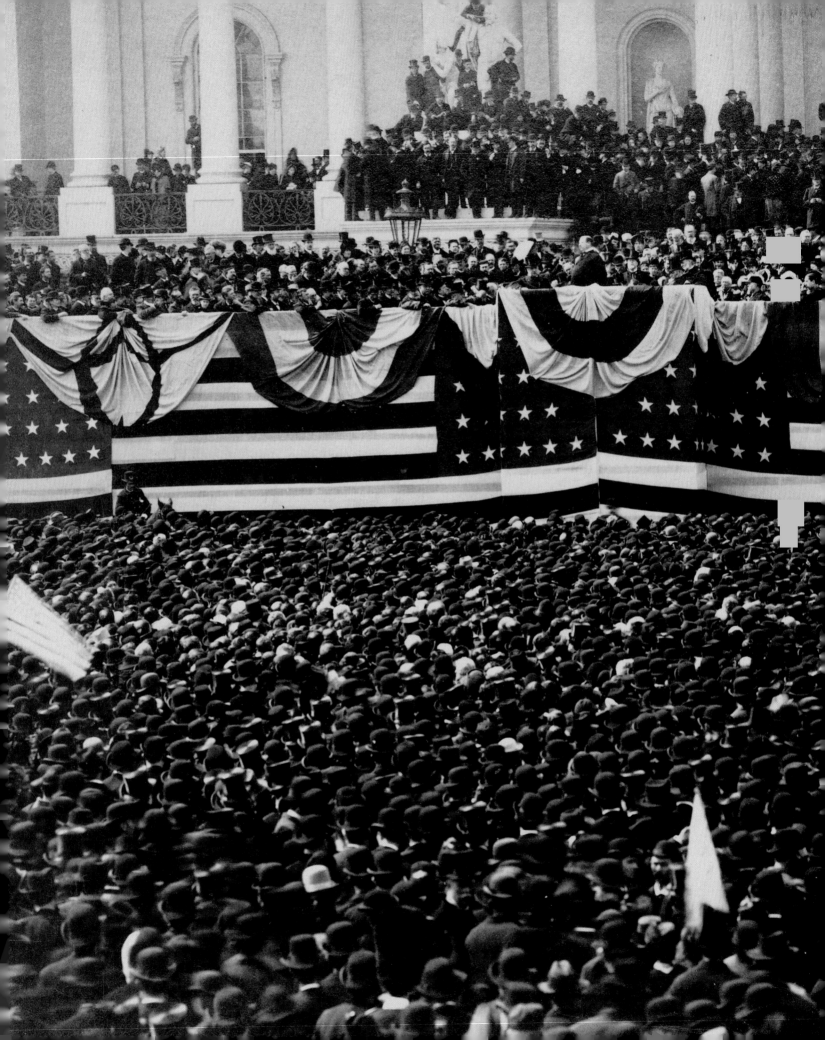

vacation. Instead, he was taken aboard a friend's yacht on the East River, where a team of five doctors and a dentist awaited him. The following day, out at sea, he was strapped to a chair against the mast, anaesthetized with nitrous oxide and ether, and then was operated on for forty-one minutes. His left upper jaw was entirely removed and a large sarcoma successfully extracted. The level of secrecy was so intense, the incident would not be known publicly until 1917.

Cleveland spent the summer resting on Cape Cod, at his summer home, Gray Gables, training himself to talk naturally with the aid of a rubber jaw. But the episode took its toll. He lost sixty pounds, his hearing was affected, and he became increasingly irritable and unwilling to compromise. The remainder of his second term was largely unsuccessful.

Cleveland managed to stretch the powers of the presidency one last time, though in a manner that would damage his reputation. It happened when workers at the Pullman Car Company went on strike the next summer, leading to outbreaks of violence in the city of Chicago. Claiming he had a presidential right to intervene, despite the direct objections of Illinois's governor, Cleveland sent in armed federal troops to assume police powers. He became the first president to assert that for the sake of the national economy, the president had the right to forcibly intervene in a labor dispute.

Cleveland's actions earned him the title of "dictator" and cost him the support of the working classes. When a band of unemployed men known as Coxey's Army became one of the earliest groups to march on Washington, a surly and unresponsive President Cleveland ordered the national guard to disperse them. He had forgotten what he understood so clearly six years earlier when he had written, "I knew that our chief executive office, if not carefully guarded, might drift, little by little, away from the people to whom it belonged." With his popularity plummeting, Cleveland ordered the White House gates to be kept locked. His administration was now largely closed off to both the public and the press. In the midterm elections of 1894, the year that Cleveland called his "year of troubles," his party lost 113 seats in Congress. "I have never been so depressed as now," Cleveland wrote.

When the Western populist William Jennings Bryant became the Democrat nominee for president in 1896, an irritable President Cleveland refused to lend his support. And with the Democratic Party hopelessly split, Republican William McKinley went on to win the election.

"I am not the sort of man people want to hear in these days," Cleveland wrote. "My beliefs and opinions are unsuited for the times."

For more than a decade he had been the dominant figure in U.S. politics. But his declining health and mounting inflexibility had ultimately undermined his ability to wield power. His greatest contribution had come early on, in his struggle with the Senate over executive privilege. By his insistence on his right to appoint the principal officers of government, Cleveland had recaptured a Constitutional power almost lost to the presidency.

"The Presidency is the repository of the people's power," he wrote. "The duty is only performed when the full exercise of the powers is insisted on."

Cleveland's inauguration—the moment of glory for the Democratic Party of 1885

Frances Folsom Cleveland

Cleveland knew Frances Folsom well; after her father died, when she was twelve, he had watched her grow up as his ward. But now, suddenly, she was more than that to him. Bright, funny, unaffected, and pretty, the twenty-one-year-old had just graduated from Wells College when the forty-nine-year-old bachelor asked her in a letter to marry him. When she made it known to the President that her answer was yes, it was decided the unlikely romance would be kept quiet while Frances and her mother went on a nine-month tour of Europe. The engagement was formally announced to the country on May 28, 1886, and five days later the marriage ceremony took place in the Blue Room. "The affair will be extremely plain and quiet," the President had decided, "with nobody but the members of the Cabinet and their wives, a very few members of the families, and one or two friends on each side perhaps—not more than twenty-five in all." The bride wore a low-necked, corded satin gown so stiff and molded it could stand up without anyone in it. There were no attendants. Cleveland had ordered many of the flowers in the conservatory forced into bloom, and the Blue Room as well as its chandelier was ablaze with bright blossoms. John Philip Sousa directed the Marine band in the wedding march, and at precisely 7:00 P.M. down the grand staircase came the bride and groom. After vows had been exchanged there was dancing in the East Room, followed by a wedding banquet in the State Dining Room. The table was decorated with a large sailing ship fashioned out of flowers and named The Hymen after the Greek god of marriage. The couple honeymooned at a mountain resort in western Maryland before Cleveland rushed back to his beloved desk.

New Year's Day at the White House, 1889 (right). Following a custom going back to the earliest days of the presidency, Grover Cleveland always held a major public reception on this day. Two months later, he would turn the house over to Benjamin Harrison and retire to private life. Whether it was New York City after his first term, or Princeton after his second (below), Cleveland's favorite refuge was always his private library.

An avid duck hunter all his life, Cleveland didn't like to be bothered with presidential cares on his hunting and fishing trips. "During my vacation," he wrote, "I am such a vagabond and lazy good-for-nothing, that I find any mental exercise a great effort."

On a camping trip in South Carolina with some Navy buddies nine months after his second term had ended, Cleveland sits just to the left of the stacked rifles. Stories were told of piles of empty whiskey bottles left behind when camps like this one were broken.

In retirement, Grover and Frances Cleveland pose with their four living children (right) having recently suffered the death of their oldest daughter, Ruth. At left is Esther, the only president's child ever to be born in the White House. Next, is the youngest, little Francis. Marion and Richard sit at the ex-President's right. Five years after Cleveland's death in 1908 at age seventy-one, Grover's "Frank," one of the most popular first ladies, married a Princeton University professor and lived happily into her eighties.

A single greenhouse was built on the west terrace in 1857, and then, over the years, many more were added, providing fresh flowers and jungle solitude for eleven presidents. The elaborate flower displays for Grover Cleveland's wedding in 1886 were products of these lush conservatories, which were demolished in the extensive renovation of 1902.

THEODORE ROOSEVELT

1901–1907

"Rough Rider"

Theodore Roosevelt (top) was a sickly child, wracked with asthma, headaches, and bouts of vomiting. Nearsightedness made him a stumbly, timid bookworm. But his loving, demanding father (above) would not accept such a son and forced him to develop his body. As an adult, Theodore was driven by the memory of his father, who died at age forty-six. "Every event in my life is tied up with him," he once said. "I almost feel as if he were present with me."

Theodore Roosevelt saw himself as a twentieth-century gladiator. Infatuated with his own strength and power, he once wrote, "No individual ever led a really worthy life unless he . . . possessed power. . . . The timid man, the lazy man . . . has lost the great fighting virtues."

The secret of Roosevelt's obsession with power lay in his sickly beginnings and his struggle to live up to the expectations of his demanding father. Raised in the Civil War era in one of the most socially prominent families in New York, he was severely nearsighted and so racked with asthma he could barely breathe. His father once told him, "Theodore, you have the mind, but you do not have the body. You must make your body." So Roosevelt began compulsively lifting weights. "I was a sickly boy, nervous and timid," he later wrote. "I had to train myself painfully and laboriously."

At sixteen he went off to Harvard. As he had been educated by private tutors, college was Roosevelt's first taste of independence, and he flourished. But in his sophomore year, his father died of stomach cancer. As the young man grieved, a new aggressiveness emerged. One day, irritated by a neighbor's dog, he pulled out his pistol and shot the animal dead. He began to ride his horse so hard he all but ruined it. And on outdoor expeditions he would drive himself to exhaustion, hiking thirty miles a day, just as his father had once done. "Oh how little worthy I am of such a father," he wrote in his diary. "I feel such a hopeless sense of inferiority to him."

Only when he married a young woman named Alice Lee was Theodore once again able to take pleasure in life. "She is so marvelously sweet, and pure and loveable and pretty," he wrote, "that I seem to love her more and more every time I see her."

But on February 12, 1884, the day after Alice gave birth to a baby girl, Roosevelt's life was shattered again. First his mother died of typhoid fever. Then within hours, twenty-two-year-old Alice also died—of childbirth complications and previously undetected Bright's disease. In his grief Roosevelt's aggressiveness went out of control. He tore every picture of Alice out of his scrapbooks and burned all her letters. And he never again mentioned his wife's name. "When my heart's dearest died," he wrote in his last reference to her, "the light went out from my life forever."

Leaving his infant daughter in the care of his sister, he headed west for the Bad Lands of Dakota to become a cattle rancher. "I owe more than I can ever express to the West," he later wrote. "I herded my own cattle, . . . killed my own food . . . shot bears, captured horse thieves. . . . No one . . . can understand the keen delight of lonely lands."

Scenes like this one in New Castle, Wyoming, became etched into the national fabric—the little man in his well-tailored suit dancing about on the speakers' platform, his tenor voice spinning higher and higher as he crowed about life, about ideals, about America. Whether exhorting his children or his people, Roosevelt's message was the same: "The joy of living is his who has the heart to demand it. Life is a great adventure, and I want to say to you, accept it in such a spirit."

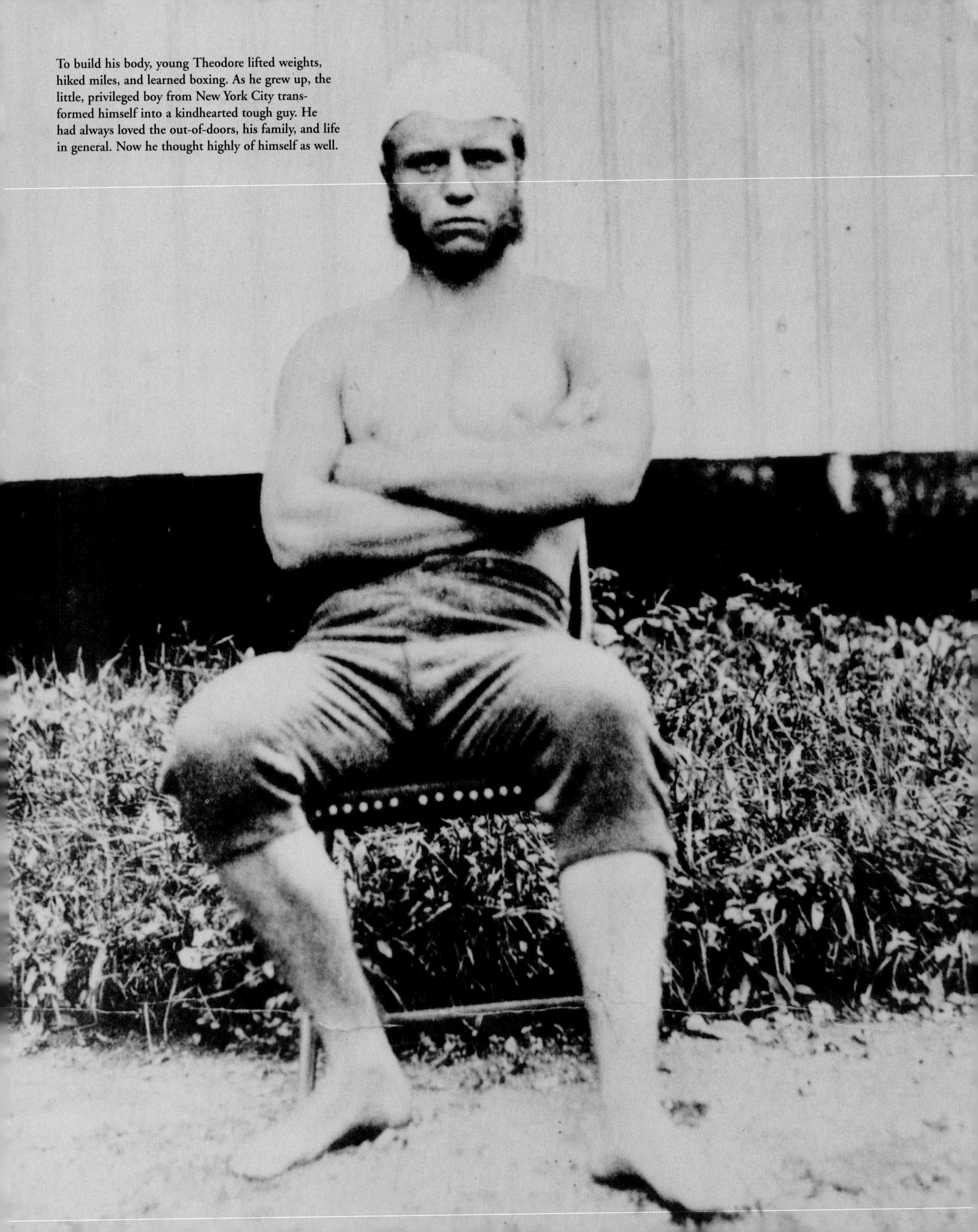

To build his body, young Theodore lifted weights, hiked miles, and learned boxing. As he grew up, the little, privileged boy from New York City transformed himself into a kindhearted tough guy. He had always loved the out-of-doors, his family, and life in general. Now he thought highly of himself as well.

Roosevelt let solitude and open spaces and intense physical labor heal his broken heart. But more important, he taught himself how to channel his aggression into a new form of energy with a purpose. "The only thing . . . to do is treat the past as past," he said. "To dwell on it, and above all to keep talking of it with anyone, would be both weak and morbid."

In 1885, on a trip back east, Roosevelt renewed an acquaintance with childhood playmate Edith Carow. The following year they were quietly married and moved into Sagamore Hill, the Long Island mansion that had been designed for Roosevelt's first wife. Here they raised not only little Alice, but eventually five more children as well. Sagamore Hill was Roosevelt's private retreat from the world and became a symbol of the man himself. Edith had little influence on the way it was decorated, and it came to look more like a hunting lodge than a home. Here, above his desk, between portraits of Lincoln and Grant, Roosevelt hung a painting of his revered father. Still trying to live up to him, Roosevelt insisted that his own children stay active and physically fit. "I would rather one of them should die," he proclaimed, "than have them grow up weaklings."

Over the next decade Roosevelt climbed his way up a spiraling series of political appointments. He was civil service commissioner under two presidents; then police commissioner of New York City; then assistant secretary of the Navy under President William McKinley. And when war with Spain erupted in 1898, he shipped off for Cuba as a lieutenant colonel in the Army. It was his chance finally to outdo his father, who in the Civil War, at the request of his wife, had reluctantly hired a substitute to fight in his place. "I did not intend to hire someone else to do my shooting for me," Theodore wrote. "I would have turned from my wife's deathbed to have answered that call."

In Cuba he fought alongside his own special regiment, which became known as the Rough Riders. And all his deep-seated aggressiveness finally had an outlet. Glorying in face-to-face combat, Roosevelt bragged to a friend, "I killed a Spaniard with my own hand, like a jack-rabbit."

His soldiers returned victorious and Roosevelt became an instant war hero. From there he experienced a meteoric rise to power. He easily won the governorship of New York. And in 1900 the Republican Party chose him to run as the vice presidential candidate alongside McKinley. The new century began with their decisive victory. But just six months into his term of office, Roosevelt received word of McKinley's assassination. At forty-two, he would be the youngest man ever to become president. "It is a dreadful thing to come into the presidency this way," he wrote. And then in a letter to his sister, he added, "I feel as if father's hand were on my shoulder."

Though he had by now far surpassed the achievements of his father, Roosevelt kept pushing himself, and in so doing he began transforming the office of the presidency. Unlike Grover Cleveland, he embraced the press, establishing the first official White House press room. He became the first president to exploit the brand-new electronic medium, the wire services, making the absolute most he could of it. And he set out to be a great national source of entertainment, making his family into a soap opera for the time and extending the presidency in so doing. He happily allowed his very active bunch of young boys and their adventures in the White House to be publicized. The time they rode their pony up to the living quarters on the second floor became a national event. And when he wanted the public's support, he did what few presidents before him had ever done—he went out and asked

Getting ready to go west and assume the life of a rancher, Theodore outfitted himself with fancy clothes, suitable for studio portraits but not for working "under the scorching mid-summer sun" or "through blinding blizzards."

Returning east, Roosevelt threw himself into government. As police commissioner of New York City, he wandered the neighborhoods incognito to uncover below-standard living conditions. "Remember," he cautioned, "do not hit at all if it can be avoided; but never hit softly."

When war with Spain flared up in Cuba, Roosevelt formed the Rough Riders. Though many were from Ivy League backgrounds like his own, "the majority of the men were Southwesterners," he wrote, who "had the cool resolute fighting temper."

Alice Lee Roosevelt

At Harvard, filling a void left by his father's early death from cancer, Theodore fell madly in love with a beautiful seventeen-year-old named Alice Lee. At first she tried to keep her distance from this wheezing asthmatic with thick glasses and a funny, high voice who smelled of chemicals from his taxidermy projects and hopped when he danced. But Roosevelt was persistent. "I cannot take my eyes off her," he wrote in his diary. "She is so pure and holy that it seems almost profanation to touch her; and yet when we are alone I cannot bear her to be a minute out of my arms." Finally she gave in. "After much pleading my own sweet, pretty darling consented to be my wife," he wrote. "The aim of my whole life will be to make her happy." Their life together lasted three years. Hours after giving birth to her first child, Alice died of Bright's disease. With little interest in ever courting again, three years later Theodore chose to marry a childhood friend, freckle-faced, red-haired Edith Carow, the young lady those close to him thought would be his wife before he met Alice and who was already practically a member of the family. Edith would bear him five children and allow him to forget.

Edith Carow Roosevelt

for it. "I don't think any President ever enjoyed himself more than I did," he said.

With the public's support, Roosevelt began redefining executive power, claiming presidential authorities not specified in the Constitution. Going far beyond Andrew Jackson or Grover Cleveland, he insisted that a president could do anything he wanted for the good of the people, except what the law specifically prohibited. "Under this interpretation of executive power I did and caused to be done many things not previously done by the President," he wrote. "I did not care a rap for the mere form and show of power; I cared immensely for the use that could be made of the substance."

Roosevelt put to use every power he could marshal toward a series of causes. As one of the country's earliest conservationists, he had a passion to preserve the American wilderness. To do so, he invoked a wartime power—the executive order. By it he forcibly acquired vast parcels of land from private hands. Then, cajoling Congress into creating the Forest Service, he doubled the number of the country's national parks and reserves.

He also used the presidential power of persuasion, settling a volatile coal strike by actually becoming part of the mediation. He backed labor unions when he found them more willing to compromise in a crisis than the company owners. And in an age when a few rich men controlled much of the nation's wealth through monopolies, Roosevelt's regulatory efforts designed to make the trusts behave better made him a hero with middle-class America.

Colonel Roosevelt (center) leads his victorious Rough Riders on their return to U.S. soil at Montauk Point, New York. The four months of training and fighting in Cuba formed the high point of Roosevelt's life and helped propel him into the White House.

The gabled mansion called Sagamore Hill in Oyster Bay, New York, became the site of an idyllic childhood for Theodore's ever-growing family. "They often went barefoot," he wrote. "They swam, they tramped, they boated, they coasted and skated in winter, they were intimate friends with the cows."

Theodore Roosevelt talks of life and joy and hope and death:

We, here in America, hold in our hands the hope of the world, the fate of the coming years; and shame and disgrace will be ours if in our eyes the light of high resolve is dimmed, if we trail in the dust the golden hopes of men. If on this new continent we merely build another country of great but unjustly divided material prosperity, we shall have done nothing; and we shall do as little if we merely set the greed of envy against the greed of arrogance, and thereby destroy the material well-being of all of us.

Only those are fit to live who do not fear to die; and none are fit to die who have shrunk from the joy of life and the duty of life. Both life and death are parts of the same Great Adventure. Never yet was worthy adventure worthily carried through by the man who put his personal safety first. Never yet was a country worth living in unless its sons and daughters were of that stern stuff which bade them die for it at need. . . . The man who is not willing to die, and the woman who is not willing to send her man to die, in a war for a great cause, are not worthy to live.

With all my heart I believe in the joy of living; but those who achieve it do not seek it as an end in itself, but as a seized and prized incident of hard work well done and of risk and danger never wantonly courted, but never shirked when duty commands that they be faced.

It makes small odds to any of us after we are dead whether the next generation forgets us. It seems to me the only important thing is to be able to feel, when our time comes to go out into the blackness, that those survivors who care for us and to whom it will be a pleasure to think well of us when we are gone, shall have that pleasure.

Splendor in the East Room—
a Theodore Roosevelt dinner
party. At right, outside the
Roosevelt White House, happy
citizens on Easter Day.

THEODORE ROOSEVELT'S WHITE HOUSE

Roosevelt's 1902 remodeling of the White House included the construction of a new West Wing, which meant tearing down the maze of greenhouses attached to the mansion, including the sprawling steam-heated conservatory shown here.

No matter how large it loomed, the White House was just too small for the twentieth century and especially for the Roosevelt family with its six children. In 1902 the Roosevelts moved out, and for six months the President's New York architect, Charles F. McKim, had his way. His charge was to modernize the old building and to make any necessary changes so that it never again would have to be altered. McKim turned the whole second floor of the old building into family living quarters, moved the offices to a new wing to the east, and enlarged the space for state functions on the first floor by adding a new West Wing. Although Edith Roosevelt insisted on holding on to some of the old furnishings, especially the Lincoln bed, most of them were put out to auction by McKim and simple, modern substitutes took their place. The White House of today had been conceived and shaped, even though future restorations would leave little of McKim's actual handiwork behind.

The East Room as it looked during Theodore Roosevelt's presidency, after the McKim renovation.

Realizing that the president had a very limited role in legislation, and overstepped it at his own peril, Roosevelt knew better than to get into a dog-fight with Congress. So he sought to make moves that were outside the congressional realm. His bold maneuvering in Central America to create the Panama Canal was classic Roosevelt. First he sent in his Navy to prop up a revolution, then did an end run around both Congress and Bogotá to get what he wanted: the Panama Canal. "I do not think the Bogotá lot of jack-rabbits should be allowed to bar one of the future highways of civilization!" he boasted. "[So] I took the canal zone and let Congress debate, and while the debate [went] on the canal [did] also."

In 1905 Roosevelt won the Nobel Peace Prize for mediating the Russo-Japanese War. But he regretted that he presided over an era of peace, and tried to leave a military mark by doubling the size of the U.S. Navy. In 1907 he made a display of power no country believed possible: he sent the American fleet around the world. He considered it his last great accomplishment during his seven and a half years in the White House. "While President I have been President," he once said proudly. "I have used every ounce of power there was in the office."

Brandishing typical Roosevelt showmanship, the President takes the controls of a giant steamshovel used in the digging of the Panama Canal. The first sitting president ever to travel outside the country, he himself had become the symbol of United States policy abroad, this bundle of energy with the big head, thick pince-nez, tiny ears, blond mustache, and heavy neck, this little man who moved like a boxer and spoke like a poet (right).

Showing the tracks of horse-drawn carriages treading their way to Theodore Roosevelt's White House, a snowfall gives a striking aura to the presidential mansion.

Because it comes rarely, snow always causes excitement in Washington. Here, during Theodore Roosevelt's presidency, newsboys pelt each other with snowballs before the Capitol.

RICHARD M. NIXON

1969–1974

Abuse of Power

Young Nixon stands shoulder to shoulder with his father, Frank, who Richard admitted taught him to be competitive and combative. "I remember my old man," President Nixon said on his very last morning in the White House. "I think that they would have called him sort of a little man, common man. He didn't consider himself that way. You know what he was? He was a streetcar motorman first, and then he was a farmer, and then he had a lemon ranch. . . . And then he was a grocer. But he was a great man, because he did his job, and every job counts up to the hilt, regardless of what happens." At the same time Nixon spoke of his Quaker mother. "Nobody will ever write a book, probably, about my mother. Well, I guess all of you would say this about your mother —my mother was a saint."

I t's very difficult to psychoanalyze oneself," Richard Nixon once said. "Most people would give me rather low grades as far as 'charisma' and 'gregariousness' and all that sort of thing that the politician is supposed to have. . . . But the essence of every great leader I have known—and I'm not saying I'm great—he was a lonely man."

Richard Milhous Nixon was born in 1913 and grew up poor in the small town of Whittier, California. His mother was a well-educated Quaker, whom he called a saint. His father was uneducated, working many jobs, and had a reputation for starting arguments with just about everyone.

Picked on as a child, Nixon wasn't comfortable around anyone outside his own family. He once said he didn't like riding the school bus "because the other children didn't smell good." He grew angry and kept his feelings bottled inside. "If your anger is deep enough," he said, "you learn [to excel]." He became his grammar school's valedictorian. In high school he became an accomplished debater. In college, even though he was unathletic, he pushed himself hard. "I just wasn't about to be a quitter," he said.

Graduating third in his class at Duke Law School, he married a California schoolteacher and cheerleading coach, Thelma Ryan, who was known by her nickname, Pat. Then, in World War II, he served ably behind the lines in the South Pacific, rising to the rank of lieutenant commander.

After the war Nixon launched a campaign for Congress. Capitalizing on the increasing conservatism of postwar America, he became the junior congressman from California. He called it the beginning of a "noncontroversial" career, but that all changed when Nixon came to serve on the House Un-American Activities Committee and ruthlessly pursued the American diplomat Alger Hiss, a suspected Communist spy. Through hard work and perseverance, he successfully discredited Hiss, but in doing so, he became known as a mean-spirited fighter who would do anything to win.

In 1952, just two years after he was elected to the Senate, thirty-nine-year-old Nixon was approached by General Dwight Eisenhower to be his vice presidential running mate. During the campaign, the immensely popular Eisenhower stayed far above the political fray, leaving the mudslinging to Nixon, who was by now renowned for it. "You read about another bribe," Nixon blasted in one campaign appearance. "You read about another gangster getting favors from government. The people are sick and tired of it . . . of an administration which instead of cleaning up is covering up scandals!"

But then Nixon himself was accused of corruption—personally profiting from a secret fund subsidized by wealthy supporters. To save his polit-

An embattled President
Nixon is framed by a
White House window.

Baby Richard

Young violinist

Trying football

Navy officer

Candidate for Congress

ical career, he went on national television. "I know that you wonder whether . . . I am going to stay on the Republican ticket, or resign," Nixon said. "Let me say this. . . . I am not a quitter."

The appearance, later called the "Checkers" speech, after his dog, worked a public relations miracle and helped Nixon regain Eisenhower's enthusiastic endorsement. And the team went on to win the election easily.

In the vice presidency Nixon was given few responsibilities. But eight years later he emerged from Eisenhower's shadow and made his own bid for the high office. Running against the charismatic John Kennedy, Nixon lost. Then, two years later, he suffered a second defeat that was even more shattering—the race for governor of California. Suddenly not even his closest friends thought he had a political future.

"As I leave you," Nixon said to a gathering of the press in California, "I want you to know, just think how much you will be missing—you don't have Nixon to kick around anymore. Because, gentlemen, this is my last press conference."

But in 1968, in a classic political comeback, Richard Nixon was once again a candidate for president. Sloughing off his old identity as a red-baiting anticommunist, he was "the new Nixon," a pragmatic spokesman for what he called "The Silent Majority." He ran on a promise to end the war in Vietnam and to restore law and order to a badly divided country.

"You are voting to restore the respect for America," he said. "And I say to you, that in our administration the American flag will not be a doormat for anybody." Implicit in Nixon's campaign speeches was a profound distrust of the nation's youth, and especially of its antiwar activists.

The election was almost as close as it had been in 1960, but this time Nixon won against Minnesota Democrat Hubert Humphrey. And at his victory celebration in New York City, he was exultant. "Having lost a close one eight years ago," Nixon said, "I can say this: winning's a lot more fun!"

From the day he arrived in the White House, however, Nixon demonstrated how much of a loner he still was. He insisted on more privacy, more free time, and more of a hierarchy in his staff than had been characteristic of former presidents. He insisted on having two free days a week when people were kept away from him, something no president had demanded since Chester Arthur. Convinced that his capacity to wield power as president was linked to an ability to prevent information from leaking out, Nixon cast a cloak of secrecy around his presidential activities. Not even his staff knew exactly what he was working on. Operating secretly through his national

Campaigning for v. p.

Finally president

Making a point

Taking advice

Always wary

security advisor, Henry Kissinger, Nixon largely bypassed the State and Defense departments. Once, he pointed to the Oval Office and said, "There's the State Department."

"We were obsessed with secrecy. As a matter of fact, I was paranoiac or almost a basket case with regard to secrecy," he later admitted. "Unpredictability is the greatest asset or weapon that a leader can have. And unless he is unpredictable, he is going to find that he loses a great deal of his power."

His presidential style alienated many, but Nixon got results, compiling a distinguished record of domestic accomplishments. And he took rightful pride in his bold initiatives abroad. "I'm the President that opened relations with China after twenty-five years of no communication," he said. And as a proponent of détente he became the first president ever to visit the Soviet Union. It was Nixon who negotiated the first arms-control agreement with the Russians, a follow-up to Kennedy's earlier test-ban treaty.

But despite his best efforts, Nixon's impressive achievements were often overshadowed by his handling of the war in Vietnam. Believing that military pressure would speed up the peace process, Nixon ordered the secret bombing of Cambodia, then Laos. And when word of it leaked out, antiwar protests virtually caged the President inside the White House.

"We must realize that that is one of the necessary adjuncts of power," he said, "Those who have power are seldom popular."

From the nation's beginning, three great powers possessed by kings were deliberately withheld from the office of president: the power to declare war, the power of the purse, and the power of immunity from legislative oversight. Richard Nixon was beginning to invade each of these areas. His presidency was being called an "imperial presidency."

Despite his unpopularity in the press, Nixon successfully ran for a second term in 1972. But on the night of June 17, operatives of his "Committee to Re-elect the President" were arrested after breaking into the Democratic Party's national headquarters at the Watergate Hotel complex in Washington. Though Nixon denied any involvement with the affair, he secretly went to work on a cover-up.

For two years Nixon used his powers as president to try to derail a mounting Watergate investigation. On October 20, 1973, he fired the Senate's special prosecutor, Archibald Cox, and transferred the investigation to the Justice Department. Attorney General Elliot Richardson, who resigned in protest, wrote that "a government of laws was on the verge of becoming a government of one man." Unbeknownst still was the fact that the illegal conduct dated back as far as 1969, and included a series of break-ins, buggings, and political "dirty tricks," as well as hush money payments, falsification of documents, and the wrongful use of the IRA.

In July 1973, Congress had learned that tape recordings existed of Nixon's conversations in the Oval Office. The voice-activated recording system had been set in place by the President himself. Nixon immediately went on the offensive to prevent the release of the tapes, claiming executive privilege, much as Grover Cleveland had done eighty-seven years earlier when he refused to turn over his files to the Senate. But unlike Cleveland's files, Nixon's tapes were pertinent to a criminal investigation. And a year later, on July 24, 1974, the Supreme Court unanimously rejected Nixon's assertion of executive privilege.

The end then came quickly. On August 5, Nixon's tape recordings proved he had been part of an illegal cover-up, an attempt to obstruct justice by using the CIA to thwart an FBI investigation. There was only one thing he could do now to stop the process from hurtling toward impeachment. Nixon informed his chief of staff, Alexander Haig, of his decision: "I said to General Haig that I would resign, but it would be with dignity and with no rancor. And then I thought a minute and I said, 'Well Al, I really screwed it up, didn't I?' He didn't have to answer."

Nixon insisted on time alone to think, write, and map strategy. His secret, voice-activated recording system was installed in the Oval Office in February 1971, and later additional recorders were positioned in Nixon's private office in the Executive Office Building, as well as in the Cabinet Room and at Camp David. A recording made during a meeting on March 22, 1973 would become known as "the smoking gun": "I want you to stonewall it. Let them plead the Fifth Amendment, cover-up, or anything else, if it'll save . . . the plan. That's the whole point."

Nixon's expression in a crowd in November 1972 reflects his confidence in being elected to a second term. When the results were in a few days later, he had swept forty-nine states, losing only Massachusetts and the District of Columbia to Senator George McGovern.

On strolls like this one outside the White House, Nixon had time to consider his presidency, finally brought down by the abuse of power proved by his own tape recordings.

President Nixon, his wife Pat, and a friend celebrate Christmas on the snowy White House grounds.

Although the White House did not change structurally during Nixon's seven years in office, the old house again needed repairs, having been worn out by its million tourists and 40,000 invited guests each year. Under the leadership of Pat Nixon, who helped raise millions of dollars to buy antiques, the house's furnishings were made more reflective of White House history. Pat took the job of first lady seriously, one day shaking hands with 1,675 DAR members. In the East Room Nixon held Sunday morning worship, and on Washington's Birthday in 1970 the room was transformed into a theater, as the Broadway cast of *1776* put on the entire show for the President and his guests. Such gaiety would be in stark contrast to the grim cloud that would envelop the White House in the Watergate years.

For Nixon, one of his proudest moments came in June of 1971, when the father of the bride escorted his daughter Tricia on her wedding day. The groom was Edward Finch Cox. The event marked the eighth time a president's daughter had been married at the White House, and the first time that the ceremony was held in the Rose Garden.

"I don't know how I got myself together, but I did and went out and read the speech. That was the resignation speech of Thursday night."

Accused of abusing presidential power, Nixon was the only president ever to resign from office. Congress would go on in the wake of his disgrace to repeal numerous statutes that had increased presidential power since FDR, rationalizing its actions by what Richard Nixon had done.

"Al Haig sort of knocked on the door," Nixon remembered. "He brought one piece of paper—there was one line on it—he said, 'You know, we forgot to do this. Would you sign it now?' 'I hereby resign the Office of President of the United States.'"

Nixon rarely spoke about Watergate. "There is no way that you could apologize," he once insisted, "that is more eloquent, more decisive, more finite than resigning the Presidency of the United States." But for the rest of his life he never forgot how his allies had dropped away, leaving him alone at the end. "In politics friendships evaporate very quickly. That was an indication of how power goes away."

With the White House behind him and the steps to the helicopter waiting, Nixon holds his hand out to his successor as Pat kisses Betty Ford goodbye. The Nixons' two daughters, Tricia and Julie, stand just behind, alongside their husbands.

On August 8, 1974, at 9:01 P.M. Richard Nixon addressed the Nation, announcing his decision to resign the office of president of the United States.

Good evening: This is the thirty-seventh time I have spoken to you from this office, where so many decisions have been made that shaped the history of this Nation. Each time I have done so to discuss with you some matter that I believe affected the national interest.

In all of the decisions I have made in my public life, I have always tried to do what was best for the Nation. Throughout the long and difficult period of Watergate, I have felt it was my duty to persevere, to make every possible effort to complete the term of office to which you elected me.

In the past few days, however, it has become evident to me that I no longer have a strong enough political base in the Congress to justify continuing that effort. As long as there was such a base, I felt strongly that it was necessary to see the constitutional process through to its conclusion, that to do otherwise would be unfaithful to the spirit of that deliberately difficult process and a dangerously destabilizing precedent for the future.

But with the disappearance of that base, I now believe that the constitutional purpose has been served, and there is no longer a need for the process to be prolonged.

I would have preferred to carry through to the finish, whatever the personal agony it would have involved, and my family unanimously urged me to do so. But the interests of the Nation must always come before any personal considerations.

. . . I have never been a quitter. To leave office before my term is completed is abhorrent to every instinct in my body. But as President, I must put the interests of America first. America needs a full-time President and a full-time Congress, particularly at this time with problems we face at home and abroad.

To continue to fight through the months ahead for my personal vindication would almost totally absorb the time and attention of both the President and the Congress in a period when our entire focus should be on the great issues of peace abroad and prosperity without inflation at home.

Therefore, I shall resign the Presidency effective at noon tomorrow. Vice President Ford will be sworn in as President at that hour in this office. . . .

I regret deeply any injuries that may have been done in the course of the events that led to this decision. I would say only that if some of my judgments were wrong —and some were wrong—they were made in what I believed at the time to be the best interest of the Nation. . . .

To have served in this office is to have felt a very personal sense of kinship with each and every American. In leaving it, I do so with this prayer: May God's grace be with you in all the days ahead.

After Nixon's resignation and departure, his chair is removed from the Oval Office.

Presidents Bush, Reagan, Carter, Ford and Nixon gather at the dedication of the Reagan Library in November 1991. Despite the permanent stain of Watergate, Nixon had by this time emerged as a valuable elder statesman. When he died in April of 1994, these same men, along with President Clinton, gathered again to pay their last respects.

James Madison

James K. Polk

THE BALANCE OF POWER

CHAPTER TEN

Although the Constitution divides federal powers among the government's three branches, the tipping of the balance depends on the personality of the president and the nature of the times.

William Howard Taft

William Jefferson Clinton

While we tend to think of the president as standing at the head of the government, he is actually immersed in an elaborate balance of powers, in which he must continuously struggle to direct the course of the nation. Suspicion of executive power goes back to the American Revolution, fought in part as an assault on the executive power of the king. The Articles of Confederation, which united the thirteen states during the war, made no provision for an executive branch, placing all executive powers in the hands of a single-house Congress, represented, when Congress was out of session, by a Committee of States. But as James Madison and others learned while serving in this Congress, such an arrangement was entirely inadequate to effective governance. At the mercy of the states, often deadlocked or adrift, Congress sorely missed the leadership of a strong executive.

To the deepest minds of the era, such as John Adams's and James Madison's, abuse of power was not a capacity exclusive to executives. Human

George Washington saw himself as a patriot king whose job it was to transcend political faction. Though the balance broke down in his second term, in his farewell address Washington called for a national recommitment to balance and warned against the "baneful effects of the spirit of party."

The balance of power was sorely tested during the administration of Andrew Johnson, the first president ever to be impeached. Though the Senate failed to convict, this was the lowest ebb in the history of the presidency to that time, and it revealed an inherent weakness in balance-of-power politics, which James Madison himself had warned against.

nature itself was deeply flawed, perhaps most so when people were massed together in groups. "[Since] those charged with the public happiness, might betray their trust," lectured Madison to the Constitutional Convention in 1787, "an obvious precaution against this danger would be to divide the trust between different bodies of men who might watch and check each other." To Madison's mind the greatest danger for abuses lay not in the executive branch, but in the legislative branch of government. The executive, he expected, would be the weaker branch, if anything in need of constitutional strengthening.

Madison's system of separated but overlapping powers presumed a basic level of comity in government—a willingness by Congress and the president to cooperate in national policymaking. If there was a design flaw in the system, it was that an independent nominating process was lacking, leaving the choice of presidential candidates too much in the hands of the national leaders in Congress. But what Madison and the other framers could not foresee was the rise of political parties in the early nineteenth century, culminating in the creation of full-scale political mobilization. Though, by definition, parties institutionalized partisanship, ironically they also offered up a fresh path toward cooperation, forging new links between the president and his political colleagues in Congress. And by securing for the president a political base that was separate from Congress, they assured his independence and thus made way for his ascendancy. Andrew Jackson, for example, made brilliant use of his party to greatly expand presidential power. His censure by the Senate in 1834 was driven in part by a raging debate in Congress about the balance of power.

A devoted disciple of Andrew Jackson, James K. Polk sought new ways to bridge the gap between the White House and Capitol Hill, laboring to balance the factions within his own party by giving "equal and exact justice" to each sectional concern. By uniting his presidential program with that of his party in Congress, he found that he could still maintain effective executive leadership.

But the presidency, designed to hold the country together and to give energy and direction to the government, grew increasingly impotent in the years after Polk, even as a deeply divided Congress offered little leadership to offset it. By mid-century, political partisanship had reached an all-time high, both between the major parties and, more ominously, within them. The Congressional Compromise of 1850, endorsed by Millard Fillmore, was the last bipartisan effort to forestall the looming crisis over slavery. It was followed by the collapse of the Whig Party, and then by a mounting schism within the Democrats. The new Republican Party, which emerged in the North in the mid-1850s, was so thoroughly sectional it was incapable of reuniting a nation hurtling toward civil war.

In making use of what he referred to as "the war powers of the government," Abraham Lincoln assumed executive powers never before assumed by any president. His uncommon leadership during the national crisis of the Civil War temporarily shifted the balance of power to the presidency. But following Lincoln's assassination, a highly partisan Republican Congress revolted against the new president, Andrew Johnson, who shared none of its passionate commitment to civil rights in the South. Determined to get the president out of the way, Congress boxed him in with a new law curtailing his ability to dismiss cabinet members. When he broke this law by dismissing his secretary of war, the House voted articles of impeachment. Though a more measured Senate failed to convict Johnson, the damage to the presidency was done. The balance of power had shifted decisively back to Congress, where it remained for most of the rest of the century.

In at least one way, this shift was tragic. The emasculated presidency of the mid- to late-nineteenth century coincided with a period of vast and unregulated industrial growth. It was a time of booming fortunes for a few, and little or no protection for the many. With no strong executive to look out for the people's interest, American government did little more than put its imprimatur on the status quo.

Under the energetic and progressive presidencies of Theodore Roosevelt and Woodrow Wilson, the balance of power once again shifted. In the opinion of Roosevelt's immediate successor, William Howard Taft, it had shifted too far—endangering, among other things, the independence of the judiciary. In his presidency and in his scholarly writings, Taft tried to redress this balance. "There is no undefined residuum of power which [the president] can exercise because it seems to him in the public interest," Taft wrote. But the momentum was against him, moving instead toward an increasingly strong presidency, in a trajectory that would lead through Franklin Roosevelt all the way to Richard Nixon.

In one sense, the resurgence of Congressional power in the post-Nixon era was a restoration of Madisonian balance, a return to checks and balances after the abuses of the "imperial presidency." But in fact a new development was occurring as well, the dawning of the age of divided government. Historically, the president's party has usually also dominated Congress, allowing for cooperative ventures in the national interest. But from 1968 to the close of the century, the national government has been divided in all but six years, with at least one house of Congress held by the party in opposition to the president. The cause of this is ticket splitting—voters refusing to vote the straight party ticket. Americans seem to have decided that a divided government offers them a measure of protection against governmental rashness. A new check and balance has been added to the Madisonian system.

Divided government can be a mixed blessing. In highly partisan times, Congress often seeks to frustrate the president's initiatives, while the president routinely vetoes the initiatives of Congress. The result can be inability to act at all. And in recent years at least two more checks and balances have contributed to the increasing stalemate—a powerful media, which now serves as a veritable fourth branch of government, and the office of the independent counsel, which came to serve almost as a fifth. The Madisonian ideal of "bodies of men who might watch and check each other" degenerated into an interlocking system of mutual antagonisms. In a period of divisiveness unmatched since the Civil War, Congress and the president have come to extreme loggerheads. And in 1998, for only the second time in our history, the House of Representatives voted to impeach the sitting president, though the Senate, as in Andrew Johnson's case, refused to convict.

And so the checks and balances proliferate, yet without the civility that James Madison took for granted. But though the Madisonian system trembles under the strain, it is a system that has survived repeated crises in the past. It is a system that continues to call out for creative solutions to the challenge of leadership in the future.

In the heyday of American political parties, one of a president's key tasks was to divide the spoils of victory. But no sooner had James Garfield begun to consider his appointments than party leaders began to try to dictate his choices. By fighting successfully to stay in charge, Garfield helped redirect the balance of power in government.

In his 1885 book, *Congressional Government*, Woodrow Wilson pointed to what he called a "radical defect" in the Madisonian system—a balance of powers so extreme it deprived American government of an adequate decision-making authority. Wilson recommended the adoption of a British-style cabinet government, in which the president would function as a figurehead. Two decades later, however, Wilson made an about-face. The problem of leadership, he now argued, could be best solved by a vastly strengthened presidency. Five years later he went on to put his words into action when he himself was elected president.

JAMES MADISON

1809–1817

Creating the Balance

He was the towering intellect of the founding fathers, but from James Madison's earliest days he was prone to sickness and exhaustion. "[I had] a constitutional liability to sudden attacks, somewhat resembling epilepsy, and suspending the intellectual functions," he wrote. "[I did] not expect a long or healthy life." Unable because of poor health to serve in the army during the Revolutionary War, Madison turned instead to government service. In the Virginia Convention, and then in the Governor's Council, he was recognized for his intellectual qualities, and he soon was fast friends with the new governor, Thomas Jefferson. With Jefferson's support, Madison was elected to the Continental Congress, where his superb leadership skills were sorely needed in wartime.

Madison's four years in Philadelphia not only revealed him as America's most gifted young administrator, they also convinced him that America's government was deeply flawed. Lacking the power to tax or to compel compliance, the national government was insufficient for its basic tasks, leaving the Confederation at the mercy of the often selfish states. At the end of the war, Madison determined to help design a better system.

In the spring of 1786, he commenced an exhaustive study of the world's governments, both past and present, with Thomas Jefferson, now in France, sending him important books on the subject. By summer he had come to a striking conclusion: The chief flaw of both ancient and modern confederacies was a lack of sufficient central authority. Unless America could devise a stronger federal government, it would be doomed to failure like all the others.

It was this message that Madison took to Philadelphia in 1787 to a national convention called to discuss the problems of America's government. Here, fifty-five state delegates would decide the nation's future. "There never was an assembly of men," Madison wrote, "who were more pure in their motives, or more . . . devoted to the object committed to them."

All agreed that the old Articles of Confederation were not working. But what kind of system could be acceptable to all the states? "Each of the objects was pregnant with difficulties," Madison wrote. "The whole formed a task more difficult than can be conceived."

The Constitutional Convention was Madison's moment of special destiny, just as the Declaration of Independence had been Thomas Jefferson's. It was Madison who proposed the all-important Virginia Plan, outlining a tripartite government with separate legislative, executive, and judicial

Madison was in his twenties (above) when he contributed to the writing of Virginia's constitution. He had grown up at Montpelier where the enormous Virginia plantation of the Madison family met the wild Appalachian frontier. His playmates in his youth were largely the children of his father's slaves. He was educated at home by his parents and then in boarding school, and at eighteen he traveled north to attend the College of New Jersey, later named Princeton, where he acquired such an extreme thirst for knowledge, he actually damaged his health by studying too hard. Nevertheless, those learning years shaped his life. Madison was a meticulous scholar, and brought a precision and a wealth of knowledge to any task he undertook.

James Madison, ten years after his great service to the country in the Constitutional Convention of 1787

Dolley at thirty-six

Up until Mrs. Madison, nobody had conceived of a role for the first lady. Dolley created one without even knowing it. A Pennsylvania starchmaker's daughter, Dolley Payne had been married to John Todd, a Quaker lawyer who had died in the yellow fever epidemic of 1793. Four years later, the much sought-after widow decided "to give my hand to the man who of all others I most admire." As wife of Thomas Jefferson's secretary of state, Mrs. Madison filled in as a hostess for the widower president. Then when her adoring husband succeeded to the high office, she came into her own. Big and buxom, she dressed up in fancy clothes—bright-colored silks and satins, tiers of jewelry, and floods of fur. Dolley used turbans and feathers and wigs and she painted her face outrageously, slapping on a combination of rouge and "pearl" powder that made her glow. She ate with gusto (ice cream in a hot pastry shell was a favorite), gambled with abandon, sniffed snuff, and spiked her punch. And everyone loved her. Possessing not an ounce of pretense, the irrepressible hostess had the wonderful ability to put people at their ease as she offered her guests compliments, fascinating chatter, and good cheer. In creating a role other first ladies would come to emulate, she made her tiny, pinched, bookish recluse of a husband seem more human and approachable.

Dolley at eighty

branches, with the legislature divided into a House and Senate. "A government composed of extensive powers," he wrote, "should be well balanced."

Unlike others at the convention who feared creating a robust presidency, Madison supported a strong and independent executive. His elaborate system of checks and balances was to guard against tyranny in any one of the different branches. "The danger of undue power in the president . . . is not to me formidable," he wrote. "I see, and *politically feel,* that that will be the weak branch of the government." He later added, in explanation, "The legislative department alone has access to the pockets of the people."

The chief opponents of a strong presidency were the old-guard states' rights republicans, men like George Mason, Elbridge Gerry, and Edmund Randolph, all three of whom would ultimately refuse to sign the Constitution. It was they who argued vehemently for a broad presidential impeachment clause, to cover such offenses as "malpractice," "neglect of duty," and even "maladministration." James Madison rejected such grounds as "vague," saying they would make presidents far too vulnerable to the political whims of their enemies. Treason and bribery, according to Madison, should be the sole grounds for presidential impeachment. When George Mason insisted on adding "or other high crimes and misdemeanors," Madison once again objected, though this time unsuccessfully.

Throughout the debates James Madison took copious notes, staying up late each night to transcribe them from his shorthand. The extra effort "nearly killed" him, he later said, but he was determined to preserve a record of the making of the Constitution. "Nor was I unaware of the value of such a contribution," he wrote, "[to] the cause of liberty throughout the world."

Finally, on September 17, after four grueling months, the Constitution was signed by a majority of the delegates. "It is impossible to consider the degree of concord which ultimately prevailed as [anything] less than a miracle," Madison wrote. For his efforts in Philadelphia and during the process of ratification that followed, James Madison would be named "The Father of the Constitution."

During George Washington's presidency, Madison served in the new federal Congress, becoming among other things the sponsor of a draft of the

At the Constitutional Convention of 1787, in Philadelphia, George Washington, unanimously elected the convention's president, looms above some of the other fifty-four delegates, including his fellow Virginian James Madison, to his left. Originally the convention had aimed to revise the Articles of Confederation. It was Madison who argued for discarding them in favor of a whole new approach.

Bill of Rights. In 1797, three years after marrying the widow Dolley Payne, he retired from government to his father's Virginia plantation, Montpelier.

But during the presidency of John Adams, Madison was shocked out of retirement by what he perceived as an unconstitutional abuse of power. At issue were the Alien and Sedition Acts of Adams's administration, which curtailed the rights of foreigners and the press during a time of national crisis and which seemed to violate everything Madison stood for. "[The bill] is a monster that must forever disgrace its parents," he wrote. "It dispenses with trial by jury; it violates the judicial system . . . and it bestows upon the President despotic power. . . . Are such measures consistent with our constitutional principles?" Determined to rescue the government he had helped create, Madison urged Thomas Jefferson to run for the presidency. When Jefferson was elected in 1800, Madison accepted the position of his secretary of state. And when Jefferson left office eight years later, it was Madison's turn to assume the presidency and to try to demonstrate the proper balance and restraint.

Madison's presidency was dominated by a crisis with Great Britain, which for years had been grossly violating American shipping rights. It was a crisis that would challenge America's system of balanced powers.

In November 1811, Madison sent an ultimatum to Britain aboard the dispatch vessel the *Hornet*. When it returned five months later with no adequate reply to his warnings, Madison sent in a war message to Congress. "To have shrunk [from war]," Madison later wrote, "would have acknowledged . . . [that] the American people were not an independent people, but colonists and vassals." But as the War of 1812 commenced, Madison faced fierce opposition from the Federalists in Congress, who derided what they called "Mr. Madison's war." Massachusetts and Connecticut went so far as to refuse to furnish their required militia quotas. Once again it was a question of national leadership: Was the federal government strong enough to lead the nation in wartime? Rallying his allies in Congress, chief among them the speaker of the House, Henry Clay, Madison effectively put down the Federalist opposition. And with executive and legislative branches working together, Madison obtained what he needed to carry out the war.

A VITAL FRIENDSHIP

In many ways they appeared to be polar opposites—Jefferson so visionary and imaginative and impulsive and passionate, Madison so analytical and cautious and dispassionate and precise. Where Jefferson was colorful, Madison was self-effacing. Where Jefferson was warm and charismatic, Madison was coolheaded but socially inept. Even physically the two men seemed each other's converse—Jefferson was tall and robustly healthy, a lover of vigorous outdoor exercise; Madison was small-statured and often sickly, a pale, indoors sort of man. And where Jefferson always poured so much of himself into everything he did, Madison almost entirely submerged his private feelings. Yet they became the best of friends. Between 1780 and 1826 the two men exchanged more than 1,200 letters, often communicating in code during times of crisis. Possessing absolute trust in each other's confidence, they were so close they could freely criticize each other, though they always showed respect even when in the deepest disagreement. Madison regularly critiqued Jefferson's simplistic faith in "the people," reminding him of the potential tyranny of majorities. He had to convince his friend of the importance of the Constitution, and much later helped steer him away from some embarrassing political alignments. Jefferson regularly influenced Madison, too, as when he persuaded him of the need for a Bill of Rights. As the bolder of the pair, he sometimes had to prod Madison's caution, and he served as the political lightning rod for their mutual activities. And so it went, from collaboration to collaboration, from the Revolutionary period, to the age of Constitution building, to the rise of political partisanship, to each man's presidency, and beyond. "The mutual influence of these two mighty minds upon each other," wrote their contemporary John Adams, "is a phenomenon, like the invisible movements of the magnet. . . . The future historian may discover [here] the solution of much of our national history not otherwise easily accountable." At the end, Jefferson called Madison his "pillar of support through life," and Madison, in turn, summed up their extraordinary relationship this way: "For a period of fifty years . . . there has not been an interruption or a diminution of mutual confidence and cordial friendship, for a single moment in a single instance." Their partnership, forged during the formative years of the American republic, stands as the most important political friendship in American history.

Here stands the shell of the President's House after the British burned it during the War of 1812. Dolley Madison escaped just before the British troops arrived, after having saved a wagonload of the mansion's treasures, including Gilbert Stuart's huge portrait of George Washington. After fires were set throughout the house and in each window, "an instantaneous conflagration took place," wrote an eyewitness, "and the whole building was wrapt in flames." Not until the gutted mansion was rebuilt under President Monroe, and its scorched sandstone exterior was painted white, did the name White House take hold for good.

Madison worked as hard for the ratification of the new Constitution as he had to create it. The Federalist Papers, *which he coauthored with Alexander Hamilton and John Jay, were eighty-five essays written to newspapers in 1787–1788, designed to convince wavering delegates of the political soundness of the Constitution. Madison's ideas were at the heart of the entire collection. Writing at a ferocious pace, at a distance from the others, Madison said there was "seldom time for a perusal of the pieces by any but the writer before they were wanted at the press and sometimes hardly by the writer himself." Thomas Jefferson called the finished collection "the best commentary on the principles of government which has ever been written." Below are excerpts from Madison's* Federalist No. 51.

To the People of the State of New York.

To what expedient then shall we finally resort for maintaining in practice the necessary partition of power among the several departments, as laid down in the constitution? The only answer that can be given is, that as all these exterior provisions are found to be inadequate, the defect must be supplied, by so contriving the interior structure of the government, as that its several constituent parts may, by their mutual relations, be the means of keeping each other in their proper places. . . . It is evident that each department should have a will of its own; and consequently should be so constituted, that the members of each should have as little agency as possible in the appointment of the members of others. . . . Ambition must be made to counteract ambition. . . . What is government itself but the greatest of all reflections on human nature? If men were angels, no government would be necessary. If angels were to govern men, neither external nor internal controuls on government would be necessary. In framing a government which is to be administered by men over men, the great difficulty is this: You must first enable the government to controul the governed; and in the next place, oblige it to controul itself. . . . The constant aim is to divide and arrange the several offices in such a manner as that each may be a check on the other. . . . In republican government the legislative authority, necessarily, predominates. The remedy to this inconveniency is, to divide the legislative into different branches; and to render them by different modes of election, and different principles of action, as little connected with each other, as the nature of their common functions, and their common dependence on the society, will admit.

From the start, however, the war went wrong for the United States, with the sole exception of some naval victories along the Canada border. As the war progressed, things took a turn for the worse, and Britain prepared for an all-out assault. "The rage and jealousy produced by our little naval triumphs," Madison wrote, "account for the gigantic force she is bringing against us on the water."

On August 17, 1814, fifty British vessels, carrying a total of 4,000 troops, anchored just thirty-five miles from the city of Washington. Five days later, President Madison, after riding into the field to rally the militia, warned Dolley to begin preparations to flee. "[You] should be ready at a moment's warning [to leave Washington]," he dashed off, "[as] it might happen that they would reach the city with the intention to destroy it."

On August 24, a hastily assembled Washington military force met the British just outside the capital city, where they were routed at what became known as the Battle of Bladensburg. Poor generalship, military cowardice, and insubordination had undermined all Madison's efforts to defend the federal city. Once inside Washington, British soldiers set fire to the Capitol and other public buildings. Close to midnight they torched the president's mansion. From his retreat on horseback, during a night of darkness and then rain, Madison watched the rising embers of one of the worst humiliations in American history.

But then the tide of war began to turn. An American victory at Baltimore harbor revived the nation's confidence and gave the country a new anthem, "The Star Spangled Banner." And in early 1815 came a conclusive victory in New Orleans, by the Tennessee general Andrew Jackson. Almost simultaneously, a peace treaty was signed in Europe. Though it seemed in some ways to settle nothing, the treaty in fact represented an important U.S. breakthrough. By standing up to Great Britain, and simply by not losing, America had won, in effect, a second war of independence. "[It illustrates] the capacity and the destiny of the United States," Madison remarked, "to be a great, a flourishing, and a powerful nation." And as Madison was forever proud to point out, he had won the war without compromising Americans' civil liberties. Even his old adversary, John Adams, had to admire the accomplishment. "Not withstanding a thousand faults and blunders," Adams wrote, "his administration has acquired more glory and established more Union, than all three predecessors put together."

In 1817, just shy of his sixty-sixth birthday, Madison finished his term as president and returned with Dolley to Montpelier. The youngest of all the founding fathers, he would outlast them all, living on for twenty more years.

All his life he had been an advocate of what he called balance, even in his view of human nature. "As there is a degree of depravity in mankind," he once wrote, "which requires a certain degree of circumspection and distrust, so there are other qualities in human nature which justify a certain portion of esteem and confidence. Republican government presupposes the existence of these qualities in a higher degree than any other form."

An aging Madison was painted in the 1820s.
"Justice is the end of government," he once
wrote. "It ever has been, and ever will be pursued,
until it be obtained, or until liberty be lost in
the pursuit."

JAMES K. POLK

1845–1849

"Young Hickory"

James Knox Polk, the grandson of a blacksmith, grew up in rural Tennessee, where his father was a successful farmer and landowner. Thin and sickly as a boy, he was allowed to pursue an education instead of farming, and he went on to graduate with honors from the newly founded University of North Carolina. He practiced law in Tennessee, then turned his attention to politics. And in 1825, just a year after marrying fellow Tennessean Sarah Childress, Polk was elected to Congress. There, through the years of the Jackson White House, he established himself as a tireless party worker who was known for his amazing memory for faces. "I don't think I was ever introduced to a man," he once said, "and talked with him ten minutes, that I ever afterwards forgot him."

Dignified and courteous, though also opinionated and secretive, Polk rose to chairman of the important Ways and Means Committee and eventually to the job of Speaker of the House. Then, after helping Martin Van Buren win the presidency in 1836, he quit Congress to make a bid for Tennessee's governorship. Polk won the election, but two years later he stumbled, failing in his bid for reelection. And when in 1843 he lost again, his political career appeared to be over.

In 1844, Polk saw a new chance—to become Martin Van Buren's vice presidential running mate. But then an unexpected event occurred. Texas had recently applied to the United States for annexation, a cause popular among Democrats and among many Whigs as well. But as the presidential campaign got under way, key Southerners began to endorse annexation as a way to spread slavery. Overnight, the issue became highly charged in much of the North, and Van Buren decided to come out publicly against immediate action on the issue.

On May 10, 1844, Polk was summoned by seventy-seven-year-old Andrew Jackson to an emergency conference at his Tennessee estate, the Hermitage. At issue was the Democratic nomination itself. "General Jackson . . . speaks in terms of deep regret at the fatal error which Mr. Van Buren has committed," Polk wrote. "He thinks the candidate . . . should be an annexation man and reside in the Southwest; and he openly expresses (what I assure you I never for a moment contemplated) the opinion that I would be the most available man."

On the surface the idea of a Polk candidacy seemed a long shot, with

This Currier and Ives lithograph of Polk was made in the year he was elected president. On August 26, 1845, he made the first entry in a diary he would keep for the rest of his term, the most extensive personal record of any American president, except for that of the brilliantly perceptive John Quincy Adams. The diary had been provoked by a conversation Polk had with his secretary of state, the details of which he later wanted to remember. "It was this circumstance which first suggested to me the idea, if not the necessity, of keeping a journal or diary of events and transactions which might occur during my Presidency. I resolved to do so & accordingly procured a blank book for that purpose on the next day, in which I have every day since noted whatever occurred that I deemed of interest." Twenty-four more volumes, each containing from 100 to 250 closely written pages, followed.

In his diary, on February 14, 1849, President Polk recorded that he had "yielded to the request of an artist named Brady, of N.Y., by sitting for my Degueryotype likeness today."

Like his political sponsor Andrew Jackson, James Polk was a rough-hewn, Western figure with extraordinary drive and seriousness of purpose. Possessing a Calvinist, frontier personality, he was also narrow and rigid and often lacking in human kindness. He was a party politician with few outside interests, and he proved his political mettle in the campaign of 1844 by his defeat of the lustrous Henry Clay. "I am fully sensible that I came into the office," Polk wrote, "not only at an earlier period of life than any of my predecessors, but perhaps, with less of the public confidence in advance than any of them." Polk is shown here as painted by George Healey in 1846.

the party dominated by far greater names: James Buchanan of Pennsylvania, Lewis Cass of Michigan, John C. Calhoun of South Carolina, and the continuing front runner, Martin Van Buren himself. But Polk was interested. "The Texas question is the all absorbing one," he wrote. "I have no hesitation in declaring that I am in favour of . . . immediate . . . annexation."

But Polk was a pro-Texas man who could appeal to all Democratic factions, and in this his candidacy suggested a new kind of balance. Perceived as an organization man commited to party consensus, at the Democratic convention in Baltimore that month, he won an unexpected upset victory on the ninth ballot. He was dubbed "Young Hickory" after his mentor, Andrew Jackson. And in the national election, where he ran largely on the issue of Texas, he offered a sharp contrast to his Whig opponent, the legendary statesman Henry Clay.

At forty-nine, Polk became the youngest man ever to assume the presidency up to that time. Leading a diverse and volatile party that included jealous rivals for the high office, he made himself a balance wheel among the factions. "I [decided to] adhere sternly to my principles without identifying myself with any faction or clique," he wrote. "If we expected my administration to be successful . . . the whole Party must be united." Determined to exercise fairness to all sections of the country, Polk took care to balance his cabinet geographically. And in his presidential program he worked hard to balance local interests. Along with Northeastern Democrats, he supported an independent treasury; along with Southerners he worked for a lower tariff; and with Westerners he advocated lower prices on government land. Then there was the subject dearest to his heart: American expansionism and "manifest destiny." Polk was determined, here too, to carry on a balanced national program, dividing his efforts between the Northwest and the Southwest. His twin goals were the settlement of the Oregon boundary with Britain, and the acquisition of Mexican-owned California, a subject closely linked to the Texas issue.

In the Northwest, Polk boldly risked war with Britain to obtain what he wanted—a fixed U.S. boundary at the forty-ninth parallel, with the sole exception of Vancouver Island. Obtaining California, however, proved to be much more difficult, ultimately requiring a war with Mexico.

Just two days following Polk's inauguration, the Mexican envoy to the United States resigned in protest, citing Polk's support for the annexation of Texas. Fearing an armed invasion of Texas by Mexico, Polk dispatched General Zachary Taylor to the region, even though it had not yet been officially admitted to the Union.

At issue as well was Mexico's long-standing refusal to settle American claims against her. When the Mexican government rebuffed Polk's efforts to reopen diplomatic ties, the President moved toward a state of war. And when a Mexican attack failed to materialize, Polk finally decided he could wait for one no longer. On May 9, 1846, he informed his cabinet that he would commence the war himself. That very same evening Polk was spared the responsibility when word arrived that the Mexican army had finally attacked. "The commanding general of the Mexican forces . . . crossed the river, invaded our territory and commenced hostilities," Polk wrote. "Mexico . . . consummated her long course of outrage against our country by . . . shedding the blood of our citizens on our own soil." Congress promptly responded to Polk's May 11 war message and granted him the means necessary for a vigorous war against Mexico.

For a year and a half, Polk's armies bludgeoned Mexico into submission, while armed forces were also dispatched to seize California. "The . . . war with Mexico was . . . forced . . . upon us," Polk insisted. "Yet it was clear that . . . we would if practicable obtain California and such other portion of the Mexican territory as would be sufficient to indemnify our claimants and to defray the expenses of the war."

Driving himself relentlessly, and taking on the work of many of his cabinet members, Polk became the first president to remain all summer in the White House, refusing to take more than a few days of vacation. "No President who performs his duty conscientiously can have any leisure," he wrote in his diary. "If he entrusts the details and smaller matters to subordinates, constant errors will occur. I prefer to supervise the whole operations of Government myself." And though he hated interruptions, he opened his office doors every morning to those seeking jobs and other favors. "I[t] requires great patience and self command to repress the loathing I feel toward a hungry crowd of unworthy office-seekers who often crowd my office," he wrote privately. "[But] I cannot insult or be rude to my fellow citizens."

By September 1847, following General Winfield Scott's capture of Mexico City, the Mexican War was effectively over. Five months later, a peace treaty was delivered to Washington, and forwarded by Polk to the Senate for acceptance. "If the treaty is ratified," Polk wrote, "there will be added to the U.S. an immense empire, the value of which . . . years hence it would be difficult to calculate."

Eventually 1.2 million square miles were added to the United States under Polk, including all the territory stretching from New Mexico to California. Opponents stressed that these lands had been acquired by an "immoral war," and would lead to huge problems in the future involving the question of the spread of slavery. But Polk responded that he had won these lands through legitimate conquest, ratified by a treaty with Mexico that included the direct payment by the United States of $15 million. And to the end of his life he considered the acquisition of these territories his greatest achievement. "The acquisition of California and New Mexico," he wrote, "are results . . . of greater consequence . . . than any . . . since the adoption of the Constitution." In fact, Polk had accomplished almost all of his original goals: he had resolved the Oregon question, acquired California, lowered the tariff, and established an independent treasury. All told, it was a remarkable presidential record, and a balanced one.

By his final year in office the President was exhausted. For four years he had held together a remarkable coalition, but it was already beginning to unravel. With the volatile issue of slavery in the new territories heating up, an issue destined to lead to the Civil War, all Polk wanted was to turn over the office to another. He had pledged from the beginning that he would serve only one term, but even if he had wished to, he could not have run again. By incessant work, by an unwillingness to delegate, and by his refusal to rest, he had destroyed his health. "They have been four years of incessant labour and anxiety," he wrote. "I am heartily rejoiced that my term is so near its close."

But though he dreamed of a happy retirement in Tennessee with Sarah, it was not to be. On his return journey home, Polk became seriously ill. Just three months after leaving office, Young Hickory was dead.

A carte de visite, based on a retouched version of the daguerreotype on page 408, shows the eleventh president's distinctive deep-set eyes and long hair. He was an opinionated but principled man of the people, intensely committed to empire building. Through Polk's war with Mexico, the United States came to include not only all of California but also the area that now encompasses New Mexico, Arizona, Utah, and Nevada.

IN HIS OWN WORDS

The following are excerpts from Polk's presidential diary:

On the death of his sponsor, Andrew Jackson:
[24th October, 1845] Received today . . . a letter from Andrew Jackson written on 6th June . . . two days before his death, and the last letter he ever wrote. . . . It will be preserved as a highly prized memorial of the friendship of the dying patriot, a friendship which had never for a moment been broken, from my early youth until the day of his death.

On Secretary of State James Buchanan:
[17th February, 1846] Mr. Buchanan . . . has discovered that he can not control me in the dispensation of the public patronage. For several weeks past he has not been pleasant in his intercourse with me. . . . His melancholy and dissatisfied manner . . . is becoming exceedingly disagreeable to me.

[13th May, 1846] Mr. Buchanan said . . . if we intended to acquire California . . . he thought it almost certain . . . England . . . would join with Mexico in the war against us. . . . I told him I would meet the war which either England or France or all the Powers of Christendom might wage, and that I would stand and fight until the last among us fell in conflict.

On the Mexican War and the issue of slavery:
[9th August, 1846] Late in the evening of Saturday, the 8th, I learned that after an excited debate in the House a bill passed that body . . . with a mischievous and foolish amendment to the effect that no territory which might be acquired from Mexico should ever be a slave-holding country. What connection slavery had with making peace with Mexico it is difficult to conceive.

On the frustrations of being a war president:
[5th February, 1847] I am in the unenviable position of being held responsible for the conduct of the Mexican War, when I have no support either from Congress or from the two officers (Scott & Taylor) highest in command in the field.

[20th March, 1847] The truth is that the old army officers have become so in the habit of enjoying their ease, sitting in parlours and on carpeted floors, that most of them have no energy. . . . If I had a proper commander of the army, who would lay aside the technical rules of war to be found in books . . . one who would go light and move rapidly, I [have] no doubt Santa Anna and his whole army could be destroyed or captured in a short time.

On Zachary Taylor:
[21st November, 1846] It is perfectly manifest that Gen'l Taylor is very hostile to the administration and seeks a cause of quarrel with it. . . . He is evidently a weak man and has been made giddy with the idea of the Presidency. . . . He is a narrow-minded, bigotted person . . . and wholly unqualified for the command he holds.

[8th November, 1848] Information received by the telegraph . . . indicate the election of Gen'l Taylor as President of the U.S. Should this be so, it is deeply to be regretted. . . . He is wholly unqualified for the station.

In this daguerreotype, taken on the south portico of the White House probably in 1849, President Polk and his wife Sarah, known as the "Spanish Donna," stand in the center. Just behind Polk is Thomas Hart Benton, and left of him is Polk's closest friend, the Postmaster General Cave Johnson. To the far left, with a smudged face, is the President's secretary of state, James Buchanan. Next to him is Buchanan's niece, Harriet Lane, and next to her is Polk's niece Joanna Rucker. The blurred figure to the right of Polk is Dolley Madison.

In 1848 Polk ordered an imposing statue of Thomas Jefferson to be moved from the Capitol rotunda and set up directly in front of the White House. An aggressive expansionist as well as a "man of the people," Polk saw himself as carrying on the Jeffersonian spirit. He was also a believer in public memorials; later that same year he himself would select the spot for the Washington Monument. Polk's Jefferson statue remained in its new location for twenty-seven years before being returned to the Capitol, the only monument to a president ever to stand outside the White House.

The daguerreotype above, of Polk and members of his cabinet by John Plumbe, Jr., is the first known photograph to be taken inside the White House. Standing are Cave Johnson, postmaster general, and George Bancroft, the Massachusetts historian whom Polk had made secretary of the navy. Seated, from the left, are John Y. Mason, attorney general; William L. Marcy, secretary of war; President Polk; and Robert J. Walker, secretary of the treasury. Below is Plumbe's view of a Washington, D.C., scene, taken about the same time. The Greek-style edifice is the Patent Office building, which today houses the National Portrait Gallery.

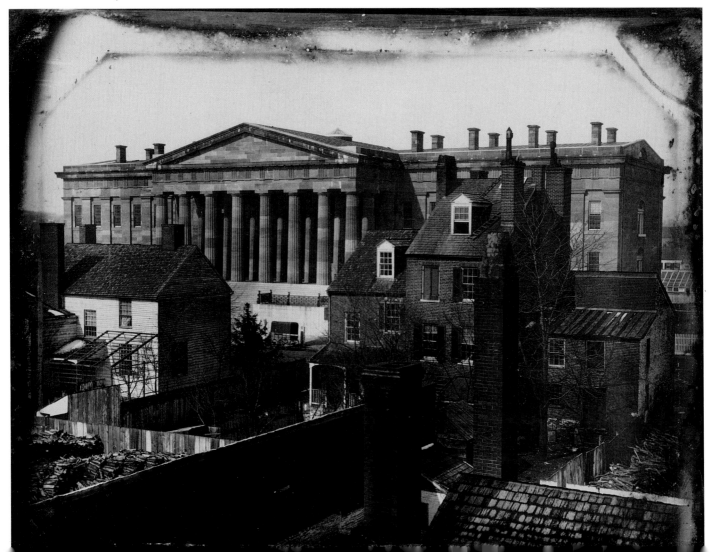

In perhaps the most revealing of all of Polk's photographic portraits, the President poses with his wife Sarah. They had met when she was a Tennessee teenager, the daughter of Major Joel Childress, a wealthy planter, tavern owner, and land speculator in Murfreesborough. Sarah loved stylish clothes, was bright and independent, and thrived in social situations. As First Lady, she banned hard liquor at her table but allowed White House guests to partake of wine.

In July 1847 the President visited Oaklands, the family home of John William Tudor Gardiner in Gardiner, Maine. This daguerreotype, which some experts identify as the eleventh president, was discovered in a collection that included views of Oaklands and the town of Gardiner.

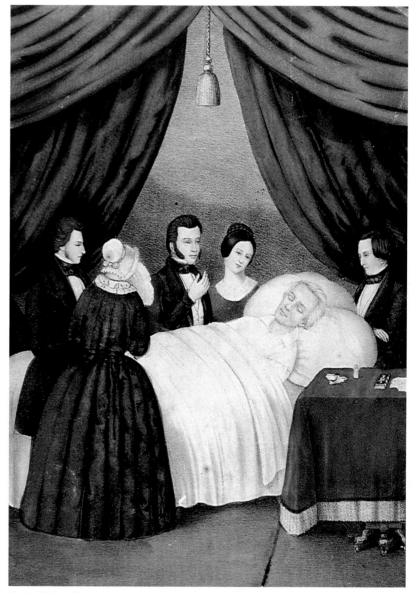

On Polk's last day in office—March 4, 1849—he assumed that the best in life lay ahead of him. "I feel exceedingly relieved that I am free from all public cares," he wrote. "I am sure I shall be a happier man in retirement than I have been during the four years I have filled the highest office." But just three and a half months later, following an emotional reunion with his mother, James K. Polk, the eleventh president, was dead.

WILLIAM HOWARD TAFT

1909–1913

Preserving the Balance

When he was seven weeks old, Louise Taft wrote about her little Willie, "He is very large of his age and grows fat every day. . . . He has such a large waist, that he cannot wear any of the dresses that are made with belts."

At high school Will played second base on the baseball team, and although he wasn't fast on his feet, he was known for his accurate throwing. He was a good dancer, too, an ability he retained throughout his life.

William Howard Taft grew up in a well-to-do Cincinnati family, the son of a highly ambitious mother and a nationally respected father. After excelling at Yale and then at the Cincinnati Law School, he practiced law in his home state and began a swift and easy climb up the Republican ladder. "Like every well-trained Ohio man," he later wrote, "I always had my plate the right side up when offices were falling."

During the Harrison administration he served as solicitor general and at the age of thirty-four he was appointed as a federal circuit judge. It was a job that the slow-moving, scholarly giant could have been contented in for the rest of his life. But if what William Taft wanted most was fretless serenity, he had chosen the wrong wife back in 1886. Helen (Nelle) Herron was as ambitious as Taft's mother, and determined that her husband would one day become president. When William McKinley in 1900 asked Taft to head up a new commission in the Philippines, Nelle saw it as a stepping stone to power and urged him to take it. "She is quite disposed to sit as a pope and direct me," he later wrote.

In the Philippines, Taft made an international name for himself by his sensitive statesmanship in presiding over the annexed islands. Then, in 1903, two years after McKinley's assassination, he was summoned back to Washington to serve as Theodore Roosevelt's secretary of war. Roosevelt immensely enjoyed having the lumbering innocent near his side. He liked Taft's happy face, his guttural laugh, his absolute honesty, and the vigorous way he acted as Roosevelt's worldwide trouble shooter and indispensable friend. "The President seems really to take much comfort that I am in his Cabinet," Taft wrote. "He is a very sweet-natured man and a very trusting man when he believes in one."

The two men shared a common viewpoint on numerous issues, including increased regulation of industry and natural resource conservation. When Roosevelt decided not to run for another term in 1908, he pushed Taft forward for the nomination. Winning the election in November by a landslide, the 300-pound charmer—so passionate and naive—could hardly believe he had been catapulted into the White House, only the second elective office he had ever held. "If I were now presiding in the Supreme Court . . . I should feel entirely at home," he wrote, "but [here] I feel just a bit like a fish out of water. . . . I pinch myself every little while to make myself realize that it is all true."

Before his presidency—which took its toll on his good humor—Taft was known for his big, sunny face that radiated friendliness and goodwill.

In March 1887, the governor of Ohio appointed Taft to the Superior Court of Cincinnati. It was the same job his father, Alphonso, had held twenty years earlier, prior to being named secretary of war, then attorney general under President Grant. Still alive, the old judge had high hopes that his son would one day sit on the Supreme Court. For William the new job was the kind of refuge he had dreamed of, a public service protected from politics, which he hated.

Theodore Roosevelt loved having Taft in his cabinet. As secretary of war, the former judge became the President's close friend and kept him smiling with his optimism and good humor. But it was Roosevelt who always got the good press. Though Taft would go on in his presidency to file more antitrust suits than TR, it is Roosevelt who is better remembered for them. He was simply much better at publicizing his actions.

From the outset Taft realized that a strong presidency was necessary. Though he agreed with much of Roosevelt's presidential agenda, he was worried about the constitutionality of his methods. "The administration of President Roosevelt, like a great crusade, awakened the people of the United States, and accomplished great advances in the . . . powers of the Federal Government," he wrote. "[But] we have a government of limited power under the Constitution, and we have got to work out our problems on the basis of law."

Defining executive power and carrying it out were, of course, two different things. Where Roosevelt was cagey and a brilliant communicator, Taft was uninterested in his public reputation. He not only shrank from criticism of any kind, he hated making decisions, and had little political savvy. "I am sorry, but I cannot be more aggressive than my nature makes me," he sighed.

As president, Taft made some real accomplishments. He promoted conservation, created the postal savings system, and exercised greater trustbusting than had Roosevelt. But he was also prone to mistakes. He failed to use patronage to instill party discipline, he alienated potential allies for no good reason, and he fired the immensely popular chief forester Gifford Pinchot, one of Roosevelt's favorites. And he had none of Roosevelt's magical way with the press, or his extraordinary energy or dispatch. "Roosevelt could always keep ahead of his work, but I cannot do it," Taft bemoaned. "I know it is a grievous fault, but it is too late to remedy it." Another time he added, "I am hopeful that a consistent, steady, quiet course . . . will ultimately convince people that [I am] . . . worthy of their respect."

In June of 1910, following a widely publicized African hunting tour, Theodore Roosevelt returned to America to find the Republican Party divided and Taft seemingly adrift. The old fighter was horrified and began saying so to fellow Republicans. "His whole attitude to me since his return has been unfriendly," Taft wrote. "I hate to be at odds with . . . Roosevelt, who made me President. . . . But, of course . . . I have to be President."

As Roosevelt became more vocal in his criticism of Taft, the bewildered chief executive could not bring himself to respond. "I am deeply hurt," Taft admitted privately. "Roosevelt was my closest friend." And to his military aide and companion Archie Butts he confided, "It is hard, very hard . . . to see a devoted friendship going to pieces like a rope of sand."

Though Roosevelt publicly claimed to still support Taft for the next election, he was already secretly planning to run for a third term, and Taft knew it. "The fact . . . is, if you were to remove Roosevelt's skull now," said the President, "you would find written on his brain '1912.'"

Roosevelt's ambitions cast a pall over the second half of Taft's presidency, as did the disastrous midterm elections, which went decisively to the Democrats. As the pressures mounted, Taft reacted by overeating more and more, eventually ballooning to 355 pounds. To escape the anxiety, he played endless rounds of golf, took long trips across the country, and grew crankier by the day. But still he refused to publicly criticize his former mentor. It was when Roosevelt began attacking the Supreme Court in his speeches, advocating the right of the public through direct balloting to override judicial decisions, that William Taft finally had had enough. Seeing himself as the protector of the constitutional balance, the former judge branded Roosevelt as a dangerous extremist. "He has leaped far ahead of the most radical leaders of the Progressive Party," he blasted. "He has not advocated the appropriation of rich men's property to distribute among the poor, but that is only

The former governor of the annexed Philippine Islands greets friends on his return to Manila in 1905 as Theodore Roosevelt's secretary of war. "Always in my heart the Philippine Islands have had the first place," Taft said. "I love the noble Filipino people."

On the stump, Taft good-naturedly spread his Republican message, all the time hating what he was doing. "A national campaign for the presidency is to me a nightmare," he complained.

Roosevelt with his toothy smile and the overweight Taft were easy targets for cartoonists. Here a *Puck* magazine cover in 1906 shows King Teddy in ermine signaling that little Prince Will is his heir apparent.

Outside the White House, Roosevelt and his successor pose on Taft's inauguration day in 1909. Compared with the vigorous, outgoing President, Taft was a slow-moving administrator, often unconscious of his surroundings. "My sin is an indisposition to labor as hard as I might," he admitted, "a disposition to procrastinate, and a disposition to enjoy the fellowship of others more than I ought." Unlike the restored friendship of John Adams and Thomas Jefferson, Taft and Roosevelt's friendship ended in a bitterness that was never overcome.

another step [away]." Later he added, "I have got to win, not for myself, but to prevent this attack on the independence of the judiciary and to prevent the triumph of [a] dangerous demagogue."

Though rank-and-file Republicans preferred Theodore Roosevelt, the old establishment swung behind Taft at the Republican convention in June, and the sitting President won the nomination. But Taft was still not to be rid of his ambitious competitor. Determined to further his progressive agenda—of child labor laws, minimum wages, health insurance, and women's suffrage—Roosevelt now abandoned the Republicans and became the candidate of the Progressive Party. "He is to be classed with the leaders of religious cults," Taft wrote in disgust. "I look upon him as I look upon a freak, almost."

Taft's leading opponent was Woodrow Wilson, who had been named in Baltimore as the Democratic nominee. Like Roosevelt, Wilson knew how to light fireworks during his campaigns, and he too, in his own way, represented the new forces of progressivism. Next to them, the drama-less, increasingly conservative Taft seemed to be courting defeat. "The people have a yearning for something startling and radical," he said, "that [I am] not likely to furnish them." Nor was he able to mount an active campaign. "I have been told that I ought to do this, ought to do that, . . . that I do not keep myself in the headlines," he commented. "I know it, but I can't do it. I couldn't if I would, and I wouldn't if I could."

In many ways it was a great relief for Taft when Woodrow Wilson, not Roosevelt, won the election in November, even though he himself finished a distant third. In a postelection appearance, Taft posed a question—"What are we to do with our ex-presidents?"—then answered it. "The proper and scientific administration of a dose of chloroform . . . might make a fitting end . . . and at the same time would secure the country from the troublesome fear that the occupant could ever come back."

Such a solution would have robbed Taft of the most fulfilling quarter of his life—first as a professor of law at Yale University, then as chief justice of the United States, the only time in our history that a president has held the other highest office. Finally content, and in the job he had always wanted, Taft lost 100 pounds and his good nature returned. Once, when asked about his troubled presidency, he responded, "I don't remember that I ever was president."

In fact, he had made important contributions to the country during his presidency. In industrial regulation, in antitrust measures, in the creation of the Department of Labor, he had made his mark. And in the establishment of the first-ever executive budget, he had strengthened the position of the president vis-à-vis Congress.

Taft all along wanted a more powerful executive office; but he also wanted to head off the threat of one that was too powerful. And though his conception of the proper constitutional balance proved too precious for its time, it would echo through the twentieth century. In the era of Richard Nixon and the "imperial presidency," Taft's point of view would take on renewed significance and urgency, an urgency more profound than even Taft had imagined. "[Mine was] a very humdrum, uninteresting administration," he once declared, "but . . . I think that . . . I can look back [with] some pleasure in having done something for the benefit of the public weal."

The new president tips his hat to the crowd, and Nelle Taft shows her delight with the world as they head for the White House after the inauguration. The ceremony was held inside the Senate Chamber because of a winter storm. After Taft's speech, the sun broke through. Below is a scene from the time of the Taft presidency. The Tafts were the last presidential family to keep a dairy cow tethered on the White House lawn.

As president, as well as in the years afterward, William Taft loved travel, especially by train (above). He was the first president to move his office out of the White House proper and into the new West Wing erected by his predecessor Theodore Roosevelt. Expanding outward on top of Roosevelt's tennis courts, Taft doubled the size of the Executive Office Building. And in 1909, at the center of the complex, he built the Oval Office, the first new state room at the White House since its inception. Later the office would be relocated within the West Wing to its present position overlooking the Rose Garden.

There is no getting around it, William Taft was big. In Hong Kong he was known as "the American giant," and in Japan his rickshaws required multiple pushers. During his years as secretary of war, Taft had struggled to reduce his weight. "I will make a conscientious effort to lose flesh," he vowed. "Were I appointed to the bench I fear I could not keep awake in my present condition." His diet worked and his weight diminished from 326 pounds to 250. But as president he was unable to control what he ate, and his weight increased to 355. Excessive eating was his only vice; he didn't drink or smoke or womanize, and he made sure to get his daily exercise. "It is not so much his bigness," wrote a close associate, "but all absence of littleness which makes him wholesomely big." And despite the 350 pounds, he was "nimble on his feet as a cat," the same friend wrote, and could look almost sleek on the dance floor in his evening clothes. More and more, however, Taft overate to compensate for his growing misery in the presidency. Increasingly fraught with worry and overcome by criticism, he often ate compulsively as a form of escape. And his trips away from Washington inevitably entailed attending banquets in his honor, where he was expected to sample the local prize dishes. Critics ridiculed that he ate his way across America. Only after leaving the presidency was Taft finally able to get his weight under control and lower it to what it had been when he graduated from Yale.

Always sensitive about his weight, Taft came to use the privacy of the golf course to hide from prying eyes. With carefully chosen partners, the president was free to putt without embarrassment (above) or flaunt his corpulence (below).

All he wanted was to be a judge, a Supreme Court judge if possible, the chief justice even, but if that was impossible, a common-pleas judge in Hamilton County, Ohio, would do just fine. He yearned for the bench because of his judicial bent of mind and because as a judge he could set the rules and could go as fast or slow as he pleased. On the bench he could procrastinate to his heart's content, could fall asleep after lunch without being criticized, could escape completely from the press, could hide his size under his robes. One of Taft's problems was that he was so genuinely nice. He was generous and polite to everyone. He couldn't bring himself to say the word no. He had a childlike quality that reflected his innocence. He liked to shop, hoping he wouldn't be recognized, but he would ask clerks and passersby, "Do you know who I am?" Sentimental, he often wept at the theater. And he eagerly awaited his vacations, forbidding any work to be brought along. He liked to duplicate his activities day after day, reveling in repetition—golf in the morning, a snooze after lunch, a sail in the afternoon, bridge after dinner. He would not do anything fast. But his superb qualities of honesty, simplicity, fidelity, and generosity, instead of standing him in good stead, often left him in trouble. Unable to figure out whom not to talk to, he talked to everyone, sometimes giving out secrets to the wrong people. He was amazed when a chance financial remark of his affected the stock market. And whenever he was reprimanded, he withdrew inside himself. Tormented by criticism, he sank into depression and irritability. During these low times, he actually apologized for being president and let people know there would soon be someone better in the office.

An airplane takes off from the Taft White House lawn in 1911.

Taft rode horseback whenever he could, preferring to ride the same course without variation. "He gets accustomed to make a turn at a given point," wrote his aide, Archie Butts, "and it is like changing the course of Niagara to try to get him to make the turn elsewhere."

On Taft's last day in office and Woodrow Wilson's first, the two shake hands. Taft came to truly hate Wilson—"that mulish enigma," he called him, "that mountain of egotism and selfishness who lives in the White House."

Chief Justice Taft

After his presidency and before his service as chief justice of the United States, Taft spent eight years teaching, writing, and lecturing. It was during this period that he wrote his classic book on the presidency, Our Chief Magistrate and His Powers. *A dispassionate presentation of his views on the presidency, it still carried signs of his hurt feelings following Roosevelt's betrayal.*

The true view of the Executive functions is, as I conceive it, that the President can exercise no power which cannot be fairly and reasonably traced to some specific grant of power . . . either in the Federal Constitution or in an act of Congress. . . . My judgement is that the view of . . . Mr. Roosevelt, ascribing an undefined residuum of power to the President is an unsafe doctrine and that it might lead under emergencies to results of an arbitrary character, doing irremediable injustice to private right. The mainspring of such a view is that the Executive is charged with responsibility for the welfare of all the people in a general way . . . and that anything that in his judgement will help the people he ought to do, unless he is expressly forbidden . . . to do it. . . . Mr. Roosevelt . . . seems to find a justification for his general view . . . in what Mr. Lincoln did during the Civil War. That Mr. Lincoln with the stress of the greatest civil war in modern times felt called upon to do things, the constitutionality of which was seriously questioned, is undoubtedly true. But Mr. Lincoln always pointed out the source of the authority which in his opinion justified his acts, and there was always a strong ground for maintaining the view which he took. . . . Mr. Lincoln never claimed that whatever authority in government was not expressly denied to him he could exercise. . . . Mr. Roosevelt, by way of illustrating his meaning as to the differing usefulness of Presidents, divides the Presidents into two classes, and designates them as "Lincoln Presidents" and "Buchanan Presidents." . . . He places himself in the Lincoln class of Presidents, and me in the Buchanan class. The identification of Mr. Roosevelt with Mr. Lincoln might . . . have escaped notice, because there are many differences between the two . . . which would give the impartial student of history a different impression.

Taft had three children—Helen, Robert, and Charles. "I have never seen [children] more natural and wholesome," wrote White House aide Archie Butts. "They have inherited the kindly, genial nature of the President and the hard common sense of the mother." Here Taft presides over his porch after some tennis between Helen and Charlie.

Taft shows his delight over a formidable lineup of grandchildren. When the first arrived, he wrote, "His face is like the face of all babies . . . but he has a fine head, and while he was small when born . . . he has shown a family trait in increasing his weight quite rapidly."

As chief justice of the United States, Taft was smiling once again. Seen here enjoying a laugh with his wife Nelle, Taft counted among his many achievements the attainment of funding for a magnificent new Supreme Court building.

A trim and contented Chief Justice Taft swings along in a jaunty manner on his way to the Supreme Court in 1924. Finally in the job he had always wanted, Taft became one of the most effective chief justices in Supreme Court history.

Second Chances

Bill was about fourteen when he was photographed with his mother, Virginia Clinton (above). She worshipped her son, never more so than when he finally fulfilled her dream for him of becoming president. Below, they pose together in 1993.

William Jefferson Clinton was born in 1946 as William Blythe III, the son of a salesman who died before his son was born and a professional nurse, Virginia Dell, who became the single greatest influence in her son's life.

From an early age his instincts drew him to politics. "Civil rights was the defining political issue of my childhood," he said, "starting when I was quite young, in the 1950s. The other thing was the fact that we got a television when I was nine years old, and I got to watch, in 1956, the Republican and Democratic Conventions. I watched the whole thing, and I was utterly fascinated by it."

In 1963, he took the last name of his stepfather, Roger Clinton, an alcoholic whose rough behavior brought out in Clinton new powers of resilience and empathy. That same year he was chosen to be part of Boys Nation, a group of young people from around the country sent to experience Washington, D.C., firsthand. There, he got to shake hands with his political hero, John F. Kennedy. The encounter changed Bill Clinton's life forever. "I was elated," said Clinton. "When I went home I had the feeling that if I worked hard and prepared myself, I could have an impact."

The following year Clinton entered Georgetown University, where he became known for his self-confidence, for his intelligence, and for being a man in a hurry. Twice elected class president, after his junior year he was hired as a part-time clerk on Capitol Hill by Arkansas Senator J. William Fulbright. And following Fulbright's example, in his senior year he won a Rhodes Scholarship. At Oxford, he studied international politics, narrowly avoided the draft, opposed the Vietnam War, and dreamt of one day entering public service.

"There is a sense of mission that most of us who grew up in the sixties feel as citizens," Clinton said. "That it is not enough for us just to pursue our own private lives; that we have a larger obligation to our community and to our country."

After his return from England, in 1970, Clinton's career advanced rapidly. At Yale Law School, he met fellow student Hillary Rodham, an active idealist whose no-nonsense working style was the perfect complement to his freewheeling charm. "'Most everything we've done has been a partnership," Clinton later said of his wife. "She is profoundly important to what I've done."

In 1972, Clinton accepted a position on the faculty of the University of Arkansas Law School and used it as a springboard into Arkansas politics. "I ran for Congress in 1974 and was defeated," Clinton recalled. "And then

Bill Clinton, who once said, "The God I believe in is the God of second chances."

Winner in a "Beautiful Baby" contest

Inspired by the televised 1956 conventions

Shaking hands with JFK

A shaggy Yale law student in 1972

An unsuccessful run for Congress in 1974

A proud Bill Clinton poses with his beloved half-brother, Roger.

IN HIS OWN WORDS

Clinton on his roots:

I never met my father. He was killed in a car wreck on a rainy road three months before I was born, driving home from Chicago to Arkansas to see my mother.

My most vivid memory of my mother and childhood was when I went to visit her at nursing school when I was three, and when my grandmother and I pulled out of the station, she knelt down by the side of the railroad tracks and cried.

My mother taught me three things: never give up; never forget where you came from; and never lose your compassion for people who are less fortunate than you are.

I was raised by my grandparents. My granddaddy ran a country store in a black neighborhood . . . and there were no food stamps then. So when his black customers, who worked hard for a living, came in with no money, he gave them food anyway and just made a note of it.

in 1976 I was attorney general, and I loved that job. Then a vacancy occurred in the governor's race, and so I ran and I won, and it was exhilarating."

Elected governor in 1978, thirty-two-year-old Bill Clinton bristled with ideas and energy. But he also made a series of political miscalculations. By seeming not to listen to his constituents, by raising licensing fees, and by giving an impression of intellectual arrogance, in 1980 he lost his bid for reelection. "I think [the loss] was good for me," Clinton later said. "It's like every other adversity in life. If you survive it, you normally come out ahead. I was very fortunate to be from a small, rural state with a lot of small towns, where people were very forthright. Because a few months after the election, I went out across the state and I'd ask what I'd done wrong. And they would tell me—in great, stunning, brutal detail. They then gave me a second chance to serve."

After winning again in 1982 and then serving another ten years as governor, Clinton, at age forty-six, ran for president. And in 1992, when his national candidacy became threatened by rumors regarding his personal life, once again he reached out to the people. With his wife at his side, Clinton confessed on national television to having had rocky times in his marriage. But it was behind them, he said, and entirely a private matter. Forcefully, he urged that the people judge him by his performance and his political record, not by his private life. His words made sense to millions of Americans, and from a position low in the polls, he soared to second place in the New Hampshire primary, earning the nickname "The Comeback Kid." Going on to win the nomination of his party, Clinton faced President George Bush and third-party candidate H. Ross Perot in the general elections. By sticking to the issues and promising the kind of change that only a young man of a new generation could bring about, Clinton won an upset victory in November with forty-three percent of the popular vote. "I felt, at the one hand, elated," he recalled. "But there was a little bit of me that felt like the dog who was chasing the pickup and finally caught it. So now what do I do? I think any person who is not a little humbled by being given this responsibility doesn't understand what he or she has got ahold of."

Clinton's presidency began with a tremendous sense of potential. One of the brightest and most empathetic politicians of the twentieth century, he was highly literate and had an instinct for the direction of history. Determined to make his mark as a Democratic reformer, he set in motion an ambitious agenda to reshape numerous social programs, including a bold central initiative to create universal health care coverage. Republicans criticized it as an over-ambitious, liberal experiment, and health care became the rallying cry for a strong political opposition. Declaring their own more conservative "Contract with America," Republicans went on to sweeping victo-

Arkansas's boyish attorney general in 1976

Governor of Arkansas in 1978

Losing the governorship in 1980

In 1981 the birth of Chelsea

Winning back the governorship in 1982

ries in the 1994 Congressional elections. Gaining control over both houses of Congress for the first time in forty years, Republicans repudiated the Clinton program and ushered in a new era of divided government, the partisanship of which had rarely been seen in modern times. The spirit of compromise—key to the workings of the Madisonian system—evaporated.

But Republicans underestimated Bill Clinton's resolve, and the power he could still wield as president. Determined to regain equal standing with Congress, Clinton adapted to the political climate, preempting some popular Republican positions, such as welfare reform, and moving closer to the nation's political center. When, twice in 1995, the government was forced to shut down, with the President and the Republican-controlled Congress at loggerheads over the budget, it was Clinton who convinced the country that the Republicans, not he, were the real radicals. And in 1996, despite negative publicity generated by an ongoing investigation into his past business dealings while governor of Arkansas, he staged one of the greatest comebacks in presidential history. In another three-way race, he won decisively in the November elections.

The Madisonian system was put to a further test at the start of Bill Clinton's second term. When the Supreme Court ruled in *Jones v. Clinton* that a sitting president could be sued for actions taken prior to his term, thereby limiting the president's traditional independence from the judiciary, Clinton was forced to testify at a civil court sexual harassment lawsuit against him. Confronted by an aggressive press corps, the President made what he later admitted were misleading statements, and insisted on keeping his entire focus on what he called "America's business." It was in this politically charged atmosphere that an independent counsel, with virtually unlimited investigative powers, intensified his scrutiny of Clinton. Intended to serve as an objective investigator, the Office of the Independent Counsel—now headed by Kenneth Starr—represented a new power that had been added to the Madisonian system of checks and balances, created in the wake of Richard Nixon's Watergate scandal. But Starr was soon caught up in the partisan warfare of Clinton's tenure, as the Madisonian system itself degenerated into one of mutual antagonism.

As Clinton's second term unfolded, Starr's inquiry broadened, turning into the most aggressive investigation ever leveled against a president. Failing to uncover incriminating evidence in what had become known as Whitewater, he shifted the focus toward Clinton's personal life. In 1998, Starr exposed a secret affair between the President and a White House intern named Monica Lewinsky, claiming that Clinton perjured himself when he denied the affair under oath in his civil case. Despite strong Democratic showings in the November midterm elections and solid, popular support, on

In 1988, Bill announces he won't run for president.

He knew he was a part of a community. . . . They believed in personal responsibility. But they also believed that the government had an obligation to help the people who were doing the best they can.

I remember where I was when Martin Luther King gave that "I had a dream" speech in 1963. I was home in Hot Springs, Arkansas, in a white reclining chair all by myself. I just wept like a baby all the way through it.

In an alcoholic family, I grew up with a much greater empathy for other people's problems than the average person has. It made me a lot more self-reliant and tougher than I might have been.

For as long as I can remember, I have loved the land, air and water of Arkansas. It's the legacy my grandparents left to me—the idea that you may not have much money and things may get really tough, but you've just go to get up each day and make the best of it.

On a plane trip to Chicago during the 1992 presidential campaign, Clinton catches some unscheduled sleep.

Clinton dances on his forty-sixth birthday in Little Rock, Arkansas, in August 1992.

At their victory celebration in November 1992, Bill and Hillary Clinton join hands with Vice President-elect Al Gore and his wife Tipper.

December 19, 1998, the Republican-controlled House of Representatives voted to impeach, initiating the only impeachment trial against a president since Andrew Johnson. The official charges were perjury and obstruction of justice, but throughout the trial the underlying dynamic was political: a struggle between the Republican revolution and Clinton's Democratic revival. It was the President's enemies who framed the debate in terms of the issue of character.

"I think a lot of the people who talk about [character] do so in ways that are quite self-serving," Clinton reflected. "Most of the people I've known who have demonstrated great character didn't go around talking about it. . . . It is important for us to remember that there is a difference between character and reputation, and that under the guise of elevating character, there are a large number of people in our country today who believe that the way they can get what they want in life is by destroying someone else's reputation. None of us is ever a complete judge of another's character; only God can fully judge that.

"Now, I made a personal mistake, which became a matter of public debate. I've tried to acknowledge my wrongdoing and say that I was sorry about it. But I also have tried to demonstrate presidential character by standing up for the interests of the country and being very strong when the interests and values of the American people were at stake. I also tried to deal with this whole impeachment controversy in a way that showed genuine devotion to the Constitution and the history of the country. I will leave it to others to determine whether I did that."

Throughout the Senate trial there loomed a more substantive issue— of exactly what constituted an "impeachable offense," and whether the President's actions in his misleading testimony during the private civil law-suit rose to the level of "high crimes and misdemeanors." Ultimately, the issue hinged on the Constitution itself, and the specter of James Madison was ever-present. If an elected president could be removed by his political enemies, scholars warned, on the basis of private misdoings and an effort to cover them up, the Madisonian system itself could be in danger of collapse.

Despite impassioned calls from many Republicans for the President's resignation, throughout the trial Clinton's job-approval ratings remained extremely high. And in the end, the Senate heeded the people. As a body it could not muster the required two-thirds vote, or even a simple majority of its members, to convict Bill Clinton of any charges.

"The American people were very good to me," Clinton said, "[and] I learned several things. I learned that there are certain rules of human conduct that apply to all of us, and when we make a mistake, whether you are president or anything else, you have to live with the consequences of your actions; nobody gets out for free. And the second thing I learned is that the Framers were smart: they designed the Constitution to prevent partisan passions from overriding common sense. The third thing was that the American people almost always get it right if they have enough time and enough information. They have this uncanny sixth sense about where things ought to be. [And] fourth, the American people were saying something besides 'We don't think the president should be impeached, and then if you do impeach him we certainly don't think he should be convicted.' What they were also really saying was, 'Okay, we know what happened—this guy made a mistake [and] he apologized to the American people—this is not what this whole impeachment thing is about. And, oh, by the way, you people are not working for us;

Elected to a second term in 1996, the year both these pictures were taken, Bill Clinton was a church-going Baptist who once thought he might become a clergyman. A masterful politician, he could remember the smallest details of people's lives, and loved drawing out of others their ideas and their energy. By close observation of seasoned politicians he had learned the key lesson of staying cool in a crisis. And a life-long habit of vigorous reading had left him able to understand and discuss almost any topic. Possessing a sharp instinct for campaigning, he could literally feel his audiences' moods. And though his speeches were often too long, he could deliver some of the most effective oratory of his generation. Indeed, despite a tendency to indiscipline at times, of all those raised during the turbulent 1960s, it was Clinton who had come the farthest the soonest. Sentimental, politically visionary, possessing immense appetites for life and for personal achievement, he embodied both the idealism and the impatience of his generation.

we hired you to work for us, not to work on each other.' And I tried to remember that.

"I have made all kinds of mistakes in my life, but I try to keep going, and the people that I love and the people with whom I work, the people from whom I learn, they gave me a second chance. And I think if we think about life as getting second chances, as long as you learn from your mistakes and you don't make the same ones again, I think it's a helpful way to look at life."

The only Democrat to be reelected president since FDR, Bill Clinton had a significant impact on American politics. He reoriented the Democratic party toward mainstream issues, including balancing the budget and reforming welfare. He genuinely cared about race relations, appointing minorities to high positions in his administration and initiating a national dialogue on race. And he appointed women to some of the highest positions in national government, including for the first time secretary of state and attorney general. He worked for peace in Ireland and the Middle East, and backed NATO's enlargement and its intervention in Kosovo. And, while highlighting the ongoing problem of America's poor, he presided over one of the strongest economic booms of the twentieth century. Bill Clinton both reflected and benefited from an increasingly tolerant America, and while most Americans deplored his personal acts in the Lewinsky case, they refused to judge his public role by his private behavior. In the end, they gave him another chance.

"[The presidency] has taught me a great deal," Clinton mused. "It's taught me the importance of being humble. I've had to ask for forgiveness in a way that most people never do in public, although nearly everybody does in private at some point during a lifetime. But it has also taught me to be less aggravated at other people, less agitated, less upset about some criticism I get. . . . I've learned a lot about giving up the little things in life so you can focus on the big things.

"And I think I've learned it in a way I never would have if I hadn't been president. If I had felt I was doing it only for myself, I'm not sure I would have had the strength to learn these things. But knowing that I was doing it for the American people helped me, and I'm very grateful for that. I think that it's something that I can carry with me for the rest of my life."

During Clinton's presidency the Madisonian system devolved into a battle of titans, with the President flanked by Speaker of the House Newt Gingrich and Senator Trent Lott (below). After the most severe attacks against any president since Andrew Johnson, Gingrich resigned, Clinton was left standing.

Clinton on the presidency:

I think that the presidency can still be a place of great influence and power; it's still the central office in the country, particularly in times of adversity or crisis. It can be in good times as well, but it requires a greater level of energy to advance. In other words, there's not an automatic deference to the presidency. There's a lot of checks, and not just in the Congress, and not just when the Congress is of the opposite party—although that certainly complicates things—but in the proliferation of press sources, in the fact that we no longer have as big a percentage of the world's wealth [as] we did in the end of the Cold War—all these things mean the energy level of the president, and the degree to which the president has thought about what the real challenges facing the country are, and specifically what the president should do about them, is more important than ever before. The president can still be very, very effective, but it requires more discipline and more care and a real plan to do that. But I still think it's the greatest job in the world and I still think it's very, very important to the American people.

Clinton shares a playful moment with his wife, Hillary, who stood loyally beside him throughout the impeachment crisis.

With First Lady Hillary Rodham Clinton looking on, on December 19, 1998, President Clinton thanks Democratic members of the House of Representatives for voting against impeachment and vows to complete his term.

On January 19, 1999, in the midst of impeachment proceedings against him, Clinton delivers his State of the Union Address (below). Twenty-four days later (right) the Senate voted not to convict.

IN HIS OWN WORDS

Clinton in early 1999 on the Office of the Independent Counsel:

We may need a little more time and we may need others to look back and judge the impact of the Office of the Special Prosecutor. I think that it's certainly led to expenditure of an enormous amount of time and resources, and diversion away from what otherwise would be the public business. And I think you have to look on a case-by-case basis to decide if you think it was worth the price that was paid. Because there was no question that this is something the Framers never would have done. James Madison believed that there should be no unaccountable power in America. The judges were the nearest thing to it, although they could be impeached. They were given lifetime terms—but quite restrictive realms of activity. Madison would never have agreed to give any executive brand of authority an unlimited budget, an unlimited tenure, and unlimited power. If you believe you get enough out of it to justify that, then you're for it; but to pretend there have been no costs to the system is quite wrong. *[On July 1, 1999, by bipartisan consensus, the twenty-one-year-old independent counsel law, The Ethics in Government Act, was quietly allowed to expire.]*

With the constitutional crisis behind him, Clinton turns to a new crisis overseas: NATO's bombing in response to the ethnic cleansing of Kosovo. Above, the President meets with his national security advisers in the Cabinet Room.

What had been long planned as a celebration of NATO's 50th anniversary became a serious work session to discuss the Kosovo crisis. Here Clinton converses with British Prime Minister Tony Blair, his closest ally. To the right, Bill Clinton steals a solitary moment.

Chronology of the U.S. Presidents

No.	President	Elected From	Date of Birth	First Lady	Vice President	Date of Death
1.	**George Washington** (F) 1789–1797	Virginia	Feb. 22, 1732	Martha Dandridge Custis Washington	John Adams	Dec. 14, 1799
2.	**John Adams** (F) 1797–1801	Massachusetts	Oct. 30, 1735	Abigail Smith Adams	Thomas Jefferson	July 4, 1826
3.	**Thomas Jefferson** (DR) 1801–1809	Virginia	Apr. 13, 1743	widower	Aaron Burr George Clinton	July 4, 1826
4.	**James Madison** (DR) 1809–1817	Virginia	Mar. 16, 1751	Dolley Payne Todd Madison	George Clinton Elbridge Gerry	June 28, 1836
5.	**James Monroe** (DR) 1817–1825	Virginia	Apr. 28, 1758	Elizabeth Kortright Monroe	Daniel D. Tompkins	July 4, 1831
6.	**John Quincy Adams** (DR) 1825–1829	Massachusetts	July 11, 1767	Louisa Johnson Adams	John C. Calhoun	Feb. 23, 1848
7.	**Andrew Jackson** (D) 1829–1837	Tennessee	Mar. 15, 1767	widower	Martin Van Buren	June 8, 1845
8.	**Martin Van Buren** (D) 1837–1841	New York	Dec. 5, 1782	widower	Richard M. Johnson	July 24, 1862
9.	**William Henry Harrison** (W) 1841	Ohio	Feb. 9, 1773	Anna Symmes Harrison	John Tyler	Apr. 4, 1841
10.	**John Tyler** (W) 1841–1845	Virginia	Mar. 29, 1790	Letitia Christian Tyler Julia Gardiner Tyler	none	Jan. 18, 1862
11.	**James K. Polk** (D) 1845–1849	Tennessee	Nov. 2, 1795	Sarah Childress Polk	George M. Dallas	June 15, 1849
12.	**Zachary Taylor** (W) 1849–1850	Louisiana	Nov. 24, 1784	Margaret Mackall Smith Taylor	Millard Fillmore	July 9, 1850
13.	**Millard Fillmore** (W) 1850–1853	New York	Jan. 7, 1800	Abigial Powers Fillmore	none	Mar. 8, 1874
14.	**Franklin Pierce** (D) 1853–1857	New Hampshire	Nov. 23, 1804	Jane Means Appleton Pierce	William R. King	Oct. 8, 1869
15.	**James Buchanan** (D) 1857–1861	Pennsylvania	Apr. 23, 1791	never married	John C. Breckinridge	June 1, 1868
16.	**Abraham Lincoln** (R) 1861–1865	Illinois	Feb. 12, 1809	Mary Todd Lincoln	Hannibal Hamlin Andrew Johnson	Apr. 15, 1865
17.	**Andrew Johnson** (R) 1865–1869	Tennessee	Dec. 29, 1808	Eliza McCardle Johnson	none	July 31, 1875
18.	**Ulysses S. Grant** (R) 1869-1877	Illinois	Apr. 27, 1822	Julia Dent Grant	Schuyler Colfax Henry Wilson	July 23, 1885
19.	**Rutherford B. Hayes** (R) 1877-1881	Ohio	Oct. 4, 1822	Lucy Webb Hayes	William A. Wheeler	Jan. 17, 1893
20.	**James A. Garfield** (R) 1881	Ohio	Nov. 19, 1831	Lucretia Rudolph Garfield	Chester A. Arthur	Sep. 19, 1881
21.	**Chester A. Arthur** (R) 1881–1885	New York	Oct. 5, 1829	widower	none	Nov. 18, 1886
22.	**Grover Cleveland** (D) 1885–1889	New York	Mar. 18, 1837	Frances Folsom Cleveland	Thomas A. Hendricks	June 24, 1908

No.	President	Elected From	Date of Birth	First Lady	Vice President	Date of Death
23.	**Benjamin Harrison** (R) 1889–1893	Indiana	Aug. 20, 1833	Caroline Scott Harrison	Levi P. Morton	Mar. 13, 1901
24.	**Grover Cleveland** (D) 1893–1897	New York	Mar. 18, 1837	Frances Folsom Cleveland	Adlai E. Stevenson	June 24, 1908
25.	**William McKinley** (R) 1897–1901	Ohio	Jan. 29, 1843	Ida Saxton McKinley	Garret A. Hobart Theodore Roosevelt	Sep. 14, 1901
26.	**Theodore Roosevelt** (R) 1901–1909	New York	Oct. 27, 1858	Edith Kermit Carow Roosevelt	Charles W. Fairbanks	Jan. 6, 1919
27.	**William Howard Taft** (R) 1909–1913	Ohio	Sep. 15, 1857	Helen Herron Taft	James S. Sherman	Mar. 8, 1931
28.	**Woodrow Wilson** (D) 1913–1921	New Jersey	Dec. 28, 1856	Ellen Louise Axson Wilson Edith Bolling Galt Wilson	Thomas R. Marshall	Feb. 3, 1924
29.	**Warren G. Harding** (R) 1921–1923	Ohio	Nov. 2, 1865	Florence Kling De Wolfe Harding	Calvin Coolidge	Aug. 2, 1923
30.	**Calvin Coolidge** (R) 1923–1929	Massachusetts	July 4, 1872	Grace Goodhue Coolidge	Charles G. Dawes	Jan. 5, 1933
31.	**Herbert Hoover** (R) 1929–1933	California	Aug. 10, 1874	Lou Henry Hoover	Charles Curtis	Oct. 20, 1964
32.	**Franklin D. Roosevelt** (D) 1933-1945	New York	Jan. 30, 1882	Anna Eleanor Roosevelt Roosevelt	John N. Garner Henry A. Wallace Harry S. Truman	Apr. 12, 1945
33.	**Harry S. Truman** (D) 1945-1953	Missouri	May 8, 1884	Elizabeth Wallace Truman	Alben W. Barkley	Dec. 26, 1972
34.	**Dwight D. Eisenhower** (R) 1953-1961	New York Pennsylvania	Oct. 14, 1890	Mamie Doud Eisenhower	Richard M. Nixon	Mar. 28, 1969
35.	**John F. Kennedy** (D) 1961–1963	Massachusetts	May 29, 1917	Jacqueline Bouvier Kennedy	Lyndon B. Johnson	Nov. 22, 1963
36.	**Lyndon B. Johnson** (D) 1963–1969	Texas	Aug. 27, 1908	Claudia Alta Taylor Johnson	Hubert H. Humphrey	Jan. 22, 1973
37.	**Richard M. Nixon** (R) 1969–1974	New York California	Jan. 9, 1913	Thelma Catherine Ryan Nixon	Spiro T. Agnew Gerald R. Ford	Apr. 22, 1994
38.	**Gerald R. Ford** (R) 1974–1977	Michigan	July 14, 1913	Betty Bloomer Warren Ford	Nelson A. Rockefeller	
39.	**Jimmy Carter** (D) 1977–1981	Georgia	Oct. 1, 1924	Rosalynn Smith Carter	Walter F. Mondale	
40.	**Ronald Reagan** (R) 1981–1989	California	Feb. 6, 1911	Nancy Davis Reagan	George W. Bush	
41.	**George W. Bush** (R) 1989–1993	Texas	June 12, 1924	Barbara Pierce Bush	J. Danforth Quayle	
42.	**William J. Clinton** (D) 1993–2001	Arkansas	Aug. 19, 1946	Hillary Rodham Clinton	Albert Gore, Jr.	

(F = Federalist, DR = Democratic-Republican, D = Democrat, W = Whig, R = Republican)

Article II of the Constitution

Section 1

The executive power shall be vested in a President of the United States of America. He shall hold his office during the term of four years, and, together with the Vice President, chosen for the same term, be elected as follows:

Each State shall appoint, in such manner as the legislature thereof may direct, a number of electors, equal to the whole number of Senators and Representatives to which the State may be entitled in the Congress; but no Senator or Representative, or person holding an office of trust or profit under the United States, shall be appointed an elector.

The electors shall meet in their respective States, and vote by ballot for two persons, of whom one at least shall not be an inhabitant of the same State with themselves. And they shall make a list of all the persons voted for, and of the number of votes for each; which list they shall sign and certify, and transmit sealed to the seat of government of the United States, directed to the President of the Senate. The President of the Senate shall, in the presence of the Senate and the House of Representatives, open all the certificates, and the votes shall then be counted. The person having the greatest number of votes shall be the President, if such number be a majority of the whole number of electors appointed; and if there be more than one who have such majority, and have an equal number of votes, then the House of Representatives shall immediately choose by ballot one of them for President; and if no person have a majority, then from the five highest on the list said house shall in like manner choose the President. But in choosing the President the votes shall be taken by States, the representation from each state having one vote; a quorum for this purpose shall consist of a member or members from two-thirds of the states, and a majority of all the States shall be necessary to a choice. In every case, after the choice of the President, the person having the greatest number of votes of the electors shall be the Vice President. But if there should remain two or more who have equal votes, the Senate shall choose from them by ballot the Vice President.

The Congress may determine the time of choosing the electors and the day on which they shall give their votes; which day shall be the same throughout the United States.

No person except a natural-born citizen, *or a citizen of the United States at the time of the adoption of this Constitution,* shall be eligible to the office of President; neither shall any person be eligible to that office who shall not have attained to the age of thirty-five years, and been fourteen years a resident with the United States.

In case of the removal of the President from office or of his death, resignation, or inability to discharge the powers and duties of the said office, the same shall devolve on the Vice President, and the Congress may by law provide for the case of removal, death, resignation, or inability, both of the President and Vice President, declaring what officer shall then act as President, and such officer shall act accordingly, until the disability be removed, or a President shall be elected.

The President shall, at stated times, receive for his services a compensation, which shall neither be increased nor diminished during the period for which he shall have been elected, and he shall not receive within that period any other emolument from the United States, or any of them.

Before he enter on the execution of his office, he shall take the following oath or affirmation: —"I do solemnly swear (or affirm) that I will faithfully execute the office of the President of the United States, and will to the best of my ability preserve, protect and defend the Constitution of the United States."

Section 2

The President shall be commander in chief of the army and navy of the United States, and of the militia of the several States, when called into the actual service of the United States; he may require the opinion, in writing, of the principal officer in each of the executive departments, upon any subject relating to the duties of their respective offices, and he shall have power to grant reprieves and pardons for offenses against the United States, except in cases of impeachment.

He shall have power, by and with the advice and consent of the Senate, to make treaties, provided two-thirds of the Senators present concur; and he shall nominate, and by and with the advice and consent of the Senate, shall appoint ambassadors, other public ministers and consuls, judges of the Supreme Court, and all other officers of the United States, whose appointments are not herein otherwise provided for, and which shall be established by law: but Congress may by law vest the appointment of such inferior officers, as they think proper, in the President alone, in the courts of law, or in the heads of departments.

The President shall have power to fill up all vacancies that may happen during the recess of the Senate, by granting commissions which shall expire at the end of their next session.

Section 3

He shall from time to time give to the Congress information of the state of the Union, and recommend to their consideration such measures as he shall judge necessary and expedient; he may, on extraordinary occasions, convene both houses, or either of them, and in case of disagreement between them, with respect to the time of adjournment, he may adjourn them to such time as he shall think proper; he shall receive ambassadors and other public ministers; he shall take care that the laws be faithfully executed, and shall commission all the officers of the United States.

Section 4

The President, Vice President and all civil officers of the United States shall be removed from office on impeachment for, and on conviction of, treason, bribery, or other high crimes and misdemeanors.

Selected Amendments

Amendment XII
[Adopted 1804]

The electors shall meet in their respective States, and vote by ballot for President and Vice President, one of whom, at least, shall not be an inhabitant of the same State with themselves; they shall name in their ballots the person voted for as President, and in distinct ballots the person voted for as Vice President, and they shall make distinct lists of all persons voted for as President, and of all persons voted for as Vice President, and of the number of votes for each, which lists they shall sign and certify, and transmit sealed to the seat of government of the United States, directed to the President of the Senate;—the President of the Senate shall, in the presence of the Senate and House of Representatives, open all certificates and the votes shall then be counted; —the person having the greatest number of votes for President shall be the President, if such number be a majority of the whole number of electors appointed; and if no person have such majority, then from the persons having the highest numbers not exceeding three on the list of those voted for as President the House of Representatives shall choose immediately, by ballot, the President. But in choosing the President, the votes shall be taken by States, the representation from each state having one vote; a quorum for this purpose shall consist of a member or members from two-thirds of the states, and a majority of all the States shall be necessary to a choice. And if the House of Representatives shall not choose a President whenever the right of choice shall devolve upon them, before the *fourth day of March* next following, then the Vice President shall act as President, as in the case of the death or other constitutional disability of the President.

The person having the greatest number of votes as Vice President shall be the Vice President, if such number be a majority of the whole number of electors appointed; and if no person have a majority, then from the two highest numbers on the list the Senate shall choose the Vice President; a quorum for the purpose shall consist of two-thirds of the whole number of Senators, and a majority of the whole number shall be necessary to a choice. But no person constitutionally ineligible to the office of President shall be eligible to that of Vice President of the United States.

Amendment XX
[Adopted 1933]

Section 1

The terms of the President and Vice President shall end at noon on the 20th day of January, and the terms of Senators and Representatives at noon on the 3d day of January, of the years in which such terms would have ended if this article had not been ratified; and the terms of their successors shall then begin.

Section 2

The Congress shall assemble at least once in every year, and such meeting shall begin at noon on the 3d day of January, unless they shall by law appoint a different day.

Section 3

If, at the time fixed for the beginning of the term of the President, the President-elect shall have died, the Vice President-elect shall become President. If a President shall not have been chosen before the time fixed for the beginning of his term, or if the President-elect shall have failed to qualify, then the Vice President-elect shall act as President until a President shall have qualified; and the Congress may be law provide for the case wherein neither a President-elect nor a Vice President-elect shall have qualified, declaring who shall then act as President, or the manner in which one who is to act shall be selected, and such persons shall act accordingly until a President or Vice President shall have qualified.

Section 4

The Congress may by law provide for the case of the death of any of the persons from whom the House of Representatives may choose a President whenever the right of choice shall have devolved upon them, and for the case of the death of any of the persons from whom the Senate may choose a Vice President whenever the right of choice shall have devolved upon them.

Section 5

Sections 1 and 2 shall take effect on the 15th day of October following the ratification of this article.

Section 6

This article shall be inoperative unless it shall have been ratified as an amendment to the Constitution by the Legislatures of three-fourths of the several States within seven years from the date of its submission.

Amendment XXII
[Adopted 1951]

Section 1

No person shall be elected to the office of President more than twice, and no person who has held the office of President, or acted as President, for more than two years of a term to which some other person was elected President shall be elected to the office of President more than once. But this article shall not apply to any person holding the office of President when this article was proposed by the Congress, and shall not prevent any person who may be holding the office of President, or acting as President, during the term within which this article becomes operative from holding the office of President or acting as President during the remainder of such term.

Section 2

This article shall be inoperative unless it shall have been ratified as an amendment to the Constitution by the legislatures of three-fourths of the several States within seven years from the date of its submission to the States by the Congress.

Amendment XXV

[Adopted 1967]

Section 1

In case of the removal of the President from office or of his death or resignation, the Vice President shall become President.

Section 2

Whenever there is a vacancy in the office of the Vice President, the President shall nominate a Vice President who shall take office upon confirmation by a majority vote of both Houses of Congress.

Section 3

Whenever the President transmits to the President pro tempore of the Senate and the Speaker of the House of Representatives his written declaration that he is unable to discharge the powers and duties of his office, and until he transmits to them a written declaration to the contrary, such powers and duties shall be discharged by the Vice President as Acting President.

Section 4

Whenever the Vice President and a majority of either the principal officers of the executive departments or of such other body as Congress may by law provide, transmit to the President pro tempore of the Senate and the Speaker of the House of Representatives their written declaration that the President is unable to discharge the powers and duties of his office, the Vice President shall immediately assume the powers and duties of the office as Acting President.

Thereafter, when the President transmits to the President pro tempore of the Senate and the Speaker of the House of Representatives his written declaration that no inability exists, he shall resume the powers and duties of his office unless the Vice President and a majority of either the principal officers of the executive department[s] or of such other body as Congress may by law provide, transmit within four days to the President pro tempore of the Senate and the Speaker of the House of Representatives their written declaration that the President is unable to discharge the powers and duties of his office. Thereupon Congress shall decide the issue, assembling within forty-eight hours for that purpose if not in session. If the Congress, within twenty-one days after receipt of the latter written declaration, or, if Congress is not in session, within twenty-one days after Congress is required to assemble, determines by two-thirds vote of both Houses that the President is unable to discharge the powers and duties of his office, the Vice President shall continue to discharge the same as Acting President; otherwise, the President shall resume the powers and duties of his office.

[Note: Passages in italic type are no longer in effect.]

A White House office, 1898

White house corridor, circa 1890

Acknowledgments

Literally hundreds of people and institutions have worked behind the scenes on this wide-ranging, five-year endeavor. First and foremost is New York Life Insurance Company. From the very start, we have had the generous support of New York Life, the sole sponsor of the companion PBS series. We thank them not only for making this project possible but also for being so wonderful to work with. Special thanks go to Sy Sternberg, the Chairman, President and Chief Executive Officer of New York Life, whose unwavering commitment to this project helped make it an unprecedented success.

We thank the entire staff and production team at Kunhardt Productions, including our colleague Charles Whittingham for bringing us together with New York Life. We give special thanks to Dyllan McGee, Kathleen Toner, and Caroline Waterlow, without whom this project would not have been possible. Each of them provided invaluable research and worked tirelessly on nearly every detail of this sometimes frustrating, always fascinating subject. Jamie Edgar, who oversaw all the original filming and post-production, and Kathryn Barnier, our creative and sensitive chief film editor for the series, each worked exhaustively on the television project, as did Michael Starobin, Robert Gold, Nancy Malin, Annastacia Mairs, Vanessa Cochran, Pam Ridder, and John Martin. We also thank Tim Hallinan and his staff for overseeing an ambitious educational outreach component. Special thanks go to Joan Caron, who not only helped in many areas of the project but also had the full responsibility of typing and correcting our manuscript and organizing all the illustrations. And we give great thanks to our designer, Elton Robinson, whose keen eye and meticulous hand were critical in a book with so many separate ingredients. Working with Elton has been a pleasure.

Throughout this venture we have also had the benefit of the support of Bill Baker and Tammy Robinson's wonderful staff at WNET. Tammy's support for the series has never wavered. Also at WNET is Bill Grant, who took on this project in 1996 with a personal passion. The series has benefited in ways too numerous to list because of his wisdom. In addition, we thank PBS and PBS Video for their part in this effort.

We thank the one and only Esther Newberg at ICM for bringing us together with Susan Petersen Kennedy and Riverhead Books, where our editor, Cindy Spiegel, has given us not only support but many insightful editorial suggestions along the way. Her dedication to this project has made it a better book. And we also want to thank Catharine Lynch, Erin Bush, and Bill Peabody at Riverhead. Our copy editor, Toni Rachiele, was painstaking in her improvements of our use of the English language. We also thank Cynthia Crippen, who is responsible for the creation of the index to this book.

Two presidential scholars reviewed the entire manuscript of this book. One was our chief academic adviser, Stephen Skowronek of Yale University. The other was presidential scholar Richard M. Pious of Barnard College and Columbia University. Both have been extremely generous with their time. In addition, our treatment of each individual president was initially critiqued by a prominent presidential scholar. A list of those authorities makes up a Who's Who of American presidential biographers, and we are proud to have been associated with each of them (though any errors or shortcomings in the final book are entirely our own). We thank Gordon Wood (Washington), Joseph Ellis (J. Adams and Jefferson), Robert Rutland (Madison), Harry Ammon (Monroe), Paul Nagel (J. Q. Adams), Robert Remini (Jackson), Donald Cole (Van Buren), Kenneth Stevens (W. H. Harrison), Michael Hoff (Tyler and Fillmore), Robert Johannsen (Polk), William Cooper (Taylor), Larry Gara (Pierce), William Gienapp (Buchanan), David Donald (Lincoln), Hans Trefousse (A. Johnson), William McFeely (Grant), Ari Hoogenboom (Hayes), Alan Peskin (Garfield), Thomas Reeves (Arthur), Jean Harvey Baker (Cleveland), Allan Spetter (B. Harrison), Lewis Gould (McKinley), John Milton Cooper (T. Roosevelt, Wilson, F. Roosevelt), Paolo Colletta (Taft), Robert Ferrell (Harding and Coolidge), Joan Hoff (Hoover), Stephen Ambrose (Eisenhower and Nixon), and Lou Cannon (Reagan). In addition, our senior historical consultant for the PBS series, David Herbert Donald, read all the biographies in an early form and his comments have been extremely helpful. Richard E. Neustadt, whom we also thank in the preface to this book, was also an early and helpful reviewer of each biography. And thanks also go to Arthur Schlesinger, Jr., and William McFeely, each of whom granted us important early interviews and was most generous with his time. The living presidents were interviewed for us by Hugh Sidey and the chapters on Gerald Ford, Jimmy Carter, George Bush, and Bill Clinton closely follow Sidey's interviews. Thanks to each of those presidents for taking the time to reflect on their lives and the presidency.

A work of this kind involves an enormous amount of research and in this area we have many to thank. In addition to the staff of Kunhardt Productions already named, several former members of our company also helped tremendously with this project, especially Heather Reilly, Patrick Feeney, Dan Klein, Lulie Haddad, Peter Trivelas, Mike DeWitt, and Tim Walker. And we would like to thank Clint Trowbridge, Sarah Horton, Michael Kunhardt, S. Martin Friedman, Tom Stone, Peter Levine and Marty Leder.

We have been aided over the past four years by numerous intern assistants, including Joe Leone, Kelly Park, Taylor Page, Jamie O'Shea, Dinah Tutein, Gretchen Hoffman, Bernard Schmidling, Peter Ortiz, Kim Forsberg, Chris Delfs, Megan Wilson, Kate Niles, Jeremy Stillman, Harriet Kirby, Katie Page, Irina Prentice, Georgia Goodhue, Lesley D'Angelo, Josh Jacobstein, Kirsten Bowen, Joanna Iadeluca, and Jill Cowan, who began as an intern before becoming a full-fledged member of our team.

In addition, we employed the help of professional researchers Jan Grenci, Cheryl Regan, Ken Kato, Mark Santangelo, and Peter Cole, all of whom did on-site research in Washington, D.C. Too numerous to name are the extraordinarily helpful persons at the many libraries and archives to which we turned for assistance. The staff of the Library of Congress in particular is to be greatly thanked for helping with innumerable requests, especially Bebe Overmiller, Deborah Evans, and Eva Shade. We also extend our thanks to Kate Flaherty, Todd Sudbrink, Lee Viveretto, Dan Linke, and Andrea Ashby, each of whom helped lead us to materials for this book. And we must mention the wonderful staff of our own public library here in Mt. Kisco, especially Mary Ayers, Wendy Bloom, Juliana Biro, and Miriam Budin, who helped with our constant requests over these many months.

Because this book depends in large measure upon the actual words of the presidents, special research went into that area. Since we were not looking just for the famous public utterances but also for the little-known, the humanly revealing, and the thematically illuminating, we tried to read virtually everything we could find. In many cases, this meant delving into unpublished manuscript sources, for which we employed transcribers to help make sense of often almost illegible handwriting. Ron Orlando, Jane Stewart, Barbara Sweet, and Judith Spikes all did tremendous service in this department. We were also helped by Holly Chase Chanetry, Roland Balibert, Sharyn Pratt, Mary Lee Fox-Roe, Martha De la Pava, Gina Nespolini, Muriel Rosso, Alice Durney, Mary Arena, Joan Stewart, Melissa Kafes, and Diane Heckler.

Writing about the modern presidents involves research into film and audio and television archives. Here we received special help from a number of individuals, including Polly Pettit, Carol Moore, Susan Hormuth, Bonnie Rowan, Diane Clater, Clark Bavin, Ron Campbell, and Lynn Watson Powers. Also, Lee Langston-Harrison, Jennifer Capps, Karen Tomlinson, and John Sykes performed helpful research for us. And we thank David Hume Kennerly and Bob McNeely for generously making their photography available.

In a general way we'd like to acknowledge the editors and staffs of the various presidential papers projects, without whose gargantuan labors over the years we could not have accomplished this job. Their work, in most cases still in progress, sets a standard for academic excellence. In particular we would like to thank Wayne Cutler at the Polk papers, Paul Bergeron at the Andrew Johnson papers, and John Y. Simon at the Grant papers, each of whom went beyond the call of duty in assisting us. And to all the curators and staffs at the presidential homes we say thank you for your kind help in our research task as well.

We also thank Neil Horstmann, Harmony Haskins, and the White House Historical Association for granting us extensive access to the mansion for photography, as well as important assistance in obtaining archival photographs. And we thank Gary Walters, Chief Usher at the White House, who has made all of our work there a pleasure.

The viewer of the series will recognize the voices we have chosen to portray the different presidents. Early on, we decided not to use actors, even though they would give the production a professional gloss. Instead, to speak the lines of the first thirty-one presidents, we chose public figures, primarily from the fields of politics and journalism. They include Walter Cronkite, Lloyd Bentsen, H. Norman Schwarzkopf, Sargent Shriver, Billy Graham, Ben Bradlee, David Gergen, Paul Simon, Morley Safer, Tom Wicker, John Glenn, George Will, Alexander Haig, James Roosevelt, Charlie Rose, Tim Russert, Don Imus, Dan Rostenkowski, Robert MacNeil, George Shultz, George Mitchell, Andrew Young, Robert Dole, James Carville, Lowell Weicker, William F. Buckley, Dale Bumpers, Howard Baker, and Colin Powell. We thank the "Washington community" for being so embracing of this project.

The 800 images in this book come from archives across the country, as can be seen in our picture credits. But we also had a head start. The Meserve-Kunhardt Collection was amassed by Frederick Hill Meserve, grandfather of one of the authors and great-grandfather of the other two. Meserve was the acclaimed scholar and expert on the photographs of Abraham Lincoln, but he was also the patient collector of presidential portraiture in general, much of which appears on these pages. We lift our hats to him and to his learned daughter and colleague Dorothy Meserve Kunhardt, who would have loved working with us on this fascinating project.

Finally we thank our wives, Katharine, Margie, and Suzy, for their love and support throughout the years of this adventure. And we salute our up-and-coming new Kunhardt generation, some of whom already have their own interest in the history of the presidents—Peter, Abby, Teddy, Jessie, George, Philip, Harry, and Clinton. We dedicate this book to all of you.

Behind the scenes at the White House, circa 1890.

Selected Bibliography

Presidential literature is notably vast; for most of the twentieth-century presidents, there are whole libraries of relevant source material. And for important earlier presidents—such as Washington, Jefferson, Jackson, and Lincoln—bibliographical guides fill entire volumes. What follows is meant as a guide into further exploration, and as a reflection of the most helpful resources that have informed the research for this book. For each president we have selected a handful of the finest biographies and historical treatments, as well as the most readily available published sources of their own words. Where such sources do not yet exist (surprisingly often), we list the names of the institutions from which we obtained photocopies of archival manuscripts. Since this book is based on a PBS television documentary, for the ten most recent presidents—Harry Truman through Bill Clinton—we have depended not so much on book and manuscript research as on film and audio and television archival research, not reflected here. The bibliographical entries for these presidents are correspondingly thinner.

General

ENCYCLOPEDIAS, DICTIONARIES, AND PRIMARY SOURCE COLLECTIONS

Cohen, Norman S. *The American Presidents: An Annotated Bibliography.* Pasadena, Calif.: Salem Press, 1989.

Degregorio, William A. *The Complete Book of U.S. Presidents.* New York: Wings Books, 1984.

Graff, Henry E. *The Presidents: A Reference History.* 2d ed. New York: Simon & Schuster, 1997.

Kane, Joseph Nathan. *Facts About the Presidents: A Compilation of Biographical and Historical Information.* New York: Wilson, 1981.

Levy, Leonard W., and Louis Fisher. *Encyclopedia of the American Presidency.* 4 vols. New York: Simon & Schuster, 1994.

Martin, Fenton, and Robert Goehlert. *American Presidents: A Bibliography.* Washington, D.C.: Congressional Quarterly, 1987.

Nelson, Michael, ed. *Congressional Quarterly's Guide to the Presidency.* 2 vols. Washington, D.C.: Congressional Quarterly, 1996.

Richardson, James D., ed. *Messages and Papers of the Presidents: 1789–1897.* 10 vols. Washington, D.C.: U.S. Government Printing Office, 1899.

———. *Messages and Papers of the Presidents: 1897–1914.* 18 vols. New York: Bureau of National Literature, 1897–1914.

Schick, Frank L. *Records of the Presidency: Presidential Papers and Libraries from Washington to Reagan.* Phoenix: Oryx Press, 1989.

The Presidency

Bailey, Thomas A. *Presidential Greatness.* New York: Appleton-Century, 1966.

Bryce, James. *The American Commonwealth.* 2 vols. Indianapolis: The Liberty Fund, 1995.

Dallek, Robert T. *Hail to the Chief.* New York: Hyperion Press, 1996.

Heale, M. G. *The Presidential Quest: Candidates and Images in American Political Culture, 1787–1852.* New York: Longman, 1982.

Hofstadter, Richard. *The American Political Tradition and the Men Who Made It.* New York: Vintage Books, reprint 1989.

Ketcham, Ralph. *Presidents Above Party: The First American Presidency, 1789–1829.* Chapel Hill, N.C.: University of North Carolina Press, 1983.

Kissinger, Henry. *Diplomacy.* New York: Simon & Schuster, 1994.

LaFeber, Walter. *The New Empire: An Interpretation of American Expansionism.* Ithaca, N. Y.: Cornell University Press, 1963.

McDonald, Forrest. *The American Presidency: An Intellectual History.* Lawrence, Kans.: University of Kansas Press, 1994.

Mayhem, David R. *Divided We Govern.* New Haven, Conn.: Yale University Press, 1991.

Milkis, Sidney M. *The Presidents and the Parties: The Transformation of the American Party System Since the New Deal.* New York: Oxford University Press, 1993.

———, and Michael Nelson. *The American Presidency: Origins and Development 1776–1993.* Washington, D.C.: Congressional Quarterly, 1994.

Miroff, Bruce. *Icons of Democracy: American Leaders as Heroes, Aristocrats, Dissenters, and Democrats.* New York: Basic Books, 1993.

Nelson, Michael. *The Presidency and the Political System.* Washington, D.C.: Congressional Quarterly, 1998.

Neustadt, Richard E. *Presidential Power And the Modern Presidents: The Politics of Leadership from Roosevelt to Reagan.* New York: Free Press, 1990.

Pious, Richard M. *The American Presidency.* New York: Basic Books, 1970.

Rose, Richard. *The Postmodern President.* Chatham, N. J.: Chatham House, 1988.

Schlesinger, Arthur M., Jr. *The Cycles of American History.* Boston: Houghton Mifflin, 1986.

———. *The Imperial Presidency.* Boston: Houghton Mifflin, 1973.

Silbey, Joel. *The Partisan Imperative: The Dynamics of American Politics Before the Civil War.* New York: Oxford University Press, 1985.

Skowronek, Stephen. *The Politics Presidents Make: Leadership from John Adams to George Bush.* Cambridge, Mass.: Belknap Press, 1993.

Tulis, Jeffrey, K. *The Rhetorical Presidency.* Princeton: Princeton University Press, 1987.

The White House

Aikman, Lonnelle. *The Living White House.* Washington, D.C.: White House Historical Association and the National Geographic Society, 1966–91.

Caroli, Betty Boyd. *Inside the White House.* New York: Canopy Books, 1992.

Freidel, Frank, and William Pencak, eds. *The White House: The First Two Hundred Years.* Boston: Northeastern University Press, 1994.

Garrett, Wendell. *Our Changing White House.* Boston: Northeastern University Press, 1995.

Guidas, John. *The White House: Resources for Research at the Library of Congress.* Washington, D.C.: Library of Congress, 1992.

Jensen, Amy La Folette. *The White House and Its Thirty-two Families.* New York: McGraw-Hill, 1958.

Seale, William. *The President's House.* 2 vols. Washington, D.C.: White House Historical Association, 1986.

———. *The White House: The History of an American Idea.* Washington, D.C.: The American Institute of Architects Press, 1992.

The White House: An Historic Guide, Washington, D.C.: White House Historical Association and National Geographic Society, 1995.

Pictorial Sources

American Heritage Pictorial History of the Presidents of the United States, The. 2 vols. New York: American Heritage Publishing and Simon & Schuster, 1968.

American Story in Art: Murals of Allyn Cox in the U.S. Capitol, The. Washington, D.C.: Daughters of the American Revolution and the U.S. Capitol Historical Society, 1986.

Andrist, Ralph, et al. *200 Years: Bicentennial Illustrated History of the United States.* New York: U.S. News & World Report, 1973.

Blaisdell, Thomas C., et al. *The American Presidency in Political Cartoons: 1776–1976.* Rev. ed. Layton, Utah, Peregrine Smith, 1976.

Collins, Kathleen. *Washingtoniana Photographs.* Washington, D.C.: Library of Congress, 1989.

Cunliffe, Marcus. *The American Heritage History of the Presidency.* New York: American Heritage, 1968.

Cunningham, Noble. *Popular Images of the Presidency.* Columbia, Mo.: University of Missouri Press, 1991.

Dowdy, Dru, ed. *National Portrait Gallery, Smithsonian Institution: Permanent Collection Illustrated Checklist.* Washington, D.C.: Smithsonian Institution Press, 1987.

Durant, John, and Alice Durant. *A Pictorial History of the Presidents.* New York: Barnes, 1955.

Heller, Joseph, ed. *War and Conflict: Selected Images from the National Archives 1765–1970.* Washington, D.C.: National Archives and Records Administration, 1990.

Jones, Cranston. *Homes of the American Presidents.* New York: McGraw-Hill, 1962.

Kloss, William. *Art in the White House.* Washington, D.C.: White House Historical Association and National Geographic Society, 1992.

Kunhardt, Dorothy Meserve, and Philip B. Kunhardt, Jr. *Mathew Brady and His World.* Alexandria, Va.: Time-Life Books, 1977.

Lorant, Stefan. *The Glorious Burden: The American Presidency.* New York: Harper & Row, 1968.

———. *The Presidency: A Pictorial History of Presidential Elections from Washington to Truman.* New York: Macmillan, 1951.

Melder, Keith. *Hail to the Candidate: Presidential Campaigns from Banner to Broadcasts.* Washington, D.C.: Smithsonian Institution Press, 1992.

Milhollen, Hirst D., and Milton Kaplan. *Presidents on Parade: The Pictorial History of the Presidents.* New York: Macmillan, 1948.

Panzer, Mary. *Mathew Brady and the Image of History.* Washington D.C.: Smithsonian Institution Press, 1997.

Pfister, Harold F., ed. *Facing the Light: Historic American Portrait Daguerreotypes.* Washington, D.C.: Smithsonian Institution Press, 1978.

Schlesinger, Arthur M., Jr. *Running for President: The Candidates and Their Images.* New York: Simon & Schuster, 1994.

Washington Past and Present: A Guide to the Nation's Capital. Washington, D.C.: United States Capitol Historical Society, 1993.

Individual Presidents

George Washington

PRIMARY SOURCES

Allen, William B. *George Washington: A Collection.* Indianapolis: The Liberty Fund, 1988.

Andrist, Ralph K., ed. *George Washington: A Biography in His Own Words.* New York: Harper & Row, 1972.

Padover, Saul, ed. *The Washington Papers: Basic Selections from the Public and Private Writings of George Washington.* New York: Grosset & Dunlap, 1955.

SECONDARY SOURCES

Elkins, Stanley M., and Eric McKitrick. *The Age of Federalism: The Early American Republic, 1788–1800.* New York: Oxford University Press, 1993.

Flexner, James Thomas. *George Washington.* 4 vols. Boston: Little, Brown, 1965-1972.

———. *Washington: The Indispensable Man.* New York: New American Library, 1974.

Freeman, Douglas Southall. *George Washington: A Biography.* 7 vols. New York: Charles Scribner's Sons, 1948–1957.

McDonald, Forrest. *The Presidency of George Washington.* Lawrence, Kans.: University Press of Kansas, 1974.

Wick, Wendy C. *George Washington: An American Icon.* Washington, D.C.: Smithsonian Institution, 1982.

John Adams

PRIMARY SOURCES

Adams, Charles, F. ed. *The Works of John Adams, Second President of the United States.* 10 vols. Boston: Little and Brown, 1850–1856.

White House Office, circa 1890

Butterfield, L. H., ed. *The Book of Abigail and John: Selected Letters of the Adams Family.* Boston: Massachusetts Historical Society, 1975.

———. *Diary and Autobiography of John Adams.* 5 vols. Cambridge, Mass.: Belknap Press, 1961–66.

Cappon, Lester J., ed. *The Adams-Jefferson Letters: The Complete Correspondence Between Thomas Jefferson and Abigail and John Adams.* 2 vols. Chapel Hill, N.C.: University of North Carolina Press, 1959.

Peabody, James Bishop, ed. *John Adams; A Biography in His Own Words.* 2 vols. New York: Harper & Row, 1973.

SECONDARY SOURCES

Brown, Ralph Adams. *The Presidency of John Adams.* Lawrence, Kans.: University Press of Kansas, 1975.

Ellis, Joseph. *Passionate Sage: The Character and Legacy of John Adams.* New York: Norton, 1993.

Nagel, Paul C. *Descent from Glory: Four Generations of the John Adams Family.* New York: Oxford University Press, 1983.

Oliver, Andrew. *Portraits of Abigail and John Adams.* Cambridge, Mass.: Belknap Press, 1967.

Shaw, Peter. *The Character of John Adams.* Chapel Hill, N.C.: University of North Carolina Press, 1976.

Smith, Page. *John Adams.* 2 vols. New York: Doubleday, 1962.

Thomas Jefferson

PRIMARY SOURCES

Betts, Edwin Morris, and James Adam Bear, Jr. *The Family Letters of Thomas Jefferson.* Charlottesville, Va.: University Press of Virginia, 1966.

Boyd, Julian, ed. *The Papers of Thomas Jefferson.* 20 vols. Princeton, N.J.: Princeton University Press, 1950–1974.

Editors of Newsweek Books, The. *Thomas Jefferson: A Biography in His Own Words.* 2 vols. New York: Newsweek, 1974.

Ford, Paul Leicester, ed. *The Writings of Thomas Jefferson.* 10 vols. New York: Putnam, 1892–1900.

Koch, Adrienne, and William Peden, eds. *The Life and Selected Writings of Jefferson.* New York: Random House, 1944.

Padover, Saul K., ed. *The Complete Jefferson.* New York: Duell, Sloan and Pearce, 1943.

———. *A Jefferson Profile as Revealed in His Letters.* New York: John Day, 1956.

Peterson, Merrill D., ed. *Thomas Jefferson: Writings.* New York: Library of America, 1984.

Smith, James Morton, ed. *The Republic of Letters: The Correspondence Between Thomas Jefferson and James Madison 1776–1826.* 3 vols. New York: Norton, 1945.

SECONDARY SOURCES

Ellis, Joseph. *American Sphinx.* New York: Knopf, 1997.

Malone, Dumas. *Jefferson and His Times.* 6 vols. Boston: Little, Brown, 1948–81.

Peterson, Merrill D. *Thomas Jefferson and the New Nation: A Biography.* New York: Oxford University Press, 1970.

James Madison

PRIMARY SOURCES

Hunt, Gaillard. *The Writings of James Madison.* 9 vols. New York: Putnam, 1900–1910.

Hutchinson, W. T., Robert A. Rutland, J. C. A. Stagg, et al., *The Papers of James Madison.* 23 vols. Charlottesville, Va.: University of Virginia Press, 1962–.

Madison, James. *Notes on the Debates in the Field Convention of 1787.* Columbus, Ohio: Ohio University Press, 1966.

Padover, Saul. *The Complete Madison.* New York: Harper & Row, 1953.

Peterson, Merrill D. *James Madison: A Biography in His Own Words.* New York: Newsweek, 1974.

Smith, James Morton, ed. *The Republic of Letters: The Correspondence Between Thomas Jefferson and James Madison 1776–1826.* 3 vols. New York: Norton, 1945.

SECONDARY SOURCES

Ketcham, Ralph L. *James Madison: A Biography.* New York: Macmillan, 1971.

White House private dining room, 1889

Rossiter, Clinton. *1787: The Grand Convention.* New York: Norton, 1966.

Rutland, Robert A. *James Madison and the Search for Nationhood.* Washington, D.C.: Library of Congress, 1981.

———. *James Madison: The Founding Father.* New York: Macmillan, 1987.

———. *The Presidency of James Madison.* Lawrence, Kans.: University Press of Kansas, 1990.

James Monroe

ARCHIVAL PRIMARY SOURCES

College of William and Mary; James Monroe Memorial Library and Museum; Library of Congress; New York Public Library

PRIMARY SOURCES

Bassett, John Spencer, ed. *The Correspondence of Andrew Jackson.* 6 vols. Washington, D.C.: Carnegie Institution, 1926.

Hamilton, Stanislaus Murray, ed. *The Writings of James Monroe.* 7 vols. New York: Putnam, 1900.

SECONDARY SOURCES

Ammon, Harry. *James Monroe: The Quest for National Identity.* New York: McGraw-Hill, 1971.

Cunningham, Noble E., Jr. *The Presidency of James Monroe.* Lawrence, Kans.: University Press of Kansas, 1995.

John Quincy Adams

PRIMARY SOURCES

Adams, Charles Francis, ed. *Memoirs of John Quincy Adams Comprising Portions of His Diary from 1795–1848.* 12 vols. Philadelphia: Lippincott, 1874–77.

Allen, David G., et al., eds. *Diary of John Quincy Adams.* 2 vols. Cambridge, Mass.: Belknap Press, 1981.

Ford, Worthington Chauncy, ed. *The Writings of John Quincy Adams.* 7 vols. New York: Greenwood Press, 1968.

Nevins, Allan, ed. *The Diary of John Quincy Adams, 1794–1845: American Diplomacy and Political, Social and Intellectual Life, from Washington to Polk.* New York: Ungar, 1951.

SECONDARY SOURCES

Bemis, Samuel Flagg. *John Quincy Adams and the Foundation of American Foreign Policy.* New York: Knopf, 1949.

———. *John Quincy Adams and the Union.* New York: Knopf, 1956.

Hargreaves, Mary. *The Presidency of John Quincy Adams.* Lawrence, Kans.: University Press of Kansas, 1985.

Nagel, Paul. *John Quincy Adams: A Public Life, A Private Life.* New York: Knopf, 1997.

Oliver, Andrew. *Portraits of John Quincy Adams and His Wife.* Cambridge, Mass.: Belknap Press, 1970.

Andrew Jackson

PRIMARY SOURCES

Bassett, John Spencer, ed. *The Correspondence of Andrew Jackson.* 6 vols. Washington, D.C.: Carnegie Institution, 1926.

Smith, Sam B., and Harriet C. Owsley, eds. *The Papers of Andrew Jackson.* 4 vols. Knoxville, Tenn.: University of Tennessee Press, 1980–.

SECONDARY SOURCES

Barber, James G. *Andrew Jackson: A Portrait Study.* Washington, D.C.: National Portrait Gallery, 1991.

———. *Old Hickory: A Life Sketch of Andrew Jackson.* Washington, D.C.: Smithsonian Institution, 1990.

Cole, Donald B. *The Presidency of Andrew Jackson.* Lawrence, Kans.: University Press of Kansas, 1993.

Parton, James. *Life of Andrew Jackson.* 3 vols. New York: Mason Brothers, 1860.

Remini, Robert V. *Andrew Jackson and the Course of the American Empire, 1767–1821.* New York: Harper & Row, 1977.

———. *Andrew Jackson and the Course of American Freedom, 1822–32.* New York: Harper & Row, 1981.

———. *Andrew Jackson and the Course of American Democracy, 1833–45.* New York: Harper & Row, 1984.

Schlesinger, Arthur M., Jr. *The Age of Jackson.* Boston: Little, Brown, 1945.

Martin Van Buren

ARCHIVAL PRIMARY SOURCE

Library of Congress

PRIMARY SOURCES

Fitzpatrick, John S., ed. *The Autobiography of Martin Van Buren* (Annual Report of the American Historical Association for the Year 1918, vol. 2). Washington, D.C., 1920.

Van Buren, Martin. *Inquiry Into the Origin and Course of Political Parties in the United States.* New York: Hurd & Houghton, 1867.

SECONDARY SOURCES

Cole, Donald B. *Martin Van Buren and the American Political System.* Princeton, N.J.: Princeton University Press, 1984.

Curtis, James C. *The Fox at Bay: The Presidency of Martin Van Buren, 1837–1841.* Lexington, Ky.: University Press of Kentucky, 1970.

Niven, John. *Martin Van Buren: The Romantic Age of American Politics.* New York: Oxford University Press, 1983.

Remini, Robert V. *Martin Van Buren and the Making of the Democratic Party.* New York: Columbia University Press, 1958.

Wilson, Major L. *The Presidency of Martin Van Buren.* Lawrence, Kans.: University Press of Kansas, 1984.

William Henry Harrison

ARCHIVAL PRIMARY SOURCES

Cincinnati Museum Center; Forbes Magazine Library; Indiana Historical Society; Library of Congress; New York Public Library; Ohio Historical Society; Transylvania University

PRIMARY SOURCES

Esarey, Logan, ed. *Messages and Letters of William Henry Harrison.* 2 vols. Indianapolis: Indiana Historical Commission, 1922.

SECONDARY SOURCES

Cleaves, Freeman. *Old Tippecanoe: William Henry Harrison and His Time.* New York: Charles Scribner's Sons, 1939.

Gunderson, Robert Gray. *The Log-Cabin Campaign.* Lexington, Ky.: University of Kentucky Press, 1957.

Peterson, Norma L. *The Presidencies of William Henry Harrison and John Tyler.* Lawrence, Kans.: University Press of Kansas, 1989.

John Tyler

ARCHIVAL PRIMARY SOURCES

Duke University; Library of Congress; University of Virginia; Virginia Historical Society; Yale University

PRIMARY SOURCE

Tyler, Lyon G. *The Letters and Times of the Tylers.* 3 vols. New York: DeCapo Press, 1884–96.

SECONDARY SOURCES

Chitwood, Oliver P. *John Tyler: Champion of the Old South.* New York: D. Appleton-Century, 1939.

Peterson, Norma L. *The Presidencies of William Henry Harrison and John Tyler.* Lawrence, Kans.: University Press of Kansas, 1989.

The Lincoln bedroom, circa 1900

James K. Polk

PRIMARY SOURCES

Nevins, Allan, ed. *Polk: The Diary of a President.* London: Longmans, Green, 1952.

Quaife, Milo M., ed. *The Diary of James K. Polk During His Presidency, 1845–49.* 4 vols. Chicago: McClurg, 1910.

Weaver, Herbert, et al., eds. *The Correspondence of James K. Polk.* 9 vols. Nashville: University of Tennessee Press, 1969–.

SECONDARY SOURCES

Bergeron, Paul H. *The Presidency of James K. Polk.* Lawrence, Kans.: University Press of Kansas, 1987.

McCormick, Eugene Irving. *James K. Polk: A Political Biography.* New York: Russell & Russell, 1922.

McCoy, Charles A. *Polk and the Presidency.* Austin, Tex.: University of Texas Press, 1960.

Sellers, Charles G. *James K. Polk: Jacksonian.* Princeton, N.J.: Princeton University Press, 1957.

———. *James K. Polk: Continentalist 1843–1846.* Princeton, N.J.: Princeton University Press, 1966.

Zachary Taylor

ARCHIVAL PRIMARY SOURCES

Historical Society of Pennsylvania; Library of Congress; Missouri Historical Society; Princeton University; University of Kentucky; Virginia Historical Society

PRIMARY SOURCE

Samson, William, ed. *Letters of Zachary Taylor from the Battlefield of the Mexican War.* Rochester, N.Y.: Gennesee Press, 1908.

SECONDARY SOURCES

Bauer, K. Jack. *Zachary Taylor: Soldier, Planter, Statesman of the Old Southwest.* Baton Rouge, La.: Louisiana University Press, 1985.

Hamilton, Holman. *Zachary Taylor: Soldier of the Republic.* Indianapolis: Bobbs-Merrill, 1941.

———. *Zachary Taylor: Soldier in the White House.* Indianapolis: Bobbs-Merrill, 1951.

Nevins, Allan. *Ordeal of the Union.* 2 vols. New York: Scribners, 1947.

Sandweiss, Martha A., Rick Stewart, and Ben W. Huseman. *Eyewitness to War: Prints and Daguerreotypes of the Mexican War, 1846–48.* Fort Worth, Tex.: Amon Carter Museum and Smithsonian Institution Press, 1989.

Smith, Elbert B. *The Presidencies of Zachary Taylor and Millard Fillmore.* Lawrence, Kans.: University Press of Kansas, 1988.

Stegmaier, Mark J. *Texas, New Mexico and the Compromise of 1850.* Kent, Ohio: Kent State University Press, 1996.

Millard Fillmore

ARCHIVAL PRIMARY SOURCES

Franklin D. Roosevelt Library; Historical Society of Pennsylvania; Library of Congress; SUNY Oswego; University of Rochester

PRIMARY SOURCE

Severance, Frank H., ed. *The Millard Fillmore Papers.* 2 vols. Buffalo: Buffalo Historical Society, 1907.

SECONDARY SOURCES

Rayback, Robert J. *Millard J. Fillmore: Biography of a President.* Buffalo: American Political Biography Press, 1959.

Smith, Elbert B. *The Presidencies of Zachary Taylor and Millard Fillmore.* Lawrence, Kans.: University of Kansas Press, 1988.

Stegmaier, Mark J. *Texas, New Mexico and the Compromise of 1850.* Kent, Ohio: Kent State University Press, 1996.

Franklin Pierce

ARCHIVAL PRIMARY SOURCE

Library of Congress

SECONDARY SOURCES

Gara, Larry. *The Presidency of Franklin Pierce.* Lawrence, Kans.: University Press of Kansas Press, 1988.

Gienapp, William E. *The Origins of the Republican Party 1852–56.* New York: Oxford University Press, 1987.

Nevins, Allan. *Ordeal of the Union.* 2 vols. New York: Scribners, 1947.

Nichols, Roy F. *Franklin Pierce: Young Hickory of the Granite Hills.* Philadelphia: University of Pennsylvania Press, 1931.

James Buchanan

ARCHIVAL PRIMARY SOURCES

College of William and Mary; Harvard University; Historical Society of Pennsylvania; Lancaster County Historical Society

PRIMARY SOURCE

Moore, John B., ed. *The Works of James Buchanan: Comprising His Speeches, State Papers and Private Correspondence.* 12 vols. New York: Antiquarian Press, reprint, 1960.

SECONDARY SOURCES

Curtis, George T. *Life of James Buchanan Fifteenth President of the United States.* New York: Harper & Row, 1883.

Gienapp, William E. *The Origins of the Republican Party 1852–56.* New York: Oxford University Press, 1987.

Klein, Phillip S. *James Buchanan: A Biography.* University Park, Pa.: Penn State University Press, 1962.

Nevins, Allan. *The Emergence of Lincoln.* 2 vols. New York: Scribners, 1950.

Smith, Elbert B. *The Presidency of James Buchanan.* Lawrence, Kans.: University Press of Kansas, 1975.

Abraham Lincoln

PRIMARY SOURCES

Basler, Roy P., et al., eds. *The Collected Works of Abraham Lincoln.* 9 vols. New Brunswick, N.J.: Rutgers University Press, 1953–55.

Basler, Roy P., ed. *The Collected Works of Abraham Lincoln, First Supplement, 1832–1865.* New Brunswick, N.J.: Rutgers University Press, 1974.

Basler, Roy P., and Christian O. Basler, eds. *The Collected Works of Abraham Lincoln, Second Supplement, 1848–1865.* New Brunswick, N.J.: Rutgers University Press, 1990.

Fehrenbacher, Don E., and Virginia Fehrenbacher, eds. *Recollected Words of Abraham Lincoln.* Stanford, Calif.: Stanford University Press, 1996.

SECONDARY SOURCES

Borritt, Gabor S. *Lincoln and the Economics of the American Dream.* Memphis: Memphis State University Press, 1978.

Current, Richard N. *The Lincoln Nobody Knows.* New York: McGraw-Hill, 1958.

Donald, David H. *Lincoln.* New York: Simon & Schuster, 1995.

———. *Lincoln Reconsidered: Essays on the Civil War Era.* New York: Knopf, 1956.

Fehrenbacher, Don E. *Lincoln in Text and Context: Collected Essays.* Stanford, Calif.: Stanford University Press, 1987.

———. *Prelude to Greatness.* Stanford, Calif.: Stanford University Press, 1962.

Kunhardt, Philip B., Jr., Philip B. Kunhardt III, and Peter W. Kunhardt. *Lincoln.* New York: Knopf, 1993.

Mellon, James. *The Face of Lincoln.* New York: Viking Press, 1979.

Meserve, Frederick Hill, and Carl Sandburg. *The Photographs of Abraham Lincoln.* New York: Harcourt, Brace, 1944.

Ostendorf, Lloyd. *Lincoln's Photographs: A Complete Album.* Dayton: Rockywood Press, 1998.

Paludan, Phillip S. *The Presidency of Abraham Lincoln.* Lawrence, Kans.: University Press of Kansas, 1994.

Andrew Johnson

PRIMARY SOURCES

Graf, Leroy P., and Ralph W. Haskins, eds. *The Papers of Andrew Johnson.* 12 vols. Nashville: University of Tennessee Press, 1967–.

Foster, Lillian, ed. *President Johnson: Life and Speeches.* New York: Richardson, 1866.

Moore, Frank, ed. *Life and Speeches of Andrew Johnson.* Boston: Little, Brown, 1865.

Welles, Gideon. *Diary of Gideon Welles.* 3 vols. Boston: Houghton Mifflin, 1911.

SECONDARY SOURCES

Castel, Albert E. *The Presidency of Andrew Johnson.* Lawrence, Kans.: University Press of Kansas, 1979.

McKitrick, Eric L. *Andrew Johnson and Reconstruction.* Chicago: University of Chicago Press, 1960.

Trefousse, Hans L. *Andrew Johnson: A Biography.* New York: Norton, 1989.

Ulysses S. Grant

PRIMARY SOURCES

Grant, U. S. *Personal Memoirs of U.S. Grant.* 2 vols. New York: Little, 1885–86.

Nevins, Allan. *Hamilton Fish: The Inner History of the Grant Administration.* New York: Dodd, Mead, 1946.

Simon, John Y., ed. *The Papers of Ulysses S. Grant.* 20 vols. Carbondale, Ill.: University of Southern Illinois Press, 1967–.

Young, J. Russell. *Around the World With General Grant.* 2 vols. New York: American News Company, 1879.

SELECTED SECONDARY SOURCES

Barber, James G. *U.S. Grant: The Man and the Image.* Washington, D.C.: National Portrait Gallery, 1985.

Catton, Bruce. *U.S. Grant and the American Military Tradition.* Boston: Little, Brown, 1954.

Frost, Lawrence A. *U.S. Grant Album: A Pictorial Biography of Ulysses S. Grant.* Seattle: Superior, 1966.

McFeely, William S. *U.S. Grant: A Biography.* New York: Norton, 1981.

Rutherford B. Hayes

PRIMARY SOURCES

Williams, Charles R., ed. *Diary and Letters of Rutherford Birchard Hayes, Nineteenth President of the United States.* 5 vols. Columbus, Ohio: Ohio Historical Society, 1922–26.

Williams, T. Harry, ed. *Hayes: Diary of a President 1875–1881.* New York: David McKay, 1964.

SECONDARY SOURCES

Hoogenboom, Ari. *The Presidency of Rutherford B. Hayes.* Lawrence, Kans.: University Press of Kansas, 1988.

———. *Rutherford B. Hayes: Warrior and President.* Lawrence, Kans.: University Press of Kansas, 1995.

James A. Garfield

PRIMARY SOURCES

Brown, Harry James, ed. *The Diary of James Garfield.* 4 vols. East Lansing, Mich.: Michigan State University Press, 1967–1981.

Hinsdale, Burke A., ed. *The Works of James Abram Garfield.* 2 vols. Boston: Osgood, 1882.

Hinsdale, Mary L., ed. *Garfield-Hinsdale Letters.* Ann Arbor, Mich.: University of Michigan Press, 1949.

Shaw, John, ed. *Crete and James: Personal Letters of Lucretia and James Garfield.* East Lansing, Mich.: Michigan State University Press, 1995.

Smith, Theodore Clark, ed. *The Life and Letters of James Abram Garfield.* 2 vols. New Haven, Conn.: Yale University Press, 1925.

Williams, Frederick D., ed. *The Wild Life of the Army: Civil War Letters of James A. Garfield.* East Lansing, Mich.: Michigan State University Press, 1964.

SECONDARY SOURCES

Doenecke, Justus D. *The Presidencies of James A. Garfield and Chester A. Arthur.* Lawrence, Kans.: University Press of Kansas, 1981.

McElroy, Richard. *James A Garfield: His Life and Times: A Pictorial History.* Canton, Ohio: Daring Books, 1986.

Peskin, Allan. *Garfield.* Kent, Ohio: Kent State University Press, 1978.

Chester A. Arthur

ARCHIVAL PRIMARY SOURCES

Chicago Historical Society; Cornell University; Free Library of Philadelphia; Indiana Historical Society; Library of Congress; New Hampshire State Historical Society; New York Historical Society; Wyoming State Archives

SECONDARY SOURCES

Doenecke, Justus D. *The Presidencies of James A. Garfield and Chester A. Arthur.* Lawrence, Kans.: University Press of Kansas, 1981.

Reeves, Thomas C. *Gentleman Boss: The Life of Chester Alan Arthur.* New York: American Political Biography Press, 1975.

Grover Cleveland

PRIMARY SOURCES

Bergh, Albert E., ed. *Addresses, State Papers and Letters.* New York: Sundial Classics, 1909.

Cleveland, Grover *Presidential Problems.* Freeport, N.Y.: Books for Libraries Press, reprint, 1971.

———. *Independence of the Executive.* Princeton, N.J.: Princeton University Press, 1913

Nevins, Allan, ed. *Letters of Grover Cleveland.* Boston: Houghton Mifflin, 1933.

Parker, George F., ed. *Writings and Speeches of Grover Cleveland.* New York: Cassell, 1892.

SECONDARY SOURCES

"Cleveland in His Hours of Ease." *Harper's Weekly*, vol. 51, June 8, 1907.

Edwards, E. Jay. "The Personal Force of Grover Cleveland." *McClure's Magazine*, November 1893, pp. 493–500.

Nevins, Allan. *Grover Cleveland: A Study in Courage.* 2 vols. New York: Dodd, Mead, 1932.

"Terrible Tale, A." *Buffalo Evening Telegraph*, July 21, 1884.

Welch, Richard. *The Presidencies of Grover Cleveland.* Lawrence, Kans.: University Press of Kansas, 1988.

Benjamin Harrison

ARCHIVAL PRIMARY SOURCE

Library of Congress

PRIMARY SOURCES

Harrison, Benjamin. *This Country of Ours.* New York: Scribners, 1897.

———, and Mary Lord Harrison, ed. *Views of an Ex-President.* Indianapolis: Bowen-Merrill, 1901.

Hedges, Charles, ed. *Speeches of Benjamin Harrison, Twenty-Third President of the United States.* New York: John W. Lovell, 1892.

SECONDARY SOURCES

Sievers, Harry J. *Benjamin Harrison: Hoosier Warrior.* New York: University Publishers, 1952.

———. *Benjamin Harrison: Hoosier Statesman.* New York: University Publishers, 1959.

———. *Benjamin Harrison: Hoosier President.* New York: University Publishers, 1968.

Socolofsky, Homer E., and Allan B. Spetter. *The Presidency of Benjamin Harrison.* Lawrence, Kans.: University Press of Kansas, 1987.

William McKinley

ARCHIVAL PRIMARY SOURCES

Library of Congress; University of Michigan

PRIMARY SOURCES

Speeches and Addresses of William McKinley: From His Election to Congress to the Present Time. New York: Appleton, 1893.

Speeches and Addresses of William McKinley: From March 1, 1897 to May 30, 1900. New York: Doubleday & McClure, 1900.

SECONDARY SOURCES

Gould, Lewis L. *The Presidency of William McKinley.* Lawrence, Kans.: University Press of Kansas, 1980.

McElroy, Richard. *William McKinley and Our America: A Pictorial History.* Canton, Ohio: Stark County Historical Society, 1996.

Morgan, H. Wayne. *William McKinley and His America.* Syracuse, N.Y.: Syracuse University Press, 1963.

Olcott, Charles. *The Life of William McKinley.* 2 vols. Boston: Houghton Mifflin, 1916.

Trask, David F. *The War with Spain in 1898.* Lincoln, Nebr.: University of Nebraska Press, 1981.

Theodore Roosevelt

PRIMARY SOURCES

Bishop, Joseph Brucklin, ed. *Theodore Roosevelt and His Time, Shown in His Letters.* 2 vols. New York: Scribners, 1920.

Butt, Archibald W. *Taft and Roosevelt: The Intimate Letters of Archie Butt.* 2 vols. New York: Doubleday, 1930.

Harbaugh, William H. *The Life and Times of Theodore Roosevelt.* New York: Oxford University Press, 1975.

———. *Power and Responsibility: The Life and Times of Theodore Roosevelt.* New York: Farrar, Straus and Cudahy, 1961.

Morrison, Elting E., and John Blum, eds. *The Letters of Theodore Roosevelt.* 8 vols. Cambridge, Mass.: Harvard University Press, 1975.

Roosevelt, Theodore. *The Strenuous Life: Essays and Addresses.* New York: Century, 1902.

SECONDARY SOURCES

Cooper, John Milton, Jr. *The Warrior and the Priest: Woodrow Wilson and Theodore Roosevelt.* Cambridge, Mass.: Belknap Press, 1983.

Gould, Lewis L. *The Presidency of Theodore Roosevelt.* Lawrence, Kans.: University Press of Kansas, 1991.

McCullough, David. *Mornings on Horseback.* New York: Touchstone, 1981.

William Howard Taft

PRIMARY SOURCES

Butt, Archibald W. *Taft and Roosevelt: The Intimate Letters of Archie Butt.* 2 vols. New York: Doubleday, 1930.

Taft, William H. *Our Chief Magistrate and His Powers.* New York: Columbia University Press, 1916.

———. *Presidential Addresses and State Papers of William Howard Taft*, 2 vols. Garden City, N.Y.: Doubleday, 1910.

SECONDARY SOURCES

Anderson, Donald F. *William Howard Taft: A Conservative's Conception of the Presidency.* Ithaca, N.Y.: Cornell University Press, 1973.

Anderson, Judith Irke. *William Howard Taft: An Intimate History.* New York: Norton, 1981.

Coletta, Paolo E. *The Presidency of William Howard Taft.* Lawrence, Kans.: University Press of Kansas, 1973.

Pringle, Henry F. *The Life and Times of William Howard Taft.* 2 vols., New York: Farrar, Straus, 1939.

Summertime at the White House, circa 1890

Woodrow Wilson

PRIMARY SOURCES

Day, Donald, ed. *Woodrow Wilson's Own Story*. Boston: Little, Brown, 1952.

Heckscher, August, ed. *The Politics of Woodrow Wilson: Selections from His Speeches and Writings*. New York: Harper & Row, 1956.

Link, Arthur, ed. *The Papers of Woodrow Wilson*. 69 vols. Princeton, N.J.: Princeton University Press, 1966–1994.

Wilson, Woodrow. *Congressional Government*. Boston: Houghton Mifflin, 1885.

———. *Constitutional Government in the United States*. New York: Columbia University Press, 1908.

SECONDARY SOURCES

Burton, David H. *The Learned Presidency: Theodore Roosevelt, William Howard Taft and Woodrow Wilson*. Rutherford, N.J.: Fairleigh Dickinson University Press, 1988.

Clements, Kendrick A. *The Presidency of Woodrow Wilson*. Lawrence, Kans.: University Press of Kansas, 1992.

Heckscher, August. *Woodrow Wilson: A Biography*. New York: Scribners, 1991.

Link, Arthur S. *Woodrow Wilson: Revolution, War and Peace*. Arlington Heights, Ill.: AHM, 1979.

Warren G. Harding

ARCHIVAL PRIMARY SOURCE

Ohio Historical Society

PRIMARY SOURCES

Schortemeier, Frederick, ed. *Rededicating America: Life and Recent Speeches of Warren G. Harding*. Indianapolis: Bobbs-Merrill, 1920.

SELECTED SECONDARY SOURCES

Ferrell, Robert H. *The Strange Deaths of President Harding*. Columbus, Mo.: University of Missouri Press, 1996.

Murray, Robert K. *The Harding Era: Warren G. Harding and His Administration*. Minneapolis: University of Minnesota Press, 1969.

Trani, Eugene P., and David L. Wilson. *The Presidency of Warren G. Harding*. Lawrence, Kans.: University Press of Kansas, 1977.

Calvin Coolidge

PRIMARY SOURCES

Coolidge, Calvin. *The Autobiography of Calvin Coolidge*. Plymouth Notch, Vt.: Calvin Coolidge Memorial Foundation, 1989.

———. *Foundations of the Republic: Speeches and Addresses*. Freeport, N.Y.: Books for Libraries Press, reprint, 1968.

Lathem, Edward, ed. *Your Son, Calvin Coolidge: A Selection of Letters from Calvin Coolidge to His Father*. Montpelier, Vt., Vermont Historical Society, 1968.

Quint, Howard H., and Robert H. Ferrell, eds. *The Talkative President: The Off-the-Record Press Conferences of Calvin Coolidge*. Amherst, Mass.: University of Massachusetts Press, 1964.

Secondary Sources

Ferrell, Robert. *The Presidency of Calvin Coolidge*. Lawrence, Kans.: University Press of Kansas, 1998.

McCoy, Donald R. *Calvin Coolidge: The Quiet President*. New York: Macmillan, 1967.

Sobel, Robert. *Coolidge: An American Enigma*. Washington, D.C.: Regnery, 1998.

Herbert Hoover

PRIMARY SOURCES

Hoover, Herbert. *American Individualism*. New York: Doubleday, Page, 1922.

———. *The Memoirs of Herbert Hoover*. 3 vols. New York: Macmillan, 1951–1952.

———. *The New Day: Campaign Speeches of Herbert Hoover*. Palo Alto, Calif.: Stanford University Press, 1928.

SECONDARY SOURCES

Burner, David. *Herbert Hoover: A Public Life*. New York: Knopf, 1979.

Fausold, Martin L. *The Presidency of Herbert Hoover*. Lawrence, Kans.: University Press of Kansas, 1985.

Wilson, Joan Hoff. *Herbert Hoover: The Forgotten Progressive*. New York: Harper & Row, 1975.

Blue Room visitors, 1893

Franklin D. Roosevelt

PRIMARY SOURCES

Roosevelt, Franklin D. *The Public Papers of Franklin D. Roosevelt, 1928–1945*. 5 vols. New York: Random House, 1930.

SECONDARY SOURCES

Burns, James MacGregor. *Roosevelt: The Lion and the Fox.* New York: Harcourt, Brace & World, 1956.

———. *Roosevelt: The Soldier of Freedom.* New York: Harcourt, Brace & World, 1956.

Freidel, Frank B. *Franklin D. Roosevelt: A Rendezvous with Destiny.* Boston: Little, Brown, 1990.

Goodwin, Doris Kearns. *No Ordinary Time: Franklin and Eleanor Roosevelt: The Home Front in World War II.* New York: Simon & Schuster, 1994.

Graff, Robert D., and Robert Emmet Ginna. *FDR.* New York: Harper & Row, 1963.

Lorant, Stefan. *FDR: A Pictorial Biography.* New York: Simon & Schuster, 1950.

Morgan, Ted. *F.D.R.* New York: Simon & Schuster, 1985.

Harry S. Truman

PRIMARY SOURCES

Public Papers of the Presidents of the United States: Harry S. Truman, 1945–53. Washington, D.C.: Government Printing Office, 1961–66.

Miller, Merle. *Plain Speaking: An Oral Biography of Harry S. Truman.* New York: Berkley, 1973.

SECONDARY SOURCES

Geis, Joseph. *Harry S. Truman: A Pictorial Biography.* New York: Doubleday, 1968.

Hamby, Alonzo L., *Man of the People: A Life of Harry S. Truman.* New York: Oxford University Press, 1995.

McCullough, David. *Truman.* New York: Simon & Schuster, 1992.

Dwight D. Eisenhower

PRIMARY SOURCES

Public Papers of the Presidents of the United States: Dwight D. Eisenhower, 1953–61. Washington, D.C.: Government Printing Office, 1957–62.

Eisenhower, Dwight D. *In Review: Pictures I've Kept: A Concise Pictorial Autobiography.* New York: Doubleday, 1969.

———. *Waging Peace: The White House Years, A Personal Account, 1956–61.* New York: Doubleday, 1965.

SECONDARY SOURCES

Ambrose, Stephen E. *Eisenhower: Soldier, General of the Army, President-elect, 1890–1952.* New York: Simon & Schuster, 1983.

———. *Eisenhower: The President.* New York: Simon & Schuster, 1984.

Greenstein, Fred. I. *The Hidden-Hand Presidency: Eisenhower as Leader.* New York: Basic Books, 1982.

John F. Kennedy

PRIMARY SOURCES

Public Papers of the Presidents of the United States: John F. Kennedy, 1961–1963. Washington, D.C.: Government Printing Office, 1962–64.

Sidey, Hugh, ed. *Prelude to Leadership: The European Diary of John F. Kennedy.* Washington, D.C.: Regnery, 1995.

SECONDARY SOURCES

Parmet, Herbert S. *Jack: The Struggles of John F. Kennedy.* New York: Dial Press, 1980.

———. *JFK: The Presidency of John F. Kennedy.* New York: Dial Press, 1983.

Reeves, Richard. *President Kennedy: Profile of Power.* New York: Simon & Schuster, 1993.

Lyndon B. Johnson

PRIMARY SOURCES

Public Papers of the Presidents of the United States: Lyndon B. Johnson, 1963–69. Washington, D.C.: Government Printing Office, 1964–70.

Beschloss, Michael R. *Taking Charge: The Johnson White House Tapes, 1963–1964*. New York: Simon & Schuster, 1997.

Miller, Merle. *Lyndon: An Oral Biography*. New York: Putnam, 1980.

SECONDARY SOURCES

Bard, Bernard. *LBJ: The Picture Story*. New York: The Lion Press, 1966.

Bornet, Vaughn D. *The Presidency of Lyndon B. Johnson*. Lawrence, Kans.: University Press of Kansas, 1983.

Dallek, Robert. *Lone Star Rising: Lyndon Johnson and His Times 1908–1960*. New York: Oxford University Press, 1991.

Kearns, Doris. *Lyndon Johnson and the American Dream*. New York: Harper & Row, 1976.

Richard M. Nixon

PRIMARY SOURCES

Public Papers of the Presidents of the United States: Richard M. Nixon, 1969–74. Washington, D.C.: Government Printing Office, 1970–75.

Nixon, Richard M. *The Memoirs of Richard Nixon*. New York: Grosset & Dunlap, 1978.

———. *Six Crises: With New Preface*. New York: Pocket Books, 1968.

SECONDARY SOURCES

Ambrose, Stephen E. *Nixon: The Education of a Politician, 1913–1962*. New York: Simon & Schuster, 1987.

———. *Nixon: The Triumph of a Politician, 1962–1972*. New York: Simon & Schuster, 1989.

———. *Nixon: Ruin and Recovery, 1973-1990*. New York: Simon & Schuster, 1991.

Gerald Ford

PRIMARY SOURCES

Public Papers of the Presidents of the United States: Gerald R. Ford, 1974–77. Washington, D.C.: Government Printing Office, 1975–78.

Ford, Gerald R. *A Time to Heal: The Autobiography of Gerald R. Ford*. New York: Harper & Row, 1979.

SECONDARY SOURCES

Cannon, James M. *Time and Chance: Gerald Ford's Appointment with History*. New York: HarperCollins, 1994.

Greene, John Robert. *The Presidency of Gerald Ford*. Lawrence, Kans. University Press of Kansas, 1995.

Jimmy Carter

PRIMARY SOURCES

Public Papers of the Presidents of the United States: Jimmy Carter, 1977–81. Washington, D.C.: Government Printing Office, 1978–82.

Carter, Jimmy. *Keeping Faith: Memoirs of a President*. New York: Bantam Books, 1982.

SECONDARY SOURCES

Hargrove, Erwin C. "Jimmy Carter: The Politics of Public Goods" in *Leadership in the Modern Presidency*, ed. Fred I. Greinstein. Cambridge, Mass.: Harvard University Press, 1988.

Kaufman, Burton I. *The Presidency of James Earl Carter, Jr*. Lawrence, Kans.: University Press of Kansas, 1993.

Ronald Reagan

PRIMARY SOURCES

Public Papers of the Presidents of the United States: Ronald Reagan, 1981–89. Washington, D.C.: Government Printing Office, 1982–90.

Reagan, Ronald. *Ronald Reagan: An American Life—The Autobiography*. New York: Simon & Schuster, 1990.

SECONDARY SOURCES

Cannon, Lou. *President Reagan: Role of a Lifetime*. New York: Simon & Schuster, 1991.

———. *Reagan*. New York: Putnam, 1982.

Muir, William K., Jr. *The Pully Pulpit: The Presidential Leadership of Ronald Reagan*. San Francisco: Institute for Contemporary Studies, 1992.

Tulis, Jeffrey. *The Rhetorical Presidency*. Princeton, N.J.: Princeton University Press, 1987.

George Bush

PRIMARY SOURCES

Public Papers of the Presidents of the United States: George W. Bush, 1989–93. Washington, D.C.: Government Printing Office, 1990–94.

Bush, George. *Looking Forward*. Garden City, New York: Doubleday, 1987.

SECONDARY SOURCES

Beschloss, Michael R., and Strobe Talbott. *At the Highest Levels: The Inside Story of the End of the Cold War*. Boston: Little, Brown, 1993.

Green, Fitzhugh. *George Bush: An Intimate Portrait*. New York: Hippocrene Books, 1989.

Bill Clinton

PRIMARY SOURCES

Public Papers of the Presidents of the United States: William J. Clinton, 1993–1996. Washington, D.C.: U.S. Government Printing Office, 1994–.

Clinton, Bill. *Between Hope and History: Meeting America's Challenges for the 21st Century*. New York: Random House, 1996.

———. "The New Covenant: Responsibility and Rebuilding the American Community." Speech at Georgetown University, Washington, D.C., October 23, 1991.

SECONDARY SOURCES

Drew, Elizabeth. *On the Edge: The Clinton Presidency*. New York: Simon & Schuster, 1994.

Maraniss, David. *First in His Class: A Biography of Bill Clinton*. New York: Simon & Schuster, 1995.

Weisberg, Jacob. "Bill Clinton's Legacy (First Draft)." *The New York Times Magazine*, January 17, 1999.

Index

White House cabinet room, 1889

White House telegraph office, 1890

Picture Sources

ii–iii: Meserve-Kunhardt Collection, Mt. Kisco, NY. iv–v: Meserve-Kunhardt Collection. vii: Library of Congress. ix: Library of Congress. xi: Hugh Sidey (all); White House (bottom). xv: Richard Neustadt

Chapter 1

2: Architect of the Capitol, Washington, DC (left); Property of the DAR, Harrison Mansion, Vincennes, IN (right). 3: Meserve-Kunhardt Collection, Mt. Kisco, NY (left); U. S. Army Photo, Courtesy Dwight D. Eisenhower Library, Abilene, KS (right). 4: Meserve-Kunhardt Collection (bottom left); The Hermitage: Home of President Andrew Jackson, Nashville, TN (middle left); The Library of Virginia, Richmond, VA (top left); The Rutherford B. Hayes Presidential Center, Fremont, OH (top second from left); Library of Congress, Washington, DC (top center and second from right); Courtesy of the McKinley Museum and National Memorial/Stark County Historical Society, Canton, OH (top right). 5: Library of Congress (left); Courtesy the Harry S. Truman Library, Independence, MO (second from left); Courtesy John F. Kennedy Library, Boston, MA (center); Courtesy George Bush Presidential Library, College Station, TX (second from right); Meserve-Kunhardt Collection (right). 6: Library of Congress. 7: National Portrait Gallery, Smithsonian

Institution/Art Resource, New York, NY. 8-9: Library of Congress (left, center); Collection of the New-York Historical Society, New York, NY (right). 10-11: Library of Congress (left); Daniel Huntington (1816-1906). *The Republican Court.* 1861. Oil on canvas, 66"x109" Gift of Crescent-Hamilton Athletic Club. 39-536-1, Brooklyn Museum of Art, Brooklyn, NY (center); Architect of the Capitol (right). 12: Architect of the Capitol (top); Meserve-Kunhardt Collection (bottom). 13: Architect of the Capitol. 14-15: Library of Congress. 16-17: Library of Congress. 18: Cincinnati Historical Society, Cincinnati, OH. 19: Meserve-Kunhardt Collection. 20: Library of Congress (top); Ohio Historical Society, Columbus, OH (bottom). 21: Library of Congress. 22: Property of the DAR, Harrison Mansion (left); Library of Congress (top); Anne S. K. Brown Military Collection, Brown University Library, Providence, RI (bottom right). 23: The President Benjamin Harrison Home, Indianapolis, IN (top); Library of Congress (bottom). 24: U. S. Grant Photo Collection, Courtesy of James A. Bultema. 25: Meserve-Kunhardt Collection. 26: Chicago Historical Society, Chicago, IL (left); Ohio Historical Society (second from left); Missouri Historical Society, St. Louis, MO (second from right); Meserve-Kunhardt Collection (right). 27: Meserve-Kunhardt Collection (top, bottom

left); U. S. Grant Photo Collection, Courtesy of James A. Bultema (bottom center, bottom right). 28-29: Library of Congress (left); Meserve-Kunhardt Collection (right). 30: Meserve-Kunhardt Collection (top, bottom);
U. S. Grant Photo Collection, Courtesy of James A. Bultema (center). 32: U. S. Grant Photo Collection, Courtesy of James A. Bultema (top left); Meserve-Kunhardt Collection (top right, bottom left, second from left, second from right, right). 33. U. S. Grant Photo Collection, Courtesy of James A. Bultema. 34: West Point Museum Collections/U. S. Military Academy, West Point, NY (top left); Meserve-Kunhardt Collection. (top right); U. S. Grant Photo Collection, Courtesy of James A. Bultema (bottom). 35: Meserve-Kunhardt Collection. 36-38: Courtesy Dwight D. Eisenhower Library (all). 39: Courtesy Dwight D. Eisenhower Library (top); National Archives Still Pictures, College Park, MD (bottom). 40-43: Courtesy Dwight D. Eisenhower Library (all). 44: Courtesy Dwight D. Eisenhower Library (left, top); Library of Congress (bottom). 45: Library of Congress (top left); National Park Service (top right); Copyright *Washington Post,* Washington, DC; reprinted by permission of D.C. Public Library (bottom left); Abbie Rowe, National Park Service, Courtesy Harry S. Truman Library (bottom right). 46-47: Courtesy Dwight D. Eisenhower Library.

Chapter 2

48: National Portrait Gallery, Smithsonian Institution/Art Resource (left); Meserve-Kunhardt Collection (right). 49: Library of Congress (left, right). 50: Collection of the James K. Polk Memorial Association, Columbia, TN (top); Meserve-Kunhardt Collection (bottom left); Library of Congress (bottom right). 51: Courtesy the Rutherford B. Hayes Presidential Center (top); Library of Congress/*U.S. News & World Report* Magazine Photograph Collection, Washington, DC (bottom). 52: Meserve-Kunhardt Collection. 53: Franklin Pierce Homestead, Hillsborough, NH. 54: New Hampshire Historical Society, Concord, NH (top); Courtesy George Eastman House, Rochester, NY (bottom). 55: Chicago Historical Society (top); New Hampshire Historical Society (bottom). 56: The Pierce Brigade, Concord, NH. 57: Meserve-Kunhardt Collection. 58: Meserve-Kunhardt Collection. 59: Lake County Historical Society, Mentor, OH. 60: Lake County Historical Society (top, bottom). 61: Library of Congress (top); Meserve-Kunhardt Collection. (bottom). 62: Library of Congress (top, bottom). 63: Library of Congress (left, right). 64: Meserve-Kunhardt Collection. (top); Lake County Historical Society (bottom). 65: Meserve-Kunhardt Collection. 66-67: Courtesy the Rutherford B. Hayes Presidential Center. 68: Ohio Historical Society (top, bottom). 69: Library of Congress. 70: Library of Congress (top); Ohio Historical

White House state dining room, 1898

The White House kitchen, 1890

Society (bottom). **71:** Library of Congress (all). **72:** Ohio Historical Society (top, bottom). **73:** Library of Congress (all). **74-75:** Library of Congress. **76:** Library of Congress (top); Ohio Historical Society (bottom). **77:** Library of Congress (top, bottom). **78:** David Kennerly Collection, Santa Monica, CA. **79:** Courtesy Gerald R. Ford Library, Ann Arbor, MI (top, bottom). **80:** Courtesy Gerald R. Ford Library (top, bottom). **81-85:** David Kennerly Collection (all).

Chapter 3
86: Beinecke Rare Book and Manuscript Library, Yale University, New Haven, CT (left); National Portrait Gallery, Smithsonian Institution/Art Resource (right) **87:** Meserve-Kunhardt Collection. (left); Courtesy Lyndon Baines Johnson Library, Austin, TX (right). 88: Library of Congress (top, bottom). **89:** Courtesy Franklin D. Roosevelt Library, Hyde Park, NY (top); Courtesy John F. Kennedy Library (bottom left); David Kennerly Collection (bottom right). **90:** Meserve-Kunhardt Collection. **91:** Meserve-Kunhardt Collection. **92:** Meserve-Kunhardt Collection. **93:** Courtesy of the U.S. Naval Academy Museum, Annapolis, MD. **94:** Library of Congress. **95:** The Photography Collection, Carpenter Center, Harvard University, Cambridge, MA. **96:** Meserve-Kunhardt Collection. **97:** Meserve-Kunhardt Collection (top); Lancaster County Historical Society, Lancaster,

PA (bottom). **98:** Library of Congress. **99:** Library of Congress. **100-117:** Meserve-Kunhardt Collection. **118:** Courtesy Lyndon Baines Johnson Library. **119:** Courtesy Lyndon Baines Johnson Library (top); *Austin Statesman,* Austin, TX (bottom). **120:** Courtesy Lyndon Baines Johnson Library (lower left, top row: left, second from left, center); *Austin Statesman* (top row: second from right, right). **121:** Courtesy Lyndon Baines Johnson Library (top row: far left, second from left, second from right and bottom right); John Bryson (top row: center); Courtesy Lyndon Baines Johnson Library, Photo by Cecil Stoughton (top row: right). **122:** Courtesy Lyndon Baines Johnson Library (top, bottom). **123:** Courtesy Lyndon Baines Johnson Library (top); Library of Congress (bottom). **124-127:** Courtesy Lyndon Baines Johnson Library (all).

Chapter 4
128: Architect of the Capitol (left); Chicago Historical Society, ICHi-22139 (right). **129:** Courtesy the Rutherford B. Hayes Presidential Center (left); Library of Congress/USN&WR Collection (right). **130:** Library of Congress (top); Meserve-Kunhardt Collection (bottom). **131:** Library of Congress (top); National Archives Still Pictures (middle); Meserve-Kunhardt Collection (bottom). **132:** Courtesy Massachusetts Historical Society, Boston, MA (top); Library of Congress

(bottom). **133:** Independence National Historical Park, Philadelphia, PA. **134:** Courtesy of the Harvard Portrait Collection, President and Fellows of Harvard College, Bequest of Ward Nicholas Boylston, 1828, to Harvard College, Cambridge, MA. **135:** Copyright 1996. Virginia Historical Society, Lora Robins Collection of Virginia Art. Richmond, VA (top); Library of Congress (bottom). **136-7:** National Park Service, Adams National Historic Site, Quincy, MA (left); White House Collection, copyright White House Historical Association, Washington, DC (center); Courtesy Massachusetts Historical Society (right). **138:** National Park Service, Adams National Historic Site. **139:** National Park Service, Adams National Historic Site. **140:** Courtesy University of Kentucky, Lexington, KY (top); Yale Collection of Western Americana, Beinecke Rare Book and Manuscript Library (bottom). **141:** Beinecke Rare Book and Manuscript Library, Yale University. **142:** Library of Congress (top); Meserve-Kunhardt Collection (bottom). **143:** The Library of Virginia (top); Library of Congress (bottom). **144:** Independence National Historical Park (top); Library of Congress (bottom). **145:** Beinecke Rare Book and Manuscript Library, Yale University. **146-147:** Library of Congress. **148:** Courtesy the Rutherford B. Hayes Presidential Center (top, bottom). **149:** Meserve-Kunhardt Collection. **150:** Courtesy the

Rutherford B. Hayes Presidential Center (top); Meserve-Kunhardt Collection. (bottom). **151:** Courtesy the Rutherford B. Hayes Presidential Center. **152:** Meserve-Kunhardt Collection (top let, top right); Courtesy the Rutherford B. Hayes Presidential Center (bottom). **153:** Courtesy the Rutherford B. Hayes Presidential Center. **154-155:** Library of Congress (left); Courtesy the Rutherford B. Hayes Presidential Center (right). **156-159:** Courtesy Jimmy Carter Library, Atlanta, GA (all). **160:** Courtesy Jimmy Carter Library (top left, bottom); Library of Congress/USN&WR Collection (top right). **161:** Library of Congress (top row); Courtesy Jimmy Carter Library (bottom). **162-163:** Library of Congress/USN&WR Collection.

Chapter 5
164: Meserve-Kunhardt Collection (left); Library of Congress (right). **165:** Courtesy FDR Library (left); Courtesy John F. Kennedy Library (right). **166:** Library of Congress (top); Property of the DAR, Harrison Mansion (bottom). **167:** Library of Congress (top, bottom). **168:** The State Department Diplomatic Reception Rooms, Washington, DC (top); National Portrait Gallery, Smithsonian Institution/Art Resource (bottom). **169:** Meserve-Kunhardt Collection. **170:** Library of Congress. **171:** National Park Service, Adams National Historic Site (all). **172:** The Connecticut Historical Society, Hartford,

CT. **173:** Mead Art Museum, Gift of William Macbeth Gallery, Amherst College, Amherst, MA. **174:** Library of Congress (top, bottom). **175:** Library of Congress. **176:** Library of Congress (top, bottom); The President Benjamin Harrison Home (center). **177:** The President Benjamin Harrison Home. **178-179:** Library of Congress (left, right). **180:** The President Benjamin Harrison Home (top, center); Library of Congress (bottom). **181:** Library of Congress (top row, center, bottom left); Meserve-Kunhardt Collection (bottom right). **182-183:** Library of Congress. **184:** Courtesy FDR Library. **185:** Courtesy FDR Library (top, bottom). **186:** Courtesy FDR Library. **187:** Courtesy FDR Library (top, center); Library of Congress (bottom). **188:** Library of Congress (top); Courtesy FDR Library (bottom). **189:** Courtesy FDR Library (left, right). **190-191:** Library of Congress. **192:** Gordon Parks, Library of Congress (top); Courtesy FDR Library (bottom). **193:** Courtesy FDR Library (top, bottom). **194:** Courtesy FDR Library (top); Library of Congress (bottom). **195:** Library of Congress (all). **196-198:** Courtesy John F. Kennedy Library (all). **199:** Library of Congress (bottom left, bottom right); Courtesy John F. Kennedy Library (top). **200:** Library of Congress (all). **201-205:** Courtesy John F. Kennedy Library (all).

Chapter 6
206-207: The Library of Virginia (far left); Library of Congress (second from left); Meserve-Kunhardt Collection (center, second from right); National Archives Still Pictures (far right). **208:** Library of Congress (top, bottom). **209:** Library of Congress/USN&WR Collection (top); National Archives, Nixon Materials Staff, College Park, MD (bottom). **210:** Meserve-Kunhardt Collection. **211:** Library of Congress (top, bottom). **212:** U.S. Senate Collection, Washington, DC. **213:** Sherwood Forest Plantation, Charles City, VA. **214:** Philipse Manor Hall State Historic Site, Courtesy NYS Office of Parks, Recreation and Historic Preservation, Waterford, NY (top); Library of Congress (center, bottom) **215:** Chicago Historical Society, ICHi-12725. **216-217:** Library of Congress. **218:** The Library of Virginia (top); Buffalo and Erie County Historical Society, Buffalo, NY (bottom). **219:** Beinecke Rare Book and Manuscript Library, Yale University. **220:** San Antonio Art League Museum, San Antonio, TX (left); Meserve-Kunhardt Collection (right). **221:** Buffalo and Erie County Historical Society. **222:** Meserve-Kunhardt Collection (left); Buffalo and Erie County Historical Society (center, right). **223:** Meserve-Kunhardt Collection. **224:**

Meserve-Kunhardt Collection. **225:** Meserve-Kunhardt Collection (top); Chicago Historical Society (bottom). **226:** Courtesy Tennessee State Museum, Nashville, TN (top); Meserve-Kunhardt Collection (bottom). **227:** Meserve-Kunhardt Collection. **228-229:** Library of Congress. **230:** Meserve-Kunhardt Collection (top left, top right); U. S. Grant Photo Collection, Courtesy of James A. Bultema (bottom). **232-233:** National Park Service, Andrew Johnson Historic Site, Greeneville, TN. **234-235:** Meserve-Kunhardt Collection (all). **236-237:** National Archives Still Pictures. **238-239:** Library of Congress (all). **240:** National Portrait Gallery, Smithsonian Institution/Art Resource (top); Library of Congress (bottom). **241-243:** Library of Congress (all). **244:** Library of Congress (top, bottom left); Meserve-Kunhardt Collection (bottom right). **245:** The Abraham Lincoln Foundation of the Union League of Philadelphia, Philadelphia, PA (left); Library of Congress (right). **246-247:** Meserve-Kunhardt Collection. **248-252:** Courtesy the Harry S. Truman Library (all). **253:** Courtesy the Harry S. Truman Library (top left; bottom left); Abbie Rowe, National Park Service, Courtesy Harry S. Truman Library (top right, center); Illinois State Historical Library, Old State Capitol Building, Springfield, IL (bottom right). **254-255:** Abbie Rowe, National Park Service, Courtesy Harry S. Truman Library. **256:** Abbie Rowe, National Park Service, Courtesy Harry S. Truman Library (top left); Courtesy the Harry S. Truman Library (top right); Courtesy Dwight D. Eisenhower Library (bottom). **257:** *St. Louis Post-Dispatch,* St. Louis, MO.

Chapter 7
258: White House Collection, copyright White House Historical Association (left); Library of Congress (right). **259:** Library of Congress (left); Courtesy Ronald Reagan Library, Simi Valley, CA (right). **260:** Library of Congress (top); Meserve-Kunhardt Collection (bottom). **261:** Library of Congress (top, bottom). **262:** The State Department Diplomatic Reception Rooms. **263:** Independence National Historical Park. **264:** Independence National Historical Park (top); Architect of the Capitol (bottom). **265:** The State Department Diplomatic Reception Rooms. **266:** Library of Congress (top); Monticello/Thomas Jefferson Memorial Foundation, Inc., Charlottesville, VA (bottom). **267:** Library of Congress (all). **268-269:** I. N. Phelps Stokes Collection, Miriam and Ira D. Wallach Division of Art, Prints and Photographs, The New York Public Library

Astor, Lenox and Tilden Foundations, New York, NY; Library of Congress (left inset); Courtesy U.S. Naval Academy Museum (right inset). **270:** Courtesy, American Antiquarian Society, Worcester, MA. **271:** Collection of the New-York Historical Society. **272:** Library of Congress. **273:** The Coolidge Collection, Forbes Library, Northampton, MA (top, bottom). **274:** The Calvin Coolidge Memorial Foundation, Plymouth, VT (top); Ohio Historical Society (bottom). **275:** Library of Congress (top, bottom); The Coolidge Collection, Forbes Library (center). **276:** Courtesy Historic Northampton, Northampton, MA (top left); Library of Congress (center, bottom); The Calvin Coolidge Memorial Foundation (top right). **277:** Courtesy Vermont Historical Society, Montpelier, VT. **278:** Courtesy Vermont Historical Society (top); Library of Congress (bottom). **279-282:** Library of Congress (all). **283:** Courtesy Herbert Hoover Presidential Library/Museum, West Branch, IA (top, bottom). **284:** Courtesy Herbert Hoover Presidential Library/Museum (top); Library of Congress (center); National Archives Still Pictures (bottom). **285-286:** Library of Congress (all). **287:** National Archives Still Pictures (bottom left); Library of Congress (upper right) **288-291:** Library of Congress (all). **291:** Library of Congress (left, right). **292:** Courtesy Ronald Reagan Library (top, bottom). **293:** Courtesy Ronald Reagan Library. **294:** Gabi Rona, courtesy Ronald Reagan Library (top); Courtesy Ronald Reagan Library (bottom). **295:** Library of Congress (top); Courtesy Ronald Reagan Library (bottom). **296-299:** Courtesy Ronald Reagan Library (all). **300:** Library of Congress (top left); Courtesy Ronald Reagan Library (top center, right, bottom). **301:** Courtesy Ronald Reagan Library.

Chapter 8
302: Courtesy of the U.S. Naval Academy Museum (left); Library of Congress (right). **303:** Library of Congress (left); Courtesy George Bush Presidential Library (right). **304:** National Archives Still Pictures (top, bottom). **305:** Courtesy John F. Kennedy Library (top); National Archives, Nixon Materials Staff (bottom). **306:** National Archives. **307:** Property of the James Monroe Museum and Memorial Library, Fredericksburg, VA. **308:** Architect of the Capitol (top); Courtesy of the Art Commission of the City of New York (bottom). **309:** Library of Congress (left); Meserve-Kunhardt Collection (right). **310:** Library of Congress (top); The State Department Diplomatic Reception Rooms (bottom). **311:** The State Department Diplomatic Reception Rooms. **312-313:** Library of

Congress. **314:** Courtesy of the McKinley Museum and National Memorial/Stark County Historical Society, Canton, OH (top, center); Meserve-Kunhardt Collection (bottom). **315:** Ohio Historical Society (top); Library of Congress (bottom left, right). **316-317:** Library of Congress. **318:** Library of Congress (left); Meserve-Kunhardt Collection (right). **319:** Library of Congress (top, center); Meserve-Kunhardt Collection (bottom). **320:** Library of Congress. **321:** Library of Congress (top, bottom left); Meserve-Kunhardt Collection (bottom right). 322-323: Meserve-Kunhardt Collection. **324:** National Archives Still Pictures. **325:** National Archives Still Pictures. **326:** Library of Congress (top, bottom); Woodrow Wilson House, National Trust for Historic Preservation, Washington, DC (center). **327:** Library of Congress (top, center); Woodrow Wilson House, National Trust for Historic Preservation (bottom). **328-329:** Library of Congress. **330:** Library of Congress (all). **331:** Woodrow Wilson House, National Trust for Historic Preservation (top); National Archives Still Pictures (bottom). **332:** Woodrow Wilson House, National Trust for Historic Preservation (left); Library of Congress (right). **333-335:** Library of Congress (all). **336:** David Kennerly Collection. **337-338:** Courtesy George Bush Presidentil Library (all). **339:** Courtesy George Bush Presidential Library (far left, second from left, top row far right, bottom right); David Kennerly Collection (top center); Courtesy Ronald Reagan Library (second from top right). **340:** Courtesy George Bush Presidential Library (top, bottom). **341:** Courtesy George Bush Presidential Library. **342:** David Kennerly Collection (top, bottom). **343:** David Kennerly Collection (top); Courtesy George Bush Presidential Library (bottom). **344-345:** David Kennerly Collection.

Chapter 9
346: Meserve-Kunhardt Collection (left); Library of Congress (right). **347:** Library of Congress (left, right). **348:** Independence National Historical Park (top left); Meserve-Kunhardt Collection (bottom left); Library of Congress (bottom right). **349:** Courtesy FDR Library (top); Courtesy Lyndon Baines Johnson Library (bottom). **350:** Meserve-Kunhardt Collection. **351:** Clermont State Historic Site, NYS Office of Parks, Recreation and Historic Preservation, Germantown, NY. **352:** Historic Hudson Valley, Tarrytown, NY (top); Library of Congress (second from top, second from bottom, bottom); The Hermitage: Home of President Andrew Jackson (center). **353:** Library of Congress.

Thanksgiving at the White House, circa 1898

Former presidents George Bush, Ronald Reagan, Jimmy Carter, Gerald Ford, and Richard Nixon gather in 1994 for photographer David Hume Kennerly. The only other time in the history of the nation when so many former presidents were alive together was 1861, when Martin Van Buren, John Tyler, Millard Fillmore, Franklin Pierce, and James Buchanan still served as elder statesmen.

In 1994 there were seven former first ladies. Above are Barbara Bush, Nancy Reagan, Rosalynn Carter, Betty Ford, Pat Nixon, and Lady Bird Johnson. The intensely private Jacqueline Kennedy Onassis died that same year.